# WATERFALLS OF MICHIGAN

### The Essential Guidebook to Michigan's Best & Easiest Waterfalls

## The Collection

### PHIL STAGG

## Waterfalls of Michigan
**The Collection**


Copyright © 2017 by Phil Stagg

Published by:

MI Falls Publishing
11765 West Cadillac Rd.
Cadillac, MI 49601
231•920•8416

www.mifalls.com

All rights reserved. No part of this publication may be reproduced, stored in a retrieval system, or transmitted, in any form or by any means, electronic, mechanical, photo-copying, recording, or otherwise, without the prior written permission of the author.

ISBN: 978-0-9971346-4-3
LCCN: 2016900613

Photography: Phil Stagg
Text: Phil Stagg
Design: Phil Stagg

Printed in the United States of America

First Printing: April 2017

## Phil Stagg

Water courses through the veins of the great state of Michigan, constantly rushing on, seeking to replenish the Great Lakes that cradle these pleasant peninsulas. As the mighty rivers and quiet streams make their way downward, they periodically tumble over hardy stone ledges, steep sandstone cliffs, or radically tilted bedrock. It's at these places, where water and stone meet, that we find some of the most picturesque scenes in Michigan. This book is the culmination of years spent documenting these waterway features.

There are many waterfalls in Michigan. In this volume we will examine many of the best and/or easiest to access waterfalls throughout the state. And only those available to the general public (according to my latest information) at the time of publication have been included. There is so much beauty to be enjoyed across Michigan. It is my intent to provide those who want to experience our watery wonders in person the very best in driving and hiking information. And for you who aren't able or don't have time to go in person, I trust that the images and descriptions that I present will transport you to a beautiful river, the sound of cascading water nearly audible, the crunching of small twigs and leaves plausible, smooth hard rock and delicate ferns almost touchable.

Come join me on a journey across Michigan. We'll examine a good selection of the waterfalls found here. Perhaps you'll grow to appreciate them and the state they are found in as much as I have!

VI

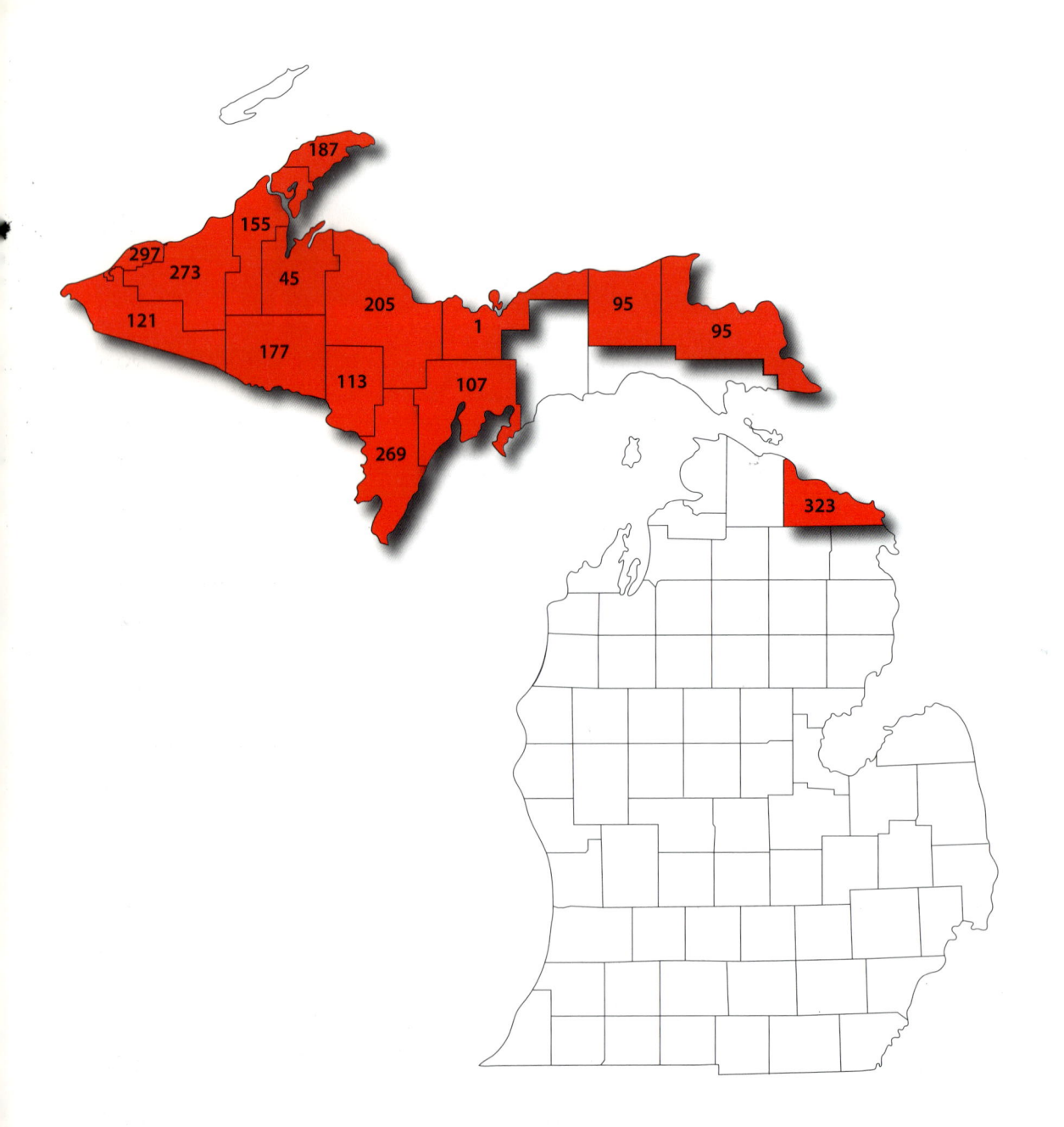

# TABLE OF CONTENTS

| CHAPTER | COUNTY | PAGE |
|---|---|---|
| | COUNTY TABLE OF CONTENTS | VIII |
| | GUIDE TO THE GUIDE | XVI |
| | WATERFALL MEMORIES | XIII |
| 1 | ALGER | 1 |
| 2 | BARAGA | 45 |
| 3 | CHIPPEWA & LUCE | 95 |
| 4 | DELTA | 107 |
| 5 | DICKINSON | 113 |
| 6 | GOGEBIC | 121 |
| 7 | HOUGHTON | 155 |
| 8 | IRON | 177 |
| 9 | KEWEENAW | 187 |
| 10 | MARQUETTE | 205 |
| 11 | MENOMINEE | 269 |
| 12 | ONTONAGON | 273 |
| 13 | PORCUPINE MOUNTAINS | 297 |
| 14 | PRESQUE ISLE | 323 |
| | INDEX | 331 |

County Table of Contents

# ALGER COUNTY MAP — 2

## AUTRAIN FALLS AREA — 4
- AUTRAIN FALLS HIKE — 4
  - 🟨 AUTRAIN FALLS (AUTRAIN RIVER) — 5

## CHAPEL FALLS AREA — 6
- CHAPEL CREEK FALLS HIKE — 7
  - 🟨 CHAPEL CREEK FALLS (CHAPEL CREEK) — 7
- CHAPEL FALLS HIKE — 8
  - 🟨 SECTION CREEK FALLS (SECTION CREEK) — 8
  - 🟩 CHAPEL FALLS (SECTION CREEK) — 9
- MOSQUITO FALLS HIKE — 10
  - 🟩 MOSQUITO FALLS (MOSQUITO RIVER) — 10
  - 🟩 MOSQUITO FALLS - UPPER (MOSQUITO RIVER) — 12
- SPRAY FALLS HIKE — 13
  - 🟩 SPRAY FALLS (SPRAY CREEK) — 13

## HURRICANE RIVER FALLS AREA — 14
- HURRICANE FALLS HIKE — 14
  - 🟨 HURRICANE FALLS (HURRICANE RIVER) — 15
  - 🟨 HURRICANE CASCADES (HURRICANE RIVER) — 16

## LAUGHING WHITEFISH FALLS AREA — 17
- LAUGHING WHITEFISH FALLS HIKE — 17
  - 🟩 LAUGHING WHITEFISH FALLS (LAUGHING WHITEFISH RIVER) — 18

## MINERS BEACH AREA — 19
- BRIDAL VEIL FALLS HIKE — 19
  - 🟩 BRIDAL VEIL FALLS (BRIDAL VEIL CREEK) — 19
- ELLIOT FALLS HIKE — 20
  - 🟩 ELLIOT FALLS: AKA MINERS BEACH FALLS (UNNAMED CREEK) — 20
  - 🟩 POTATO PATCH FALLS (UNNAMED CREEK) — 21
- MINERS FALLS HIKE — 22
  - 🟩 MINERS FALLS (MINERS RIVER) — 22
  - 🟩 LITTLE MINERS FALLS (LITTLE MINERS RIVER) — 24

## MUNISING FALLS AREA — 25
- LAKESHORE FALLS HIKE — 26
  - 🟩 LAKESHORE FALLS #1 (UNNAMED CREEK) — 27
  - 🟩 LAKESHORE FALLS #2 (UNNAMED CREEK) — 28
- MEMORIAL FALLS HIKE — 29
  - 🟩 MEMORIAL FALLS (UNNAMED CREEK) — 29
  - 🟩 OLSON FALLS AKA: TANNERY FALLS (TANNERY CREEK) — 30
- MUNISING FALLS HIKE — 31
  - 🟩 MUNISING FALLS (MUNISING FALLS CREEK) — 31

## ROCK RIVER FALLS AREA — 32
- ROCK RIVER FALLS HIKE — 32
  - 🟩 ROCK RIVER FALLS (ROCK RIVER) — 33
- SILVER FALLS HIKE — 34
  - 🟨 SILVER FALLS AKA: SILVER BELL FALLS (NELSON CREEK) — 34

## SABLE FALLS AREA — 35
- SABLE FALLS HIKE — 35
  - 🟩 SABLE FALLS (SABLE CREEK) — 36

## SCOTT FALLS AREA — 37
- SCOTT FALLS HIKE — 37
  - 🟨 SCOTT FALLS (SCOTT CREEK) — 38

## WAGNER FALLS AREA — 39
- ALGER FALLS HIKE — 39
  - 🟩 ALGER FALLS (ALGER CREEK) — 40
- HORSESHOE FALLS HIKE — 41
  - 🟩 HORSESHOE FALLS (STUTTS CREEK) — 41
- WAGNER FALLS HIKE — 42
  - 🟩 WAGNER FALLS (WAGNER CREEK) — 42

VIII

## WHITEFISH FALLS AREA ........................................................................................ 43
   WHITEFISH FALLS HIKE ................................................................................................. 43
      🟨 WHITEFISH FALLS (WEST BRANCH - WHITEFISH RIVER) .............................................. 43

# BARAGA COUNTY MAP    46

## CANYON FALLS AREA ........................................................................................... 47
   CANYON FALLS HIKE ...................................................................................................... 47
      🟩 CANYON FALLS (STURGEON RIVER) .......................................................................... 48
   OGEMAW FALLS HIKE .................................................................................................... 49
      🟩 OGEMAW FALLS (OGEMAW CREEK) ............................................................................. 49

## FALLS RIVER AREA ............................................................................................... 50
   FALLS RIVER - LOWER HIKE ........................................................................................... 51
      🟩 CASCADING FALLS (FALLS RIVER) .............................................................................. 52
      🟨 BARE HOLE FALLS (FALLS RIVER) .............................................................................. 53
   FALLS RIVER - MIDDLE HIKE ........................................................................................... 54
      🟨 MITTEN HOLE FALLS (FALLS RIVER) ........................................................................... 55
      🟩 BIG HOLE FALLS (FALLS RIVER) .................................................................................. 56
      🟩 SECRET HOLE FALLS (FALLS RIVER) .......................................................................... 57
      🟩 CHUTE FALLS (FALLS RIVER) ...................................................................................... 58
   FALLS RIVER - UPPER HIKE ............................................................................................ 59
      🟩 POWER HOUSE FALLS (FALLS RIVER) ....................................................................... 59

## HURON RIVER AREA .............................................................................................. 60
   BIG ERICK'S FALLS HIKE ................................................................................................. 61
      🟨 BIG ERICK'S FALLS (HURON RIVER) ............................................................................ 61
   BIG FALLS HIKE .............................................................................................................. 62
      🟩 BIG FALLS (HURON RIVER - EAST BRANCH) ............................................................... 62
   EAST BRANCH FALLS HIKE ............................................................................................. 63
      🟩 EAST BRANCH FALLS (HURON RIVER - EAST BRANCH) ............................................ 63
   ERICK'S FALLS HIKE ...................................................................................................... 64
      🟨 ERICK'S FALLS (HURON RIVER - WEST BRANCH) ..................................................... 64
   LETHERBY FALLS HIKE .................................................................................................. 65
      🟩 LETHERBY FALLS (HURON RIVER - WEST BRANCH) .................................................. 65
   LETHERBY - UPPER FALLS HIKE ..................................................................................... 66
      🟩 LETHERBY FALLS - UPPER (HURON RIVER - WEST BRANCH) .................................. 66
   RAVINE RIVER ROAD FALLS HIKE ................................................................................... 67
      🟨 RAVINE RIVER ROAD FALLS (UNNAMED TRIBUTARY) ............................................... 67

## SILVER RIVER - LOWER AREA ............................................................................. 68
   ABUTMENT FALLS HIKE .................................................................................................. 68
      🟩 ABUTMENT FALLS (SILVER RIVER) ............................................................................. 69
   SILVER FALLS HIKE ........................................................................................................ 70
      🟩 SILVER FALLS - LOWER (SILVER RIVER) ................................................................... 70

## SILVER RIVER - MIDDLE AREA ............................................................................ 71
   SILVER RIVER - MIDDLE HIKE ......................................................................................... 71
      🟩 SILVER FALLS - MIDDLE #8 (SILVER RIVER) .............................................................. 72
      🟩 GOMANCHE FALLS (GOMANCHE CREEK) ................................................................... 73

## SILVER RIVER - UPPER AREA ............................................................................. 74
   BARAGA FALLS HIKE ..................................................................................................... 76
      🟩 HERMAN FALLS (SILVER RIVER) ................................................................................. 77
      🟩 BARAGA FALLS (SILVER RIVER) ................................................................................. 78
   SILVER FALLS - UPPER HIKE .......................................................................................... 79
      🟩 SILVER FALLS - UPPER (SILVER RIVER) .................................................................... 79

## SLATE RIVER - LOWER AREA ............................................................................. 80
   BLACK SLATE FALLS HIKE ............................................................................................. 81
      🟩 QUARTZITE FALLS (SLATE RIVER) ............................................................................. 81
      🟩 BLACK SLATE FALLS (SLATE RIVER) ......................................................................... 82
   SLATE RIVER FALLS HIKE .............................................................................................. 83
      🟩 SLATE RIVER FALLS (SLATE RIVER) .......................................................................... 83
      🟩 ECSTASY FALLS - LOWER (SLATE RIVER) ................................................................ 84
      🟩 ECSTASY FALLS (SLATE RIVER) ................................................................................. 85

IX

- ■ KUCKUK'S FALLS  (SLATE RIVER)..................................................................86
- **SLATE RIVER - UPPER AREA** .................................................................**87**
  - THE GRADE FALLS HIKE .......................................................................88
    - ■ THE GRADE FALLS  (UNNAMED TRIBUTARY) ..........................................88
  - VICTORY FALLS HIKE ...........................................................................89
    - ■ VICTORY FALLS  (SLATE RIVER) .......................................................89
- **TIBBETS FALLS AREA** ..........................................................................**90**
  - TIBBETS FALLS HIKE .............................................................................90
    - ■ TIBBETS FALLS  (STURGEON RIVER) ..................................................91
- **TIOGA FALLS AREA** ..............................................................................**92**
  - TIOGA PARK FALLS HIKE .....................................................................92
    - ■ TIOGA PARK FALLS  (TIOGA RIVER) ..................................................93

# CHIPPEWA & LUCE COUNTY MAP — 96

- **TAHQUAMENON FALLS AREA** ..............................................................**98**
  - TAHQUAMENON FALLS - LOWER HIKE .................................................99
    - ■ LOWER TAHQUAMENON FALLS #1  (TAHQUAMENON RIVER) ..............100
    - ■ LOWER TAHQUAMENON ISLAND FALLS #1  (TAHQUAMENON RIVER) ...101
    - ■ LOWER TAHQUAMENON FALLS #2  (TAHQUAMENON RIVER) ..............102
    - ■ LOWER TAHQUAMENON ISLAND FALLS #2  (TAHQUAMENON RIVER) ...103
  - TAHQUAMENON FALLS - UPPER HIKE ..................................................104
    - ■ TAHQUAMENON FALLS - UPPER  (TAHQUAMENON RIVER) ................104

# DELTA COUNTY MAP — 108

- **HAYMEADOW FALLS AREA** ................................................................**110**
  - HAYMEADOW FALLS HIKE ..................................................................110
    - ■ HAYMEADOW FALLS  (HAYMEADOW CREEK) ...................................111
  - RAPID RIVER FALLS HIKE ....................................................................112
    - ■ RAPID RIVER FALLS  (RAPID RIVER) .................................................112

# DICKINSON COUNTY MAP — 114

- **IRON MOUNTAIN AREA** ......................................................................**115**
  - FUMEE FALLS HIKE .............................................................................115
    - ■ FUMEE FALLS  (FUMEE CREEK) ........................................................115
  - PIERS GORGE HIKE .............................................................................116
    - ■ SECOND PIER  (MENOMINEE RIVER) .................................................116
    - ■ MISICOT FALLS  AKA: THIRD PIER  (MENOMINEE RIVER) ...................117
- **ROCK DAM FALLS AREA** ...................................................................**118**
  - ROCK DAM FALLS HIKE ......................................................................118
    - ■ ROCK DAM FALLS  (PINE CREEK) .....................................................119

# GOGEBIC COUNTY MAP — 122

- **BLACK RIVER FALLS AREA** ................................................................**124**
  - GREAT CONGLOMERATE FALLS HIKE ................................................124
    - ■ GREAT CONGLOMERATE FALLS  (BLACK RIVER) ..............................124
  - MAPLE CREEK HIKE ............................................................................125
    - ■ MANAKIKI FALLS  (MAPLE CREEK) ..................................................125
    - ■ MAPLE CREEK FALLS #1 (MAPLE CREEK) .........................................126
  - POTAWATOMI FALLS HIKE .................................................................127
    - ■ POTAWATOMI FALLS (BLACK RIVER) ...............................................127
    - ■ GORGE FALLS (BLACK RIVER) .........................................................129
  - RAINBOW FALLS HIKE .......................................................................130
    - ■ RAINBOW FALLS  (BLACK RIVER) ....................................................130
  - SANDSTONE FALLS HIKE ...................................................................132

County Table of Contents

- ■ SANDSTONE FALLS (BLACK RIVER) .................................................................. 132

## GABBRO FALLS AREA — 133
- GABBRO FALLS HIKE ............................................................................................. 133
  - ■ GABBRO FALLS (BLACK RIVER) .................................................................... 134
- ROOT BEER FALLS HIKE ........................................................................................ 135
  - ■ ROOT BEER FALLS (PLANTER CREEK) ........................................................ 135
- SUNDAY LAKE FALLS HIKE .................................................................................. 136
  - ■ SUNDAY LAKE FALLS (PLANTER CREEK) ................................................... 136

## INTERSTATE FALLS AREA — 137
- INTERSTATE FALLS HIKE ...................................................................................... 137
  - ■ INTERSTATE FALLS (MONTREAL RIVER) .................................................... 138
- PETERSON FALLS HIKE ......................................................................................... 139
  - ■ PETERSON FALLS (MONTREAL RIVER) ....................................................... 139

## KAKABIKA FALLS AREA — 140
- KAKABIKA FALLS HIKE .......................................................................................... 140
  - ■ KAKABIKA FALLS #1 (ONTONAGON RIVER - WEST BRANCH) ................. 141

## MEX-I-MIN-E FALLS AREA — 142
- MEX-I-MIN-E FALLS HIKE ....................................................................................... 142
  - ■ MEX-I-MIN-E FALLS (ONTONAGON RIVER - MIDDLE BRANCH) ............... 143

## POWDERHORN FALLS AREA — 144
- POWDERHORN FALLS HIKE .................................................................................. 144
  - ■ POWDERHORN FALLS - LOWER (POWDER MILL CREEK) ........................ 145

## SAXON FALLS AREA — 146
- SAXON FALLS HIKE ................................................................................................ 146
  - ■ SAXON FALLS - LOWER (MONTREAL RIVER) ............................................. 147
- SUPERIOR FALLS HIKE .......................................................................................... 148
  - ■ SUPERIOR FALLS (MONTREAL RIVER) ........................................................ 148

## YONDOTA FALLS AREA — 149
- JUDSON FALLS HIKE .............................................................................................. 149
  - ■ JUDSON FALLS (SLATE RIVER) ...................................................................... 150
- MARSHALL FALLS HIKE ......................................................................................... 151
  - ■ MARSHALL FALLS (MARSHALL CREEK) ...................................................... 151
- NELSON CANYON FALLS HIKE ............................................................................. 153
  - ■ NELSON CANYON FALLS (NELSON CREEK) ............................................... 153
- YONDOTA FALLS HIKE ........................................................................................... 154
  - ■ YONDOTA FALLS (PRESQUE ISLE RIVER) ................................................... 154

# HOUGHTON COUNTY MAP — 156

## HOGGER FALLS AREA — 157
- HOGGER FALLS HIKE ............................................................................................. 158
  - ■ STURGEON FALLS - WB #1 (WEST BRANCH - STURGEON RIVER) ......... 158
  - ■ STURGEON FALLS - WB #2 (WEST BRANCH - STURGEON RIVER) ......... 159
  - ■ STURGEON FALLS - WB #3 (WEST BRANCH - STURGEON RIVER) ......... 160
  - ■ STURGEON FALLS - WB #4 (WEST BRANCH - STURGEON RIVER) ......... 161
  - ■ STURGEON FALLS - WB #5 (WEST BRANCH - STURGEON RIVER) ......... 162
  - ■ HOGGER FALLS (WEST BRANCH - STURGEON RIVER) ............................ 163

## HUNGARIAN FALLS AREA — 164
- DOUGLASS HOUGHTON FALLS HIKE .................................................................. 165
  - ■ DOUGLASS HOUGHTON FALLS (HAMMELL CREEK) ................................. 165
- HUNGARIAN FALLS HIKE ....................................................................................... 166
  - ■ HUNGARIAN LOWER FALLS (DOVER CREEK) ............................................. 166
  - ■ HUNGARIAN MIDDLE FALLS (DOVER CREEK) ............................................ 167
  - ■ HUNGARIAN UPPER FALLS (DOVER CREEK) .............................................. 168

## JUMBO FALLS AREA — 169
- JUMBO FALLS HIKE ................................................................................................ 169
  - ■ JUMBO FALLS (JUMBO RIVER) ....................................................................... 170

County Table of Contents

| | |
|---|---|
| **QUEEN ANNE'S FALLS AREA** | **171** |
|    QUEEN ANNE'S FALLS HIKE | 171 |
|       ■ QUEEN ANNE'S FALLS  (SLAUGHTERHOUSE CREEK) | 172 |
| **STURGEON FALLS AREA** | **173** |
|    STURGEON FALLS HIKE | 174 |
|       ■ STURGEON FALLS  (STURGEON RIVER) | 174 |
| **WYANDOTTE FALLS AREA** | **175** |
|    WYANDOTTE FALLS HIKE | 175 |
|       ■ WYANDOTTE FALLS  (MISERY RIVER) | 176 |

# IRON COUNTY MAP — 178

| | |
|---|---|
| **CRYSTAL FALLS AREA** | **180** |
|    CHICAGON FALLS HIKE | 180 |
|       ■ CHICAGON FALLS  (CHICAGON CREEK) | 181 |
| **DUPPY FALLS AREA** | **182** |
|    DUPPY FALLS HIKE | 182 |
|       ■ DUPPY FALLS  (JUMBO RIVER) | 183 |
|       ■ DUPPY FALLS - MIDDLE  (JUMBO RIVER) | 184 |
|       ■ DUPPY FALLS - UPPER  (JUMBO RIVER) | 185 |
| **HORSERACE RAPIDS AREA** | **186** |
|    HORSERACE RAPIDS HIKE | 186 |
|       ■ HORSERACE RAPIDS  (PAINT RIVER) | 186 |

# KEWEENAW COUNTY MAP — 188

| | |
|---|---|
| **EAGLE RIVER AREA** | **190** |
|    EAGLE RIVER FALLS HIKE | 190 |
|       ■ EAGLE RIVER FALLS  (EAGLE RIVER) | 190 |
|    FENNERS FALLS HIKE | 191 |
|       ■ FENNERS FALLS  (EAGLE RIVER) | 191 |
|    JACOBS FALLS HIKE | 192 |
|       ■ JACOBS FALLS  (JACOBS CREEK) | 192 |
|    TEN FOOT FALLS HIKE | 193 |
|       ■ TEN FOOT FALLS  (EAGLE RIVER) | 193 |
| **HAVEN FALLS AREA** | **194** |
|    HAVEN FALLS HIKE | 194 |
|       ■ HAVEN FALLS (HAVEN CREEK) | 194 |
| **MANGANESE FALLS AREA** | **195** |
|    FANNY HOOE FALLS HIKE | 195 |
|       ■ FANNY HOOE FALLS  (FANNY HOOE CREEK) | 195 |
|    MANGANESE FALLS HIKE | 196 |
|       ■ MANGANESE FALLS  (MANGANESE CREEK) | 196 |
| **MONTREAL FALLS AREA** | **197** |
|    MONTREAL FALLS HIKE | 197 |
|       ■ MONTREAL FALLS - LOWER  (MONTREAL RIVER) | 198 |
|       ■ MONTREAL FALLS - MIDDLE  (MONTREAL RIVER) | 199 |
|       ■ MONTREAL FALLS - UPPER  (MONTREAL RIVER) | 200 |
| **SILVER RIVER FALLS AREA** | **201** |
|    SILVER RIVER FALLS HIKE | 201 |
|       ■ SILVER RIVER FALLS (SILVER RIVER) | 201 |
| **TOBACCO FALLS AREA** | **202** |
|    TOBACCO FALLS HIKE | 202 |
|       ■ TOBACCO FALLS - LOWER  (TOBACCO RIVER) | 202 |
|       ■ TOBACCO FALLS - UPPER  (TOBACCO RIVER) | 203 |

County Table of Contents

# MARQUETTE COUNTY MAP (NORTH)    206
# MARQUETTE COUNTY MAP (SOUTH)    208

## ALDER FALLS AREA .......................................................................................... 210
   ALDER FALLS HIKE ............................................................................................ 210
      🟩 ALDER FALLS  (ALDER CREEK) ............................................................... 211

## BLACK RIVER FALLS AREA ............................................................................... 212
   BLACK RIVER FALLS HIKE ................................................................................ 212
      🟩 BLACK RIVER FALLS  (BLACK RIVER) ................................................... 213

## BULLDOG FALLS AREA ..................................................................................... 214
   BULLDOG FALLS HIKE ...................................................................................... 214
      🟩 BULLDOG FALLS #1  (YELLOW DOG RIVER) ......................................... 216
      🟩 BULLDOG FALLS #2  (YELLOW DOG RIVER) ......................................... 217
      🟩 BULLDOG FALLS #3  (YELLOW DOG RIVER) ......................................... 218
      🟩 BULLDOG FALLS #4  (YELLOW DOG RIVER) ......................................... 219
      🟩 BULLDOG FALLS #5  (YELLOW DOG RIVER) ......................................... 220
      🟨 BULLDOG FALLS #6  (YELLOW DOG RIVER) ......................................... 221
      🟨 BULLDOG FALLS #7  (YELLOW DOG RIVER) ......................................... 222
      🟨 BULLDOG FALLS #8  (YELLOW DOG RIVER) ......................................... 223
      🟩 WEST BRANCH FALLS #1  (YELLOW DOG RIVER - WEST BRANCH) .... 224
      🟩 WEST BRANCH FALLS #2  (YELLOW DOG RIVER - WEST BRANCH) .... 225

## CARP RIVER FALLS AREA .................................................................................. 226
   CARP RIVER FALLS HIKE .................................................................................. 226
      🟩 MORGAN FALLS  (MORGAN CREEK) ..................................................... 227
      🟥 CARP RIVER FALLS #1  (CARP RIVER) ................................................... 228
      🟨 CARP RIVER FALLS #2  (CARP RIVER) ................................................... 229
      🟨 CARP RIVER FALLS #3  (CARP RIVER) ................................................... 230
      🟩 CARP RIVER FALLS #4  (CARP RIVER) ................................................... 231
      🟨 CARP RIVER FALLS #5  (CARP RIVER) ................................................... 232
      🟩 CARP RIVER FALLS #6  (CARP RIVER) ................................................... 233

## CARP RIVER - UPPER FALLS AREA ................................................................... 234
   UPPER CARP RIVER FALLS HIKE ..................................................................... 234
      🟨 CARP RIVER FALLS - UPPER #1  (CARP RIVER) .................................... 235
      🟩 CARP RIVER FALLS - UPPER #2  (CARP RIVER) .................................... 236

## DEAD RIVER FALLS AREA ................................................................................. 237
   DEAD RIVER FALLS HIKE .................................................................................. 237
      🟨 DEAD RIVER CASCADES  (DEAD RIVER) .............................................. 238
      🟨 DEAD ISLAND FALLS - LOWER  (DEAD RIVER) .................................... 239
      🟨 DEAD ISLAND FALLS  (DEAD RIVER) ..................................................... 240
      🟩 DEAD POOL FALLS  (DEAD RIVER) ........................................................ 241
      🟩 DEAD POOL FALLS - UPPER  (DEAD RIVER) ......................................... 242
      🟩 DEAD HOOK FALLS  (DEAD RIVER) ....................................................... 243
      🟩 DEAD PLUNGE FALLS  (DEAD RIVER) ................................................... 244
      🟩 STONY MILLS FALLS  (DEAD RIVER) ..................................................... 245
   LOWER DEAD RIVER FALLS HIKE .................................................................... 246
      🟨 DEAD RIVER FALLS - LOWER #1  (DEAD RIVER) .................................. 246
      🟨 DEAD RIVER FALLS - LOWER #2  (DEAD RIVER) .................................. 247
   REANY FALLS HIKE ........................................................................................... 248
      🟨 REANY FALLS  (REANY CREEK) .............................................................. 248

## FORTY FOOT FALLS AREA ................................................................................ 249
   FORTY FOOT FALLS HIKE ................................................................................ 250
      🟩 FORTY FOOT FALLS  (CLIFF RIVER) ...................................................... 250

## GARLIC FALLS AREA ......................................................................................... 251
   GARLIC FALLS HIKE .......................................................................................... 251
      🟨 GARLIC FALLS  (BIG GARLIC RIVER) ..................................................... 252
   GARLIC FALLS - UPPER HIKE ........................................................................... 253
      🟨 GARLIC FALLS - UPPER #1  (BIG GARLIC RIVER) ................................. 253
      🟩 GARLIC FALLS - UPPER #2  (BIG GARLIC RIVER) ................................. 254

XIII

## County Table of Contents

### GWINN AREA .................................................................................................. 255
- ESCANABA RIVER FALLS HIKE ............................................................................. 255
  - ■ FIRST FALLS (EAST BRANCH ESCANABA RIVER) ................................................. 255
  - ■ SECOND FALLS (EAST BRANCH ESCANABA RIVER) ............................................ 256

### MORGAN MEADOWS FALLS AREA ............................................................ 257
- MORGAN MEADOWS FALLS HIKE ........................................................................ 257
  - ■ MORGAN MEADOWS FALLS (MORGAN CREEK) ................................................. 258

### PINNACLE FALLS AREA ............................................................................. 259
- PINNACLE FALLS HIKE ........................................................................................ 259
  - ■ PINNACLE FALLS (YELLOW DOG RIVER) ........................................................... 260

### TRESTLE FALLS AREA ............................................................................... 261
- TRESTLE FALLS HIKE .......................................................................................... 261
  - ■ TRESTLE FALLS (DEAD RIVER) ........................................................................... 262

### WARNER FALLS AREA .............................................................................. 263
- SCHWEITZER FALLS HIKE .................................................................................... 263
  - ■ SCHWEITZER FALLS (SCHWEITZER CREEK) ....................................................... 263
- WARNER FALLS HIKE .......................................................................................... 264
  - ■ WARNER FALLS (WARNER CREEK) ................................................................... 264

### YELLOW DOG FALLS AREA ....................................................................... 265
- BIG PUP FALLS HIKE ........................................................................................... 265
  - ■ BIG PUP FALLS (BIG PUP CREEK) ...................................................................... 266
- YELLOW DOG FALLS HIKE .................................................................................. 267
  - ■ YELLOW DOG FALLS #1 (YELLOW DOG RIVER) ............................................... 268

# MENOMINEE COUNTY MAP ............................................................ 270

### PEMENE FALLS AREA ............................................................................... 271
- PEMENE FALLS HIKE .......................................................................................... 272
  - ■ PEMENE FALLS (MENOMINEE RIVER) ............................................................... 272

# ONTONAGON COUNTY MAP ........................................................... 274

### AGATE FALLS AREA .................................................................................. 276
- AGATE FALLS HIKE ............................................................................................. 276
  - ■ AGATE FALLS (WEST BRANCH - ONTONAGON RIVER) .................................... 277

### BONANZA FALLS AREA ............................................................................ 278
- BONANZA FALLS HIKE ....................................................................................... 278
  - ■ BONANZA FALLS (BIG IRON RIVER) ................................................................. 279

### BOND FALLS AREA ................................................................................... 280
- BOND FALLS HIKE .............................................................................................. 280
  - ■ BOND FALLS (MIDDLE BRANCH - ONTONAGON RIVER) ................................ 281
  - ■ BOND FALLS - UPPER (MIDDLE BRANCH - ONTONAGON RIVER) .................. 283

### CASCADE FALLS AREA ............................................................................. 284
- CASCADE FALLS HIKE ........................................................................................ 284
  - ■ CASCADE FALLS (CASCADE CREEK) ................................................................. 284

### LITTLE TRAP FALLS AREA ........................................................................ 285
- LITTLE TRAP FALLS HIKE .................................................................................... 285
  - ■ LITTLE TRAP FALLS (ANDERSON CREEK) ......................................................... 286

### O-KUN-DE-KUN FALLS AREA ................................................................... 287
- O-KUN-DE-KUN FALLS HIKE .............................................................................. 287
  - ■ PEANUT BUTTER FALLS (BALTIMORE RIVER) ................................................... 288
  - ■ O-KUN-DE-KUN FALLS (BALTIMORE RIVER) .................................................... 289
- SANDSTONE CREEK FALLS HIKE ........................................................................ 290
  - ■ SANDSTONE CREEK FALLS (SANDSTONE CREEK) ........................................... 290
- VICTORIA DAM FALLS HIKE ............................................................................... 291
  - ■ VICTORIA DAM FALLS (ONTONAGON RIVER - WEST BRANCH) ..................... 291

XIV

### PENN FALLS AREA — 292
- PENN FALLS HIKE .......... 293
  - 🟩 PENN FALLS - LOWER  (FIRESTEEL RIVER - EAST BRANCH) .......... 294
  - 🟩 PENN FALLS - UPPER  (FIRESTEEL RIVER - EAST BRANCH) .......... 295

# PORCUPINE MOUNTAINS MAP — 298
- EXPLORERS FALLS HIKE .......... 300
  - 🟨 EXPLORERS FALLS  (LITTLE CARP RIVER) .......... 301
- NONESUCH FALLS HIKE .......... 302
  - 🟨 NONESUCH FALLS  (IRON RIVER) .......... 302
- PRESQUE ISLE FALLS HIKE .......... 303
  - 🟩 PRESQUE ISLE KETTLES  (PRESQUE ISLE RIVER) .......... 303
  - 🟩 MANABEZHO FALLS  (PRESQUE ISLE RIVER) .......... 304
  - 🟩 MANIDO FALLS  (PRESQUE ISLE RIVER) .......... 305
  - 🟩 NAWADAHA FALLS  (PRESQUE ISLE RIVER) .......... 306

### CARP RIVER AREA — 307
- CARP RIVER HIKE .......... 307
  - 🟩 BATHTUB FALLS  (CARP RIVER) .......... 308
  - 🟩 BIG CARP FALLS  (CARP RIVER) .......... 309
  - 🟩 SHINING CLOUD FALLS  (CARP RIVER) .......... 310

### LITTLE CARP RIVER AREA — 311
- LITTLE CARP RIVER HIKE .......... 311
  - 🟩 OVERLOOKED FALLS  (LITTLE CARP RIVER) .......... 312
  - 🟩 GREENSTONE FALLS  (LITTLE CARP RIVER) .......... 313

### TRAP FALLS AREA — 314
- TRAP FALLS AREA HIKE .......... 314
  - 🟩 TRAP FALLS  (CARP RIVER) .......... 315

### UNION RIVER AREA — 316
- LITTLE UNION RIVER HIKE .......... 316
  - 🟩 LITTLE UNION GORGE FALLS  (LITTLE UNION RIVER) .......... 317
  - 🟩 LITTLE UNION GORGE FALLS - LOWER  (LITTLE UNION RIVER) .......... 318
  - 🟩 ARTISTS FALLS #1  (LITTLE UNION RIVER) .......... 319
  - 🟨 ARTISTS FALLS #2  (LITTLE UNION RIVER) .......... 320
  - 🟩 INSPIRATION FALLS  (LITTLE UNION RIVER) .......... 321
- UNION RIVER HIKE .......... 322
  - 🟨 UNION MINE FALLS  (UNION RIVER) .......... 322

# PRESQUE ISLE COUNTY MAP — 324
### OCQUEOC FALLS AREA — 326
- OCQUEOC FALLS HIKE .......... 326
  - 🟨 OCQUEOC FALLS  (OCQUEOC RIVER) .......... 327

The Guide to the Guide

*Full Color* **County Maps** *have Area Map Breakdowns.*

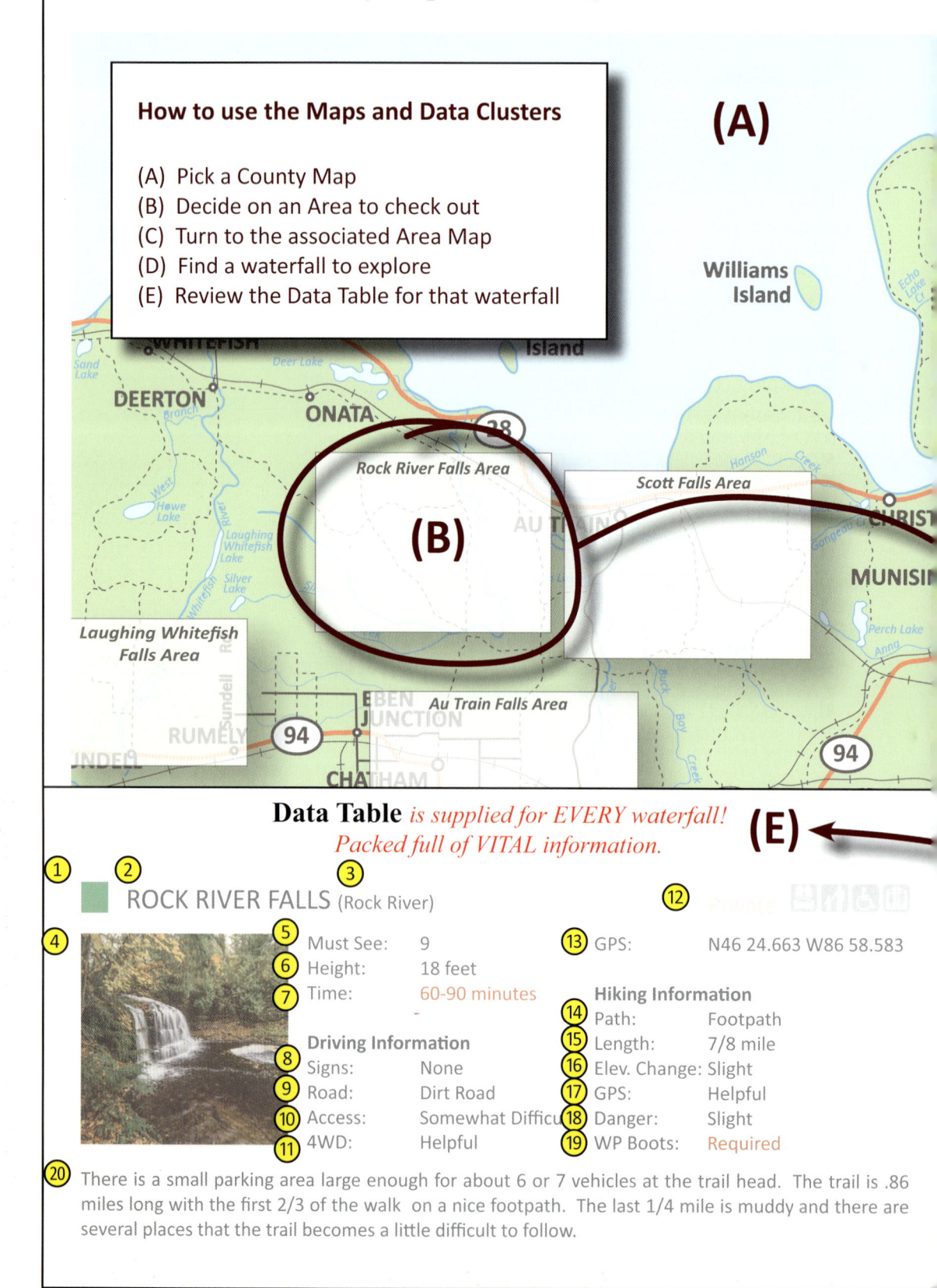

**How to use the Maps and Data Clusters**

(A) Pick a County Map
(B) Decide on an Area to check out
(C) Turn to the associated Area Map
(D) Find a waterfall to explore
(E) Review the Data Table for that waterfall

**Data Table** *is supplied for EVERY waterfall!*
*Packed full of VITAL information.* **(E)**

**ROCK RIVER FALLS** (Rock River)

| | |
|---|---|
| Must See: | 9 |
| Height: | 18 feet |
| Time: | 60-90 minutes |

**Driving Information**
| | |
|---|---|
| Signs: | None |
| Road: | Dirt Road |
| Access: | Somewhat Difficult |
| 4WD: | Helpful |

| | |
|---|---|
| GPS: | N46 24.663 W86 58.583 |

**Hiking Information**
| | |
|---|---|
| Path: | Footpath |
| Length: | 7/8 mile |
| Elev. Change: | Slight |
| GPS: | Helpful |
| Danger: | Slight |
| WP Boots: | Required |

There is a small parking area large enough for about 6 or 7 vehicles at the trail head. The trail is .86 miles long with the first 2/3 of the walk on a nice footpath. The last 1/4 mile is muddy and there are several places that the trail becomes a little difficult to follow.

XVI

The Guide to the Guide

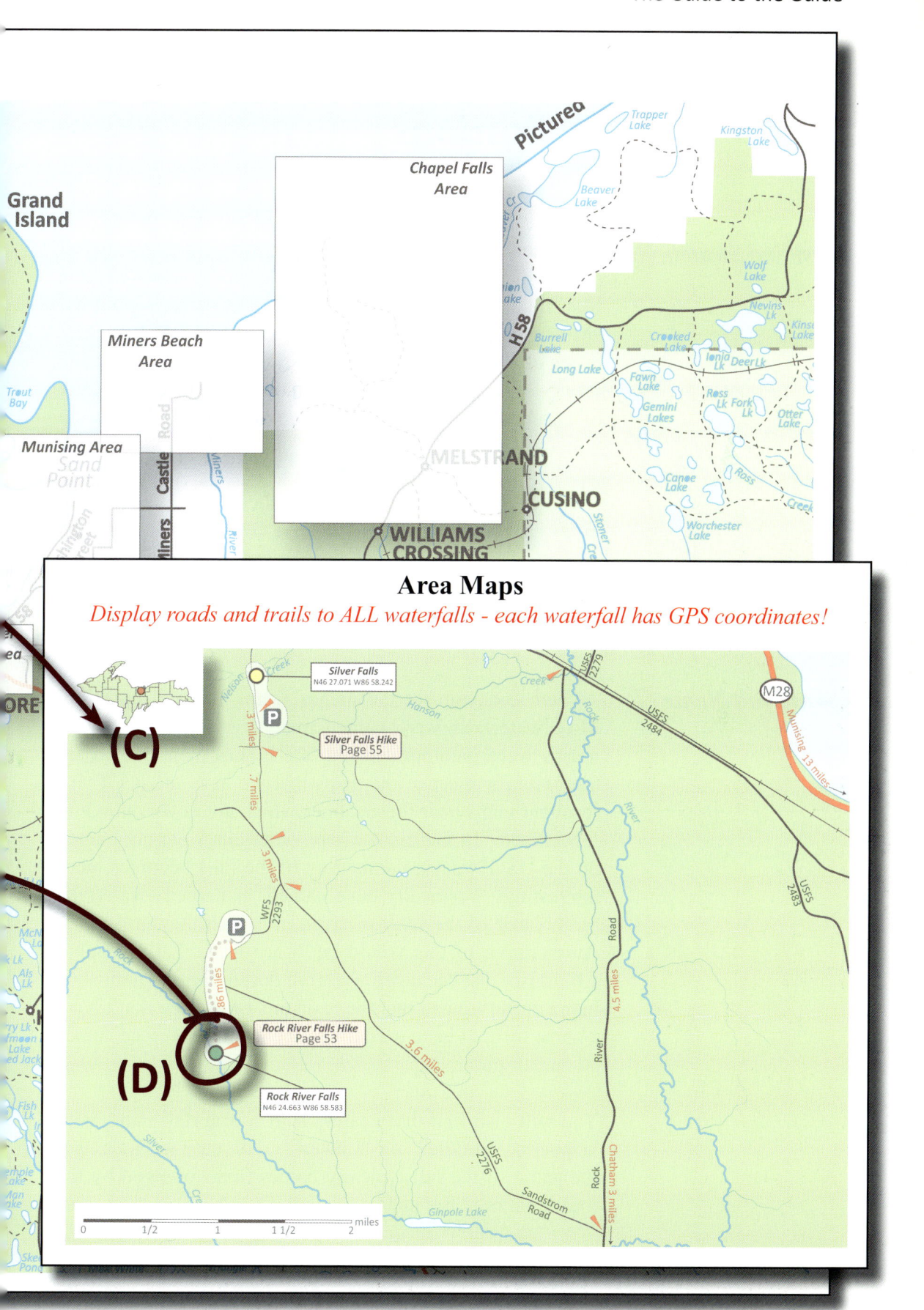

## Area Maps
*Display roads and trails to ALL waterfalls - each waterfall has GPS coordinates!*

XVII

# Data Table
## Definitions

***Must See Swatch*** ①  The colored square in the upper, left corner of the Waterfall Data Tables corresponds with the color in the Waterfall Area Map for each particular waterfall and is derived from the "Must See" rating. Those waterfalls with a "Must See" rating of 1-3 are "Red" waterfalls. "Yellow" waterfalls have ratings of 4-6, and "Green" waterfalls are rated 7-10. Think of the "Must See Colors" as you would a standard traffic light.

Green: GO!! You've got to check these out!
Yellow: SLOW DOWN!! These are OK waterfalls, perhaps it'll be nice to visit once or twice.
Red: STOP!! These are waterfalls, or at least considered waterfalls by some, but unless you are a die-hard waterfall fan, you probably won't enjoy them.

***Waterfall Name*** ② "Where did you get the names from?" Good question! Most waterfalls were named many years ago and those names were incorporated into the USGS maps which are the basis for most of the maps that we have today. These resultant maps bear those names which are now commonly recognized. In the cases where waterfalls were not named on the USGS maps, the naming of the falls becomes more interesting. I typically have named "unnamed" waterfalls by the area of the river or creek on which they are found. An example of this would be "Carp River Falls - Upper #3". Also, just because a waterfall doesn't have a published name doesn't mean that the residents of an area don't have a name for it. I have tried to use the locally accepted names whenever possible.

You will also find that I rarely start a waterfall name with "Upper", "Middle", or "Lower". For ease of indexing, the name of the fall typically comes first, followed by the locational modifier and/or number if applicable.

Most of the waterways on which waterfalls are found have long established names. Just like waterfalls, there are some small creeks that have no published names, but do have locally accepted names. I have used these names whenever known.

**③ *Waterway Name***

A small picture of each waterfall is attached. Some waterfalls are on posted, private land. If I wasn't able to receive permission to photograph the waterfall, there is obviously no picture.

**④ *Waterfall Picture***

Each waterfall is rated on a 1-10 scale, with one being the least desirable and 10 being the most. The following is the guideline I use:

**⑤ *Must See Rating***

10. Gorgeous! Great eye appeal! Inspiring! One of the best waterfalls in Michigan.
9. Excellent waterfall! You will want to make many repeat visits.
8. Very nice waterfall! Very popular!
7. Nice waterfall. Worth coming back to see several times.
6. An above average waterfall. Might want to see it again.
5. A nice all-around waterfall. Perhaps worth a repeat visit.
4. An OK waterfall. Probably not worth coming back to.
3. Don't have your hopes too high - it's not that good.
2. Avid waterfall enthusiasts may want to check it out just to say that they did.
1. It's water. It's falling. Who cares?

The "Must See" rating is my attempt at describing only the visual desirability of each waterfall. It doesn't take into account the difficulty in getting to the waterfall. There are some very nice waterfalls that require a substantial hike over rough terrain. The difficulty in reaching the waterfall doesn't figure into "Must See" rating.

Everyone has their own taste in waterfalls. What I am looking for in a waterfall is a visually pleasing setting combined with water that is falling at angles and with rates in keeping with the overall genre of the waterfall. Consistency and lack of obvious flaws is also important.

There may be times when you disagree with my rating. Keep in mind that water level, season, temperature, weather conditions, sun position, and even frame of mind affect the

# The Guide to the Guide

visual desirability of any waterfall at any point in time.

I have included the "Must See" rating to offer you a standardized method of comparing waterfalls so that you have some idea of which waterfalls you may wish to view.

*Waterfall Height* ⑥ This is an estimate of the height of the waterfall in feet. This is a potentially poor piece of information. Let me explain. If a waterfall has a free drop of 20 feet, flattens out for 20 to 30 feet of river length and then it has small cascading drops of 4 to 6 inches per drop for another 20 feet of accumulated drop, there would be a total drop of 40 feet. When viewing the waterfall, some people may consider just the free drop as the waterfall height, while others may include the additional 20 feet of cascades downstream. I tried to include the "normal" waterfall portion of the falls in my height estimates. I think of most waterfalls as viewable from one location. If a portion of the waterfall is not photogenic, then I may not have included that part in the overall height of the waterfall.

*Hike Time* ⑦ How much time should you plan for a hike? I have included an estimated amount of minutes or hours to plan for a hike. I am assuming that a hike entails a leisurely walk to and from the waterfall and includes an "appropriate" amount of time for viewing the waterfall.

*Is there a Sign?* ⑧ Most waterfalls have no signs announcing their presence. The waterfalls that do, have signs that are made by the Federal Government, the State of Michigan, counties, and some by private individuals.

*Worst Road Type* ⑨ In the process of driving to a waterfall the roads typically go from good to worse. So the road that a waterfall is accessed from will tell you what to expect for the worst driving conditions on your waterfall quest.

*Accessibility* ⑩ There is a wide variety of difficulty when it comes to finding a particular waterfall. A waterfall on a main road with signs announcing its presence is very easy to find. The more turns that are required off of a main road, the more difficult or complicated it becomes to find.

*Is a 4WD needed?* ⑪ You will find it easier to drive to some waterfalls with a 4WD vehicle. High clearance vehicles are sometimes needed.

Ghosted Symbols     Activated Symbols     **(12) *Quick Reference***

Private            Private

The "activated symbols" are the ones (if any) that apply to this particular waterfall.

**Private** This waterfall is on private land and more often than not the land is posted and the waterfall is not accessible to the public. *Note that this information is to the best of my knowledge. There very well may be more waterfalls on private land, but since it was not posted I was unaware. Be respectful of property owners and follow their wishes.*

- The waterfall can be viewed from a vehicle.
- A particularly kid-friendly waterfall.
- Wheelchair accessible
- Bathroom facilities are available, normally at the beginning of the hike. There will be flush, composting, or vault toilets.

The GPS coordinate for the waterfall is written in degrees and minutes.

**(13) *GPS Coordinate***

There are a variety of hiking trails that you will encounter. Expect everything from graded and paved trails to narrow dirt footpaths to no paths at all! Note that sometimes there will be one type of path at the beginning of the hike and another one entirely by the end. The worst type of path to the waterfall is listed here.

**(14) *Type of Path***

This is the length of the hike to the falls. Remember to double the length for a round trip estimate. Some hikes have a number of waterfalls along the route. The length for any particular waterfall along that hike is the distance from the vehicle to that waterfall, typically including the previous waterfalls found along the way.

**(15) *Hike Length***

Many waterfalls involve a change in elevation, either along the hike or climbing down into a ravine to the waterfall.

**(16) *Elevation Change***

Do you need a handheld GPS to find this waterfall? If so, make sure that you are using a reliable GPS and are familiar with its functions and use. Don't forget to take spare batteries. Having a compass with you is a great backup as well.

**(17) *GPS Needed?***

XXI

# The Guide to the Guide

***Danger*** (18)   Viewing waterfalls has some inherit danger; walking along potentially wet or icy paths or boardwalks, hiking over uneven ground and climbing into and out of ravines and gorges, standing at the brink of a fifty foot waterfall, navigating moss covered rocks near swift moving waters. Yes, caution is always important. But some waterfalls are more difficult to view or get to, so I trust this "Danger" category will help you to decide which waterfalls are right for you to view.

***Waterproof Boots?*** (19)   I prefer to keep my feet dry on waterfall hikes. If there are muddy trails or rivers or creeks that need to be forded I recommend wearing waterproof boots. I wear calf high boots when needing something more than my ankle high waterproof hiking shoes.

***Description*** (20)   Find out a little more about the waterfall or hike in this brief description.

## *Waterfall Etiquette*

Proper waterfall etiquette begins with a proper attitude toward people and the environment. Many waterfalls in the Upper Peninsula are on private land. Fortunately for us, many of the land owners allow individuals to drive on their property, park on it, and hike across it.

1) NEVER trespass on posted property. Obey all signs. The private property rights of all land owners must be respected.

2) Don't invade someone's personal space. Just because there isn't a "No Trespassing" sign doesn't mean that you can drive up next to their house, park your vehicle, and walk across their back yard to a waterfall just behind their house. Use common sense. Have proper waterfall etiquette. Do unto others as you would want them to do unto you. This timeless principle always holds true.

There are some waterfalls that are "OK" to view, but they are also quite close to residences. Be quiet and considerate. Be courteous and respectful.

3) Clean up after yourself. I know of a land owner that doesn't allow waterfall enthusiasts onto his land because every year he removes several bags of garbage from around the waterfall on his property. We must do better. Don't leave anything behind on your hikes. In fact, help clean up after others. If we all would do our part, I believe that more land owners would allow us to view the beauty that resides within their estates.

Respecting land owners and the environment in which the wonderful waterfalls of Michigan reside must be our top priority. Forsaking these principles will result in the loss of access to more and more waterfall locations. We must not let that happen.

# Waterfall Memories

| Waterfall | Page | Date | Memory |
|---|---|---|---|
| | | | |
| | | | |
| | | | |
| | | | |
| | | | |
| | | | |
| | | | |
| | | | |
| | | | |
| | | | |
| | | | |
| | | | |
| | | | |
| | | | |
| | | | |
| | | | |
| | | | |
| | | | |
| | | | |
| | | | |
| | | | |
| | | | |
| | | | |
| | | | |
| | | | |
| | | | |
| | | | |
| | | | |
| | | | |
| | | | |
| | | | |
| | | | |
| | | | |
| | | | |
| | | | |
| | | | |
| | | | |
| | | | |
| | | | |

# Waterfalls Memories

| Waterfall | Page | Date | Memory |
|---|---|---|---|
| | | | |
| | | | |
| | | | |
| | | | |
| | | | |
| | | | |
| | | | |
| | | | |
| | | | |
| | | | |
| | | | |
| | | | |
| | | | |
| | | | |
| | | | |
| | | | |
| | | | |
| | | | |
| | | | |
| | | | |
| | | | |
| | | | |
| | | | |
| | | | |
| | | | |
| | | | |
| | | | |
| | | | |
| | | | |
| | | | |
| | | | |
| | | | |
| | | | |
| | | | |
| | | | |
| | | | |
| | | | |
| | | | |

# CHAPTER 1
# ALGER COUNTY

# Alger County Map

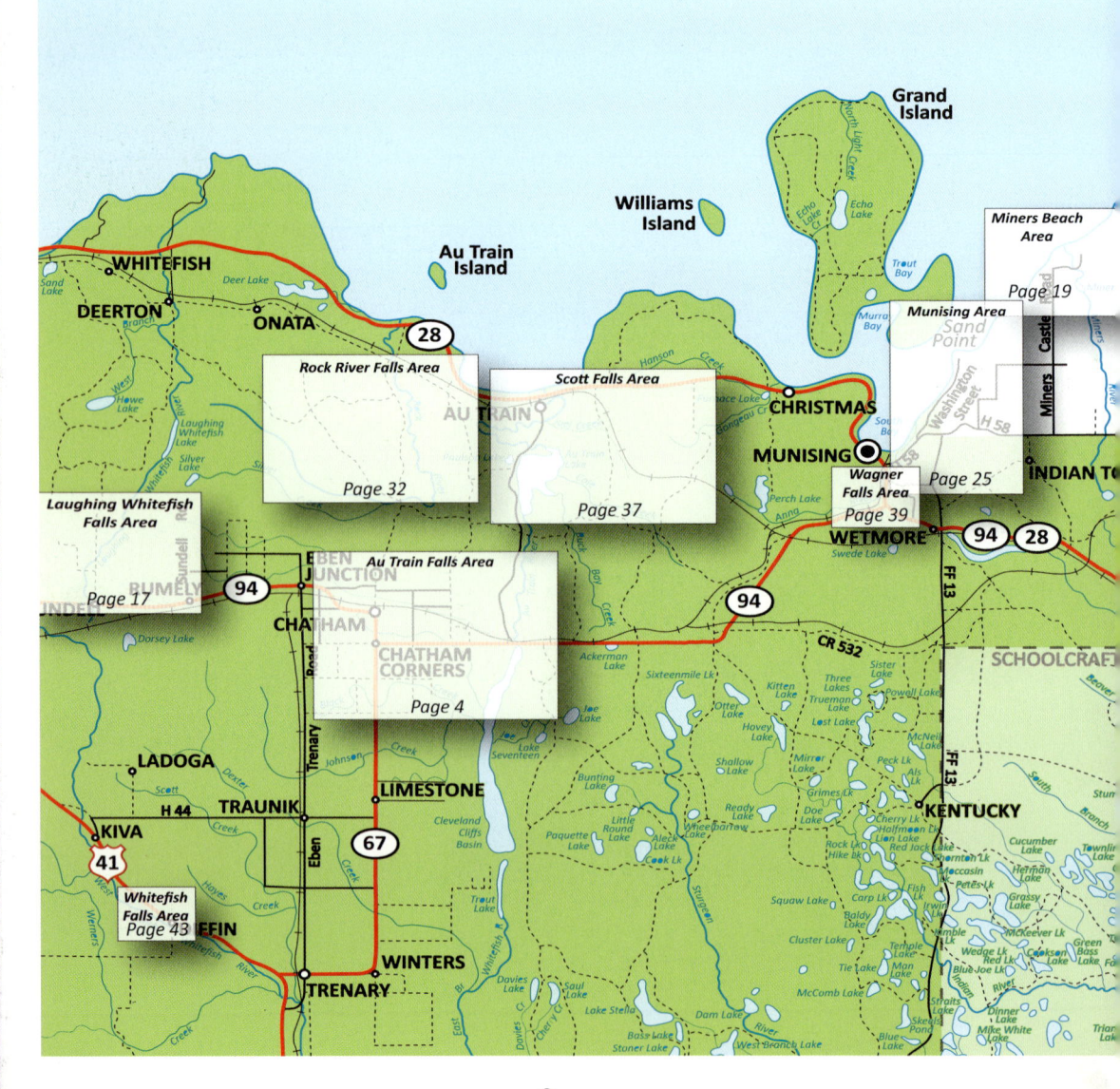

GRAND MARAIS
Hurricane Falls Area
Page 14
Sable Falls Area
Page 35
Chapel Falls Area
Page 6
H 58
CR 60
77
28
94
Pictured Rocks National Lakeshore
Grand Sable Lake
Trapper Lake
Beaver Lake
Kingston Lake
Preacher Lake
Wolf Lake
Nevins Lk
Kinsey Lake
Burrell Lake
Crooked Lake
Long Lake
Mocassin Lake
Lavender Lake
Buck Lake
Fox Lk
Panther Lk
Carter Lake
Mallard Lake
Teal Lake
Bearfoot Lake
McKay Lake
Cloverleaf Lake
Lake Nita
Gypsy Lake
Grass Lake
Sand Lake
Loon Lake
Deadman Lake
Adams Trail
GREEN HAVEN
Niemi Lake
Weber Lake
Line Lake
Sitka Lake
Sullivan Lake
Bluegill Lake
Mitchell Lake
Moose Lake
Havestock Creek
Blood Creek
Sucker River
Hurricane River
Rhody Cr
SCHOOLCRAFT COUNTY
Fawn Lake
Gemini Lakes
Ross Lk
Fork Lk
Otter Lake
Mahoney Lake
Sucker Lake
Lost Lake
Snyder Lake
Twin Lakes
Dutch Fred Lake
Canoe Lake
Worchester Lake
Driggs Lake
MELSTRAND
CUSINO
WILLIAMS CROSSING
AN MEER
HINGLETON
STAR
CRAIGHTON
WALSH
SENEY
Stoner Creek
Creighton River
Marsh Creek
Driggs River
Little Fox River
Fox River
Camp Seven Cr
East Branch
Cold Creek
Grondon Creek
Star Creek
Prairie Creek
Commencement Creek
West Branch
Walsh Creek
Holland Ditch
Manistique River
Hickey Creek
Hay Meadow Creek
Stutts Creek
North Branch
Lily Lake
Sand Lake
Clear Lake
Beaton Lake
Crooked Lake
Steuben Lake
STEUBEN
East Lake
Neighbor Lake
Pine Creek
A-Two Pool
C-Two Pool
I Pool
H Pool
G Pool
C Pool
B Pool
A Pool
M Pool
T Pool
GERMFASK
Sand Cr
Grays River
Delta Creek
Kennedy Lake
Stewart Lake
Holland Creek
0
2.5
5
7.5
10
miles

# AuTrain Falls Area

## AuTrain Falls Hike

**AuTrain Falls:** These are a series of cascades that extend 100 yards and are found north and south of the access road bridge that spans the river by the power house. None of the drops are spectacular in height or volume of water, but the typically shallow river allows for walking back and forth across the river and exploring the various drops up close.

**WARNING!** If a siren sounds, get to high ground immediately. This is a warning that the sluice gates upstream will be opened and a large volume of water will be heading downstream.

**Directions:** Turn east onto a service drive off of AuTrain Forest Lake Road (USFS 2278) just north of M-94. Drive down the access drive to the gate. Park. Walk past the normally locked gate down to the bridge that crosses the AuTrain River. The cascading drops can be seen both upstream and downstream from the bridge.

# AuTRAIN FALLS (AuTrain River)   Private

| | | | |
|---|---|---|---|
| Must See: | 6 | GPS: | N46 20.328 W86 51.131 |
| Height: | 10 feet | | |
| Time: | 15-45 minutes | | |

**Hiking Information**
Path: Blacktop Service Drive

**Driving Information**
| | | | |
|---|---|---|---|
| Signs: | Small | Length: | 100 yards |
| Road: | Secondary Road | Elev. Change: | Moderate |
| Access: | Easy | GPS: | N/A |
| 4WD: | N/A | Danger: | Slight |
| | | WP Boots: | If wading in the river |

View from the bridge that crosses the river. Waterproof boots are recommended if desiring to wade out in the 3 to 6 inch deep river. Underwater plant growth makes the rocks slippery in the riverbed. *(see lower picture)*

ALGER COUNTY

AuTrain Falls Area

AuTrain Falls

5

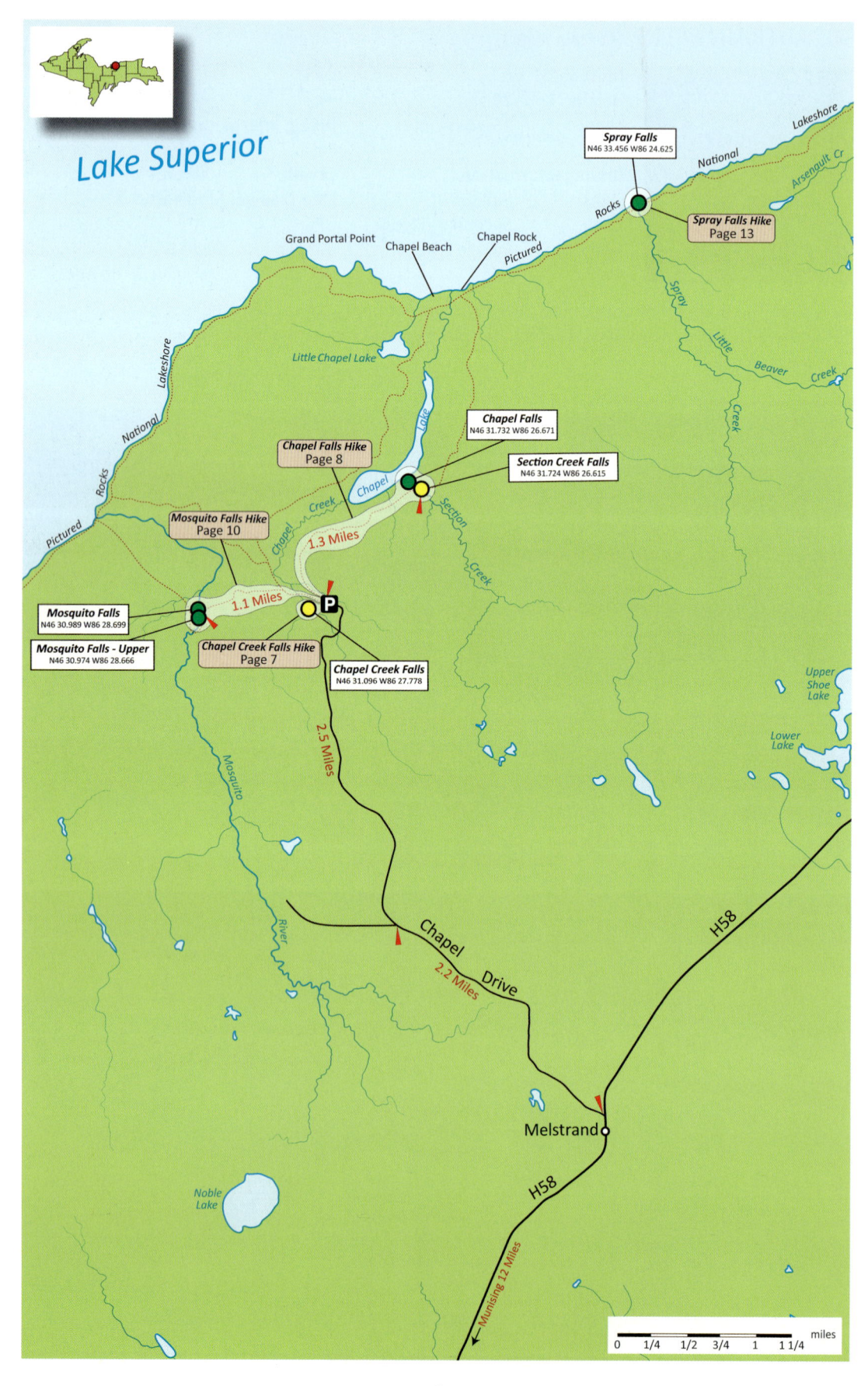

# Chapel Falls Area

**ALGER COUNTY**

Chapel Falls Area

### Chapel Creek Falls Hike

Most visitors that use the Chapel Falls Trailhead parking area are intent on hiking to Chapel Falls, Mosquito Falls, Chapel Beach or one of the many back country campgrounds. Few have Chapel Creek Falls in mind. The rest of the hiking destinations are over a mile away and yet Chapel Creek Falls can nearly be seen from the parking lot!

*Chapel Creek Falls:* Erosion in the shape of a horseshoe is the hallmark of canyons in the Pictured Rocks National Lakeshore. The relatively soft sandstone is susceptible to being worn rapidly by rivers and creeks as they plunge over the edge of cliffs. Chapel Creek follows this pattern. Chapel Creek cascades down into a canyon that is lined with smooth sandstone walls 30 feet tall. The falls start with a 5 foot sheer drop, then rapidly cascade down as the creek enters the canyon. Wild flowers abound below the falls. The creek divides into a few smaller channels that meander through the base of the canyon until the walls gently squeeze closer together and the creek resumes its course.

*Directions:* Follow the driving directions for Chapel Falls Hike. Park. Hike along the tributary (that runs under the road by the parking lot) downstream. This tributary merges with Chapel Creek about 150 yards downstream from the falls. A couple of periodically used paths descend from the cliff's edge down to the creek near the juncture. Hike upstream through the canyon to the falls.

## CHAPEL CREEK FALLS (Chapel Creek)                              Private

| | | | |
|---|---|---|---|
| Must See: | 6 | GPS: | N46 31.096 W86 27.778 |
| Height: | 25 feet | | |
| Time: | 20-45 minutes | **Hiking Information** | |
| | | Path: | Slight Footpath |
| **Driving Information** | | Length: | 200 yards |
| Signs: | None | Elev. Change: | Moderate |
| Road: | Dirt Road | GPS: | Helpful |
| Access: | Somewhat Difficult | Danger: | Moderate |
| 4WD: | Helpful | WP Boots: | Recommended |

Be careful getting down to the base of the falls. The canyon walls are fairly steep and about 20 feet high at the junction of Chapel Creek and the tributary that runs near the parking lot. There are also many fallen trees to navigate around heading up through the canyon to the wide, open area around the falls.

ALGER COUNTY

Chapel Creek Falls

Chapel Falls Area

### Chapel Falls Hike

The first snowflakes of the season swirled through the air. The hardwoods reluctantly dropped their golden leaves as the wind played tug-o'-war with the branches. And here I was, standing on the wooden viewing platform high above Chapel Falls, the tallest of all the waterfalls in the Pictured Rocks National Lakeshore. What a sight!

**Section Creek Falls:** Just before the path reaches Chapel Falls it crosses Section Creek. Section Creek Falls is immediately downstream from the bridge. Leave the path and follow the bank for a better view. Continuing downstream, the top of Chapel Falls is visible. Be careful, there is no fencing here, and Chapel Falls drops about 80 feet. Hike back to the path and follow it to the viewing deck for Chapel Falls.

**Chapel Falls:** The walk to Chapel Falls is relatively flat and the path is wide and well kept. It is a 1.3 mile hike to the "main" viewing deck (the one just past Section Creek Falls). There is another, smaller viewing deck before reaching the bridge over Section Creek. A short spur trail ends right next to the cliff edge for a closer view of Chapel Falls.

*Directions:* Take H 58 northeast out of Munising. Turn left (northwest) onto Chapel Drive (dirt road) and follow it for 2.2 miles. Stay to the right at the "Y", and travel for another 2.9 miles to the end of the road. This last section can be a bit rough, so be aware. There are vault toilets, a nice sized parking area and a bulletin board with camping information and directions here. The trail head for Mosquito Falls is to the left and the nicer path leading to Chapel Falls is to the right. Follow the trail to the right for 1.3 miles to Chapel Falls (Section Creek Falls is less than .1 miles before Chapel Falls).

## SECTION CREEK FALLS (Section Creek)     Private

| | | | |
|---|---|---|---|
| Must See: | 5 | GPS: | N46 31.724 W86 26.615 |
| Height: | 10 feet | | |
| Time: | 1 to 1.5 hours | Hiking Information | |
| | | Path: | Good Footpath |
| Driving Information | | Length: | 1.3 Miles |
| Signs: | None | Elev. Change: | Slight |
| Road: | Dirt Road | GPS: | Helpful |
| Access: | Somewhat Difficult | Danger: | Moderate |
| 4WD: | Helpful | WP Boots: | Helpful |

Section Creek Falls are easily seen on the way to Chapel Falls, as the path crosses Section Creek just above the falls. This serves as a nice "appetizer" for Chapel Falls. The soft, cascading water flowing downstream from the footbridge lets you know that you are almost to one of the best waterfalls in Michigan! Beware of steep drops in this area. Keep children close.

# CHAPEL FALLS (Section Creek)

Private

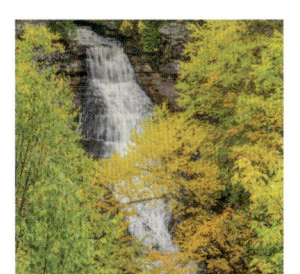

| | | | |
|---|---|---|---|
| Must See: | 10 | GPS: | N46 31.732 W86 26.671 |
| Height: | 80 feet | | |
| Time: | 1 1/2 to 2 hours | **Hiking Information** | |
| | | Path: | Good Footpath |
| **Driving Information** | | Length: | 1.3 Miles |
| Signs: | None | Elev. Change: | Slight |
| Road: | Dirt Road | GPS: | Helpful |
| Access: | Somewhat Difficult | Danger: | Moderate |
| 4WD: | Helpful | WP Boots: | Helpful |

Even though it is off of the beaten path, Chapel Falls is an internationally recognized destination. This is another of the MUST SEE attractions in Alger County. Chapel Falls has the largest drop of any of the Pictured Rocks National Lakeshore waterfalls. Be careful if taking children with you. There are some very steep drops with little guarding in the falls area.

*Chapel Falls as seen from the bottom of the cliff. A narrow path winds its way alongside the canyon face. This path is at the top of the bowl. Getting to the path is a bit of a trick. Find a spot along the top of the canyon where there is a safe climb down to the path. The path leads around the base of the cliff to just below the top of the waterfall.*

*Although it looks as if this photo was taken from the middle of the creek, I was actually set up on the edge of the bank. Climb down the very steep hill from the base of the cliff (see picture above). Much of this area is wet and soft. Waterproof boots are highly recommended. Once down to the bottom of the hill, head to the left (toward the base of the falls).*

9

Chapel Falls Area

### Mosquito Falls Hike

Mosquito Falls is a very popular waterfall that is found from the same parking lot as Chapel Falls. Make sure to continue past Mosquito Falls to the Upper Mosquito Falls. It is just a short distance upstream from Mosquito Falls, and is quite nice!

There is a somewhat tricky left turn that must be made on the trail fairly early on after leaving the Chapel Falls parking area. There are also a couple of hills that must be climbed, with roots and rocks holding the dirt in place. When finally arriving at Mosquito Falls, the trail will be at the top of the falls. (To view both of the "main" falls from the other side of the river, continue on the trail, past the Upper Falls to a bridge that crosses the river. Follow the trail on the other side back, first to the Upper Falls and then on to Mosquito Falls. The trail will be quite high above the river when arriving back at Mosquito Falls, but climbing down into the ravine from west side of the river isn't as difficult as from the east.) The trail crosses the river after the upper falls and doubles back downstream.

*Directions:* Use driving directions from the Chapel Falls Hike. From the parking lot for Chapel Falls, the trail head for Mosquito Falls is to the left. Waterproof boots are advisable for this hike, as there are some soft spots along the first 1.1 miles of the hike.

## MOSQUITO FALLS (Mosquito River)    Private

| | | | |
|---|---|---|---|
| Must See: | 7 | GPS: | N46 30.989 W86 26.699 |
| Height: | 14 feet | | |
| Time: | 1 to 1 1/2 hours | **Hiking Information** | |
| | | Path: | Unimproved Footpath |
| **Driving Information** | | Length: | 1.1 Miles |
| Signs: | None | Elev. Change: | Moderate |
| Road: | Dirt Road | GPS: | Helpful |
| Access: | Somewhat Difficult | Danger: | Moderate |
| 4WD: | Helpful | WP Boots: | Recommended |

The 1.1 mile hike meanders along a sometimes muddy and root filled trail. There are a couple of not-so-obvious turns at trail intersections. It is a good idea to bring your GPS along on this hike.

This beautiful cascading drop with sandstone walls banks off to the west, presenting itself with distinction. Yellow and green colors dominate the landscape in autumn. The fragrance of freshly fallen leaves - exhilarating. The constant sound of water falling - calming.

It's easier to access the river's edge from the west side of the river. To get there, follow the trail past the waterfall. You'll quickly come upon the upper drop and then a footbridge which crosses the river and doubles back to this waterfall. Leave the path and find a way down into the ravine. It's steep, but not as difficult to descend as the eastern side. The picture above was taken from the river's edge on the west side of the river. The shots on the facing page were taken from the east side. Here, the waterfall drops down into a shallow, 15 foot deep gorge. Climb down the steep bank through small, scrubby pine trees to get to this level.

Chapel Falls Area

*The ground at river's edge is very soft. Waterproof boots really should be worn if getting down to this level. Note the sandstone walls arching out from either side of the waterfall. Wildflowers are profuse in the water rich soil below the falls, especially on the west side of the river.*

Chapel Falls Area

## ■ MOSQUITO FALLS - UPPER (Mosquito River)     Private

| | | | |
|---|---|---|---|
| Must See: | 7 | GPS: | N46 30.974 W86 28.666 |
| Height: | 12 feet | | |
| Time: | 1 1/4 to 1 3/4 hours | **Hiking Information** | |
| | | Path: | Unimproved Footpath |
| **Driving Information** | | Length: | 1.2 Miles |
| Signs: | None | Elev. Change: | Moderate |
| Road: | Dirt Road | GPS: | Helpful |
| Access: | Somewhat Difficult | Danger: | Moderate |
| 4WD: | Helpful | WP Boots: | Recommended |

A footbridge crosses the Mosquito River just upstream from the falls. The trail doubles back along the river to allow access to both sides of the river at the falls. Note the difference between the rock wall lined canyon at Mosquito Falls and the river here that flows basically at the surrounding grade.

*Note the dead tree trunk leaning up against the waterfall. Waterfalls are notorious for collecting debris. Keep that in mind, especially when visiting waterfalls rarely seen. The look of a waterfall can change dramatically with downed trees and branches clogging the area. Over time, sometimes within a year, nature will break them down and the look will once again change.*

Chapel Falls Area

### Spray Falls Hike

**Spray Falls:** Spray Falls is one of the iconic waterfalls located along the Pictured Rocks National Lakeshore. It is commonly seen on postcards, brochures and billboards. The 70 foot drop into Lake Superior makes it one of the highest waterfalls in Michigan.

*Directions:* (The easiest way to view Spray Falls is by boat. Boat tours are offered May through October by Pictured Rocks Cruises, Inc., located in downtown Munising. Call (906) 387-2379 or check their website at *http://www.picturedrocks.com/Home.php* for more information. **NOTE: Not all of the boat tours travel all the way to Spray Falls.** Verify that the tour you are interested in will be viewing Spray Falls. It is the furthest point of interest on the tour, and is therefore sometimes cut out in the interest of time.

## SPRAY FALLS (Spray Creek)　　　　　　　　　　　Private

| | | | |
|---|---|---|---|
| Must See: | 8 | GPS: | N46 33.456 W86 24.625 |
| Height: | 70 feet | | |
| Time: | 2-3 hours | **Hiking Information** | |
| | | Path: | N/A |
| **Driving Information** | | Length: | N/A |
| Signs: | None | Elev. Change: | N/A |
| Road: | Secondary Road | GPS: | N/A |
| Access: | Easy | Danger: | Slight |
| 4WD: | N/A | WP Boots: | N/A |

The driving/hiking information listed is for taking the boat tour. I highly recommend it! There are wonderful sights all along the Pictured Rocks National Lakeshore that you will thoroughly enjoy. Spray Falls can also be viewed from along the Lakeshore Trail.

ALGER COUNTY

Spray Falls

Hurricane River Falls Area

ALGER COUNTY

## Hurricane Falls Hike

County Road H 58 underwent a major overhaul from 2009-2011. Hills were lowered, valleys filled in, turns smoothed out, tree lines moved back, and the entire stretch from Munising to Grand Marais is now paved. A gorgeous bridge was built over the Hurricane River next to the rustic U.S.F.S. campground. Come and listen to the babbling waterfall. Enjoy the expansive Lake Superior beach. Hike down to see the historic Au Sable Lighthouse.

**Hurricane Falls:** The small 5 foot cascade ends in a sandy bottomed stretch of river. Just down river from here a nice footbridge crosses the river.

**Hurricane Cascades:** As the Hurricane River emerges from the forest and enters the beach, it cascades down 4 feet over a multitude of small sandstone drops before it snakes out to Lake Superior.

**Directions:** These small waterfalls can be found near the entrance to the Hurricane River U.S.F.S. Campground. Follow H 58 south and west past Sable Falls for about 10.5 miles. A paved road into the campground is found just east of the Hurricane River bridge. (Look for the road that is next to the bridge. There is a second entrance/camping area. Don't stop at this one!) A paved parking lot is immediately on the left. Drive past this to a dirt day use parking area. Picnic tables and grills are nearby. Park here. Head toward Lake Superior. The river is on the left. The falls are a couple of hundred yards upriver from the beach.

*Au Sable Lighthouse*  *Sunset at the lake*   *Shipwrecks nearby*   *Beautiful Lake Superior*

14

Hurricane River Falls Area

## HURRICANE FALLS (Hurricane River)

Private

| | | | |
|---|---|---|---|
| Must See: | 5 | GPS: | N46 39.914 W86 10.049 |
| Height: | 5 feet | | |
| Time: | 10-30 minutes | **Hiking Information** | |
| | | Path: | Footpath |
| **Driving Information** | | Length: | 100 yards |
| Signs: | None | Elev. Change: | Slight |
| Road: | Secondary Road | GPS: | N/A |
| Access: | Somewhat Difficult | Danger: | Slight |
| 4WD: | N/A | WP Boots: | N/A |

This waterfall is tucked away into the woods close to the day use parking area at the Lower Hurricane Campground. Since Hurricane Falls is so close to Lake Superior, you may want to spend some time on the beach here as well!

Consider visiting the Au Sable Point Lighthouse while here. It is a 1.5 mile hike each way. You can either walk the beach or take the "foot traffic only" road. Both will take you directly to the lighthouse.

*The trail to the obvious overlook of the falls from the day use parking lot is well-trodden*

ALGER COUNTY

Hurricane Falls

15

Hurricane River Falls Area

### HURRICANE CASCADES (Hurricane River)                                   Private

| | | | |
|---|---|---|---|
| Must See: | 4 | GPS: | N46 39.959 W86 10.070 |
| Height: | 4 feet | | |
| Time: | 15-30 minutes | **Hiking Information** | |
| | | Path: | Footpath |
| **Driving Information** | | Length: | 100 yards |
| Signs: | None | Elev. Change: | Slight |
| Road: | Secondary Road | GPS: | N/A |
| Access: | Easy | Danger: | Slight |
| 4WD: | N/A | WP Boots: | N/A |

The bridge that spans the Hurricane River can be seen in the above picture. These rapids tumble over sandstone ledges as the river rushes across the beach to Lake Superior. Sunsets can be enjoyed by the river, as seen just below. Several small cascades can be viewed from the bridge looking upstream. *(bottom picture)*

ALGER COUNTY

Hurricane Cascades

16

Laughing Whitefish Falls Area

### Laughing Whitefish Falls Hike

This 100 foot tall cascading/sliding waterfall is impressive in its height, while simple in its shape. The water races down the long escarpment to rejoin the quiet river at the base of the falls. This is considered by some to be the best waterfall in Michigan! It is one of just a handful of waterfalls that I rate a 10 on my Must See scale!

Keep in mind that the Dorsey Road is only plowed the first 2 miles. Hiking during the winter and early spring means parking about .8 miles back from the "normal" parking area.

At the parking lot is a picnic area with a hand pump for water. There is a vault toilet as well. The DNR runs this location. For more information visit their web site. http://www.michigandnr.com/parksandtrails/Details.aspx?id=422&type=SPRK

*Directions:* From M-94, turn north onto Dorsey Road and follow it for 2.8 miles to the nice circular parking area. (Note: Dorsey Road becomes a dirt road and can be quite bumpy after the first 2 miles. After .3 miles on the bumpy road it turns to the east and continues for another .5 miles.) Hike .5 miles to the falls on the nicely maintained footpath.

### LAUGHING WHITEFISH FALLS (Laughing Whitefish River) Private

Must See: 10
Height: 100 feet
Time: 1 to 1.5 hours

GPS: N46 23.041 W87 4.145

**Driving Information**
Signs: Near Entrance
Road: Dirt Road
Access: Fairly Easy
4WD: Helpful

**Hiking Information**
Path: Improved Path
Length: .5 miles
Elev. Change: Moderate
GPS: N/A
Danger: Slight
WP Boots: N/A

During the year, Laughing Whitefish Falls puts on a variety of faces. During spring melt the river will fill the riverbed from wall to wall, white frothing water cascading down the steep slide. As summer comes along and the dry season slows the rivers, the waterfall moves further and further to the east, leaving most of the rock face exposed and dry.

There are three viewing decks, each one further down the falls. To reach the bottom viewing deck requires descending MANY steps. Make sure that you pace yourself.

*Looking down from the top of the tall falls*

18

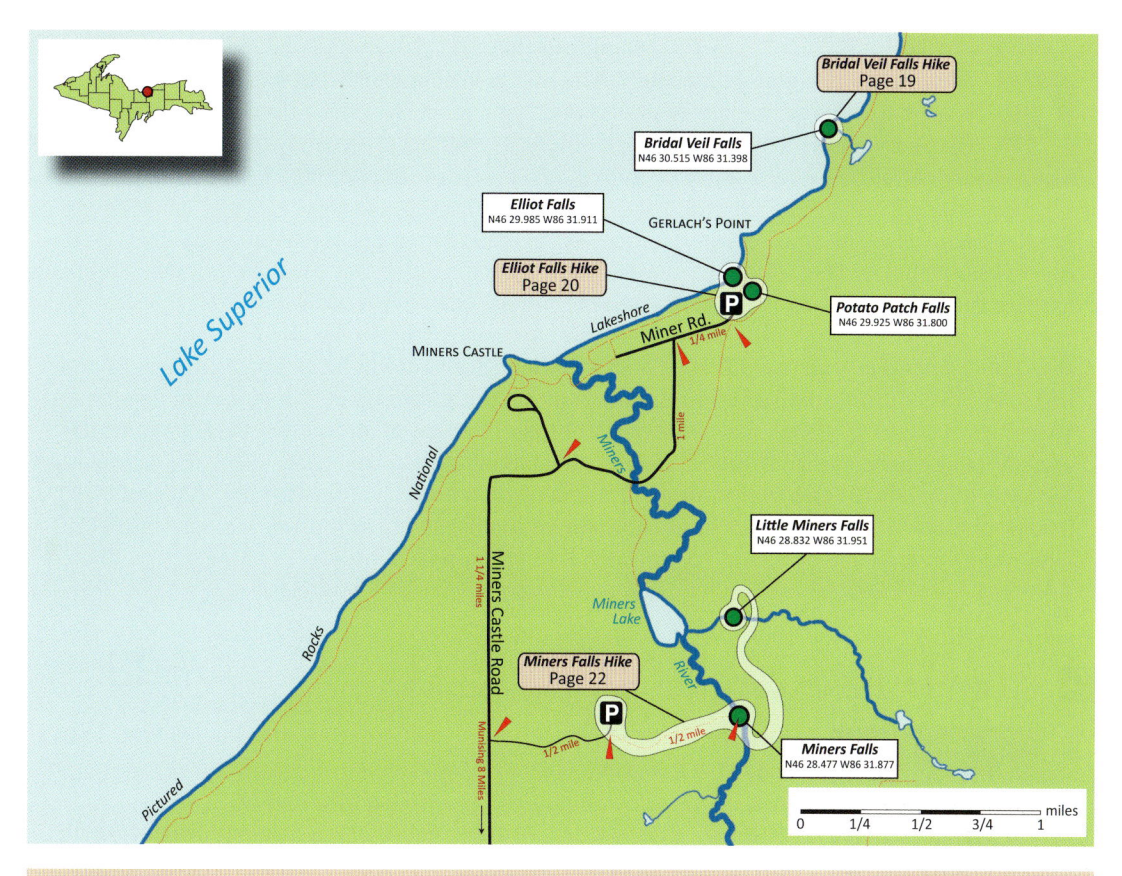

# Miners Beach Area

## Bridal Veil Falls Hike

**Bridal Veil Falls:** The falls are best viewed by taking the Pictured Rocks Boat Tour. Beavers have built a dam 50 yards upstream from the wooden footbridge over Bridal Veil Creek. This has greatly reduced the volume of water to this waterfall. During the drier months, this traditionally beautiful waterfall is drastically affected, so the best time to schedule this trip is in the spring during the snow melt or after heavy rains. Call for dates and times of operation at (906) 387-2379 or check their web site at *http://www.picturedrocks.com* for more information.

## BRIDAL VEIL FALLS (Bridal Veil Creek)   Private

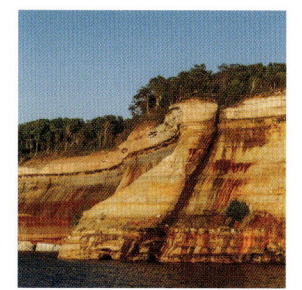

| | | | |
|---|---|---|---|
| Must See: | 7 | GPS: | N46 30.515 W86 31.398 |
| Height: | 134 feet | | |
| Time: | 3-4 hours | **Hiking Information** | |
| | | Path: | N/A |
| **Driving Information** | | Length: | N/A |
| Signs: | None | Elev. Change: | N/A |
| Road: | Side | GPS: | N/A |
| Access: | Easy | Danger: | Slight |
| 4WD: | N/A | WP Boots: | N/A |

Bridal Veil Falls has been featured in many postcards and other literature promoting Michigan and Pictured Rocks National Lakeshore. Unfortunately, a beaver dam upstream has greatly reduced the volume of water that flows here. The best viewing times are in the spring or after a large rainfall. It is easily best viewed from the lake. It can also be seen in the distance from Miners Castle. *This shot was taken from the Pictured Rocks Cruises.*

Traditionally, this waterfall would fan out and run down the face of the rock, spreading out like a bride's veil. This trickle is but a small portion of the water that once greeted Lake Superior mariners.

Miners Beach Area

ALGER COUNTY

### Elliot Falls Hike

***Elliot Falls:*** This cute little waterfall makes up in character what it lacks in height. This is a great waterfall for family picnics and outings. A short hike from the parking lot to the beach allows even the youngest among us to thoroughly enjoy this scenic spot. The beach, the waterfall, the interesting rock formations, the trees - altogether a lovely setting!

***Potato Patch Falls:*** The small creek that drops off of the Pictured Rocks Plateau into Miners Basin is very seasonal in its flow. There are times that it is running well and yet at other times there is hardly a trickle. Try viewing in the spring or after heavy, soaking rain showers.

***Directions:*** Continue north on CO H 13 past the Miners Falls turnoff for another 2 1/4 miles until the road "T's". Turn to the right and continue to the end of the road. There will be parking on both sides of the road. Park. Hike to the north to Lake Superior. Elliot Falls will be seen to the east around a slight bend in the shoreline. Back at the parking area, a trail heads off to the northeast. Follow it. It quickly rises up the escarpment, climbing up to the top of the plateau. After following it most of the way up, there is a narow footpath on the left that winds along the base of the cliff face. Follow it around a bend and Potato Patch Falls will appear shortly.

## ELLIOT FALLS: AKA Miners Beach Falls (Unnamed Creek)      Private

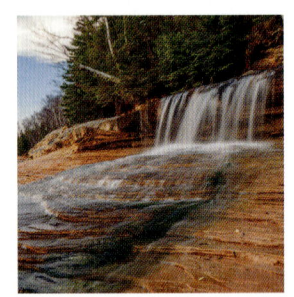

| | | | |
|---|---|---|---|
| Must See: | 7 | GPS: | N46 29.985 W86 31.911 |
| Height: | 6 feet | | |
| Time: | 15-60 minutes | **Hiking Information** | |
| | | Path: | Unimproved Footpath |
| **Driving Information** | | Length: | 200 yards |
| Signs: | None | Elev. Change: | Slight |
| Road: | Dirt Road | GPS: | N/A |
| Access: | Somewhat Difficult | Danger: | Slight |
| 4WD: | N/A | WP Boots: | N/A |

Even though Elliot Falls is a small waterfall, it is located in a gorgeous setting. You really owe it to yourself to check out the shoreline in the evening. Nothing is so beautiful as this stretch of water, sandstone and trees lit up by the setting sun.

Lake Superior has risen in recent years and eroded this shoreline dramatically. Every year brings about change.

Elliot Falls

Miners Beach Area

## POTATO PATCH FALLS (Unnamed Creek)  Private

| | | | |
|---|---|---|---|
| Must See: | 7 | GPS: | N46 29.925 W86 31.800 |
| Height: | 30 feet | | |
| Time: | 15-30 minutes | **Hiking Information** | |
| | | Path: | Semi-improved footpath |
| **Driving Information** | | Length: | 150 yards |
| Signs: | None | Elev. Change: | Moderate |
| Road: | Dirt Road | GPS: | N/A |
| Access: | Somewhat Difficult | Danger: | Moderate |
| 4WD: | N/A | WP Boots: | Recommended |

Climb the steep trail northeast from the parking lot. Just before reaching the top of the escarpment, a footpath will be seen following the base of the cliff face in both directions. Turn left (north). The path will drop back down a little, turn a corner and Potato Patch Falls will come into view just ahead. If you're fortunate and it has been raining there may be a good stream flowing as seen in these shots!

The waterfall drops in an unobstructed arc to the top of the rubble field. From there it quickly descends down a slippery and often debris filled waterway. Climbing down the embankment is not recommended as the ground is very wet and soft. You also want to be careful not to damage the lovely wildflowers that grow profusely in the area. It's best to stay on the narrow footpath which, as can be seen in the lower photo, winds along the cliff face and behind the waterfall to the far side.

Note: This waterfall can slow seasonally to a trickle.

*Trailhead to Potato Patch Falls*

ALGER COUNTY

Potato Patch Falls

Miners Beach Area

## Miners Falls Hike

Miners Falls is one of my favorite waterfalls to photograph! The torrent of water pouring down into Miners Basin is impressive, but so is the rock filled waterway as Miners River continues its course from the waterfall. The gorge decked out in golden leaves during October is a glorious sight! Add to it the constant sound of falling water and the pungent scent of newly fallen leaves. Hike along the 1/2 mile trail at first light with a touch of frost in the air and you have the makings of a wonderful day!

I have included Little Miners Falls in this hike, but it is really is an extension if you so desire. The hike to Miners Falls is straightforward and quite easy. Continuing on to Little Miners Falls is not! Keep that in mind when deciding how far to go on this hike.

*Directions:* From H 58, turn north on Miners Castle Road. In about 3.75 miles turn right (east) onto the well marked dirt road heading to Miners Falls. In about 1/2 mile it ends at a nice parking lot with vault toilets and picnic tables. Hike the 1/2 mile long well maintained trail to Miners Falls. Wooden stairs lead down to a very nice overlook. (Optional: Continue on to Little Miners Falls. From the top viewing deck get down to Miners River. You are above the top of Miners Falls, so be careful. Ford the river if it's not flowing too swiftly. Once again, be careful! On the far side of the river, the bank rises rapidly. Climb up out of the gorge for about 1/8 mile until the ground levels out with small rolling knolls and you are into the easy hiking hardwood forest. Turn left, paralleling Miners River downstream. In about 1/2 mile the ground will drop down into another gorge (shallower than the Miners River Gorge) when you intersect Little Miners River. Cross the river and head downstream to the top of the cliff. Follow it northerly until there is an obvious route down into Miners Basin (it's within a couple hundred yards of Little Miners River). Once into the gorge, follow the base of the cliff back to Little Miners River and Little Miners Falls.)

Warning! The second half of this hike is a serious hike through dense back country with no trails and generally no cell coverage. Take plenty of water and supplies for emergencies.

## MINERS FALLS (Miners River)          Private

| | | | |
|---|---|---|---|
| Must See: | 9 | GPS: | N46 28.477 W86 31.877 |
| Height: | 40 feet | | |
| Time: | 45-60 minutes | **Hiking Information** | |
| | | Path: | Improved Footpath |
| **Driving Information** | | Length: | 1/2 mile |
| Signs: | Sign near Entrance | Elev. Change: | Moderate |
| Road: | Dirt Road | GPS: | N/A |
| Access: | Somewhat Easy | Danger: | Slight |
| 4WD: | N/A | WP Boots: | N/A |

Miners River vaults itself into Miners Basin at the extreme end of the canyon. Miners Basin begins extremely narrow at this point, but continues to widen out all the way to Lake Superior. A viewing platform near the top of the falls offers limited viewing, but a great view of the falls is had from the lower wooden deck that is accessed via a wooden stairway. On the next page is a view from the riverbed. Rising air currents typically lift a mist from the base of the falls next to the wall on the right. The remnants of a third viewing deck can be seen below the lower platform. Visitors venturing down to get the closest look at the falls would often leave a little damp! Perhaps that is why the Park Service didn't replace that deck when it was eroded away.

22

Miners Beach Area

Picnic Facilities at the Trailhead

ALGER COUNTY

Miners Falls

Miners Beach Area

## LITTLE MINERS FALLS (Little Miners River)

Private

| | | | |
|---|---|---|---|
| Must See: | 8 | GPS: | N46 28.832 W86 31.951 |
| Height: | 40 feet | | |
| Time: | 3-4 hours | **Hiking Information** | |
| | | Path: | None |
| **Driving Information** | | Length: | 1.25 miles |
| Signs: | None | Elev. Change: | Major |
| Road: | Dirt Road | GPS: | Required |
| Access: | Somewhat Difficult | Danger: | Major |
| 4WD: | N/A | WP Boots: | Required |

This waterfall is impressive! It is very similar in appearance to Memorial and Olson Falls. The volume of water may be a little greater than those falls, but they all drop 30 to 40 feet with an undercut "cave" behind the falls.

There are no trails to this waterfall. However, the beauty of the waterfalls in this secluded land make the hike well worth the while. There is a large amount of sandstone eroded from behind the waterfall, creating a pseudo cave - perfect for a nice picnic before the return trip. Just make sure that you leave nothing but footprints.

Note the oh-so-typical horseshoe shaped and heavily eroded sandstone wall that Little Miners Falls flows over.

Note: There are vault toilets at the trailhead, NOT THE WATERFALL!

ALGER COUNTY

Little Miners Falls

24

Munising Falls Area

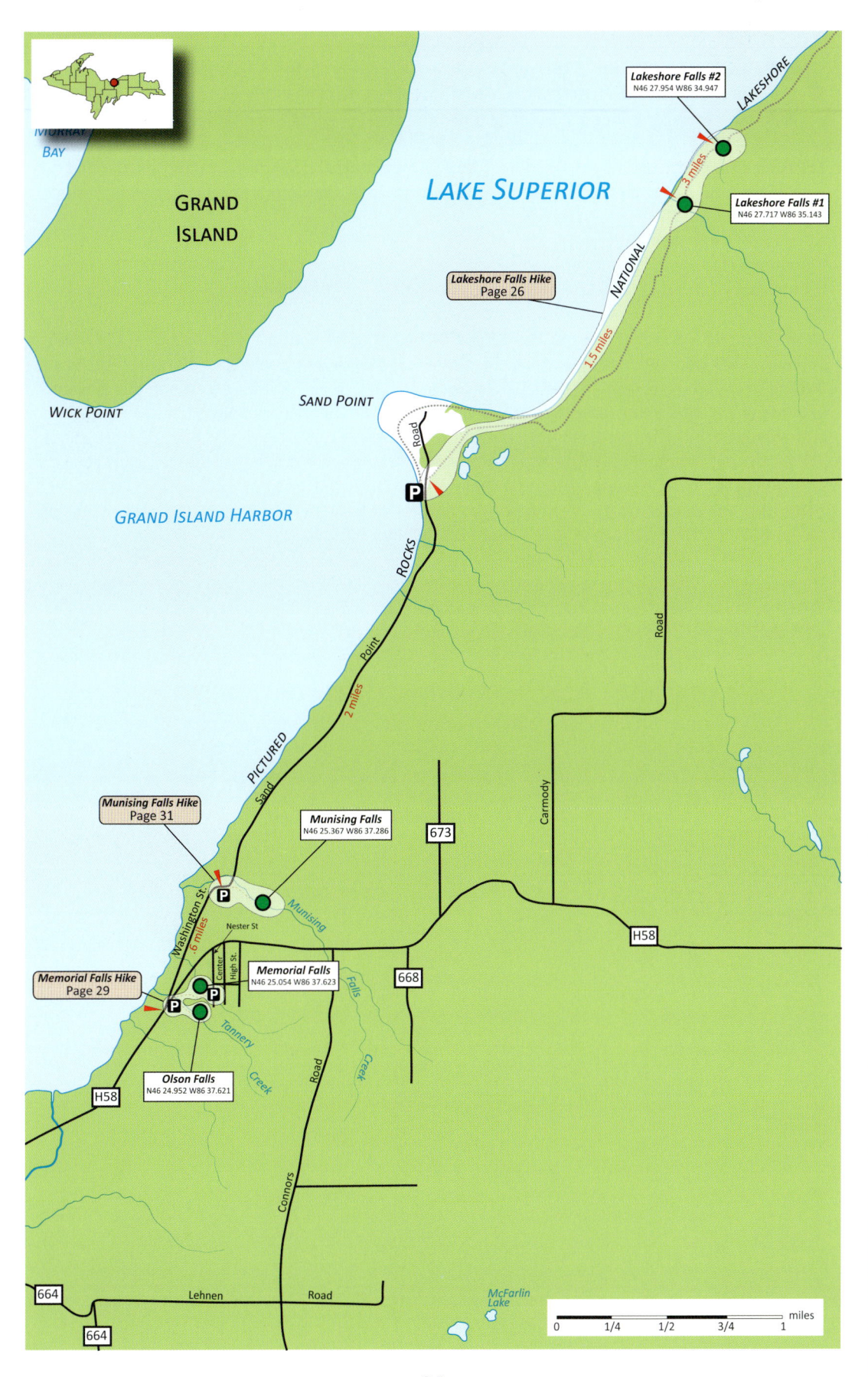

ALGER COUNTY

25

Munising Falls Area

### Lakeshore Falls Hike

***Lakeshore Falls #1***: * This remote waterfall is rarely visited. It is a 50 foot sheer drop off of the top of the Pictured Rocks National Lakeshore cliff. It drops into a small splash pool and then continues a steep slide down the bedrock for about another 80 feet.

***Lakeshore Falls #2:*** * Just like Lakeshore Falls #1, this waterfall is very remote and surrounded by rugged terrain. Although the volume of water is not large, the drop is spectacular, and presents itself nicely.

*Caution:* This portion of the hike can be dangerous. There is no trail most of the way. The terrain is quite steep at times. Fallen dead trees must be navigated. Wet bedrock can be very slippery.

*Directions:* Near the end of Sand Point Road is a parking lot with a great beach and bathroom facilities. Park here. Across the road is the Sand Point Marsh Trail trailhead. Follow it to the east, staying to the left. (A branch to the right loops through the Sand Point Marsh. Along this elevated walkway many interesting facts about the marsh and its inhabitants are pointed out.) Follow the shoreline (which can be accessed from the Sand Point Marsh Trail - it runs close to the shore about 2/3 of the way from the parking lot to the Lakeshore Trail) to the northeast until the cliffs start to rise along the shore, making further progress impossible. The small cliff can be climbed at this point (it is 4-6 feet tall here). The rest of the hike is not easy. To the right (east) is the main cliff face, which is a sheer vertical rise of around 20 to 80 feet in this area. To the left (west), there is a second cliff face which drops straight down into Lake Superior. The land in between these cliffs drops off toward the shore, sometimes quite steeply. Follow this corridor to the waterfalls. This is NOT an easy hike. There is no trail, and dead trees have fallen haphazardly along the way. The waterfalls are fed by small creeks which can easily be crossed.

Munising Falls Area

## LAKESHORE FALLS #1 (Unnamed Creek)

Private

| | | | |
|---|---|---|---|
| Must See: | 8 | GPS: | N46 27.717 W86 35.143 |
| Height: | 50 feet | | |
| Time: | 2.5 to 3.5 hours | **Hiking Information** | |
| | | Path: | None |
| **Driving Information** | | Length: | 1.5 miles |
| Signs: | None | Elev. Change: | Major |
| Road: | Secondary Road | GPS: | Required |
| Access: | Easy | Danger: | Extreme |
| 4WD: | N/A | WP Boots: | Recommended |

Hiking to this waterfall is very difficult. Careful planning and much caution must be used in attempting to visit this beautiful waterfall. I had wanted to see if there really was a waterfall here for some time. What an exhilarating sight to come upon the lovely drop after a long hike fighting off the mosquitoes and hiking along the often steep embankment. Viewing of the waterfall must also be done from the severely angled debris field.

After the creek makes it's 50 foot free fall over the sandstone face it continues to race down the slippery rock toward Lake Superior, some 100 yards to the west.

*Bathrooms are found at the parking area.*

ALGER COUNTY

Lakeshore Falls #1

27

Munising Falls Area

ALGER COUNTY

### LAKESHORE FALLS #2  (Unnamed Creek)

Private

| | | | |
|---|---|---|---|
| Must See: | 8 | GPS: | N46 27.954 W86 34.947 |
| Height: | 50 feet | | |
| Time: | 2.5 to 3.5 hours | **Hiking Information** | |
| | | Path: | None |
| **Driving Information** | | Length: | 1.8 miles |
| Signs: | None | Elev. Change: | Major |
| Road: | Secondary Road | GPS: | Required |
| Access: | Easy | Danger: | Extreme |
| 4WD: | N/A | WP Boots: | Recommended |

Once getting to Lakeshore Falls #1, it is only another 1/3 mile to this spectacular waterfall! This is on a larger creek than #1 so the volume of water will be greater than the first one. It is also slightly less steep terrain than #1, yet finding much of anything flat here is a challenge. What a gorgeous view, however! The free-falling water with the ribbed, undercut sandstone cliff towering overhead with the classic horseshoe shape is awe inspiring. Revel in the solitude.

*Bathrooms are found at the parking area.*

Lakeshore Falls #2

28

### Memorial Falls Hike

Tucked into sandstone canyons not far from a residential area, these waterfalls are under the care of the Michigan Nature Association (MNA). They have graciously opened up both of these waterfalls for public viewing so abide by their wishes and stay on the trails.

There is access to Memorial Falls from H 58 as well as Nester Street. It is a shorter walk to Memorial Falls from Nester Street, but hiking to both Memorial and Olson Falls can be more easily accomplished from H 58.

*Memorial Falls:* A small cascade is followed by a sheer drop into a large horseshoe shaped basin. Fine sand surrounds the splash pool. Soft underlying rock and sand has eroded away from behind the falls, opening up a large, undercut "cave" area.

*Olson Falls:* Memorial and Olson Falls look like twins. Perhaps it is because of their proximity and because they share similar sized creeks and the same bedrock. Here at Olson Falls another large, horseshoe shaped canyon receives the waterfall plunge of over 30 feet. The thin, wispy water falling can be mesmerizing.

*Directions*: There is a small parking spot (it looks like a short 2-track or driveway) off of H 58, near the intersection of Washington Street. Park here. The trail head is just north of here. The trail splits almost immediately. There is a small sign for each waterfall. Memorial Falls is to the left and Olson Falls is to the right. Each waterfall is about a 1/4 mile hike from here. The trails are narrow, unimproved footpaths, but quite easy to follow. Be on the alert as they drop into the canyons. Be aware of some steep drops.

## MEMORIAL FALLS (Unnamed Creek)                           Private

| | | | |
|---|---|---|---|
| Must See: | 8 | GPS: | N46 25.054 W86 37.623 |
| Height: | 40 feet | | |
| Time: | 30-60 minutes | **Hiking Information** | |
| | | Path: | Footpath |
| **Driving Information** | | Length: | 1/4 mile |
| Signs: | Small - Obscure | Elev. Change: | Moderate |
| Road: | Secondary Road | GPS: | Helpful |
| Access: | Easy | Danger: | Moderate |
| 4WD: | N/A | WP Boots: | Helpful |

Memorial Falls was recently made available to the public. What a great asset to the community! Be careful as the trail narrows on its downward trek to the bottom of the canyon. There are steep drops and care needs to be taken. That said, this waterfall, found just 1/4 mile in from H 58 is a lovely waterfall that can be viewed from various angles. It's one of those taller waterfalls that can be viewed intimately, even walking around behind the falls beneath the eroded sandstone overhead. As always, beware of falling rocks.

*Note the undercut sandstone*

*The trail to the waterfall*

29

Munising Falls Area

## OLSON FALLS  AKA: TANNERY FALLS  (Tannery Creek)   Private

| | |
|---|---|
| Must See: | 7 |
| Height: | 35 feet |
| Time: | 30-60 minutes |

**Driving Information**

| | |
|---|---|
| Signs: | Small-Obscure |
| Road: | Secondary Road |
| Access: | Easy |
| 4WD: | N/A |

| | |
|---|---|
| GPS: | N46 24.952 W86 37.621 |

**Hiking Information**

| | |
|---|---|
| Path: | Footpath |
| Length: | 1/4 mile |
| Elev. Change: | Moderate |
| GPS: | Helpful |
| Danger: | Moderate |
| WP Boots: | Helpful |

The name of this waterfall was recently changed from Tannery Falls to Olson Falls in honor of Rudolph M. Olson. The Michigan Nature Association (MNA), the owners of the land, wanted to honor Rudy Olson, one of their members. His grave is alongside the trail to the falls with a small rectangular bronze plaque marking the spot. Olson Falls and Memorial Falls are both part of a nature preserve that the MNA allows visitors to enjoy.

It's hard to believe that Munising is just a couple miles away when standing out here in the untamed beauty of nature. There is nothing but footprints to suggest that civilization is nearby. And that's the way it should be.

30

Munising Falls Area

ALGER COUNTY

### Munising Falls Hike

***Munising Falls:*** This popular waterfall destination is at the southwest end of the Pictured Rocks National Lakeshore. Along with an information center, there are rest rooms available here. The 1/4 mile long path to the falls is covered with asphalt. There are 3 viewing decks. The main deck is wheelchair accessible. There are also viewing decks built up higher on either side of the falls.

*Directions*: From H 58, turn north onto Washington Street. The large parking lot for Munising Falls is 1/2 mile down on the right (east). The trail to the falls starts between the bathrooms and the information center.

## MUNISING FALLS (Munising Falls Creek)   Private

| | | | |
|---|---|---|---|
| Must See: | 9 | GPS: | N46 25.367 W86 37.286 |
| Height: | 50 feet | | |
| Time: | 20-40 minutes | **Hiking Information** | |
| | | Path: | Improved Path |
| **Driving Information** | | Length: | 1/4 mile |
| Signs: | Sign at Parking Lot | Elev. Change: | Slight |
| Road: | Secondary Road | GPS: | N/A |
| Access: | Easy | Danger: | Slight |
| 4WD: | N/A | WP Boots: | N/A |

Munising Falls is perhaps the most popular waterfall in Munising - likely because it bears the name of the town, is close to downtown, and has a large, paved parking lot with bathroom facilities and an information center at the southwestern end of the Pictured Rocks National Lakeshore. And, maybe most importantly, it's a beautiful waterfall!

Munising Falls

31

Rock River Falls Area

## Rock River Falls Hike

**Rock River Falls:** Although it requires driving down dirt roads and hiking nearly a mile with some portions of the trail being wet and muddy, this is a waterfall that you will really want to visit. The classic cascading ribbons of water fan out slightly as they fall, creating a sense of fullness and portraying beautiful symmetry.

The trail leads to the base of the waterfall, but it can also be viewed from the top of the ledge. There is no railing, so be careful.

*Directions:* Rock River Road runs between USFS 2484 and Chatham. From Rock River Road, turn west onto Sandstrom Road (USFS 2276). Follow it for 3.6 miles. USFS 2293 turns to the left. (The sign was quite worn when I was there in the spring of 2010.) Within about .5 miles a small turnoff area will appear for the trail head to Rock River Falls. Park on either side of the road, leaving room for others to park or drive on through. The hike is .86 miles long and starts off very nice, but by the end, the trail is muddy and sometimes difficult to see.

## ROCK RIVER FALLS (Rock River)   Private

| | | | |
|---|---|---|---|
| Must See: | 9 | GPS: | N46 24.663 W86 58.583 |
| Height: | 18 feet | | |
| Time: | 60-90 minutes | **Hiking Information** | |
| | | Path: | Footpath |
| **Driving Information** | | Length: | 7/8 mile |
| Signs: | None | Elev. Change: | Slight |
| Road: | Dirt Road | GPS: | Helpful |
| Access: | Somewhat Difficult | Danger: | Slight |
| 4WD: | Helpful | WP Boots: | Required |

There is a small parking area large enough for about 6 or 7 vehicles at the trail head. The trail is .86 miles long with the first 2/3 of the walk on a nice footpath. The last 1/4 mile is muddy and there are several places where the trail becomes a little difficult to follow.

I love hiking out to this gem of a waterfall! Finding the trailhead can feel like an accomplishment. And then after hiking the deteriorating trail and wondering if the waterfall will ever appear, it will suddenly be heard off to the right after gaining entrance to the shallow gorge! And there's the beautiful waterfall coming into view! This is a delight that demands to be enjoyed time and again!

33

Rock River Falls Area

### Silver Falls Hike

*Silver Falls:* My son, Nathan, has referred to this waterfall as "Terror Falls", so named after the number of mosquitoes that we encountered there in June of 2009. The fall is couched in a steep ravine that serves as a funnel for debris. A dead tree was obstructing the view in 2009. By 2010 the branches had started to break down and not take up so much of the "visual space" of the falls.

*Directions:* Use the same directions as Rock River Falls. Where USFS 2293 turns to the left, continue on straight for .3 miles. Stay to the right. Drive another .7 miles. At this point the main road turns to the left and a 2-track continues on straight. Follow the 2-track for .3 miles. There will be a place to park on the right (1 or maybe 2 vehicles wide). Park here. Continue on foot another 1/8 mile down the abandoned 2-track to Nelson Creek. The creek is small enough to step across. The falls are to the right and can't be missed. You will be at the top of the falls. Climb down either steep side of the ravine to get to the base of the falls.

## SILVER FALLS AKA: Silver Bell Falls (Nelson Creek)

Private

| | | | |
|---|---|---|---|
| Must See: | 6 | GPS: | N46 27.071 W86 58.242 |
| Height: | 28 feet | | |
| Time: | 15-20 minutes | **Hiking Information** | |
| | | Path: | Abandoned 2-track |
| **Driving Information** | | Length: | .12 mile |
| Signs: | None | Elev. Change: | Moderate |
| Road: | 2-track | GPS: | Helpful |
| Access: | Difficult | Danger: | Moderate |
| 4WD: | Helpful | WP Boots: | Helpful |

This fan-shaped fall looks nice when there is a decent quantity of water flowing - especially in contrast to the lush green moss that hangs on the face of the gorge.

The 2-track to the waterfall used to end at the creek. If you weren't careful, you could drive right into it. Recently, trees have been transplanted directly into the 2-track, eliminating that danger. Just keep that in mind as the obvious hiking route from the parking area may become less obvious!

*Note the debris collected at the base of the fall*

*The gorge looking downstream*

# Sable Falls Area

## Sable Falls Hike

Grand Marais stands watch over the entrance to the eastern end of the Pictured Rocks National Lakeshore. Tourists flock here each year to experience Sable Falls, the Grand Sable Dunes, the Log Slides, Au Sable Light House, Lake Superior beaches, amazing sunsets, and the camping experiences available along the lakeshore.

**Sable Falls:** This is a spectacular waterfall featuring a series of cascades that starts with the most spectacular drop and then teases the eye downstream, making for an extremely pleasing visual treat. Even as the Tahquamenon waterfalls provide the foundation for the Upper Peninsula waterfalls at its eastern end, so Sable Falls is the gateway waterfall to the central and western portions of the U.P. where virtually all of Michigan's waterfalls reside.

*Directions:* Turn left onto H-58 west in the center of Grand Marais. Follow it for 1.4 miles. Turn right at the sign for Sable Falls into a large parking area with a nice bathhouse. A well-marked path takes you to the waterfall. There are a fair number of wooden steps with a couple of viewing decks along the way. If you would like, continue past the waterfall on the path that deteriorates to a well-worn footpath. It soon ends at a beach on Lake Superior. Grand Marais can be seen in the distance to the right, and the Grand Sable Dunes rise from the shoreline to the left.

*The trailhead to the falls*

*The creek cuts through sandstone*

*Looking down the river*

Sable Falls Area

## SABLE FALLS (Sable Creek)

Private

| | | | |
|---|---|---|---|
| Must See: | 9 | GPS: | N46 40.091 W86 0.857 |
| Height: | 25 feet | | |
| Time: | 30-60 minutes | | |

**Driving Information**
| | |
|---|---|
| Signs: | Well Marked |
| Road: | Main Road |
| Access: | Easy |
| 4WD: | N/A |

**Hiking Information**
| | |
|---|---|
| Path: | Improved Footpath |
| Length: | 1/4 mile |
| Elev. Change: | Moderate |
| GPS: | N/A |
| Danger: | Slight |
| WP Boots: | N/A |

This waterfall needs to be on the short list for anyone at all interested in waterfalls. This easy to access waterfall is seldom overrun with tourists, and yet is a beautiful example of a Michigan waterfall. Several viewing decks offer a nice selection of different views of the waterfall.

Sable Falls starts with this wonderful cascade and then proceeds to churn and tumble as it continues is fast descent down the narrow river. Sable River marks the transition between beach and sand dunes. East of the river, miles of beach stretch all the way to Grand Marais. Immediately west of the river, the Grand Sable Dunes take over, their steep sandy hillsides reaching down to the edge of the pounding Lake Superior surf.

36

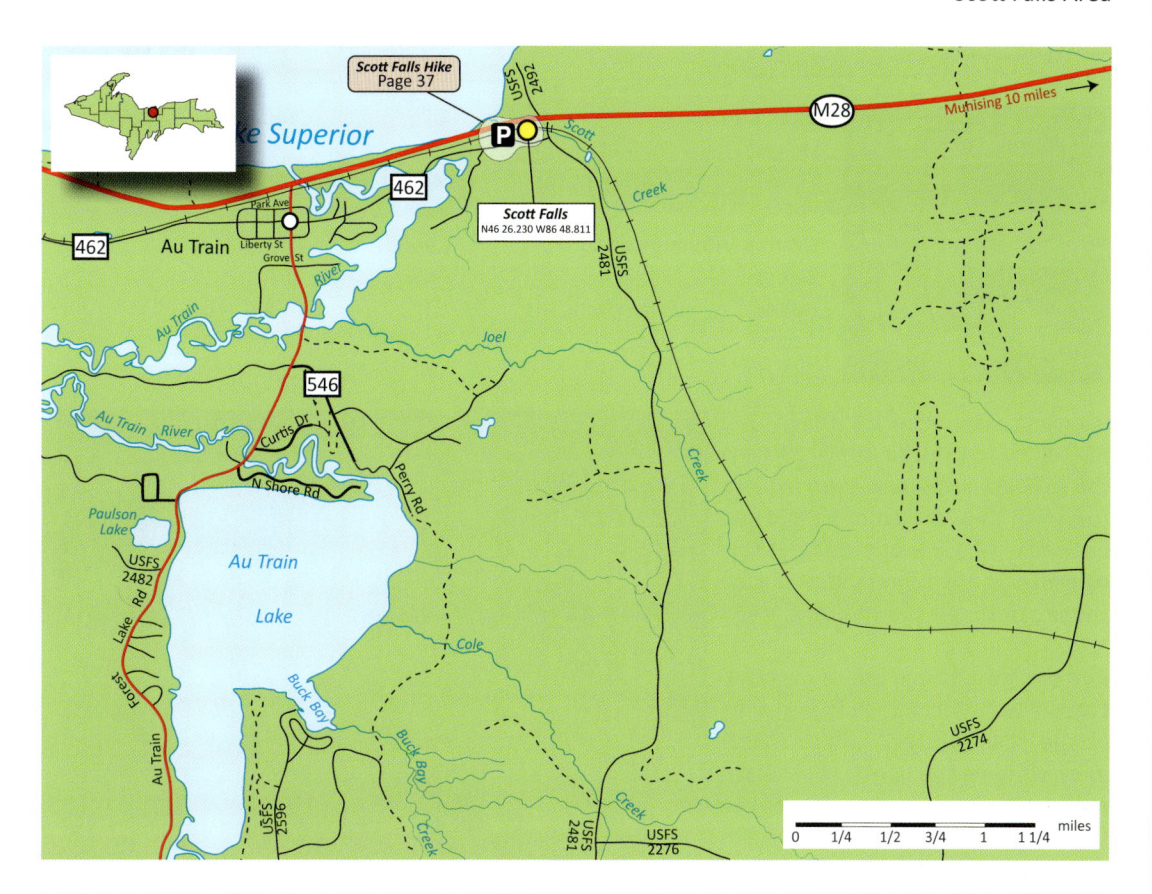

### Scott Falls Hike

**Scott Falls:** This is a fun little waterfall! It is easy to find and generally safe to play around. This is a great family waterfall destination.

*Directions:* This very easy to find waterfall is located between Christmas and Au Train on M-28. There is a roadside park on the lakeshore just to the east of Au Train. Another 100 yards to the east of the park and south of M-28 is Scott Falls. Pull off of M-28 onto the south shoulder. The waterfall will be visible from the vehicle.

## SCOTT FALLS (Scott Creek)

Private

| | | | |
|---|---|---|---|
| Must See: | 6 | GPS: | N46 26.230 W86 48.811 |
| Height: | 12 feet | | |
| Time: | 5-15 minutes | **Hiking Information** | |
| | | Path: | N/A |
| **Driving Information** | | Length: | N/A |
| Signs: | Small | Elev. Change: | N/A |
| Road: | Main Road | GPS: | N/A |
| Access: | Easy | Danger: | N/A |
| 4WD: | N/A | WP Boots: | May be Helpful |

Park and view from the road. You may also cross the creek to view the falls up closer and even explore the small cave tucked in behind the waterfall. Check it out in the winter as well. The ice formations can be very interesting!

This has always been one of my boys' favorite waterfalls! They love playing in the shallow creek where marsh marigolds line the banks. The splash pool and moss covered cave walls give their car-bored muscles something to do after a long drive! You may need waterproof boots to get over the creek to the base of the falls.

Over the past several years, this creek has sometimes dried up. A culvert upstream has periodically plugged up and the creek then diverted to Au Train Lake. Hopefully this will be a seldom event, and the waterfall will continue to run nicely in the years to come.

Wagner Falls Area

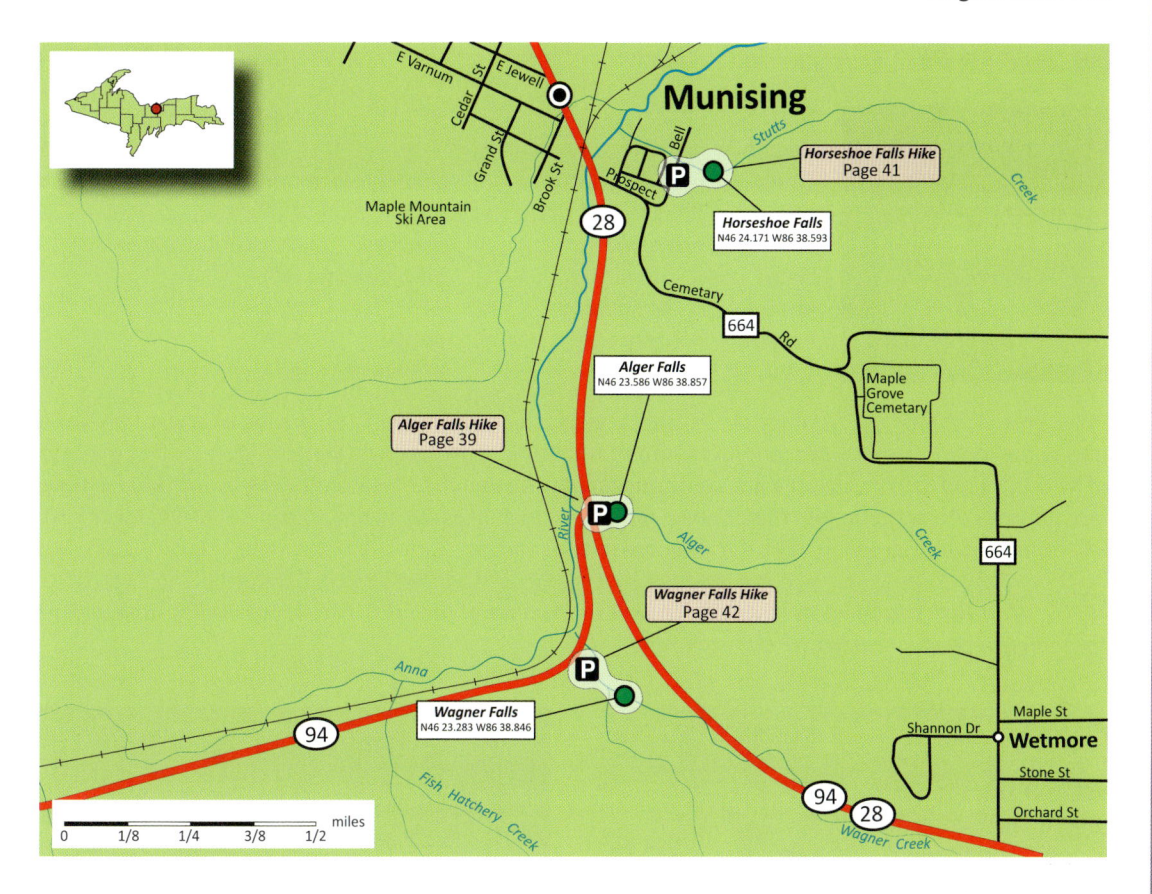

ALGER COUNTY

### Alger Falls Hike

***Alger Falls:*** Alger Falls is one of the best known waterfalls in the Munising area since it is easily viewed from M-28 just south of Munising. A green road sign announces its presence.

*Directions:* Alger Falls is located on the east side of M-28 near the M-94 intersection. There is room to pull off onto the shoulder of M-28 with enough space for 2 or 3 vehicles. Look for a small sign announcing the waterfall. Be careful if you want to get to the base of the waterfall or view it from the sides of the hillside. The area near Alger Falls is very wet and spongy. Water seeps into the area from the slopes on either side of the falls. It seems that the ground on the right (south) side of the falls is a little easier to get across.

Wagner Falls Area

## ALGER FALLS (Alger Creek)  Private

| | | | |
|---|---|---|---|
| Must See: | 7 | GPS: | N46 23.586 W86 38.857 |
| Height: | 30 feet | | |
| Time: | 1-5 minutes | **Hiking Information** | |
| | | Path: | N/A |
| **Driving Information** | | Length: | View from Vehicle |
| Signs: | Small Sign | Elev. Change: | N/A |
| Road: | Main Road | GPS: | N/A |
| Access: | Very Easy | Danger: | N/A |
| 4WD: | N/A | WP Boots: | N/A |

"Welcome to Munising!" That is how I always feel as I head past Alger Falls, driving westward on M-28 during the long, sweeping descent just south of Munising. The roadside waterfall gives a first glimpse of how the waterfalls in the area are doing, judging by the volume of water flowing over the sandstone face and into the undergrowth filled valley. Sitting just east of M-28 by the junction of M-94, Alger Falls can be viewed by merely pulling off to the side of the road.

NOTE: Wear waterproof boots if desiring to walk to the base of the falls. The steep hillsides surrounding the waterfall seep groundwater constantly.

From the center of the river looking upstream. The river was especially low for this shot.

40

Wagner Falls Area

ALGER COUNTY

### Horseshoe Falls Hike

Although it costs a little to view the falls, the beauty of the falls and the experience afforded are worth the expense, in my opinion! The waterfall is privately owned and access to it is limited to the normal tourist season. Check out their web site at http://www.uppermichiganwaterfalls.com for more information. You may also contact the gift shop at (906) 387-2635.

*Horseshoe Falls:* A distinctly angled sheer drop lands on a moss covered plateau that alternately cascades and slides down to the creek below. The viewing deck at the base of the falls offers a wonderful place to enjoy the beauty of the falls and eroded sandstone face.

*Directions:* Turn east onto Prospect Street off of M-28 near the southern end of Munising. Prospect Street very quickly turns to the left where it becomes Bell Avenue. The gift shop is on the right.

## HORSESHOE FALLS  (Stutts Creek)                                         Private

| | | | |
|---|---|---|---|
| Must See: | 8 | GPS: | N46 24.171 W86 38.593 |
| Height: | 35 feet | | |
| Time: | 20-45 minutes | **Hiking Information** | |
| | | Path: | Improved Path |
| **Driving Information** | | Length: | 200 yards |
| Signs: | Billboard | Elev. Change: | Slight |
| Road: | Side Road | GPS: | N/A |
| Access: | Very Easy | Danger: | None |
| 4WD: | N/A | WP Boots: | N/A |

Horseshoe Falls is privately owned. Access the falls through a nicely maintained gift shop. Price of admission was $6 ($12/vehicle) the last time I went. There is a fish pond and nature information along the path to the falls. This is a great place to bring children.

41

Horseshoe Falls

Wagner Falls Area

### Wagner Falls Hike

Wagner Falls is one of the premier waterfalls in the Munising area. It is easily accessed. A well maintained wooden walkway leads to the falls where there is a wonderful viewing deck. Several benches along the way allow for resting as needed.

**Wagner Falls:** The cascading waterfalls with a longer free drop toward the base of the falls presents itself nicely with a slight bend in the creek below the falls allowing a straight on view from the viewing deck. Several downed trees angle across the falls. They have become part of the "look" of Wagner Falls over the years.

*Directions:* From M-28 turn southwest onto M-94. The parking lot for Wagner Falls is on the left (southeast) side of the road. There is also overflow parking provided on the right. The walkway to the falls is only about 100 yards long.

## WAGNER FALLS (Wagner Creek)   Private

| | | | |
|---|---|---|---|
| Must See: | 9 | GPS: | N46 23.283  W86 38.846 |
| Height: | 25 feet | | |
| Time: | 15-30 minutes | **Hiking Information** | |
| | | Path: | Improved Path |
| **Driving Information** | | Length: | 100 yards |
| Signs: | Large Sign | Elev. Change: | Slight |
| Road: | Main Road | GPS: | N/A |
| Access: | Very Easy | Danger: | None |
| 4WD: | N/A | WP Boots: | N/A |

A gravel lot directly off of M-94 offers plenty of parking for tourists to Wagner Falls. During peak tourist seasons, there is an overflow parking area across the road. A nicely constructed viewing deck provides the perfect angle for viewing the falls. This is one of the nicest waterfalls in Alger County and draws a good number of visitors each year. Be sure to take the time to stop here!

A small tributary joins Wagner Creek just below Wagner Falls. The steep waterway has some small cascades that can be seen from the walkway while on the way to Wagner Falls.

Whitefish Falls Area

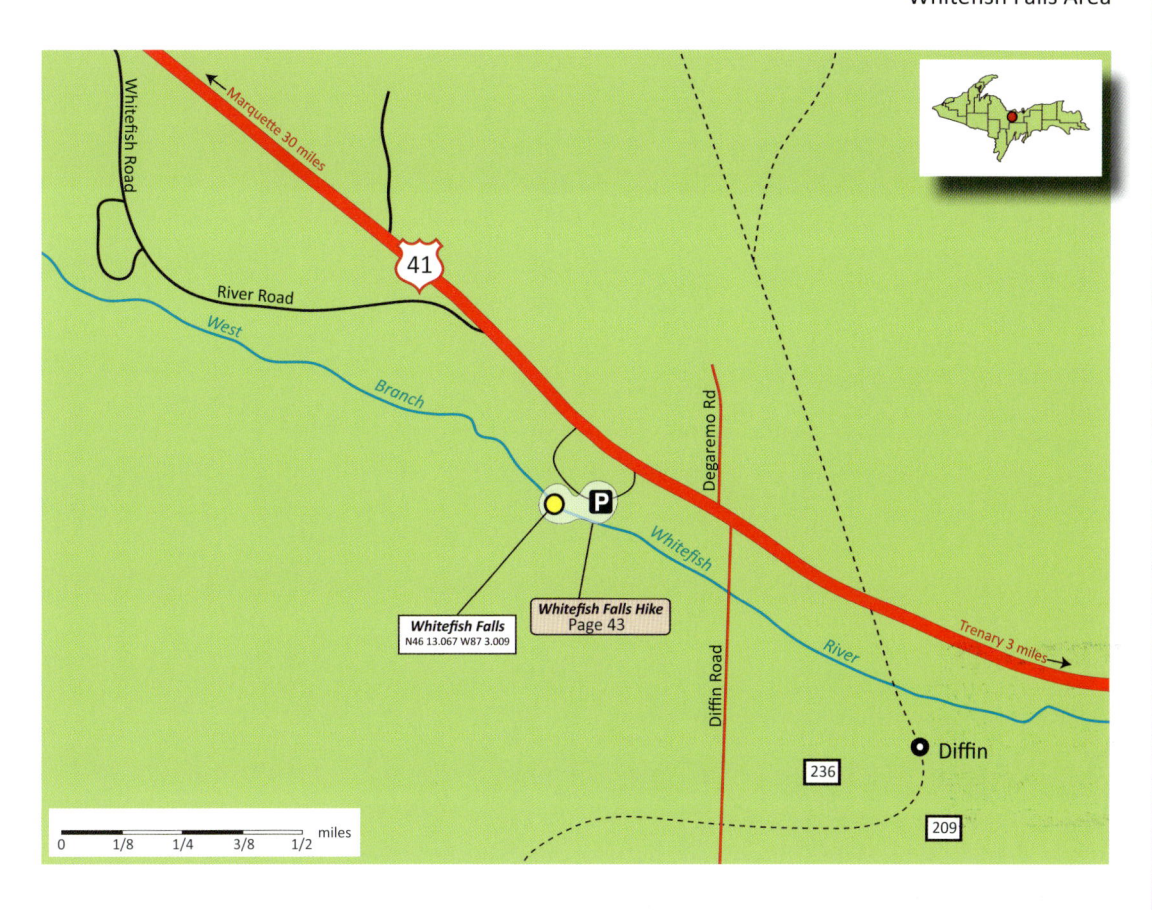

## Whitefish Falls Hike

**Whitefish Falls:** Whitefish Falls is a series of cascading drops over a short stretch of the West Branch of the Whitefish River. A short walk through cedars ends with a nice view of the tiered drops.

*Directions:* Travel west on US-41 a little over 3 miles west of Trenary. As you drive, you will pass Diffin Road on the left. Turn left at the next road. It is unnamed and meanders through a campground. Park at an old concrete area. It looks like there may have been an old road here. A footpath cuts into the forest near here. Follow the short trail to the river. The falls are downstream.

### WHITEFISH FALLS (West Branch - Whitefish River)   Private

| | |
|---|---|
| Must See: | 5 |
| Height: | 10 feet |
| Time: | 15-25 minutes |

**Driving Information**

| | |
|---|---|
| Signs: | None |
| Road: | Dirt Road |
| Access: | Fairly Easy |
| 4WD: | N/A |

| | |
|---|---|
| GPS: | N46 13.067 W87 03.009 |

**Hiking Information**

| | |
|---|---|
| Path: | Narrow Footpath |
| Length: | 100 yards |
| Elev. Change: | Slight |
| GPS: | N/A |
| Danger: | Slight |
| WP Boots: | Helpful |

Park at the old circular blacktop area. It is just a short walk to the river via a dirt trail. The trail brings you out to the top of the falls. There are several cascades to enjoy.

ALGER COUNTY

# CHAPTER 2
# BARAGA COUNTY

# Baraga County Map

Canyon Falls Area

### Canyon Falls Hike

Canyon Falls Roadside Park at the trail head to the falls features drinking water, toilets, picnic tables and charcoal grills. This wonderful facility sets the tone for a hike to Canyon Falls on a semi-improved footpath.

*Directions:* US-41 crosses the Sturgeon River 2.9 miles north of the intersection of M-28 and 1.4 miles south of Alberta. Just north of the bridge is a very nice roadside park on the west side of the road. The trailhead to the falls is toward the southern end of the parking lot. The trail is fairly flat, although there are a couple low areas that must be crossed. These are covered with planks that are very slippery when wet. At Canyon Falls there is a nice railed area for viewing the falls.

Canyon Falls Area

## CANYON FALLS (STURGEON RIVER)     Private

| | | | |
|---|---|---|---|
| Must See: | 8 | GPS: | N46 37.355 W88 28.600 |
| Height: | 15 feet | | |
| Time: | 30-45 minutes | Hiking Information | |
| | | Path: | Improved Footpath |
| Driving Information | | Length: | .4 miles |
| Signs: | Roadside Park | Elev. Change: | Slight |
| Road: | Main | GPS: | N/A |
| Access: | Very Easy | Danger: | Slight |
| 4WD: | N/A | WP Boots: | N/A |

Canyon Falls has been referred to as "The Grand Canyon of Michigan". Although this comparison is a bit of a stretch, the box canyon that starts at the waterfall is a beautiful natural feature that everyone should make an effort to visit. The incredible rock formations are as intriguing as the falls themselves and are well worth the time it takes to explore them.

Wooden rails line the edge of the main viewing area to provide safety from the raw power of the waterfall and sheer canyon walls. However, keep small children close.

*Canyon Falls as seen from the far side of the river. The stonework built by the public works program years ago can be seen along the canyon's edge.*

*Looking back at Canyon Falls from further along the North Country Trail*

## Ogemaw Falls Hike

A short walk followed by a relatively easy climb down a fairly steep embankment ends at this beautiful little waterfall. The main cascade pours into a spill pool with a second, smaller drop emptying out of a narrow, shallow spot between two rocky segments of the pool rim. The creek then turns hard to the right, flowing along an interestingly smooth and rounded hump of bedrock.

*Directions:* From US-41, turn west onto Baraga Plains Road (.5 miles north of Alberta). In 1.5 miles, the road crosses Ogemaw Creek. Just before the bridge, the shoulder of the road widens out. Park by the wooden sign for the waterfall. A faint footpath runs through the woods. The creek is at the base of a short, but somewhat steep, forested hillside.

## OGEMAW FALLS (OGEMAW CREEK)    Private

| | | | |
|---|---|---|---|
| Must See: | 7 | GPS: | N46 38.752 W88 30.448 |
| Height: | 10 feet | | |
| Time: | 15-30 minutes | Hiking Information | |
| | | Path: | Unimproved Footpath |
| Driving Information | | Length: | 100 yards |
| Signs: | At Trailhead | Elev. Change: | Moderate |
| Road: | Secondary | GPS: | N/A |
| Access: | Somewhat Easy | Danger: | Moderate |
| 4WD: | N/A | WP Boots: | Recommended |

Signs have been placed at various waterfalls around the county by the Baraga County Visitor's Bureau. One of them is here. The trail down to the waterfall has several places that can be slippery and there is a short but steep climb down at the waterfall itself, so do be careful on this short hike. Wade across the shallow creek to view both of the drops from the best vantage point.

Ogemaw Creek widens out into a good sized pond before narrowing down again and flowing through a culvert below Baraga Plains Road on its way to the waterfall. The pond can be easily seen on the left and serves as a good landmark for the waterfall.

# Falls River Area

**BARAGA COUNTY**

**L'ANSE**

**Bare Hole Falls**
N46 45.198 W88 27.228

**Cascading Falls**
N46 45.183 W88 27.164

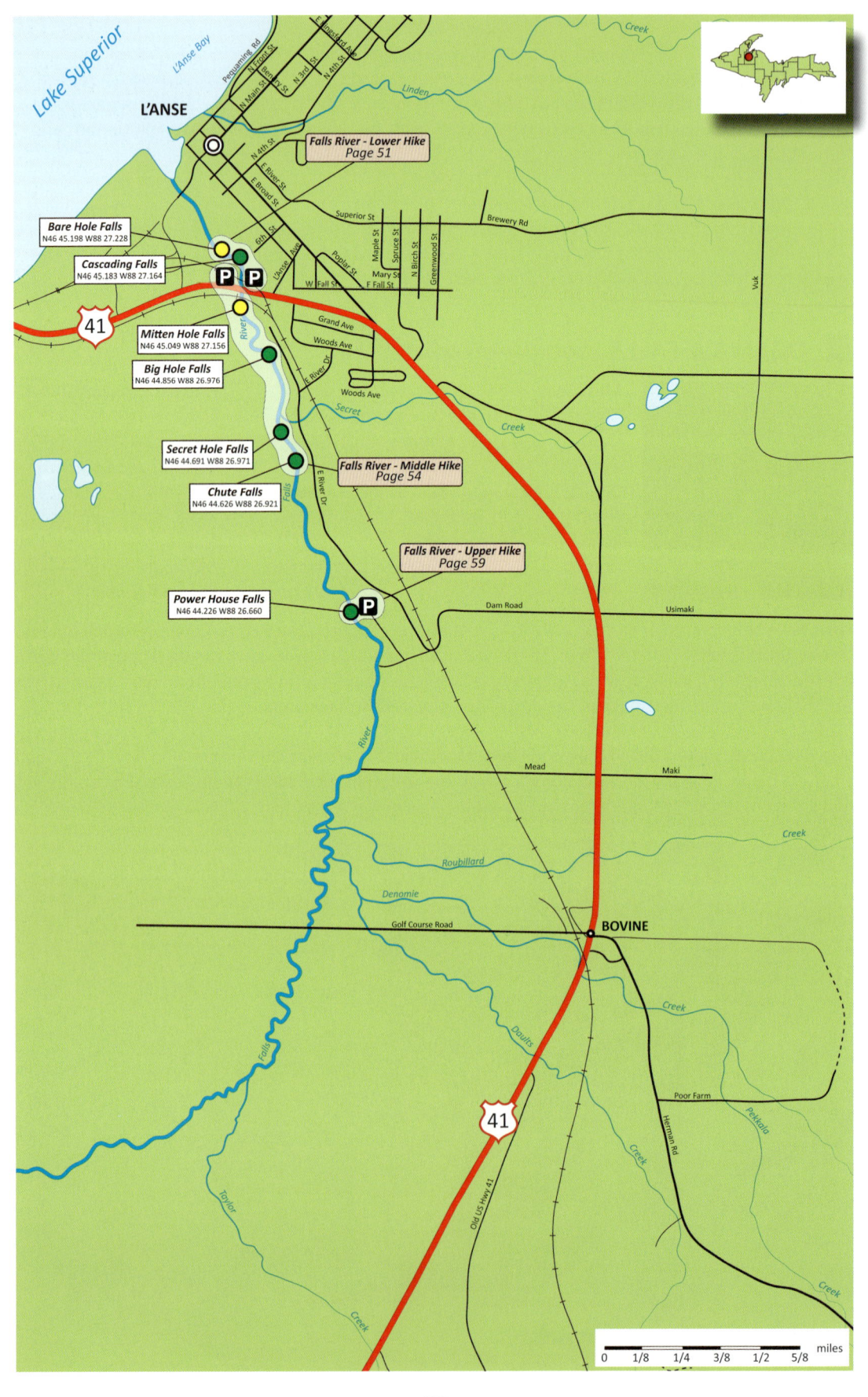

**Mitten Hole Falls**
N46 45.049 W88 27.156

**Big Hole Falls**
N46 44.856 W88 26.976

**Secret Hole Falls**
N46 44.691 W88 26.971

**Chute Falls**
N46 44.626 W88 26.921

**Power House Falls**
N46 44.226 W88 26.660

**Falls River - Lower Hike** Page 51

**Falls River - Middle Hike** Page 54

**Falls River - Upper Hike** Page 59

**BOVINE**

### Falls River - Lower Hike

The lower falls on the Falls River are the batch of falls north of US-41. These are the easiest to access on the Falls River, and Bare Hole Falls as well as Cascading Falls are very nice to view! The waterfalls on the Falls River are a local attraction for the youth of the area since they are so close to the village. It is also not uncommon to see fishermen along the banks of the river.

**Cascading Falls:** A stretch of cascades begins just down river from the train trestle. I prefer to view this waterfall from higher up the hillside, rather than from the river's edge as usual.

**Bare Hole Falls:** Bare Hole Falls is a complicated "slide waterfall" with cascades falling off of either side of the slide. It lies at the bottom of a steep ravine.

*Directions:* This stretch of river can be reached by several different routes.
1) US-41 crosses the Falls River just west of the Burger King. Park on the east side of the bridge. There is ample room to pull off of the busy highway. Walk north along the river (downstream) following the blue blazed footpath. (This is my favorite parking spot and hiking information is based on this option.)
2) Drive to the center of the L'Anse by taking E. Broad Street from US-41 (you will drive under the "Welcome" sign). Turn left at the light (N. Main Street). Just before crossing the Falls River, the road deteriorates into what seems more like a glorified parking lot. A factory is on the left. Drive over that direction. There will be places to park along the river. Walk south (upstream) along the river to view the waterfalls. This route will take you along the east side of the river. The falls are best viewed from this side.
3) There is a snowmobile trail that winds along the eastern top of the ravine overlooking the Falls River. On the side of this trail there is an iron bench set in the ideal place for viewing Cascading Falls. This is a very scenic location for those not able to traverse hillsides. (This is the route required to allow for wheelchair access.)

*Note: Restrooms are available at nearby establishments.*

Falls River Area

## CASCADING FALLS (FALLS RIVER)     Private

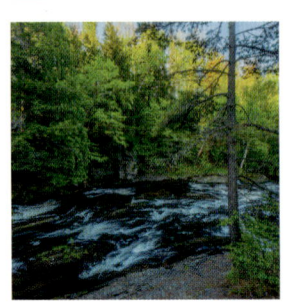

| | | | |
|---|---|---|---|
| Must See: | 7 | GPS: | N46 45.183 W88 27.164 |
| Height: | 20 feet | | |
| Time: | 10-20 minutes | Hiking Information | |
| | | Path: | Footpath |
| Driving Information | | Length: | .13 miles |
| Signs: | Sign on US-41 | Elev. Change: | Moderate |
| Road: | Highway | GPS: | N/A |
| Access: | Very Easy | Danger: | Moderate |
| 4WD: | N/A | WP Boots: | N/A |

AKA "Lower Falls", Cascading Falls is best viewed from the east side of the river. The western side is more rugged, less accessible, and since the river turns sharply to the west at the base of the waterfall, it is difficult to view the waterfall from that side.

The river widens out after it passes beneath the train trestle and begins its descent down the many cascades that stretch out over nearly 100 yards. The rocky island in the middle of the river is topped when the river is running strong.

From the rough dirt road that runs nearby it is possible to maneuver a wheelchair to the overlook.

*\* Hiking information is based on parking along US-41*

*This is the view from the bench that sits atop the high bank on the eastern side of the river.*

BARAGA COUNTY

Cascading Falls

52

## BARE HOLE FALLS (FALLS RIVER)  Private

| | | | |
|---|---|---|---|
| Must See: | 6 | GPS: | N46 45.198 W88 27.228 |
| Height: | 15 feet | | |
| Time: | 20-40 minutes | **Hiking Information** | |
| | | Path: | Unimproved Footpath |
| **Driving Information** | | Length: | 250 yards |
| Signs: | Sign on US-41 | Elev. Change: | Moderate |
| Road: | Highway | GPS: | N/A |
| Access: | Very Easy | Danger: | Moderate |
| 4WD: | N/A | WP Boots: | N/A |

The river narrows and turns hard to the west below Cascading Falls. It then widens out again while rushing over Bare Hole Falls. This waterfall is a multi-faceted drop, with a plunge on the northern side and a slower, cascading side to the south.

I was informed that young people in the '40s and '50s would skinny dip here, hence the name!

\* Hiking information is based on parking along US-41

The plunge on the northern side of the waterfall can be seen peeking through this gap in the trees.

53

Falls River Area

## Falls River - Middle Hike

This hike includes the waterfalls south of US-41 and north of Power House Falls. These are all fairly closely spaced together. There are private residences along this stretch of river. Be respectful of the owners. These are beautiful waterfalls to be enjoyed, but please be kind, quiet, and clean. And always obey all "No Trespassing" signs.

*Mitten Hole Falls:* A glimpse of the waterfall can be had while driving over the Falls River on US-41. After crossing the road and railroad trestle, it is a little climb down to the edge of the river. The falls span the river with a ledge fall of about 4 feet that is randomly broken up by taller segments of rock.

*Big Hole Falls:* This large, cascading waterfall is tapered from an 18 foot drop on the right to about a third of that on the left. A nice fishing hole exists below the falls.

*Secret Hole Falls:* Beautiful waterfall! The wonderful cascading drops are perfectly segmented, as though it were engineered by a master waterfall designer!

*Chute Falls:* Large rock masses on either side of the waterfall constrict the width of the river to about 5 feet and send the river shooting through the resulting gap.

*Directions:* Park along the side of US-41 on the western side of the bridge over the Falls River. (This is the same general parking area described in one of the Lower Falls Hikes.) Carefully cross US-41 and the railroad trestle on foot. (The road is normally quite busy.) Walk along the edge of the river. Take care to be considerate as there are houses along the river. Always respect private property.

*In the springtime the river flows with so much water that kayakers will put in at Power House Falls and chute the waterfalls all the way to Lake Superior!*

Falls River Area

## MITTEN HOLE FALLS (FALLS RIVER)     Private

| | | | |
|---|---|---|---|
| Must See: | 6 | GPS: | N46 45.049 W88 27.156 |
| Height: | 6 feet | | |
| Time: | 10-20 minutes | Hiking Information | |
| | | Path: | Unimproved Footpath |
| Driving Information | | Length: | 100 yards |
| Signs: | None | Elev. Change: | Moderate |
| Road: | Main | GPS: | N/A |
| Access: | Very Easy | Danger: | Moderate |
| 4WD: | N/A | WP Boots: | N/A |

BARAGA COUNTY

The riverbed is composed of slate, some of which is above water during most of the year. Mitten Hole Falls can be viewed nicely from several of these dry rocks. This is the first of the waterfalls listed in the Middle Falls Hike which starts just 100 yards uphill from here on the other side of US-41.

My youngest son, Luke, was 6 years old when I first took him to this waterfall. He wandered into a nest of yellow jackets while we were there. Neither he, nor I will forget this waterfall which we still refer to as "Yellow Jacket Falls". (I'm thankful to say that I've never encountered any other stinging insects during my hikes in the Upper Peninsula - obviously excluding mosquitoes and ticks which aren't technically stinging insects anyway!)

*Note the water level difference between this winter shot and the fall scene above!*

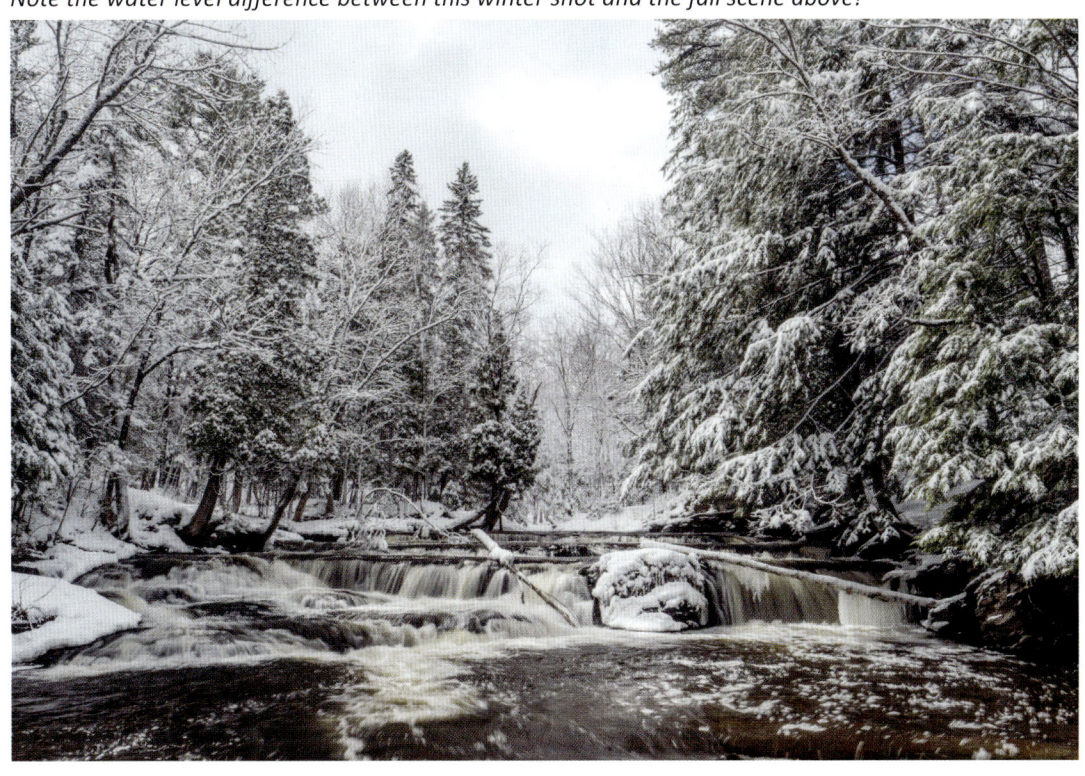

55

Mitten Hole Falls

Falls River Area

## BIG HOLE FALLS (FALLS RIVER)　　　　　　　　　　　　　　Private

| | | | |
|---|---|---|---|
| Must See: | 7 | GPS: | N46 44.856 W88 26.976 |
| Height: | 18 feet | | |
| Time: | 30-45 minutes | Hiking Information | |
| | | Path: | Unimproved Footpath |
| Driving Information | | Length: | .36 miles |
| Signs: | None | Elev. Change: | Moderate |
| Road: | Main | GPS: | N/A |
| Access: | Very Easy | Danger: | Moderate |
| 4WD: | N/A | WP Boots: | N/A |

Angled bedrock is suddenly cut away into an increasingly deeper section of the river, fragmented layers of slate glistening black. Along the side of the waterfall the squared off ends are stacked up with tree supporting soil softening the crest of the unrelenting hard slate below.

A promontory stands tall in the center of the waterfall, its glistening black head rising above the white frothy rivulets most of the year. The river cascades down both sides, the left side also tapering away from the center, with that portion of the river running sideways before turning and spilling down the shorter side of the waterfall.

*The river runs at one of its lowest levels that I've seen in this November picture.*

BARAGA COUNTY

Big Hole Falls

## SECRET HOLE FALLS (FALLS RIVER)

Private

| | | | |
|---|---|---|---|
| Must See: | 8 | GPS: | N46 44.691 W88 26.971 |
| Height: | 8 feet | | |
| Time: | 50-75 minutes | Hiking Information | |
| | | Path: | Unimproved Footpath |
| Driving Information | | Length: | .57 miles |
| Signs: | None | Elev. Change: | Moderate |
| Road: | Main | GPS: | N/A |
| Access: | Very Easy | Danger: | Moderate |
| 4WD: | N/A | WP Boots: | N/A |

Hike another .21 miles from Big Hole Falls to this, my favorite waterfall on the Falls River! The rich, cascading water flows with powerful lines around underlying black bedrock in this slightly rounded waterfall.

The waterfall gets its name from Secret Creek, which empties into the Falls River nearby. The river starts cascading with small drops, quickly increasing in height and culminating in a nicely defined waterfall situated next to a good sized home on the eastern side on the river.

*Early morning light streams through the trees, lighting up the river below the lovely falls.*

Falls River Area

## CHUTE FALLS (FALLS RIVER)    Private

| | | | |
|---|---|---|---|
| Must See: | 7 | GPS: | N46 44.626 W88 26.921 |
| Height: | 6 feet | | |
| Time: | 60-90 minutes | Hiking Information | |
| | | Path: | Unimproved Footpath |
| Driving Information | | Length: | .66 miles |
| Signs: | None | Elev. Change: | Moderate |
| Road: | Main | GPS: | N/A |
| Access: | Very Easy | Danger: | Moderate |
| 4WD: | N/A | WP Boots: | N/A |

Hike another .1 miles upstream from Secret Hole Falls to this unique waterfall on the Falls River. The river here is squeezed down to a width of about 5 feet as the water chutes between two large masses of rock. A tangle of rocks below the falls tend to collect tree debris and help to contribute to the always changing look of this waterfall.

A stairway has been built down into the gorge on the eastern side. Several houses can be seen along that side of the river along here.

*Looking downstream from the top of the falls.*

*Note: This waterfall has another commonly used name, but isn't appropriate for this family friendly book.*

*Minor rapids extend downstream from the waterfall.*

### Falls River - Upper Hike

***Power House Falls:*** This is the most easily viewed waterfall in Baraga County. The waterfall is located at the end of the dirt road leading to the abandoned power house. The beautiful, cascading waterfall is adjacent to the power house.

*Directions:* Drive south of L'Anse on US-41 to Power Dam Road. Follow Power Dam Road west. The road will turn hard to the left, then back to the right and cross some railroad tracks. The black top ends with the main road turning to the right, while a dirt road continues on straight. Follow the dirt road. (Sometimes in the spring, the road will be closed by the village when deep ruts develop from spring rains and thawing winter snows.) Another dirt road will intersect from the northwest. Turn right and follow this to its end. The boarded up remains of the electric power house are here, right next to the Power House Falls. Park here.

## POWER HOUSE FALLS (FALLS RIVER)   Private

| | | | |
|---|---|---|---|
| Must See: | 8 | GPS: | N46 44.226 W88 26.660 |
| Height: | 13 feet | | |
| Time: | 5-15 minutes | Hiking Information | |
| | | Path: | N/A |
| Driving Information | | Length: | N/A |
| Signs: | Near Entrance | Elev. Change: | N/A |
| Road: | Gravel | GPS: | N/A |
| Access: | Easy | Danger: | N/A |
| 4WD: | N/A | WP Boots: | N/A |

The Power House Falls are easily viewed from a vehicle. The old, concrete, boarded up power house doesn't add to the aesthetics of the waterfall, but it does lend a sense of historical significance as many waterfalls have been tapped for their power from years gone by to the present.

Next to the gray building, the Falls River cascades down beautifully in this popular waterfall on the Falls River. The parking lot right next to the river means that it is easily accessible, with no hiking needed to enjoy its beauty.

*Note: The dirt road down to the waterfall is not plowed in the winter, so you will need to hike about .3 miles to get to the waterfall then.*

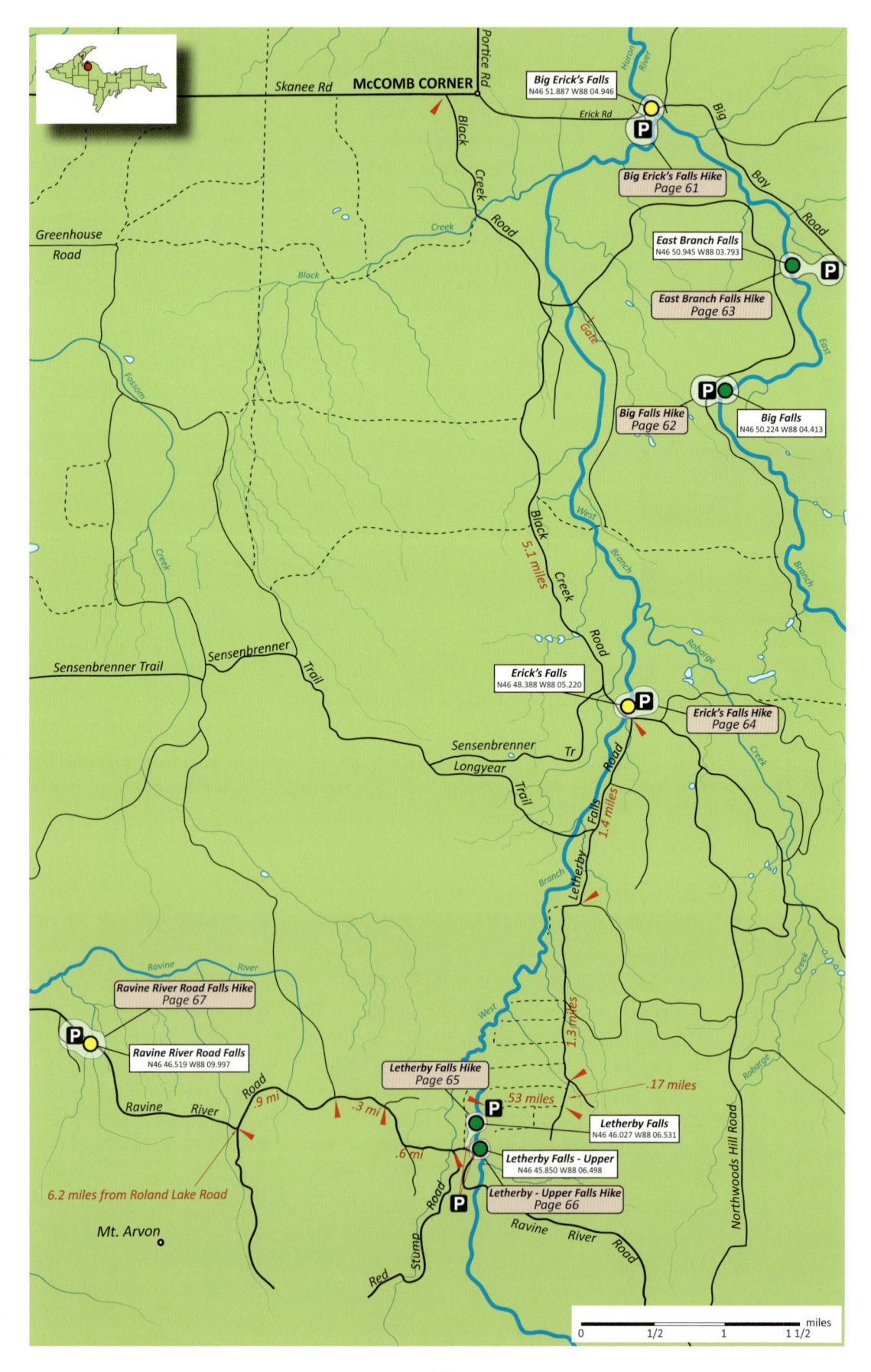

# Huron River Area

**BARAGA COUNTY**

- Big Erick's Falls — N46 51.887 W88 04.946
- Big Erick's Falls Hike — Page 61
- East Branch Falls — N46 50.945 W88 03.793
- East Branch Falls Hike — Page 63
- Big Falls Hike — Page 62
- Big Falls — N46 50.224 W88 04.413
- Erick's Falls — N46 48.388 W88 05.220
- Erick's Falls Hike — Page 64
- Ravine River Road Falls Hike — Page 67
- Ravine River Road Falls — N46 46.519 W88 09.997
- Letherby Falls Hike — Page 65
- Letherby Falls — N46 46.027 W88 06.531
- Letherby Falls - Upper — N46 45.850 W88 06.498
- Letherby - Upper Falls Hike — Page 66

McCOMB CORNER

Skanee Rd, Portice Rd, Erick Rd, Big Bay Road, Black Creek Road, Sensenbrenner Trail, Longyear Trail, Letherby Falls Road, Northwoods Hill Road, Ravine River Road, Red Stump Road, Greenhouse Road

5.1 miles, 1.4 miles, 1.3 miles, .17 miles, .53 miles, .9 mi, .3 mi, .6 mi

6.2 miles from Roland Lake Road

Mt. Arvon

0 — 1/2 — 1 — 1 1/2 miles

60

Huron River Area

### Big Erick's Falls Hike

A nice campground, sporting pit toilets and a generous parking lot, is located near the waterfalls. A good section of the grass along the shoreline is mowed, making it relatively easy to walk down the length of the falls.

**Big Erick's Falls:** The main cascade is located just below the bridge. It is segmented, with regularly spaced sections spilling water over the short ledge.

*Directions:* Follow Skanee Road to the east. At the end of the road, Portice Road turns left and Erick Road (gravel) turns to the right. Follow Erick Road east to the bridge that passes over the Huron River. Park next to the bridge in the large parking lot. Walk across the road (north) to the falls.

## BIG ERICK'S FALLS (HURON RIVER)    Private

| | | | |
|---|---|---|---|
| Must See: | 6 | GPS: | N46 51.887 W88 04.946 |
| Height: | 3 feet | | |
| Time: | 5-10 minutes | Hiking Information | |
| | | Path: | Unimproved Footpath |
| Driving Information | | Length: | 50 yards |
| Signs: | None | Elev. Change: | Slight |
| Road: | Gravel | GPS: | N/A |
| Access: | Easy | Danger: | Slight |
| 4WD: | Helpful | WP Boots: | Recommended |

The waterfall is split into four separate falls by three evenly spaced rock promontories creating nicely proportioned falls. There is a nice gravel parking area adjacent to the bridge. Pit toilets are across the road from the parking lot. Fisherman's trails meander along the river's edge.

BARAGA COUNTY

Big Erick's Falls

61

Huron River Area

### Big Falls Hike

**Big Falls:** The East Branch of the Huron River widens out and flows around an island situated at the top of the falls. The resultant split waterfall is nicely symmetrical. Remnants of campfires and a flat, pleasing viewing area at the base of the falls show that this is a favorite picnicking area.

*Directions:* From near the eastern end of Skanee Road turn right (south) onto Black Creek Road. Drive 1.7 miles to N46 50.763 W88 05.956. Turn left (east) onto a good dirt road. Big Falls is 2.1 miles from this intersection. The Western Branch of the Huron River will appear in about .2 miles. Caution! The river must be forded here. If the river is running too high this might not be possible. After crossing the river turn left at the first "Y". Then turn right at the next "Y". Park @ N46 50.241 W88 04.415. There is a small obvious parking spot here. This is just above the waterfall. Climb down the steep 30 foot high bank to the base of the falls.

## BIG FALLS (HURON RIVER - EAST BRANCH)   Private

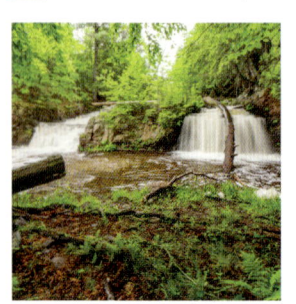

| | | | |
|---|---|---|---|
| Must See: | 9 | GPS: | N46 50.224 W88 04.413 |
| Height: | 18 feet | | |
| Time: | 15-30 minutes | Hiking Information | |
| | | Path: | Unimproved and STEEP |
| Driving Information | | Length: | 100 yards |
| Signs: | None | Elev. Change: | Steep Climb - 30 feet |
| Road: | Good Dirt | GPS: | Recommended |
| Access: | Somewhat Difficult | Danger: | Moderate |
| 4WD: | Helpful | WP Boots: | None |

A beautiful split cascade surrounds an island in the middle of the 50 foot wide river. There are multi-tiered cascades splashing down either side. A nice spill pool below the waterfall butts up to a flat, pine covered picnic area.

Two channels have been cut through the angular bedrock layers, one on either side of the river. The channels start 40 feet back from the edge of the falls. The eastern side is a series of stair steps, while the western side makes just two small drops before plunging down 10 feet into the spill pool.

*More volume pours over the near side of the river*

*Looking down on the waterfall from the steep hill*

62

Huron River Area

### East Branch Falls Hike

***East Branch Falls:*** The boulder strewn river drops 10 feet in several cascades that ends in the river that is then split in half by a 20 foot wide island. Cedars shroud the rugged rock walls that line the river's sides. The setting, as much as the waterfall, calls for a "Must See" rating of 7.

Directions: Follow Erick Road east past the Huron River. Park in a nice sized pullout area by the very nice bridge that crosses an unnamed creek. Cross over the bridge to the turnout large enough for three or four vehicles and park there. The parking area is at GPS location N46 51.006 W88 03.406. Hike across a berm and small creek. Follow the abandoned roadway. (Old orange/pink ribbons were hanging in strategically placed locations along the way when I was here in 2010.) Use a GPS at the end of the road to navigate through the forest. There is no path here. Scramble down about 20 feet of rock near the falls to the river's edge. Follow the river upstream from East Branch Falls for 1/4 mile.

## EAST BRANCH FALLS (HURON RIVER - EAST BRANCH)           Private

| | | | |
|---|---|---|---|
| Must See: | 7 | GPS: | N46 50.945 W88 03.793 |
| Height: | 4 feet | | |
| Time: | 45-60 minutes | Hiking Information | |
| | | Path: | None |
| Driving Information | | Length: | .36 miles |
| Signs: | None | Elev. Change: | Moderate |
| Road: | Gravel | GPS: | Required |
| Access: | Somewhat Difficult | Danger: | Moderate |
| 4WD: | Helpful | WP Boots: | Recommended |

Situated with 20 foot tall walls of cracked, layered basalt, the waterfall cascades over a tapered mass of rock, sliding into a pool that splits around an island covered with stones, boulders, and wild flowers. As a backdrop to the waterfall, hardwoods and pines lend their colors.

Huron River Area

### Erick's Falls Hike

***Erick's Falls:*** Black Creek Road is a good gravel road that acts as a main truck route for the logging industry. An unusually nice bridge spans the West Branch of the Huron River just upstream from Erick's Falls. It is sometimes referred to by locals as the "Million Dollar Bridge". The waterfall, cascading over jagged rocks, is close to a gravel parking lot on the east side of the river. This stretch of river is favored by fishermen.

***Erick's Cascades:*** A calm, black pool gives way to a small cascade that spans the river. Although it is a small drop, the setting is idyllic. Pine scented air. Open forest floor. A shallow, babbling river. This is a great family area!

***Directions:*** Turn right on Black Creek Road off of Skanee Road. (This is just west of Erick Road.) Follow the road for 5.1 miles. The road crosses the West Branch of the Huron River on a very nice bridge. Park just east of the bridge. The Erick's Falls are just north of the bridge.

## ERICK'S FALLS (HURON RIVER - WEST BRANCH)    Private

| | | | |
|---|---|---|---|
| Must See: | 6 | GPS: | N46 48.388 W88 05.220 |
| Height: | 5 feet | | |
| Time: | 5-15 minutes | Hiking Information | |
| | | Path: | Unimproved Footpath |
| Driving Information | | Length: | 100 feet |
| Signs: | None | Elev. Change: | Slight |
| Road: | Gravel | GPS: | N/A |
| Access: | Somewhat Difficult | Danger: | Slight |
| 4WD: | Helpful | WP Boots: | N/A |

Smooth hewn rocks sit quietly by the constantly rushing falls. These falls are just below the bridge.

Huron River Area

## Letherby Falls Hike

**Letherby Falls:** You can hear the waterfall before seeing it! Leave the old gravel road at the obvious sound of water falling. Climb down the somewhat steep hill to approach Letherby Falls from the spill pool directly below the falls.

*Directions:* Letherby Falls can be accessed from both sides of the river. I prefer the route on the West Side.

*Preferred Route (West Side):* Turn south off of Skanee Road onto Roland Lake Road (dirt). Follow it to the end (2.9 miles). Turn right (west) onto Ravine River Road for 4.0 miles. Go straight @ N46 46.797 W88 10.770 for 2.2 miles. Turn left @ N46 45.995 W88 08.627 for .9 miles. Veer right @ N46 46.169 W88 07.784 for .3 miles. Veer right @ N46 46.120 W88 07.334 for .6 miles. Veer left @ N46 45.852 W88 06.741 for .1 miles. Turn onto a connecting "road" @ N46 45.866 W88 06.658 and park. Hike 150 yards (north) to a "T". Hike to the right (east). In 50 yards, the road turns to the north. Hike another 120 yards. The waterfall is not that far from the "road". In fact, Letherby Falls can usually be heard while hiking down the "road".

*Alternate Route (East Side):* Turn south on Black Creek Road off of Skanee Road. Turn right on Letherby Falls Road just past the bridge at Erick's Falls. There is a sign for "Letherby Falls" at this corner. After 1.4 miles turn right (west). Follow this road generally southward for 1.3 miles. Turn right (south). In .17 miles veer right (west). Follow the 2-track to the end (.53 miles). Park. Walk 175 yards down an embankment and across a little creek to the falls. Use a GPS unit as there is no trail.

## LETHERBY FALLS (HURON RIVER - WEST BRANCH)   Private

| | | | |
|---|---|---|---|
| Must See: | 8 | GPS: | N46 46.027 W88 06.531 |
| Height: | 15 feet | | |
| Time: | 40-60 minutes | Hiking Information | |
| | | Path: | Old road then none |
| Driving Information | | Length: | .22 miles |
| Signs: | None | Elev. Change: | Moderate |
| Road: | Gravel Road | GPS: | Required |
| Access: | Difficult | Danger: | Moderate |
| 4WD: | Helpful | WP Boots: | Recommended |

The West Branch of the Huron River flows over a unique igneous mass here at Letherby Falls. Two slits eroded into the basalt disgorge the water in twin tails of frothing white. The rock face has circular and footprint shaped imprints scattered over it. Below the initial spill pool the river drops another 2 feet to finish the waterfall. Continue downstream just another 100 yards to see the Letherby Cascades.

This is a beautiful waterfall, but it is not easily viewed. Uneven rocks and tangled undergrowth run all the way up to the river's edge.

*NOTE: The USGS has "Letherby Falls" located about 1 mile downstream from here. That is NOT ACCURATE! There is no waterfall there. It is one of several such errors found in Michigan USGS maps.

BARAGA COUNTY

Letherby Falls

Huron River Area

### Letherby - Upper Falls Hike

**Letherby Falls - Upper:** This is the easiest to access out of all the "Letherby" Falls. Park at the entrance to an ATV trail. Hike down the steep trail 100 yards to the base of the waterfall. It is easy to view the waterfall. The terrain is flat and free from undergrowth. This is a locally favorite waterfall.

*Directions:* Turn south off of Skanee Road onto Roland Lake Road (dirt). Follow it to the end (2.9 miles). Turn right (west) onto Ravine River Road for 4.0 miles. Go straight @ N46 46.797 W88 10.770 for 2.2 miles. Turn left @ N46 45.995 W88 08.627 for .9 miles. Veer right @ N46 46.169 W88 07.784 for .3 miles. Veer right @ N46 46.120 W88 07.334 for .6 miles. Veer left @ N46 45.852 W88 06.741 for .2 miles. Park at the entrance to an ATV trail @ N46 45.841 W88 06.564. Drive an ATV (or hike) 300 feet down the hill to the base of the falls.

## LETHERBY FALLS - UPPER (HURON RIVER - WEST BRANCH) Private

| Must See: | 8 | GPS: | N46 45.850 W88 06.498 |
|---|---|---|---|
| Height: | 14 feet | | |
| Time: | 10-30 minutes | Hiking Information | |
| | | Path: | ATV Trail |
| Driving Information | | Length: | 100 yards |
| Signs: | None | Elev. Change: | Moderate |
| Road: | Gravel | GPS: | Recommended |
| Access: | Somewhat Difficult | Danger: | Slight |
| 4WD: | Helpful | WP Boots: | Helpful |

A long, choppy slide ends with a short 1 foot drop into a 30 foot square spill pool. Cedar trees line the sides of the river.

# Huron River Area

### Ravine River Road Falls Hike

***Ravine River Road Falls:*** Watch carefully along the south side of Ravine River Road. The falls can be seen facing the road from about 100 feet upstream.

*Directions:* Turn south off of Skanee Road onto Roland Lake Road (dirt). Follow it to the end (2.9 miles). Turn right (west) onto Ravine River Road for 4.0 miles (to N46 46.797 W88 10.770). Go straight for .75 miles. Park alongside Ravine River Road near where a culvert channels the tributary below the road. Ravine River Road Falls are a mere 100 feet upstream.

## RAVINE RIVER ROAD FALLS (UNNAMED TRIBUTARY)   Private

| | | | |
|---|---|---|---|
| Must See: | 6 | GPS: | N46 46.519 W88 09.997 |
| Height: | 5 feet | | |
| Time: | 5-10 minutes | **Hiking Information** | |
| | | Path: | None |
| **Driving Information** | | Length: | 100 feet |
| Signs: | None | Elev. Change: | Minor |
| Road: | Gravel | GPS: | Helpful |
| Access: | Somewhat Difficult | Danger: | Slight |
| 4WD: | Helpful | WP Boots: | N/A |

A straight drop into a couple of jutting pieces of bedrock send up rooster tails from this easy to find waterfall. Although it is a bit of a drive to get out to this waterfall, it is one of the closest waterfalls to a road in Baraga County.

*Parking near the falls*

**BARAGA COUNTY**

Ravine River Road Falls

67

# Silver River - Lower Area

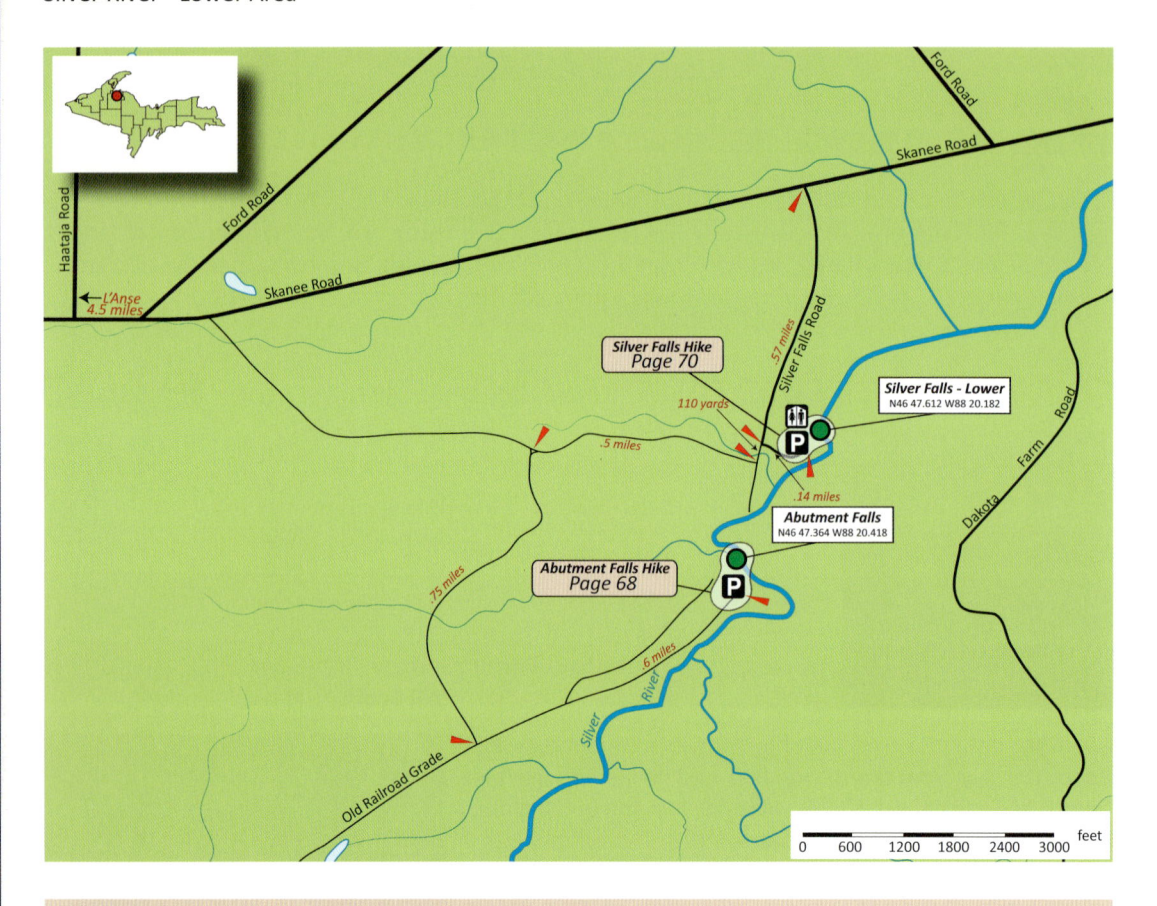

## Abutment Falls Hike

An old railroad grade runs along the Silver River, ending at the waterfall. Old concrete abutments still stand on both sides of the river, helping you to envision where the railroad bridged the waterway.

*Directions:* From Skanee Road, turn south on Silver Falls Road for .57 miles. Continue on straight for 110 yards. Turn right (west) on a 2-track for .5 miles. Turn left (south) on another 2-track for .75 miles until it reaches a "T". Turn left (east) for .6 miles. Park near the river. (This last .6 miles is along a very narrow 2-track. It's the old railroad grade.) The waterfall is straight ahead and downstream. Hike downstream for some better views. Be careful crossing the exposed bedrock. It can be quite slippery, and it angles down toward the top of the waterfall. A fisherman's trail winds along the shoreline. Follow it a short distance to view the waterfall from the base. The best views of the waterfall are probably from the other side. Either ford the river (I haven't tried yet) or hike in along the far side of the river. I believe it would be quite a long hike with no trail on that side.

## ABUTMENT FALLS (SILVER RIVER)

Silver River - Lower Area

Private

| | | | |
|---|---|---|---|
| Must See: | 8 | GPS: | N46 47.364 W88 20.418 |
| Height: | 15 feet | | |
| Time: | 10-20 minutes | Hiking Information | |
| | | Path: | N/A |
| Driving Information | | Length: | 50 feet |
| Signs: | None | Elev. Change: | Minor |
| Road: | 2-track | GPS: | Helpful |
| Access: | Difficult | Danger: | Moderate |
| 4WD: | Helpful | WP Boots: | N/A |

The Silver River rushes through the narrowed river with old concrete abutments squeezing in from either side. It then widens and smooths out, running along the base of slanted, flat, and slippery-when-wet bedrock. The river tilts, sliding down sideways into a gorge in a splashing cascade.

Note the photo below sporting a solitary Spotted Touch-Me-Not, one of my favorite flowers to see at waterfalls. They are so delicate and beautiful! They love water, so they are commonly seen in lowlands. Sometimes they grow in patches, their unique bell-shaped, bright flowers dominating the foreground! There is so much beauty to be enjoyed in this great state of Michigan! If only we look about us...

*Slender beauty in a harsh environment*

*Looking downstream from the abutments*

BARAGA COUNTY

Abutment Falls

Silver River - Lower Area

## Silver Falls Hike

**Silver Falls - Lower:** Slippery rocks line the sides of the falls allowing for an intimate view of the falls. Hike down a fairly well used fisherman's trail downstream from the parking lot to the falls.

*Directions:* From Skanee Road, turn south on Silver Falls Road for .57 miles. The main road turns left, while a lesser travelled road continues straight. Turn left. The road will end in .12 miles at a good sized parking area. There is a vault toilet here. Silver Falls - Lower is downstream. Follow the narrow foot trail on the north side of the parking lot to the falls.

### SILVER FALLS - LOWER (SILVER RIVER)                     Private

| | | | |
|---|---|---|---|
| Must See: | 7 | GPS: | N46 47.612 W88 20.182 |
| Height: | 20 feet | | |
| Time: | 20-30 minutes | Hiking Information | |
| | | Path: | Slight Footpath |
| Driving Information | | Length: | 150 yards |
| Signs: | None | Elev. Change: | Minor |
| Road: | Dirt | GPS: | N/A |
| Access: | Somewhat Easy | Danger: | Slight |
| 4WD: | N/A | WP Boots: | Recommended |

The river churns through a narrow channel in a picturesque setting well-loved by local fishermen. A well-worn path leads through a rocky stretch of forest, crossing a wet patch or two on the way to the base of the falls. Both of the waterfalls here are easily accessed from the good sized parking area. A vault toilet built here is testimony to the popularity of this off-the-road "roadside park".

*Bare bedrock lies all along the chute, smoothed over time by water and ice*

70

Silver River - Middle Area

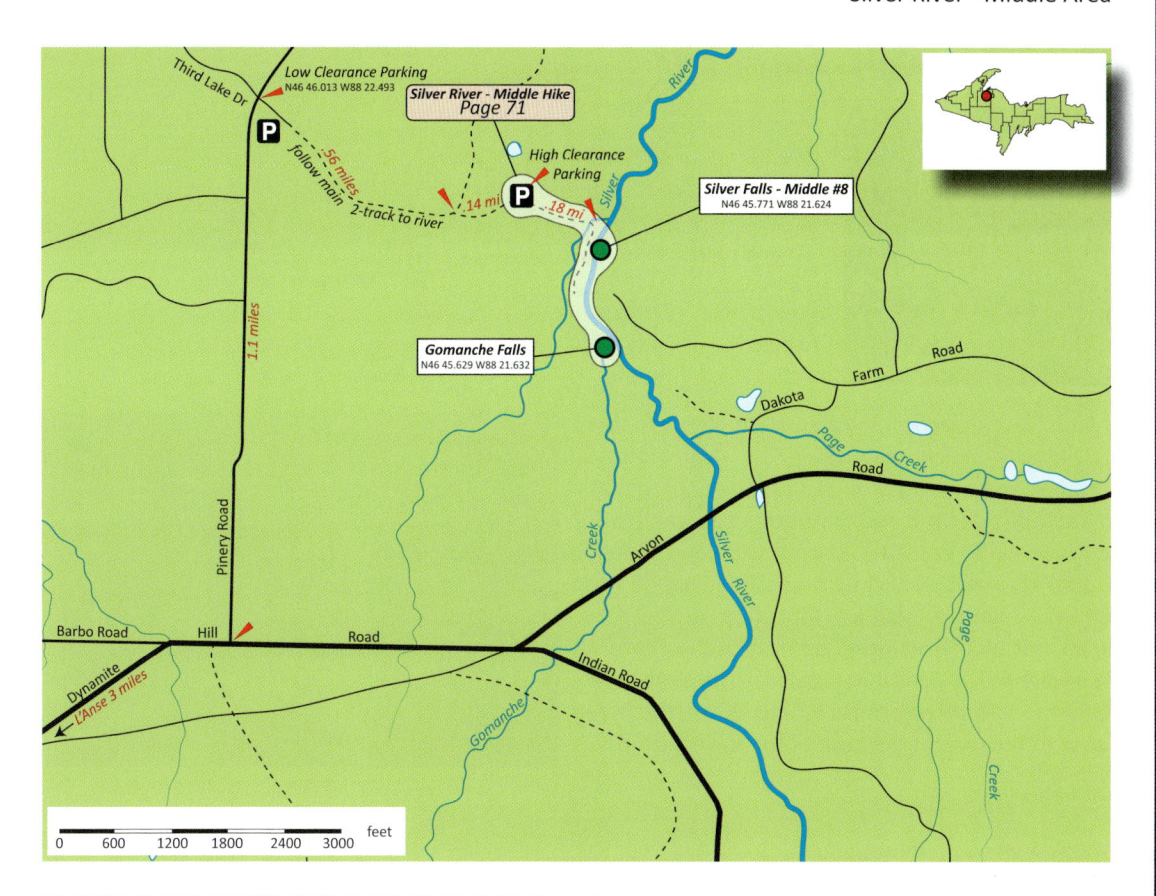

## Silver River - Middle Hike

The Silver River runs through a gorge with a steep wall that guards the river from casual observers. Fortunately, a nice footpath winds along the top of the gorge wall. There are several waterfalls to be seen along the hike to Gomanche Creek. We take a look at one of them in this guidebook (Middle #8). For more information about the rest of the waterfalls around here, see Book 3 in the Waterfalls of Michigan series.

*Directions:* From Dynamite Hill Road turn north onto Pinery Road. Drive 1.1 miles. (The road will jog right and then left again) Third Lake Road is to the left. If you don't have a good clearance vehicle then park on the right (N46 46.013 W88 22.493). High clearance vehicles can drive southeast down the 2-track for .56 miles. The 2-track turns hard to the left. Turn right here onto another 2-track. Follow it for .14 miles. Park on the left of the trail (N46 45.849 W88 21.820). There is room here for one vehicle. Hike .16 miles down the 2-track past the steep, sandy, rutted area and on to the river. Continue to hike along the river to Gomanche Creek, which empties into Silver River immediately after dropping over Gomanche Falls.

Silver River - Middle Area

## 🟩 SILVER FALLS - MIDDLE #8 (SILVER RIVER)   Private

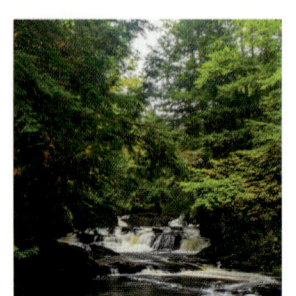

| | | | |
|---|---|---|---|
| Must See: | 7 | GPS: | N46 45.771 W88 21.624 |
| Height: | 15 feet | | |
| Time: | 25-40 minutes | Hiking Information | |
| | | Path: | ATV trail |
| Driving Information | | Length: | .19 miles |
| Signs: | None | Elev. Change: | Moderate |
| Road: | 2-track | GPS: | Recommended |
| Access: | Difficult | Danger: | Moderate |
| 4WD: | Helpful | WP Boots: | N/A |

Almost immediately upon arriving at the river, there is a lovely 3-drop waterfall. The river starts by dividing and running around a slightly domed mass. It cascades down 8 feet on both sides, pauses for a dozen yards, cascades down a wide and pleasing 6 foot rippled and slightly horseshoe shaped drop and then finishes with a 1 foot drop 25 feet later. A 20 foot bluff is snuggled up next to the center of the waterfall, making it impossible to hike the river's edge up the three drops. Climb down the steep bank to the river at the base of the lowest drop.

*Looking back downstream from the waterfall*

\*Note: Hiking Information in the Data Table assumes a high clearance vehicle that parked at the top of the sandy hill along the 2-track. Add .7 miles if parking just off of Pinery Road.

*Notice the three drops, nicely framed in this stretch of river*

Silver River - Middle Area

# GOMANCHE FALLS (GOMANCHE CREEK)   Private

| | | | |
|---|---|---|---|
| Must See: | 7 | GPS: | N46 45.629 W88 21.632 |
| Height: | 13 feet | | |
| Time: | 45-65 minutes | Hiking Information | |
| | | Path: | None |
| Driving Information | | Length: | .37 mile |
| Signs: | None | Elev. Change: | Moderate |
| Road: | 2-track | GPS: | Recommended |
| Access: | Difficult | Danger: | Moderate |
| 4WD: | Helpful | WP Boots: | Recommended |

Gomanche Creek makes a double drop into a narrow gorge just before it falls several more feet as it empties into Silver River. There is a very nice viewing area that would be a perfect spot for a picnic. The entire area is composed of crumbling slate.

The best viewing of Gomanche Falls is from the south side of the creek. This requires wading across from the north. Therefore waterproof boots are recommended if wanting to get over to the far side.

*Silver River can be seen just downstream*

*Note: Hiking Information in the Data Table assumes a high clearance vehicle that parked at the top of the sandy hill along the 2-track. Add .7 miles if parking just off of Pinery Road.

*Amazing fragmented layers of slate splay out on the northern side of the waterfall*

BARAGA COUNTY

Gomanche Falls

73

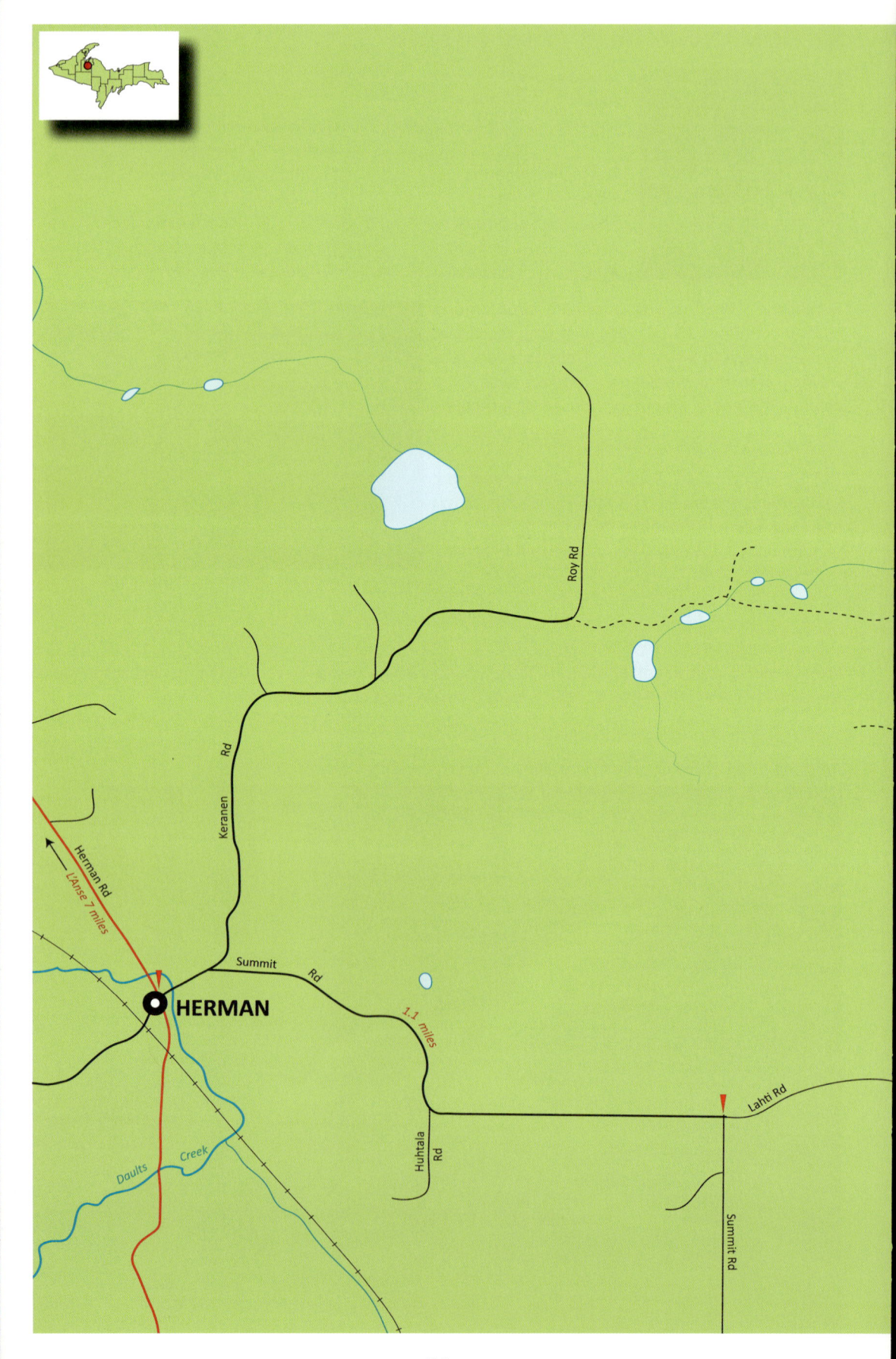

Silver River - Upper Area

BARAGA COUNTY

BARAGA COUNTY

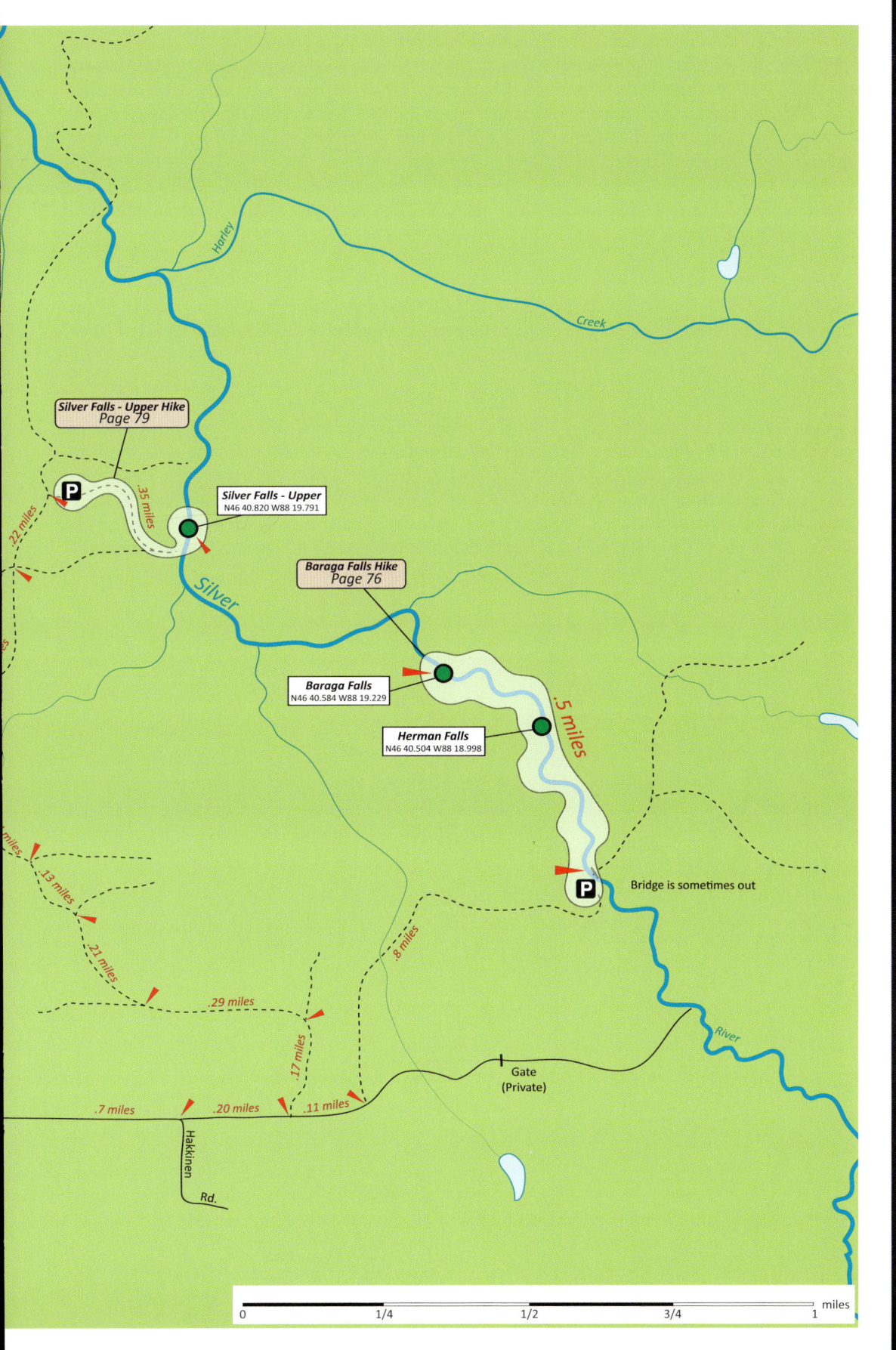

**Silver Falls - Upper Hike**
Page 79

**Silver Falls - Upper**
N46 40.820 W88 19.791

**Baraga Falls Hike**
Page 76

**Baraga Falls**
N46 40.584 W88 19.229

**Herman Falls**
N46 40.504 W88 18.998

Bridge is sometimes out

Gate (Private)

Hakkinen Rd.

.35 miles
.22 miles
.5 miles
.13 miles
.21 miles
.29 miles
.17 miles
.8 miles
.7 miles
.20 miles
.11 miles

Harley Creek
Silver
River

miles
0  1/4  1/2  3/4  1

75

Silver River - Upper Area

### Baraga Falls Hike

The hike to these waterfalls, downstream from the parking area, is one of my favorite secluded waterfall hikes. Even though there is no trail, the hike is not oppressive. This area contains a mature hardwood forest. This means that the undergrowth is kept at bay, and walking is mostly unobstructed. There are, however, rolling hills to be climbed, and very large boulders strewn about at random to be navigated around.

***Herman Falls:*** The river falls over an amazingly sheer slab of stone. This is not a common sight and begs to be viewed!

***Baraga Falls:*** "Take your breath away!" What a way to end an incredible hike! A gorgeous cascade tumbles down the perfectly proportioned waterfall. Rocks are strewn through the riverbed below the falls with a large, 6 foot boulder situated ideally in the middle of the river as an ideal specimen for a photographic accent. This waterfall should be on the very short list for any serious waterfall enthusiast.

***Directions:*** From Herman, which is 7 miles southeast of L'Anse, drive northeast on Keranen Road and then turn right (east) almost immediately onto Summit Road. When Summit turns to the right (about 1 mile) keep going straight (east) on Lahti Road (dirt) for 1 mile. Turn left. A high clearance vehicle may be required for this stretch of road. Follow the road to the river. A wooden bridge over the river is normally closed. Park here. Follow the river downstream to the waterfalls. I have hiked down both sides of the river. I prefer the eastern side. I think it is any easier hike, although I like to photograph the falls from both sides. During most of the year it is possible to find places to carefully cross the river on exposed rocks.

Silver River - Upper Area

## HERMAN FALLS (SILVER RIVER)　　　　　　　　　　Private

| | | | |
|---|---|---|---|
| Must See: | 8 | GPS: | N46 40.504 W88 18.998 |
| Height: | 18 feet | | |
| Time: | 1-1 1/2 hours | Hiking Information | |
| | | Path: | None |
| Driving Information | | Length: | .35 miles |
| Signs: | None | Elev. Change: | Moderate |
| Road: | Dirt | GPS: | Required |
| Access: | Difficult | Danger: | Minor |
| 4WD: | Helpful | WP Boots: | Recommended |

I was shocked the first time I saw this waterfall! I had no idea that there would be a vertical wall waterfall on the Silver River. What a beautiful situation. It reminds me of a miniature Manabezho Falls. Most of the drop is sheer.

Unfortunately, as is often the case, this waterfall acts as a giant garbage collector for tree debris. A large fallen tree lays along the base. It has been diminishing in size over the past several years, and in time, or with some human intervention, it will eventually be gone. This could be a spectacular waterfall to photograph without the distraction.

I would love to see this waterfall during spring melt! I suspect that the flow would run wall to wall over this wide face.

BARAGA COUNTY

Herman Falls

Silver River - Upper Area

## BARAGA FALLS (SILVER RIVER)   Private

| | | | |
|---|---|---|---|
| Must See: | 9 | GPS: | N46 40.584 W88 19.229 |
| Height: | 20 feet | | |
| Time: | 1 1/2-2 hours | Hiking Information | |
| | | Path: | None |
| Driving Information | | Length: | .56 miles |
| Signs: | None | Elev. Change: | Moderate |
| Road: | Dirt | GPS: | Required |
| Access: | Difficult | Danger: | Minor |
| 4WD: | Helpful | WP Boots: | Recommended |

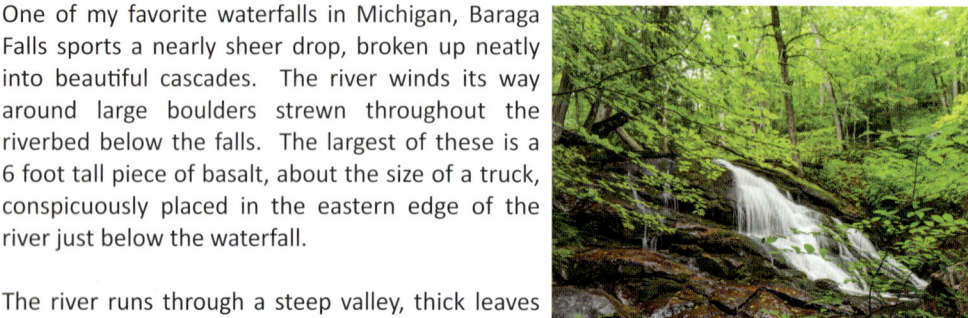

One of my favorite waterfalls in Michigan, Baraga Falls sports a nearly sheer drop, broken up neatly into beautiful cascades. The river winds its way around large boulders strewn throughout the riverbed below the falls. The largest of these is a 6 foot tall piece of basalt, about the size of a truck, conspicuously placed in the eastern edge of the river just below the waterfall.

The river runs through a steep valley, thick leaves mulching the saplings struggling for light beneath their towering parents. Maple and birch turn the landscape to an earthy gold, nature's Midas returning year after year to touch the land with a crisp display that few can rival! Here and there a cedar tree adds a green accent.

78

Silver River - Upper Area

### Silver Falls - Upper Hike

**Silver Falls - Upper:** The Upper Falls flow over two main cascades. The trail follows the river to the top of the falls, then works its way down to the base. Downed tree debris tends to accumulate among the rocks below the falls.

*Directions:* From Herman, drive east/northeast on Summit/Keranen Road. Stay on Summit Road until it turns hard to the right. Continue on straight on Lahti Road for .9 miles. Turn left onto a bumpy road (high clearance recommended). A maze of logging trails heads north from here. Stay on the "main road". Use the area map to help you stay on the correct trail. In 1.6 miles, turn right. Park near the berm that shortly blocks the 2-track. Hike down the switchback path for about .35 miles. Fifty yards before the river is a worn down berm. Just before the berm is an old parking spot on the left. Head into that area. A pine tree on the right has red and blue stripes painted on it. That is the trail head. It is a faint path. The path leads to the river and then turns down river to the top of the falls. There is about 100 feet of elevation change on this hike.

## SILVER FALLS - UPPER (SILVER RIVER)     Private

| | | | |
|---|---|---|---|
| Must See: | 8 | GPS: | N46 40.820 W88 19.791 |
| Height: | 30 feet | | |
| Time: | 15-30 minutes | Hiking Information | |
| | | Path: | Unimproved Footpath |
| Driving Information | | Length: | .39 miles |
| Signs: | None | Elev. Change: | Elevated |
| Road: | 2-track | GPS: | Required |
| Access: | Difficult | Danger: | Minor |
| 4WD: | Required | WP Boots: | Helpful |

Although it is not easy to find, this is a locally popular waterfall destination. Keep in mind that it's about a 100 foot change in elevation from the parking spot. Enjoy the shaded river bank where the footpath winds through mature hardwoods and evergreens.

The 40 foot wide riverbed houses huge rock sections. The river runs through hardwoods, golden yellow in autumn. However, along the side the river, evergreens dominate the foliage. The falls drop 10 feet, splitting around a mounded rock. A pool below the first drop empties on the far side of the river into a narrow crevasse formed between the river bedrock and a large boulder that broke off and is wedged up against the rock face by a number of similarly sized boulders. A narrow pool runs back sideways along the face before the river continues its journey downstream with several small drops added as a parting gift.

*Low water level in October*

*The top cascade can just be seen from down here*

# Slate River - Lower Area

**BARAGA COUNTY**

- Karschney Rd
- Heikkinen Rd
- Townline Rd
- Koski Road
- Biltonen Road
- Marzal Rd
- Bayview Road
- Skanee Road
- Townline Rd
- Collins Rd
- Skanee Road
- Arvon Road

Lake Superior
Bendry Point
Snug Harbor
Huron Bay
Echo Harbor
Silver River
Slate River
Bella Lake
Bella Creek
Lake

L'Anse 9 miles

**Slate River Falls Hike — Page 83**

**Slate River Falls**
N46 49.874 W88 15.126

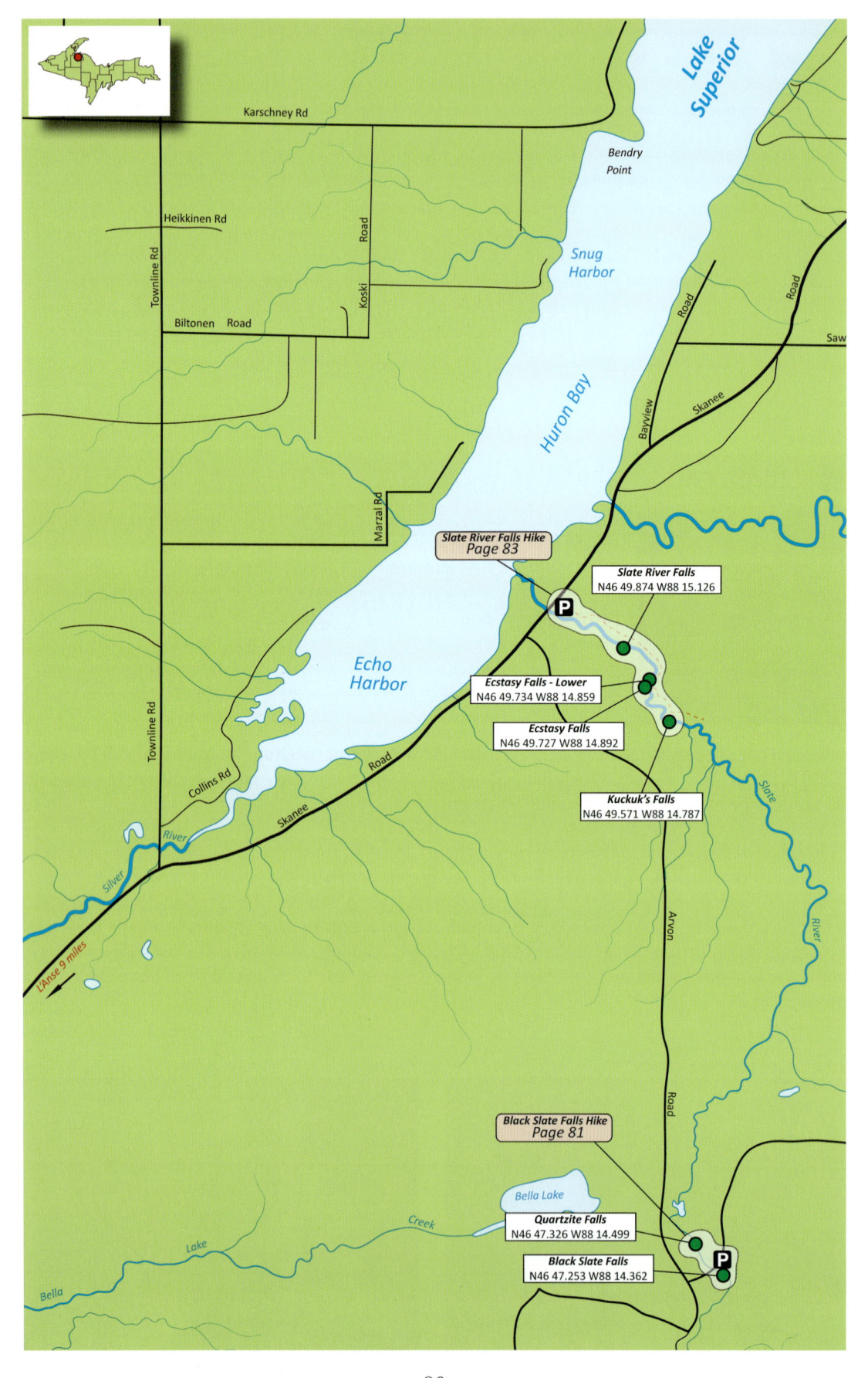

**Ecstasy Falls - Lower**
N46 49.734 W88 14.859

**Ecstasy Falls**
N46 49.727 W88 14.892

**Kuckuk's Falls**
N46 49.571 W88 14.787

**Black Slate Falls Hike — Page 81**

**Quartzite Falls**
N46 47.326 W88 14.499

**Black Slate Falls**
N46 47.253 W88 14.362

80

Slate River - Lower Area

### Black Slate Falls Hike

Quartzite Falls and the Black Slate collection of falls are easily accessed and occur in a fairly tame section of the Slate River. An interesting oddity is seen on the short hike to Quartzite Falls. A narrow vein of white rock runs for a ways down the middle of the Slate River, looking like a painted center line for dividing water traffic!

*Directions:* Turn southeast onto Arvon Road off of Skanee Road. (This is the first main dirt road southwest of the Slate River.) Follow Arvon Road in a generally southerly direction for about 3.5 miles. Turn left onto another dirt road. About 200 yards down the road is a bridge that crosses the Slate River. Park on the (far) east side of the bridge. Hike along the ATV trail to the north, following the river downstream to Quartzite Falls. When done, hike back along the trail to the vehicle. Now follow the river (either side) up river from the bridge to Black Slate Falls.

## QUARTZITE FALLS (SLATE RIVER)    Private

| | | | |
|---|---|---|---|
| Must See: | 7 | GPS: | N46 47.326 W88 14.499 |
| Height: | 10 feet | | |
| Time: | 15-25 minutes | Hiking Information | |
| | | Path: | ATV Trail |
| Driving Information | | Length: | 175 yards |
| Signs: | None | Elev. Change: | Minor |
| Road: | Gravel | GPS: | N/A |
| Access: | Somewhat Easy | Danger: | Slight |
| 4WD: | N/A | WP Boots: | N/A |

While hiking down the ATV trail to the falls, watch for a unique geological feature. It looks like someone painted a bright, white center line down the river! It's a surprisingly uniform vein of white rock. Of course, it's best to view when the river is low!

The waterfall appears suddenly, as the river cuts deep into the black slate bedrock. A 20 foot wide horseshoe shaped cascade stair-steps the river down into an 8 foot high steep-walled gorge. The waterfall continues to slide down flat layers for about 75 feet below the cascade. The river then flushes into a large swimming hole at the base of the slide.

*The trail from the bridge to Quartzite Falls*

*Walking along the side of the waterfall*

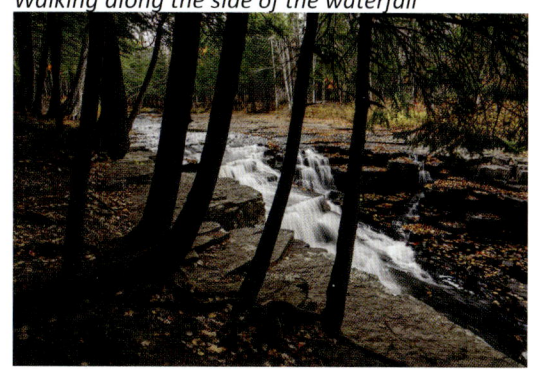

BARAGA COUNTY

Quartzite Falls

81

Slate River - Lower Area

## BLACK SLATE FALLS (SLATE RIVER)　　　　　　　　Private

| | | | |
|---|---|---|---|
| Must See: | 7 | GPS: | N46 47.253 W88 14.362 |
| Height: | 5 feet | | |
| Time: | 10-20 minutes | Hiking Information | |
| | | Path: | Slight Footpath |
| Driving Information | | Length: | 100 yards |
| Signs: | East Side of Bridge | Elev. Change: | Minor |
| Road: | Gravel | GPS: | N/A |
| Access: | Somewhat Easy | Danger: | Slight |
| 4WD: | N/A | WP Boots: | N/A |

The waterfall can be seen from the bridge, but to view it better, follow the riverbed on either side of the river. The shot to the right was taken from the western bank. It is easier to follow this bank upstream from here. The eastern side gets quite boggy and there are many downed trees as well as thick brush to contend with.

The 30 foot wide river cascades down closely spaced stair steps of slate bedrock. Beautiful birch trees on both sides of the river stretch out golden arms each October.

*A LARGE boulder sits downstream from the waterfall*

## Slate River Falls Hike

Slate River Falls is a wonderful waterfall secreted away at the base of a long, steep, winding ravine. A large sandy area provides for great viewing of the falls and a nice place to take a break after completing this somewhat rigorous hike. Continue upstream when conditions allow to view more waterfalls! (The ravine is very steep and runs down to the river in most places, so there is no river's edge to walk along. During high water, the river may be too deep and fast to wade in.)

*Directions:* Coming from L'Anse on Skanee Road, cross the Slate River bridge (there is a big, wooden sign announcing the Slate River) and immediately turn right (southeast) on a dirt road. The road doesn't go far, but be looking to your left for a hiking trail that quickly starts climbing the hillside. Park and hike the trail. After 5-10 minutes you will see that you have been paralleling the Slate River, but at a much higher elevation. Nearing the waterfall, the trail dives down into the ravine that it had been running along the top of. This is the most dangerous part of the hike. Be careful on this steep hill, as it seems to be about 100 feet tall and it is easy to start sliding down the hill. With this warning in mind, this (Slate River Falls) is the easiest waterfall to get to on this hike! Climb up above Slate River Falls on the near side of the river and continue upstream, often hiking right up the riverbed to the rest of the falls. After Kuckuk's Falls, I always leave the river, climb up to the top of the ravine (now manageable), and follow the footpath along the top of the ravine back to the vehicle.

## SLATE RIVER FALLS (SLATE RIVER)   Private

| | | | |
|---|---|---|---|
| Must See: | 8 | GPS: | N46 49.874 W88 15.126 |
| Height: | 25 feet | | |
| Time: | 45-60 minutes | Hiking Information | |
| Driving Information | | Path: | Unimproved Footpath |
| Signs: | None | Length: | .30 miles |
| Road: | Dirt | Elev. Change: | Major |
| Access: | Somewhat Easy | GPS: | Recommended |
| 4WD: | Helpful | Danger: | Moderate |
| | | WP Boots: | Recommended |

The walk is fairly strenuous, but the view of the falls is worth it. There is a nice sized landing area to view the falls from. It is a great place for a picnic!

At the end of the trail there is a steep hill (maybe 100 feet high) that needs to be climbed down. There are no steps and only a slight trail. This hike is not for the faint of heart or unsteady of foot.

*The viewing area is on the east side of the river*

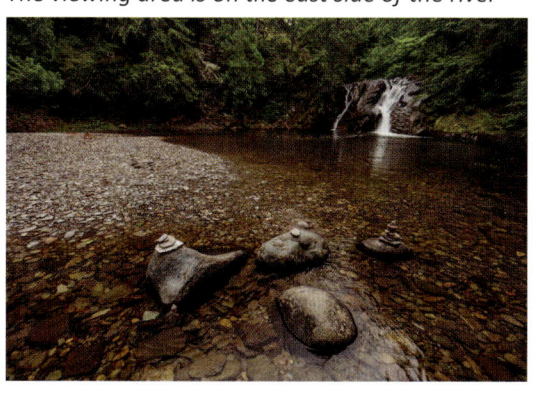

*Note the difference in water volume!*

83

## ECSTASY FALLS - LOWER (SLATE RIVER)  Private

| | | | |
|---|---|---|---|
| Must See: | 8 | GPS: | N46 49.734 W88 14.859 |
| Height: | 10 feet | | |
| Time: | 2 1/4-2 3/4 hours | Hiking Information | |
| | | Path: | Footpath then none |
| Driving Information | | Length: | .61 miles |
| Signs: | None | Elev. Change: | Major |
| Road: | Dirt | GPS: | Required |
| Access: | Somewhat Easy | Danger: | Elevated |
| 4WD: | N/A | WP Boots: | Required |

Follow the riverbed upstream from Slate River Falls past several drops to the Lower Ecstasy Falls. It is much narrower, and more spectacular than Ecstasy Falls (just upstream from here) during low water periods.

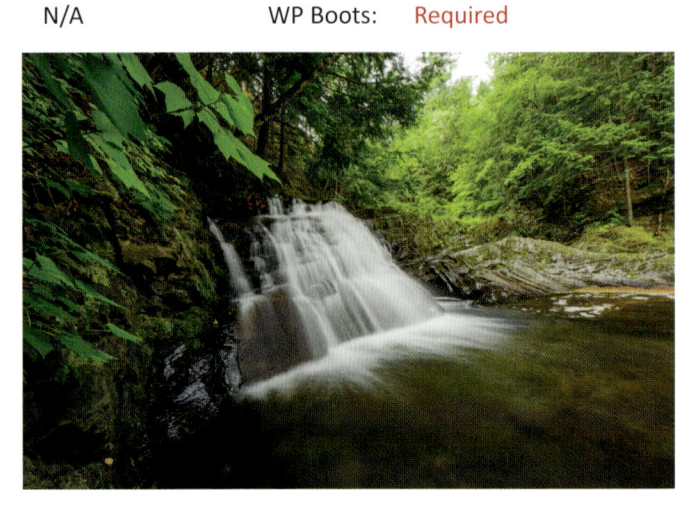

The Lower Ecstasy Falls is a very traditional, 8 foot, slightly rounded cascading waterfall with a small 2 foot drop below the spill pool. There is a convenient stony viewing area along the side and below the main drop. When the river is high it may be under water.

Slate River - Lower Area

## ECSTASY FALLS (SLATE RIVER)                                   Private

| | | | |
|---|---|---|---|
| Must See: | 7 | GPS: | N46 49.727 W88 14.892 |
| Height: | 12 feet | | |
| Time: | 2 1/2-3 hours | Hiking Information | |
| | | Path: | Footpath then none |
| Driving Information | | Length: | .64 miles |
| Signs: | None | Elev. Change: | Major |
| Road: | Dirt | GPS: | Required |
| Access: | Somewhat Easy | Danger: | Elevated |
| 4WD: | N/A | WP Boots: | Required |

Just 50 yards upstream from Lower Ecstasy Falls, the river runs wall to wall, much wider than at the Lower Falls. It, therefore, takes a lot more water to fill out the wide cascades. I haven't seen it in these conditions yet. A difficulty in viewing this waterfall with high water is getting to it! The river can be dangerous, as much of the hiking needs to take place in the riverbed.

Although there are four cascades in this set of falls, the most prominent drops are a parallel batch of cascades that have rounded fronts like dams bulging to the bursting point. Water spills over them at random points when the water level is low, as seen here.

85

BARAGA COUNTY

Ecstasy Falls

Slate River - Lower Area

## KUCKUK'S FALLS (SLATE RIVER) — Private

| | | | |
|---|---|---|---|
| Must See: | 8 | GPS: | N46 49.571 W88 14.787 |
| Height: | 14 feet | | |
| Time: | 4-4 1/2 hours | Hiking Information | |
| | | Path: | Footpath then none |
| Driving Information | | Length: | .92 miles |
| Signs: | None | Elev. Change: | Major |
| Road: | Dirt | GPS: | Required |
| Access: | Somewhat Easy | Danger: | Elevated |
| 4WD: | N/A | WP Boots: | Required |

It's quite a stretch between Ecstasy Falls and here. But the hike up the river ends with this great waterfall!

The river makes a hairpin turn as soon as it falls over the main cascades. It then quickly shoots down another 4 feet of small drops and slides to continue on its way down through a flatter section of riverbed. The steep ravine is much calmer at this point in the river. Climb up the left side of the river to the footpath that follows the top of the ravine. It is a much faster hike back to the vehicle!

86

# Slate River - Upper Area

**BARAGA COUNTY**

These waterfalls are in the Slate River - Lower Area (Page 81)

Arvon Road

.78 miles

Arvon Slate Quarry

1.75 miles

Arvon Road

Victory Falls
N46 46.379 W88 13.520

Slate

Victory Falls Hike
Page 89

1.11 miles

"Turkey Tracks"

.45 miles

Arvon Road

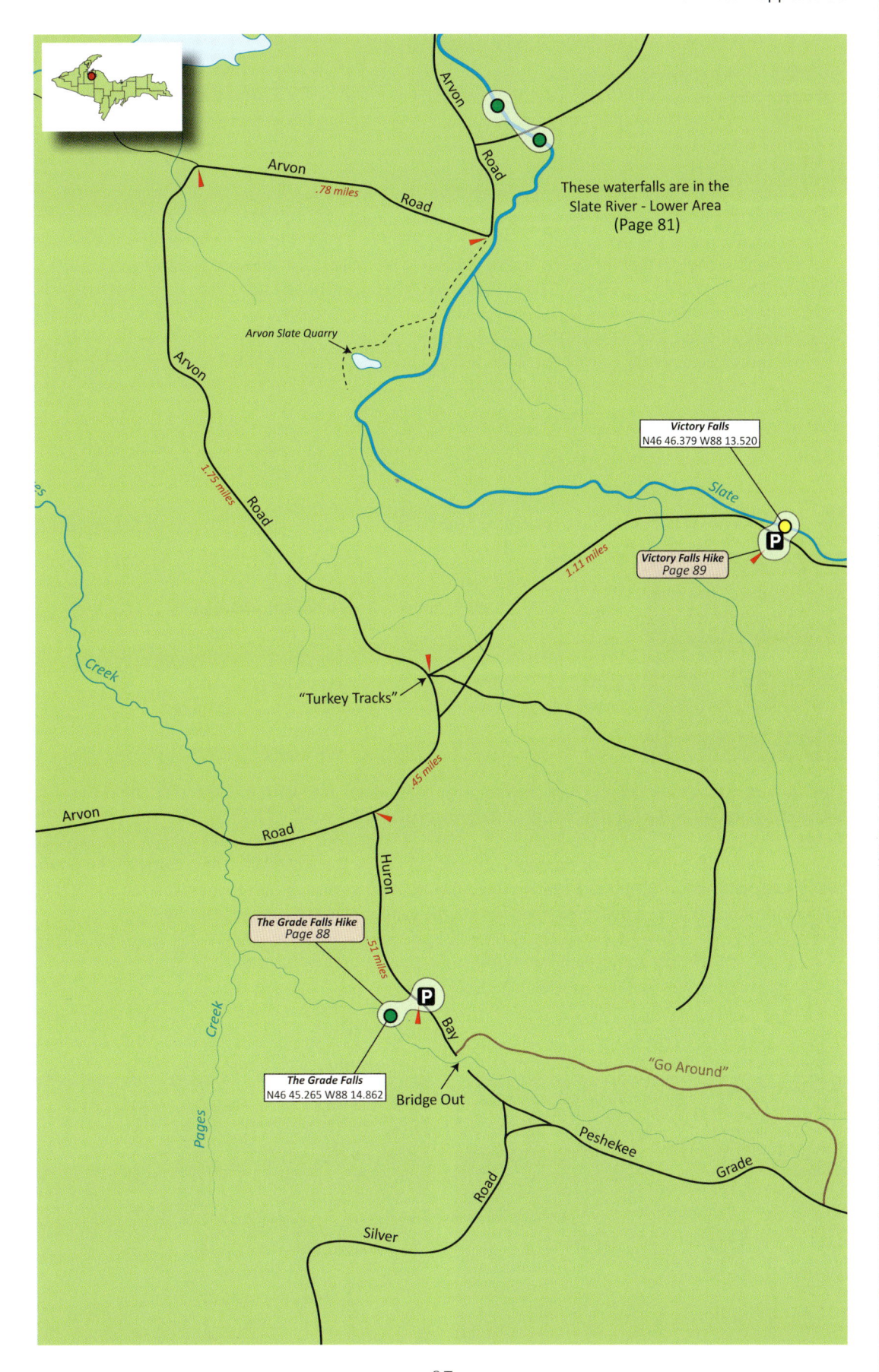

Huron

The Grade Falls Hike
Page 88

.51 miles

Creek

Pages Creek

The Grade Falls
N46 45.265 W88 14.862

Bridge Out

Bay

"Go Around"

Peshekee Grade

Road

Silver

87

Slate River - Upper Area

### The Grade Falls Hike

The Huron Bay - Peshekee Grade is an old railroad grade turned into a road. This portion of the grade follows the southern side of a mountain that is 3 miles west of Mount Arvon. The runoff from this unnamed mountain is carried into Pages Creek via a small tributary. This is where The Grade Falls are found.

*Directions:* Turn southeast onto Arvon Road off of Skanee Road. (This is the first main dirt road southwest of the Slate River.) Follow Arvon Road in a generally southerly direction for 3.7 miles. Arvon Road turns to the right (west). Follow it for .78 miles. Arvon turns to the left. Follow it for 1.75 miles. Turn right (south) at the Turkey Tracks. In .45 miles turn left onto another gravel road (Huron Bay - Peshekee Grade). In .51 miles park on the left (northeast) side of the road. There is an old 2-track and a bit of a clearing here - probably from logging activity. Hike southwest to the GPS coordinates for The Grade Falls. There are some old overgrown logging trails that may be of help on the short hike downhill toward the waterfall. It's only 130 yards, but there is no trail or signage.

## THE GRADE FALLS (UNNAMED TRIBUTARY)   Private

| | | | |
|---|---|---|---|
| Must See: | 7 | GPS: | N46 45.265 W88 14.862 |
| Height: | 12 feet | | |
| Time: | 20-40 minutes | Hiking Information | |
| | | Path: | None |
| Driving Information | | Length: | 130 yards |
| Signs: | None | Elev. Change: | Minor |
| Road: | Gravel | GPS: | Required |
| Access: | Difficult | Danger: | Minor |
| 4WD: | N/A | WP Boots: | N/A |

After parking, cross the road and hike the faint logging trail down toward the waterfall. It's 130 yards with mostly no trail and a fair amount of undergrowth along the way.

A large boulder sits to the side of the rocky stream just above the waterfall. The tributary then pours over a solid rock ridge and enters a gently sloped ravine. It flows through the stone-filled waterway that meanders in the midst of a peaceful, open forest. It's a great place to enjoy a waterfall!

This tributary can dry up during summer months. Try to go after a good rain.

*The waterway up above the waterfall*

*The beautiful, open forest below the waterfall*

Slate River - Upper Area

### Victory Falls Hike

With no road signs throughout most of the Huron Mountains, it can make driving very confusing. Follow the directions, however, and have fun discovering another of the little known water features in Michigan's back country. This is another waterfall on the Slate River. Fortunately, there is a good gravel road that runs close to the river at this point.

*Directions:* Turn southeast onto Arvon Road off of Skanee Road. (This is the first main dirt road southwest of the Slate River.) Follow Arvon Road in a generally southerly direction for 3.7 miles. Arvon Road turns to the right (west). Follow it for .78 miles. Arvon Road turns to the left. Follow it for 1.75 miles. Turn left (northeast) at the Turkey Tracks. In 1.11 miles pull off the side of the road (N46 46.342 W88 13.537). There is no obvious parking spot or trail here. Hike through the woods to the north for 85 yards to N46 46.379 W88 13.520.

## VICTORY FALLS (SLATE RIVER)   Private

| | | | |
|---|---|---|---|
| Must See: | 6 | GPS: | N46 46.379 W88 13.520 |
| Height: | 8 feet | | |
| Time: | 15-25 minutes | Hiking Information | |
| | | Path: | None |
| Driving Information | | Length: | 85 yards |
| Signs: | None | Elev. Change: | Minor |
| Road: | Gravel | GPS: | Required |
| Access: | Difficult | Danger: | Minor |
| 4WD: | N/A | WP Boots: | N/A |

There is no trail to the falls, but it is a short 85 yard hike to the river.

Angular sheets of slate lie fractured across the 20 foot wide river. Passages have been cut on either side of the river at the top of the waterfall. They taper in toward each other, meeting near the base of the waterfall where the "V" shaped waterfall plunges a final 2 feet into a shallow channel. Eight feet later, the rocky mass that makes up the 40 foot long cascading waterfall gives way to a pleasant spill pool (possibly nice for swimming), shrouded by birch and cedar.

As the water level rises, the "V" becomes submerged, and the waterfall widens out, filling out more of the rocky riverbed.

*The obvious "V" in the river*

*The rugged bedrock creates unique patterns*

Tibbets Falls Area

## Tibbets Falls Hike

***Tibbets Falls:*** There are no highly-defined drops in this stretch of river. Instead, the bedrock of the river is tilted at an awkward angle, creating interesting lines and patterns. The waterfall begins with a cascading drop and continues in a series of aggressive rapids.

*Directions:* Drive north on W Plains Road off of M-28 or west on N Section 16 Road from US-141. Drive north from the intersection of E Plains Road and N Section 16 Road 1.81 miles. A white post with "Tibbets Falls" is located by a gravel road on the left (west). Turn left and drive .22 miles. Turn left on a NARROW 2-track. Follow it .47 miles to a parking area at the end of the road. There is a steep downhill trail to the falls. (Be prepared to park short of the end of the road and walk the rest of the way if your vehicle has clearance issues.)

# TIBBETS FALLS (STURGEON RIVER)

Private

| | | | |
|---|---|---|---|
| Must See: | 6 | GPS: | N46 34.874 W88 35.347 |
| Height: | 8 feet | | |
| Time: | 20-40 minutes | Hiking Information | |
| | | Path: | Unimproved Footpath |
| Driving Information | | Length: | 100 yards |
| Signs: | Small | Elev. Change: | Moderate |
| Road: | 2-track | GPS: | Helpful |
| Access: | Difficult | Danger: | Moderate |
| 4WD: | Recommended | WP Boots: | Recommended |

It's a 100 yard hike from the circular parking area to the river. The North Country Trail winds along the top of the gorge up above the Sturgeon River. A spur trail connects the parking lot to the NCT. There are several places along the NCT that you can get down to the river's edge. Most of these are quite steep descents. The easiest way down is to follow the NCT downstream past the main cascades. When the river turns more northerly the trail has dropped down closer to the river. Find a safe way down to the river and follow it back upstream to the falls.

*The "main" drop - up above the corner cascades*

91

Tioga Falls Area

### Tioga Park Falls Hike

The roadside park has vault toilets and a water hand pump. There is also a nice sign describing many of the unique features in Baraga County. A unique footbridge spans the Tioga River and offers a nice view of the cascades from there.

*Tioga Park Falls:* Hike from the parking lot down a somewhat rough footpath. It quickly enters an old forest with little undergrowth. The trail then meets up with the river and follows it upstream. The undergrowth here is thicker. The falls will be around a bend in the river. The lazy river is fairly wide and slow below the falls.

*Directions:* From US-41, turn south into the roadside park next to the bridge over the Tioga River. Park here. There are signs from the parking lot giving directions to Tioga Park Falls. Follow the trail at the rear of the park that winds through the woods and then to the left, where the trail then meets the river and follows it upstream to the falls.

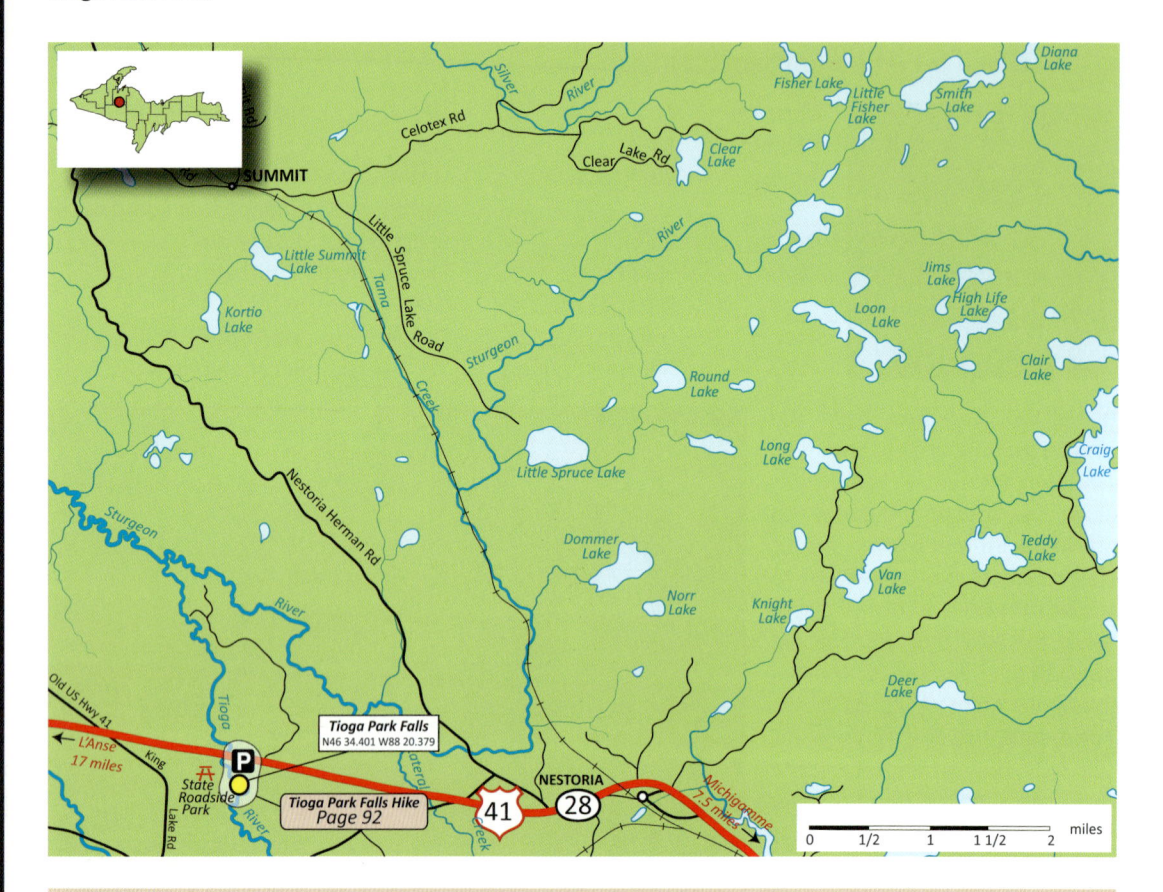

## TIOGA PARK FALLS (TIOGA RIVER)

Private

| | | | |
|---|---|---|---|
| Must See: | 4 | GPS: | N46 34.401 W88 20.379 |
| Height: | 3 feet | | |
| Time: | 15-30 minutes | Hiking Information | |
| | | Path: | Unimproved Footpath |
| Driving Information | | Length: | .17 miles |
| Signs: | Roadside Park | Elev. Change: | Slight |
| Road: | Main | GPS: | N/A |
| Access: | Very Easy | Danger: | Slight |
| 4WD: | N/A | WP Boots: | N/A |

Hike along the faint trail found at the back of the roadside park along Tioga River upstream and around a corner in the river. An old, gnarly tree sits next to the waterfall. Its roots sprawl along the rocky river bank, looking for soil. Above the falls is an outcropping of rock that can be climbed on for a closer look at the river and waterfall.

*The small drop, seen from the side near the large tree that overlooks the waterfall*

93

BARAGA COUNTY

# CHAPTER 3
# CHIPPEWA & LUCE COUNTY

# Chippewa & Luce County Map

Ile Parisienne
CANADA
UNITED STATES OF AMERICA
Sault Ste Marie
Sault Ste Marie
Lake George
Pendills Lake
West 6 Mile Road
River
Waiska
221
Charlotte River
Lake Nicolet
Waiska River
W Br
75
129
Little Munuscong River
H40
Big
48
River
Munuscong Lake
Pickford
CHIPPEWA COUNTY
MACKINAC COUNTY
Munuscong
East Br
River
48
Pine
48
McKay Creek
129
134
Moran
Cedarville
De Tour Village
134
Marquette Island
La Salle Island
Hay Lake
St. Ignace
Mackinaw Island
Lake Huron
Pointe Aux Pins
75
0 3 6 9 12 miles

# Tahquamenon Falls Area

CHIPPEWA & LUCE COUNTY

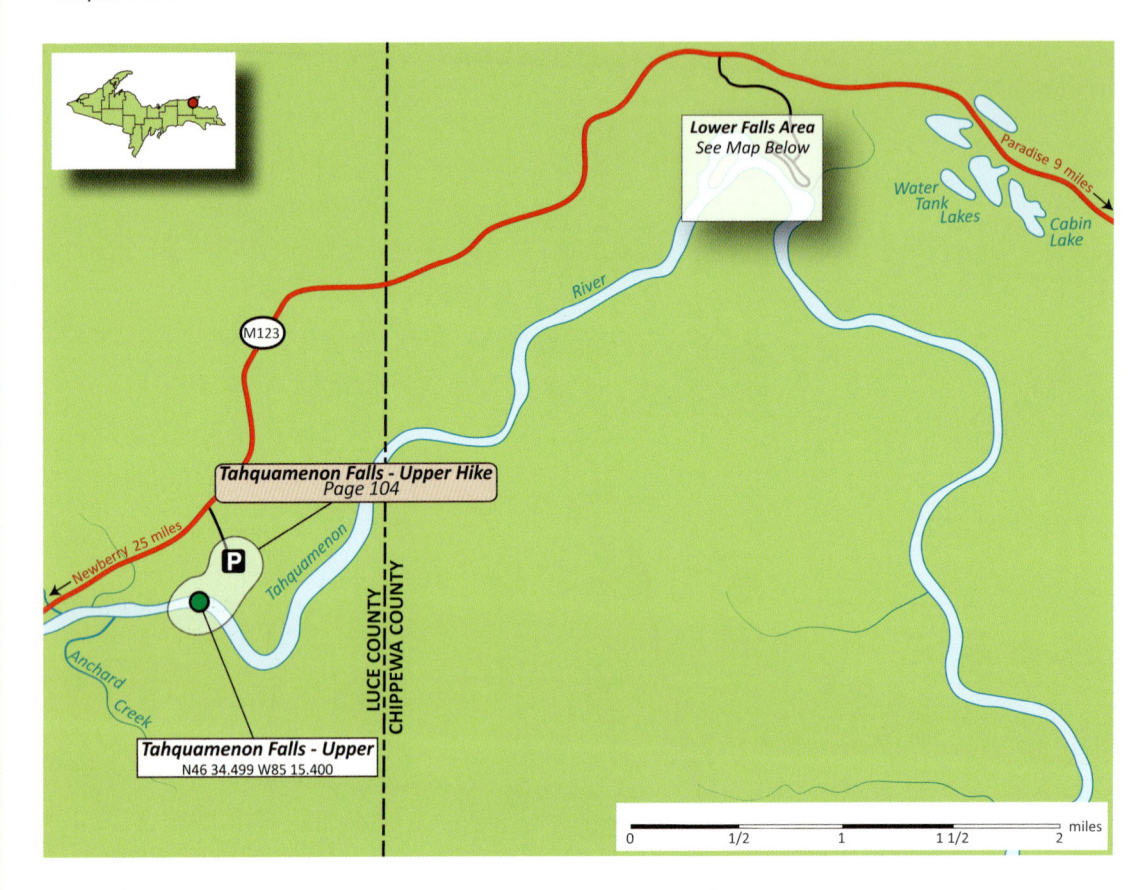

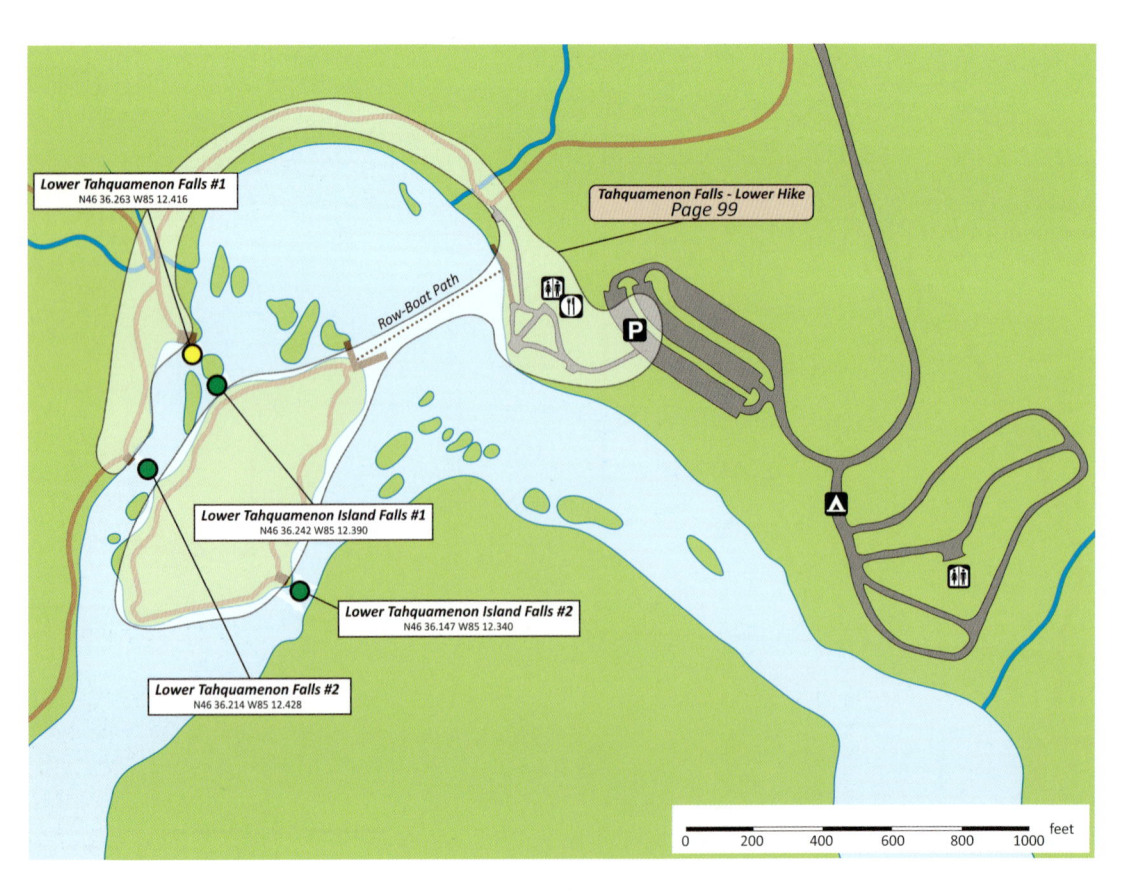

**Lower Falls Area** — See Map Below

Paradise 9 miles
Water Tank Lakes
Cabin Lake
River
M123
Newberry 25 miles
Anchard Creek
Tahquamenon
LUCE COUNTY | CHIPPEWA COUNTY

**Tahquamenon Falls - Upper Hike**
Page 104

**Tahquamenon Falls - Upper**
N46 34.499 W85 15.400

0 — 1/2 — 1 — 1 1/2 — 2 miles

**Lower Tahquamenon Falls #1**
N46 36.263 W85 12.416

**Tahquamenon Falls - Lower Hike**
Page 99

Row-Boat Path

**Lower Tahquamenon Island Falls #1**
N46 36.242 W85 12.390

**Lower Tahquamenon Island Falls #2**
N46 36.147 W85 12.340

**Lower Tahquamenon Falls #2**
N46 36.214 W85 12.428

0 — 200 — 400 — 600 — 800 — 1000 feet

98

### Tahquamenon Falls - Lower Hike

Take time to enjoy the natural beauty here at the lower set of cascades on the Tahquamenon River. Although not as spectacular as the Upper Falls, these falls each have their own unique attributes that attract many visitors each year. The Lower Falls allow for more intimate viewing of each of the cascades. A beautiful campground is located just downstream from the falls. Parking for day hikes to the falls is a short walk from rest room facilities and a well stocked gift store.

***Lower Tahquamenon Falls #1:*** The largest of the viewing decks located along the riverside walkway commands a "front-row" view of the waterfall. Falling 7 feet in a frothing gush of foaming water, the waterfall often sends up a mist that dampens the wooden platform and anyone standing on it.

***Lower Tahquamenon Island Falls #1:*** Best viewed from the island, Lower Tahquamenon Island Falls #1 is a nicely formed, round fronted cascading waterfall. It is bordered to the north by a wooded outcropping and to the south by bare bedrock. Numerous photographs have been taken with visitors standing or sitting to the left of the falls.

***Lower Tahquamenon Falls #2:*** Just beyond the viewing deck for Lower Tahquamenon Falls #1 is another nice wooden platform that looks out upon one of my favorite drops on the Tahquamenon River. Crafted by a Master Artist, the bedrock drops a mere 3 feet, but in a unique, sawtooth fashion. I love to photograph the resulting zigzag ribbons of water.

***Lower Tahquamenon Island Falls #2:*** This is actually a double drop. Twin 10 foot falls make for a total of 20 feet of elevation change. This is the only waterfall on the southeast segment of the Tahquamenon River. This accounts for the tallest of the Lower Falls. It is best appreciated from the island. A nicely constructed wooden deck overlooks the falls just off of the footpath that encircles the island. This waterfall can be viewed in the distance from the first observation area encountered west of the day use parking area as well.

*Directions:* From M-123, turn south into the well marked Lower Falls entrance. A Michigan State Park permit is required to enter. Turn right before the campground to enter the day-use parking area. Follow the asphalt walkway past the gift shop to the falls. Near the beginning of the hike is the rowboat rental. This is the only access to the island. From the island, all of the falls can be seen. And the tallest of the falls, Lower Tahquamenon Island Falls #2, is best seen from the island.

*Trail to the Lower Falls*

*The trail in the winter*

*Trail on the island*

*Parking lot at sunrise*

Tahquamenon Falls Area

## LOWER TAHQUAMENON FALLS #1 (Tahquamenon River)   Private

| | | | |
|---|---|---|---|
| Must See: | 6 | GPS: | N46 36.263 W85 12.416 |
| Height: | 7 feet | | |
| Time: | 45-90 minutes | **Hiking Information** | |
| | | Path: | Improved Footpath |
| **Driving Information** | | Length: | 1/4 mile |
| Signs: | Excellent | Elev. Change: | Minor |
| Road: | Main | GPS: | N/A |
| Access: | Very Easy | Danger: | Slight |
| 4WD: | N/A | WP Boots: | N/A |

This is the waterfall that is most easily viewed from the "main" viewing deck along the river. In fact, the waterfall is so close that the wooden platform is often moist from the mist that rises up and is carried along by prevailing winds. The trail that continues upstream from the viewing deck runs along the side of the waterfall, offering another look at the tannin stained waterfall. There is also a nice view of the waterfall from the island.

*The view from the island*

*A wintry look from the river's edge walkway*

*A close-up of the largest cascade as seen from the island.*

100

# Tahquamenon Falls Area

## LOWER TAHQUAMENON ISLAND FALLS #1 (Tahquamenon River)   Private

| | | | |
|---|---|---|---|
| Must See: | 7 | GPS: | N46 36.242 W85 12.390 |
| Height: | 8 feet | | |
| Time: | 45-90 minutes | Hiking Information | |
| | | Path: | Improved Footpath |
| Driving Information | | Length: | 1/4 mile |
| Signs: | Excellent | Elev. Change: | Minor |
| Road: | Main | GPS: | N/A |
| Access: | Very Easy | Danger: | Slight |
| 4WD: | N/A | WP Boots: | N/A |

Get up close and personal with this lovely narrow waterfall that flows next to the island. Rent one of the rowboats to take the short trip across the river to the island that is situated in the center of the lower falls. From the boat landing area, take the footpath to the right along the north side of the island to this waterfall. You'll first see the lower rapids with this beautiful waterfall immediately following. Layered sandstone is abundant along the river's edge in this area and in fact makes up the bedrock for the waterfalls and rapids. Take time to enjoy the unique natural structure!

*Island Falls #1 as seen from the island*

*Through the fog - view from the "main" deck*

*Snow capped evergreens get a fresh layer of snow as they stand watch over a chilly Taquamenon River*

CHIPPEWA & LUCE COUNTY

Lower Tahquamenon Island Falls #1

101

Tahquamenon Falls Area

## LOWER TAHQUAMENON FALLS #2 (Tahquamenon River)    Private

| | | | |
|---|---|---|---|
| Must See: | 7 | GPS: | N46 36.214 W85 12.428 |
| Height: | 3 feet | | |
| Time: | 45-90 minutes | Hiking Information | |
| | | Path: | Improved Footpath |
| Driving Information | | Length: | 1/4 mile |
| Signs: | Excellent | Elev. Change: | Minor |
| Road: | Main | GPS: | N/A |
| Access: | Very Easy | Danger: | Slight |
| 4WD: | N/A | WP Boots: | N/A |

I love the angular drops of Lower #2! The patterns of root beer colored water flowing over the slightly irregularly fronted rock faces are wonderful to photograph. Make sure to view them from both sides of the river. I prefer the view of this particular waterfall from the riverside pathway as opposed to the island. Some venturous souls wade across the river, especially when it's running low in the summer. This is the place that they typically cross. Please note that this is not recommended! The river can be deadly. Swirling eddies and dangerous undertows have claimed many victims over the years.

*Looking down from the island side of the river*

*Freezing the falling water*

*My favorite vantage point is from the last viewing deck along the main pathway*

CHIPPEWA & LUCE COUNTY

Lower Tahquamenon Falls #2

102

Tahquamenon Falls Area

## LOWER TAHQUAMENON ISLAND FALLS #2 (Tahquamenon River)   Private

| | | | |
|---|---|---|---|
| Must See: | 8 | GPS: | N46 36.147 W85 12.340 |
| Height: | 20 feet | | |
| Time: | 45-90 minutes | Hiking Information | |
| | | Path: | Improved Footpath |
| Driving Information | | Length: | 1/4 mile |
| Signs: | Excellent | Elev. Change: | Minor |
| Road: | Main | GPS: | N/A |
| Access: | Very Easy | Danger: | Slight |
| 4WD: | N/A | WP Boots: | N/A |

Two 10 foot drops make for a beautiful waterfall that can only be adequately enjoyed by viewing from the island in the middle of the Tahquamenon River. Rent a rowboat for a small fee to gain access to the island. This waterfall is to the left (south) of the docking area. I have often seen fishermen working the base of the waterfall.

*The view from the island*

*Standing above the fall, looking downstream*

*Zooming in on the waterfall from the viewing area by the gift store. The island is on the right.*

CHIPPEWA & LUCE COUNTY

Lower Tahquamenon Island Falls #2

103

Tahquamenon Falls Area

### Tahquamenon Falls - Upper Hike

Tahquamenon Falls - the most popular waterfall in Michigan. The name is usually associated with the Upper Falls, the largest and most picturesque waterfall on the Tahquamenon River. Downstream, the Lower Falls surround an island which, although creating a unique viewing experience, splits the volume of water flowing over those drops.

*Directions:* About 3.5 miles southwest of the Lower Falls entrance turn south into the well marked Upper Falls entrance. No camping is allowed at this end of the Tahquamenon Falls State Park. State Park vehicle permits are required for entry. Park in the wonderfully maintained blacktop parking area. Follow the well manicured walkway. The path "Y's". To the left (downstream), a gorge-top viewing deck is met almost immediately. One hundred yards further, a long winding stairway works down to the river's edge well below the falls. To the right (upstream) of the "Y" are two viewing areas (these are wheelchair accessible) before the trail drops down a long set of stairs to a platform that is right at the top of the falls. The brink is the most popular place from which to view the falls.

### ■ TAHQUAMENON FALLS - UPPER (Tahquamenon River)    Private

| | | | |
|---|---|---|---|
| Must See: | 10 | GPS: | N46 34.499 W85 15.400 |
| Height: | 40 feet | | |
| Time: | 45-90 minutes | Hiking Information | |
| | | Path: | Improved Footpath |
| Driving Information | | Length: | 1/4 mile |
| Signs: | Excellent | Elev. Change: | Slight to Major |
| Road: | Main | GPS: | N/A |
| Access: | Very Easy | Danger: | Slight to Moderate |
| 4WD: | N/A | WP Boots: | N/A |

Five viewing areas exist, from this far look down at the river's edge *(thumbnail)*, to three stops along the paved path above the falls, to a sometimes mist covered overlook at the brink. The stops along the way to the brink are wheelchair accessible. The view from the river below the falls and at the waterfall's edge both require a substantial climb down well maintained stairways. Benches are provided for resting along the climbs.

104

Tahquamenon Falls Area

*Part of the stairway at the river's edge downstream*   *Looking down at the stairs to the brink deck*

*View from the brink deck before sunrise on a cold winter night*

CHIPPEWA & LUCE COUNTY

*Tahquamenon Falls - Upper*

Tahquamenon Falls Area

CHIPPEWA & LUCE COUNTY

*The walkway along the top of the gorge*

*Autumn brings many visitors to view the colors*

*The view from the gorge-top viewing deck furthest downstream (left of the "T")*

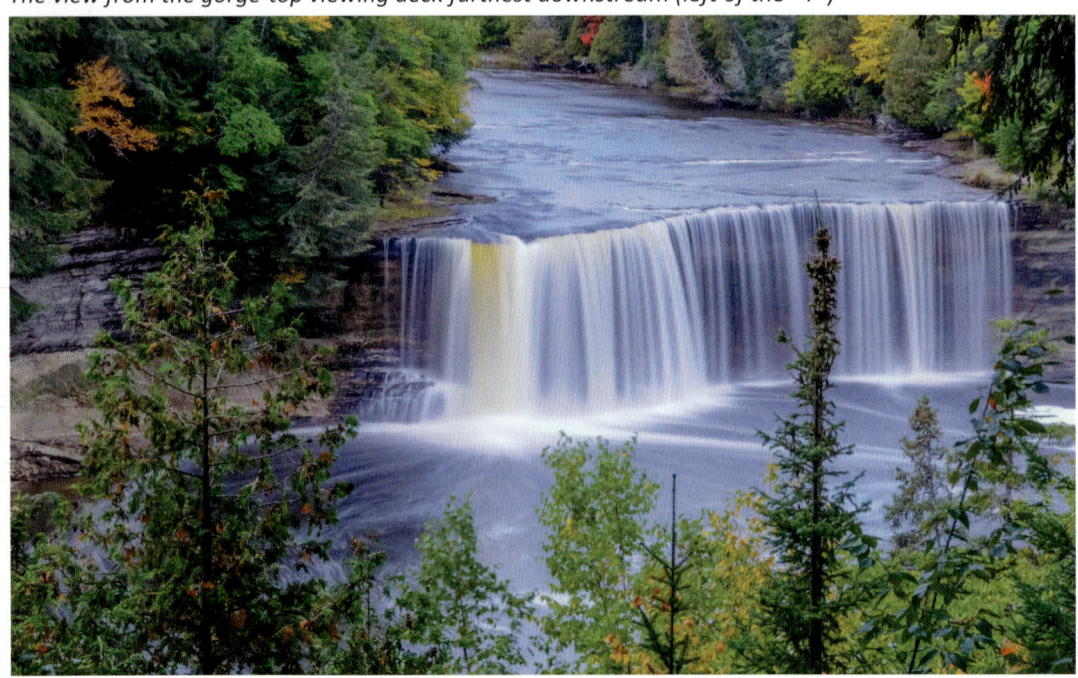

Tahquamenon Falls - Upper

106

# CHAPTER 4
# DELTA COUNTY

# Delta County Map

DELTA COUNTY

# Haymeadow Falls Area

## Haymeadow Falls Hike

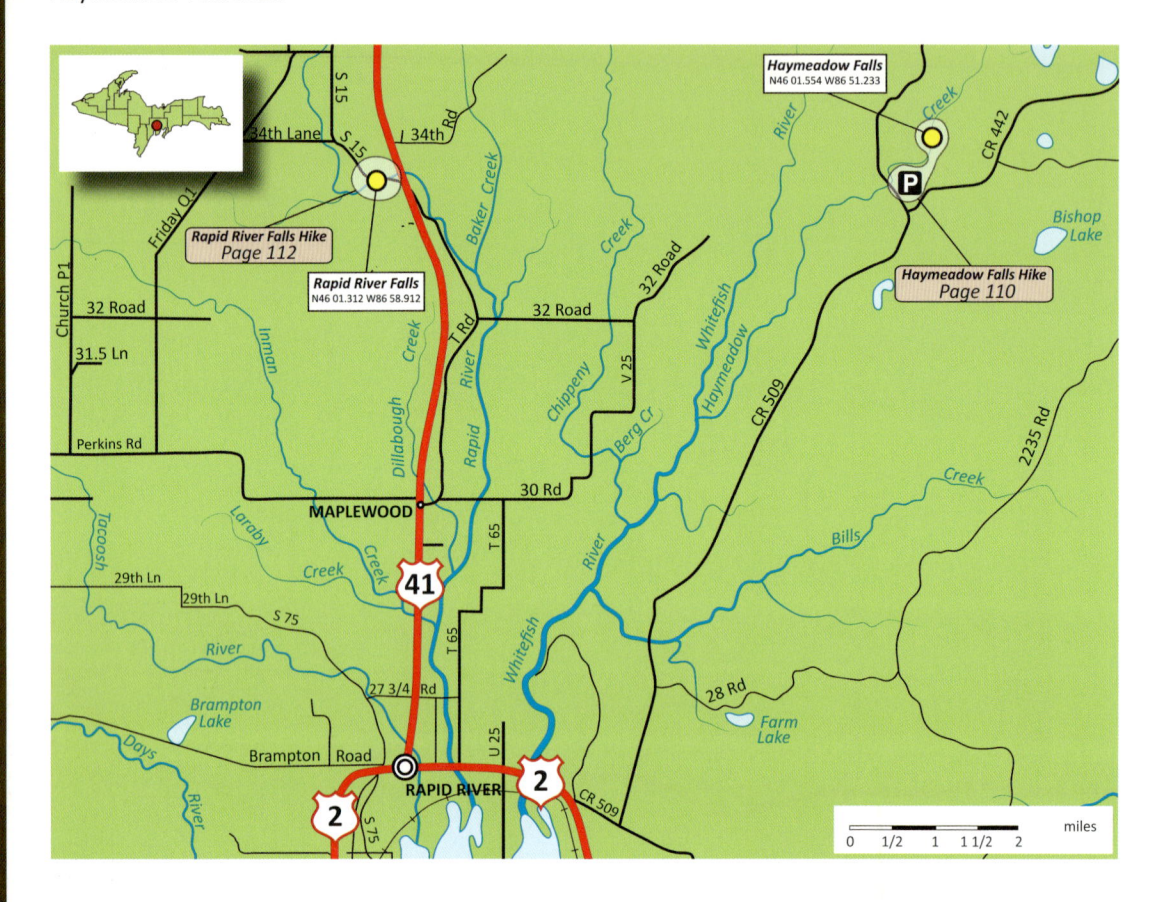

***Haymeadow Falls Hike:*** Enjoy the beautiful looping trail through a conifer forest across mostly flat terrain. Narrow boardwalks span the lowest lying areas. Downstream from the falls is a narrow bridge that crosses the creek. Most of my shots were taken from the other side where I was able to climb down a small bank to the creek. The riverbed is made up of layers of flat, black rock. The falls occur where a layer of this rock has been undercut and broken off.

*Directions:* Drive east on US-2 from Rapid River. As the road makes a large sweeping bend to the south, turn left (southeast) onto CR 509. In .6 miles turn left to stay on CR 509. Stay on CR 509 for another 8.5 miles. Just before the road crosses Haymeadow Creek there is an entrance into a campground. A sign, "Hiawatha National Forest Campground - Haymeadow Creek", is next to the road into the campground. Once into the campground loop there is a sign stating that there is a trail to Haymeadow Falls. Park in one of the small pull off areas near the trailhead that is about 3/4 of the way through the campground. Start the hike at the well marked trailhead. About 100 yards from the trailhead is a side trail. There are two arrows here pointing in different directions. Turn left and follow the trail to the waterfall.

## HAYMEADOW FALLS (Haymeadow Creek)  Private

| | | | |
|---|---|---|---|
| Must See: | 5 | GPS: | N46 01.554 W86 51.233 |
| Height: | 2 feet | | |
| Time: | 15-30 minutes | Hiking Information | |
| | | Path: | Semi-Improved Footpath |
| Driving Information | | Length: | .3 miles |
| Signs: | In the Park | Elev. Change: | Slight |
| Road: | Secondary | GPS: | None |
| Access: | Easy | Danger: | Slight |
| 4WD: | N/A | WP Boots: | Recommended |

After parking at the small Forest Campground, hike the easy 1/3 mile to the falls. There are some wet areas along the hike. Although there are planks laid down across the worst areas, it is still advisable to wear waterproof footwear. Be sure to view the waterfall from the footbridge that spans the river as well as the riverbank next to the falls. Greenery abounds during the summer months.

Look for the memorial marker placed alongside the trail near the falls.

*The trail leads through the forest until reaching the river. It then winds along the riverbed to the falls*

*A look at the falls from the far side of the river with spotted touch-me-nots in the foreground*

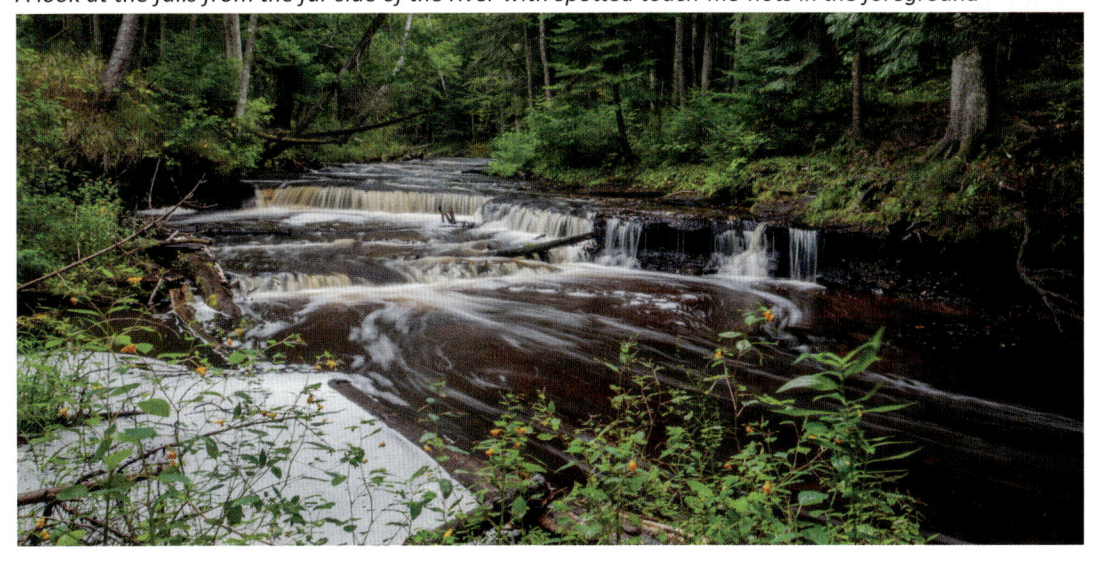

Haymeadow Falls Area

### Rapid River Falls Hike

***Rapid River Falls:*** This is a barrier free and kid friendly waterfall destination. There is a wonderful park with a paved walkway to the waterfall. Grills, picnic tables, swing sets, slides - what more do you want? Vault toilets? Benches to view the falls? Yep, this place has them all!

The bedrock is composed of limestone as is typical in Delta County. There are four distinct drops, with the largest one falling about 2 feet.

***Directions:*** Drive north on US-41 from Rapid River for about 7 miles. Turn left (west) on S 15 just before crossing the bridge over Rapid River. The park is .3 miles on the left at N46 01.343 W86 58.967.

## RAPID RIVER FALLS (Rapid River)    Private

| | | | |
|---|---|---|---|
| Must See: | 5 | GPS: | N46 01.312 W86 58.912 |
| Height: | 3 feet | | |
| Time: | 5-15 minutes | Hiking Information | |
| | | Path: | Paved Footpath |
| Driving Information | | Length: | 150 yards |
| Signs: | In the Park | Elev. Change: | Slight |
| Road: | Secondary | GPS: | None |
| Access: | Easy | Danger: | Slight |
| 4WD: | N/A | WP Boots: | N/A |

*Low water during a dry autumn*   *High water during spring*    *Enjoy the beautiful park*

*A typical look during the summer months*

# CHAPTER 5
# DICKINSON COUNTY

# Dickinson County Map

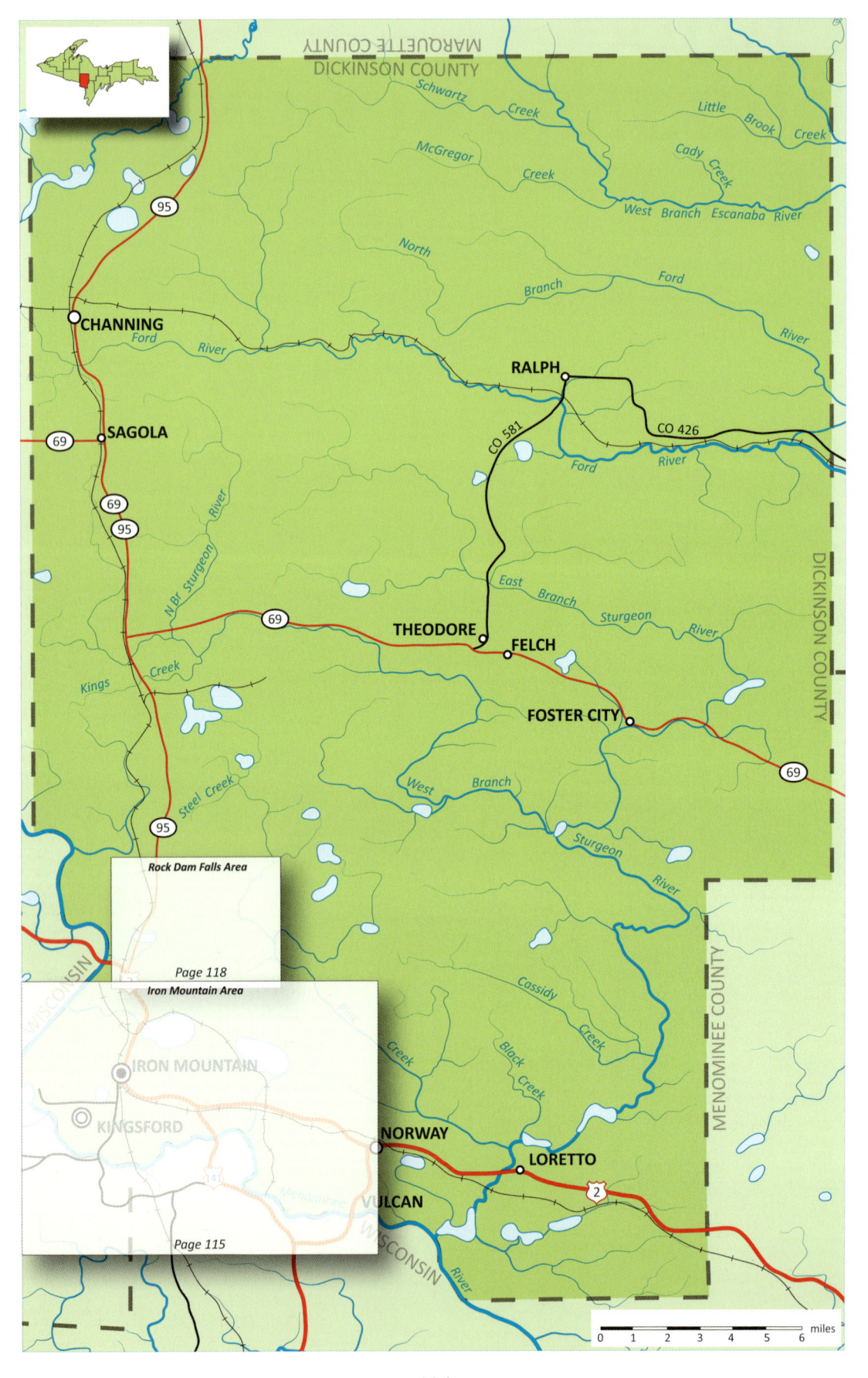

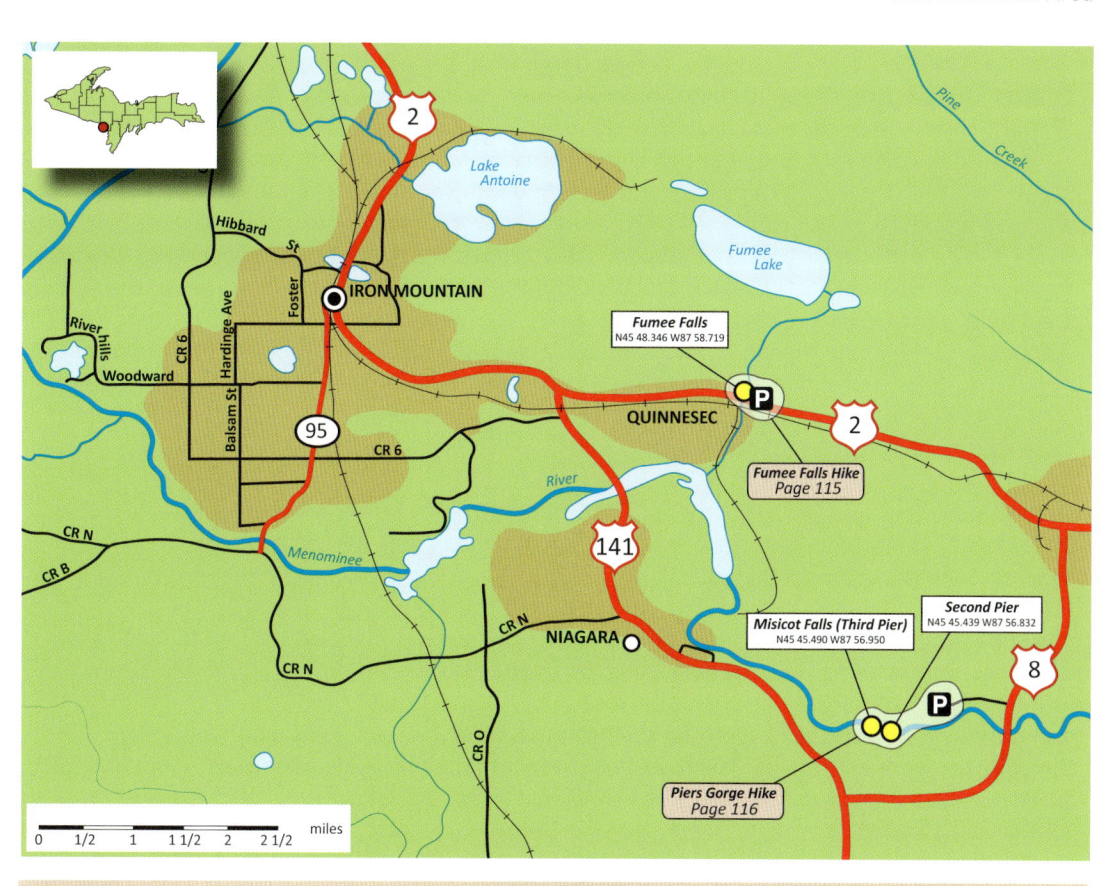

Iron Mountain Area

## Fumee Falls Hike

**Fumee Falls:** The small creek cascades down about 20 feet in full view of US-2.

*Directions:* About 4 miles east of Iron Mountain and 4 miles west of Norway on US-2 is the unincorporated community of Quinnesec. The Helen Z. Lien Roadside Park is found on the north side of the road where Fumee Creek flows beneath the road. Park here. Fumee Falls can be seen from the vehicle.

## FUMEE FALLS (FUMEE CREEK)

Private

| | | | |
|---|---|---|---|
| Must See: | 6 | GPS: | N45 48.346 W87 58.719 |
| Height: | 20 feet | | |
| Time: | 5-15 minutes | Hiking Information | |
| | | Path: | N/A |
| Driving Information | | Length: | N/A |
| Signs: | Good sign | Elev. Change: | Slight |
| Road: | Main | GPS: | None |
| Access: | Very easy | Danger: | N/A |
| 4WD: | N/A | WP Boots: | N/A |

The roadside park located below the falls is a popular picnic area and a great place for families. The bridge over the creek is wheelchair accessible.

# Piers Gorge Hike

Winding along next to the Menominee River is a trail through the Piers Gorge. It is not a difficult hike since it is relatively flat and well groomed. And as a bonus, there are some interesting rock formations to enjoy during the hike. Along the trail are signs labeled "First Pier", "Second Pier", "Third Pier" and "Fourth Pier". These "piers" refer to rocky formations that give a semblance of a pier. The first three are within 1/2 mile of the trailhead, while Pier 4 is about 1 mile further down the trail. Although these drops have been labeled as waterfalls, they are basically aggressive rapids, with none of the pizzazz of a "typical" waterfall. This is one of the more used trails in the Upper Peninsula. It is common to see a number of individuals, of all ages, taking advantage of the nicely shaded walk. There are several locations along the path that are used to "put in" for white water rafting. I describe just the "best" two piers in this guide. The other piers as well as many more waterfalls in the central portion of the U.P. are documented in Book 2 of the Waterfalls of Michigan guidebook series.

*Second Pier:* This drop is also known as "The Sisters" or "Twin Sisters" by those who enjoy white water rafting or kayaking. This is the second best drop in the gorge with interesting splays of water falling around jagged, rocky fingers.

*Misicot Falls (Third Pier):* The best of the drops on this stretch of river, the 8 foot Misicot Falls is best viewed from a small hill that rises along the riverbank.

*Directions:* In Norway, head south on US-8 from US-2 for 2 miles. Turn right (west) onto Piers Gorge Road. Drive to the end of the road (about 1 mile). The trailhead for the Piers Gorge Trail will be obvious. Park and hike down the well maintained trail to the Piers.

## SECOND PIER (MENOMINEE RIVER)    Private

| | | | |
|---|---|---|---|
| Must See: | 4 | GPS: | N45 45.439 W87 56.832 |
| Height: | 2 feet | | |
| Time: | 30-45 minutes | Hiking Information | |
| | | Path: | Improved path |
| Driving Information | | Length: | .3 miles |
| Signs: | "Piers Gorge" | Elev. Change: | Minor |
| Road: | Dirt | GPS: | Helpful |
| Access: | Somewhat easy | Danger: | Slight |
| 4WD: | N/A | WP Boots: | N/A |

Also known as "The Sisters", it is a short drop, only a couple of feet, but it has interesting character with sharp rock fingers slicing through the falling river.

A shallow gorge ends at this point. As the river bends 50 yards downstream from the waterfall, the rocky bedrock walls drop down to the river's edge.

# MISICOT FALLS AKA: THIRD PIER (MENOMINEE RIVER) Private

| | | | |
|---|---|---|---|
| Must See: | 6 | GPS: | N45 45.490 W87 56.950 |
| Height: | 8 feet | | |
| Time: | 45-60 minutes | Hiking Information | |
| | | Path: | Improved path |
| Driving Information | | Length: | .5 miles |
| Signs: | "Piers Gorge" | Elev. Change: | Moderate |
| Road: | Dirt | GPS: | Helpful |
| Access: | Somewhat easy | Danger: | Slight |
| 4WD: | N/A | WP Boots: | N/A |

Misicot Falls is laid out nicely, as seen from the top of a cliff that borders the river's edge. It can also be viewed from water level downstream of the overlook. The river makes an "S" curve with the waterfall marking its start.

The river falls over jagged mounds of bedrock as the river bends around a sheer wall of rock on the Wisconsin side of the river.

*The footpath wanders close to the river at this point*

*Looking down into the gorge not far from the "Third Pier" sign*

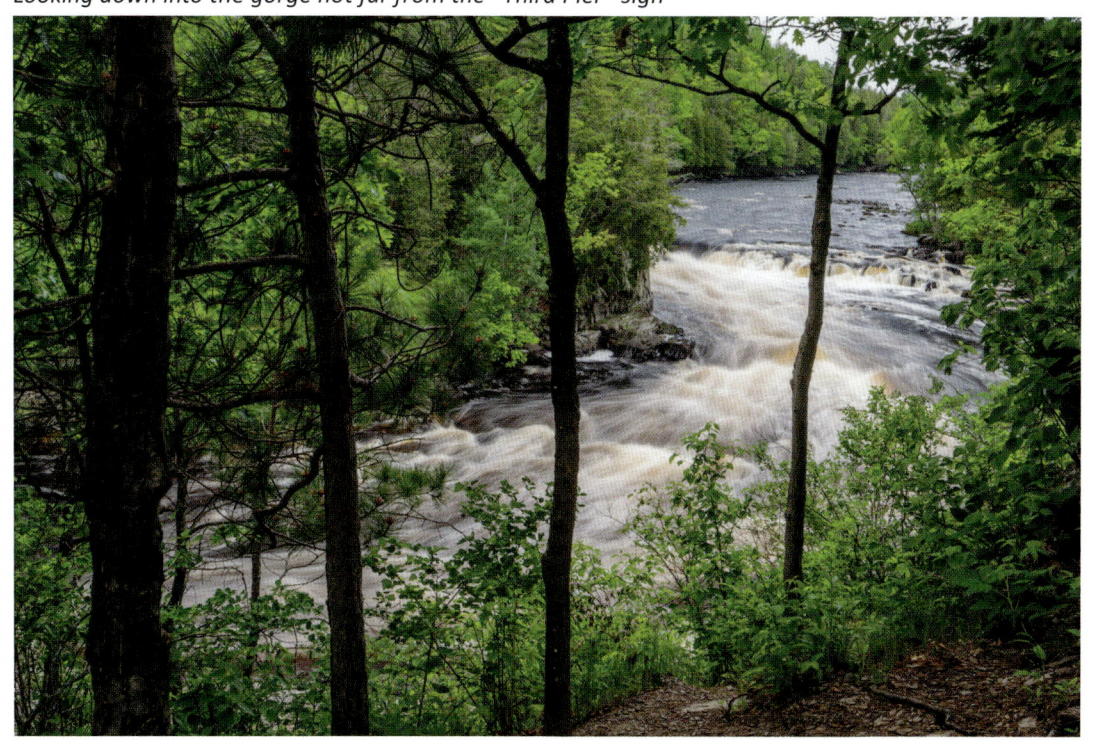

Rock Dam Falls Area

### Rock Dam Falls Hike

**Rock Dam Falls:** A relatively easy waterfall to find (once you know the way) is discovered at the end of a drive down some decent dirt roads. The short hike through somewhat dense shrubbery leads across rickety looking foot bridges and meanders past the spillpool at the base of the drawn out waterfall.

*Directions:* Travel north from US-2 on M-95 for 1.3 miles. Turn right on Old Carney Lake Road (east) for 2.3 miles (the pavement ends after about 1 mile - stay on the main road). Stay left at N45 53.555 W88 01.182 for 2.7 miles (ignore the numerous side trails). Turn into the circle drive at N45 54.059 W87 59.013 for 75 yards. Park. An obvious, though narrow footpath heads through the undergrowth from the far end of the circle. The falls can be heard from the parking area.

## ROCK DAM FALLS (PINE CREEK)    Private

| | |
|---|---|
| Must See: | 6 |
| Height: | 12 feet |
| Time: | 20-40 minutes |

**Driving Information**

| | |
|---|---|
| Signs: | None |
| Road: | Dirt |
| Access: | Somewhat Difficult |
| 4WD: | Helpful |

| | |
|---|---|
| GPS: | N45 54.058 W87 58.891 |

**Hiking Information**

| | |
|---|---|
| Path: | Narrow Footpath |
| Length: | 150 yards |
| Elev. Change: | Slight |
| GPS: | Helpful |
| Danger: | Slight |
| WP Boots: | Recommended |

A heavily travelled narrow footpath leads to the base of the falls and beyond. Ladder bridges span the creek at several points. The creek tumbles in cascades around moss encrusted boulders before ending in a 30 foot wide spill pool. A 70 foot cliff to the right overlooks the falls. A large amount of deciduous trees makes this a beautiful autumn destination. Follow the trail that leads to the top of the falls to view the upper cascades. Continue up the trail to see what appears to be a mass of gray-white marble infused with flecks of burnt red.

*A portion of the footpath and one of the bridges*

*The top cascade up near the "white bedrock"*

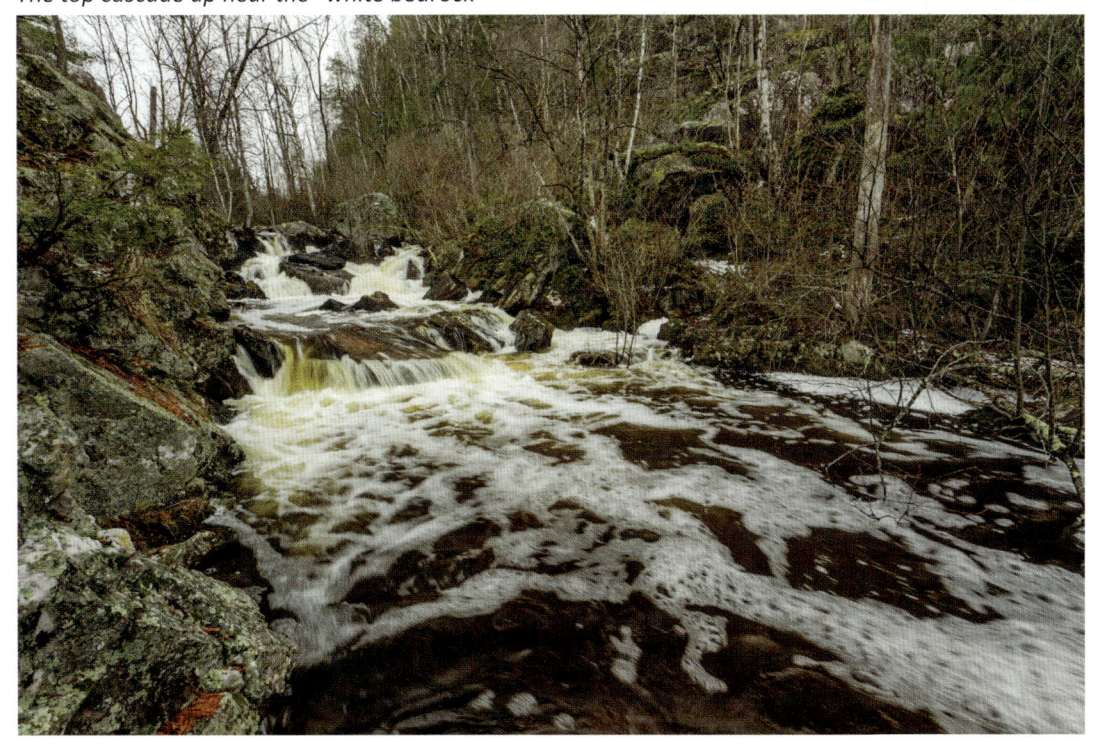

119

DICKINSON COUNTY

# CHAPTER 6
# GOGEBIC COUNTY

# Gogebic County Map

SILVER CITY
107
64
Park
Road
WHITE PINE
18 miles
64
BERGLAND
West
Branch
Ontonagon
River
Ontonagon
River
45
38
GREENLAND
26
38
MASS
ROCKLAND
26
East
Branch
Ontonagon
River
Middle
Branch
Ontonagon
River
South
Branch
Ontonagon
River
Baltimore
River
28
20 miles
EWEN
BRUCE CROSSING
64
WOOD
Lake
Gogebic
Gogebic County
Ontonagon County
TROUT CREEK
28
9 miles
45
Yondota Falls
Area
Page 149
PAULDING
Bond
Flowage
2
Kakabika
Falls Area
Page 140
28 miles
10 miles
Mex-i-min-e Falls Area
WATERSMEET
Page 142
Gogebic County
WISCONSIN
Cisco
Lake
2
CR-B
CR-B
Cutoff Road
CR-K
Lac
Vieux
Desert
45
CR-E
CR-S

Black River Falls Area

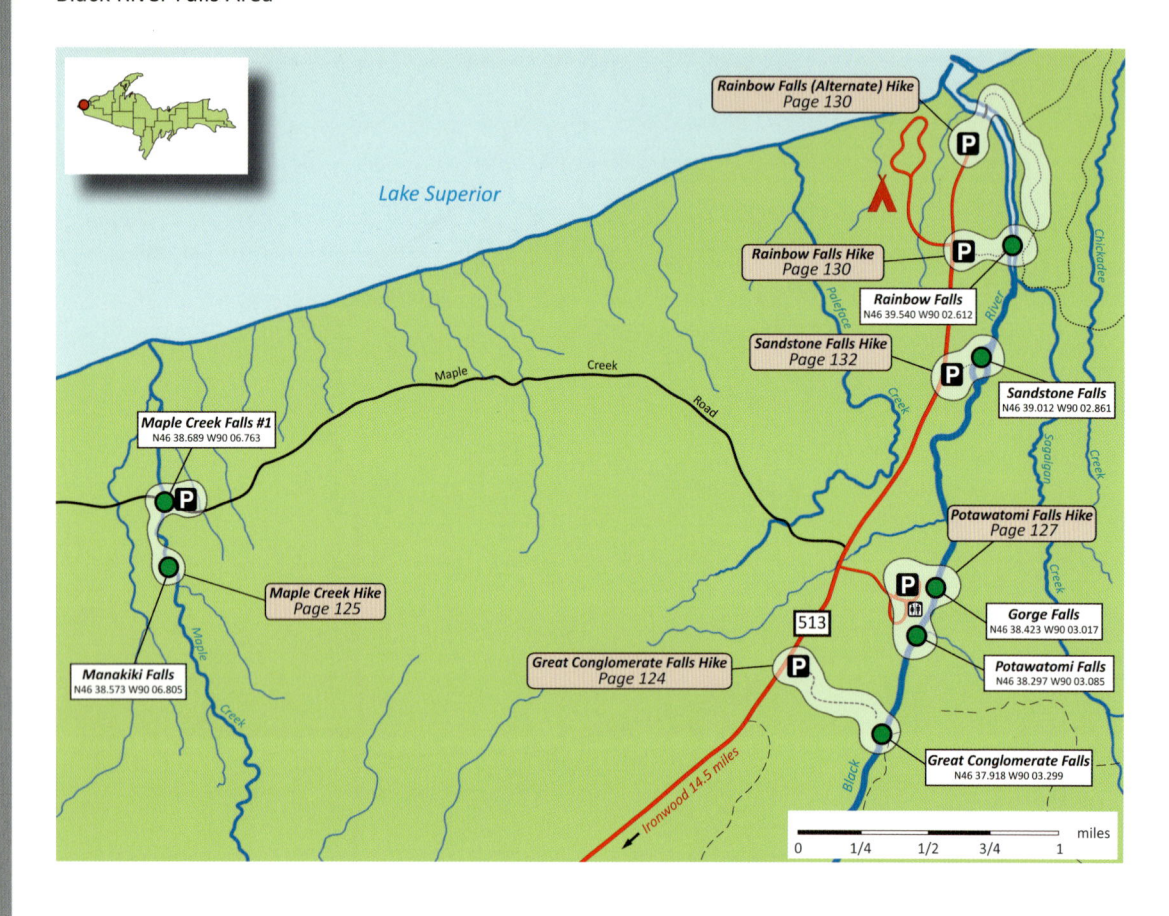

### Great Conglomerate Falls Hike

**Great Conglomerate Falls:** A large protruding section of conglomerate divides the waterfall into two distinct drops. A wooden guardrail was strategically placed around a natural observation area, but tree growth is starting to hinder an unobstructed view.

*Directions:* Follow CR 513 northerly toward Lake Superior. Turn right (east) at the sign for the waterfall. Park in the small parking lot. A very nice footpath leads 3/4 mile to the waterfall.

## GREAT CONGLOMERATE FALLS (BLACK RIVER)           Private

| | | | |
|---|---|---|---|
| Must See: | 7 | GPS: | N46 37.918 W90 03.299 |
| Height: | 30 feet | | |
| Time: | 30-60 minutes | Hiking Information | |
| | | Path: | Improved Footpath |
| Driving Information | | Length: | 3/4 mile |
| Signs: | Good Sign | Elev. Change: | Moderate |
| Road: | Secondary | GPS: | N/A |
| Access: | Very Easy | Danger: | Slight |
| 4WD: | N/A | WP Boots: | N/A |

The hike is fairly flat until right at the end and then around forty steps lead down to the observation area. There are some benches along the way to give your feet a rest. The North Country Trail intersects the trail near the waterfall. Follow the NCT a short distance upstream and you will find a place where it is possible to scramble down to the river's edge near the base of the falls.

### Maple Creek Hike

Maple Creek flows northward to Lake Superior, roughly paralleling the Black River which is about 3 miles to the east. This small creek passes through a gorge, areas with rocky outcroppings, as wells as some calmer terrain. This easily accessed, though seldom traversed strip of land has become one of my favorite hikes in Michigan. There are some sheer drops and steep hillsides, some of which are water saturated and muddy. Be very careful!

*Manakiki Falls:* Climbing, sometimes slipping down a wet, steep leaf covered hillside is the best means of getting down into the gorge. The other side of the creek is a sheer rock wall which provides a nice backdrop for the waterfall that slides down along the sharply angled riverbed.

(Head back to the bridge and continue following the creek to the north.)

*Maple Creek Falls #1:* Just north of the bridge, work your way down to the bottom of the gorge. Wade through the 1 foot deep creek that fills the gorge from wall to wall. Hike upstream and around a turn in the gorge to view the falls.

*Directions:* Follow CR-513 northerly toward Lake Superior. Turn left (west) onto Maple Creek Road (dirt). Follow it for 3.1 miles to the bridge that crosses over Maple Creek. Park on the right (north) just before the bridge. There is room for several vehicles here. Hike across the bridge. While crossing the bridge, look down to the left. Maple Creek Falls #1 can be seen falling into a deeper section of the gorge. After crossing the bridge there are faint footpaths that lead both ways along the river. I typically head upstream (left) first, travelling to the Manakiki Falls before backtracking, crossing the road and then following the creek to the north to the Maple Creek Falls. (There are times when Maple Creek Road is gated. You can park at the gate and hike in. Just keep in mind that this will greatly increase the hiking distance.)

## MANAKIKI FALLS (MAPLE CREEK)    Private

| | | | |
|---|---|---|---|
| Must See: | 7 | GPS: | N46 38.573 W90 06.805 |
| Height: | 25 feet | | |
| Time: | 30-45 minutes | Hiking Information | |
| | | Path: | Slight Footpath |
| Driving Information | | Length: | .3 miles |
| Signs: | None | Elev. Change: | Moderate |
| Road: | Dirt | GPS: | Helpful |
| Access: | Easy | Danger: | Moderate |
| 4WD: | N/A | WP Boots: | Required |

From the vehicle, cross the bridge to the west. Don't be too concerned with following a path. There is just the faintest of footpaths along the creek. Follow the creek upstream (south) for about 1/3 mile. Climb down the steep ravine to the base of Manakiki Falls. The hillside is made up of moist, spongy, leaf covered soil with sticks and other obstacles to avoid. Manakiki Falls is a nicely sloped slide waterfall with solid rock for a backdrop. What a pleasant surprise to stumble onto this beautiful waterfall tucked away. The splash pool at the bottom of the falls quietly swirls as the water takes its rest from the rapid descent it has just made. Then gravity takes over again, drawing the creek downward towards its next drop 1/4 mile later.

## MAPLE CREEK FALLS #1 (MAPLE CREEK)

Private

| | | | |
|---|---|---|---|
| Must See: | 7 | GPS: | N46 38.689 W90 06.763 |
| Height: | 15 feet | | |
| Time: | 15-30 minutes | **Hiking Information** | |
| | | Path: | Slight Footpath |
| **Driving Information** | | Length: | 50 yards |
| Signs: | None | Elev. Change: | Moderate |
| Road: | Dirt | GPS: | N/A |
| Access: | Easy | Danger: | Moderate |
| 4WD: | N/A | WP Boots: | Required |

This is the first waterfall heading north from the vehicle. Maple Creek Falls #1 can be seen while crossing the bridge. In fact, it is nearly under the bridge, slightly upstream! Take the faint footpath to the north and climb carefully down to the bottom of the gorge. The waterfall is not visible from here because of the rock formation that blocks the view of the falls. To get to the base of the falls, follow the creek back upstream and around a corner in the gorge. The creek takes up the entire width of the gorge, so the only way to follow it back upstream is to walk in the water. Wade through the approximately 1 foot deep creek to view the falls.

### Potawatomi Falls Hike

The most visited waterfalls on the Black River are Potawatomi and Gorge Falls. They also happen to be the closest waterfalls to the parking lots. I wonder if this is coincidental? Nice paved driveways and parking areas greet visitors. A paved path runs next to pit toilets on its way to the wheelchair accessible viewing deck for Potawatomi Falls.

*Potawatomi Falls:* The falls are 1/8 mile from the parking lot. The main viewing area is barrier free. There are 58 wooden steps to the lower viewing platform. This waterfall feels a bit distant from the platforms, but the majesty of the falls, especially when it is running strong with spring runoff or fall rains, makes this a wonderful waterfall to view. The riverbed is very wide above the falls but is seldom covered edge to edge.

*Gorge Falls:* Like Potawatomi Falls, Gorge Falls is 1/8 mile from the left (north) end of the parking lot. There are 76 steps down to the main wooden viewing deck. The tiered waterfall is made up of three cascading drops and the viewing deck is at the perfect angle for appreciating all three cascades at once!

*Directions:* Heading north on CR 513 (toward Lake Superior) turn right (east) into the Gorge/Potawatomi Falls driveway. The parking lots for these two waterfalls are connected by this common drive. The parking lot to the left is my favorite and is marked by an arrow directing you to Gorge Falls. Park at the far end (south) of the blacktopped parking lot to be centered between the two falls.

## POTAWATOMI FALLS (BLACK RIVER)

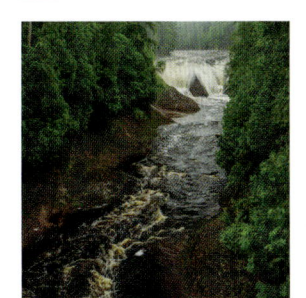

Private

| | | | |
|---|---|---|---|
| Must See: | 8 | GPS: | N46 38.297 W90 03.085 |
| Height: | 40 feet | | |
| Time: | 15-30 minutes | Hiking Information | |
| | | Path: | Improved Path |
| Driving Information | | Length: | 1/8 mile |
| Signs: | Good Sign | Elev. Change: | Slight |
| Road: | Secondary | GPS: | N/A |
| Access: | Very Easy | Danger: | Slight |
| 4WD: | N/A | WP Boots: | N/A |

The Potawatomi were a tribe of Indians, cousins to the Ojibwe that lived in various portions of Michigan as well as Wisconsin. Potawatomi means "People of the place of the fire", referring to a fire kept burning perpetually, or perhaps to their place of honor in intertribal powwows. It is a privilege to have such a wonderful waterfall named after these proud inhabitants of our state.

This area of the U.P. ranks as one of my favorites! The waterfalls on the Black River hold a special place in my heart. Perhaps my winter hike into the five waterfalls in this stretch has something to do with it. The ruggedness of the land along the Black River has been tamed by improved trails and wooden boardwalks and viewing decks. But lest you think that this area is void of raw, natural beauty, a short drive over to Maple Creek will set you straight. This creek has the slightest of footpaths, and the multiple clambers down to the creek require agility and care.

The Potawatomi/Gorge Waterfall Scenic Area is perfect for family outings. Picnic tables and charcoal grills are strategically placed amongst old growth pines near the parking area. Well defined paths, with stairs when needed, lead to Potawatomi and Gorge Falls. Wooden guard rails line the cliff edges to provide protection. There is even a paved, wheelchair accessible path to the main overlook at Potawatomi Falls. A set of pit toilets is also located nearby.

Black River Falls Area

*The beautifully maintained walkway to the falls*    *Several interpretive signs are set along the way*

## GORGE FALLS (BLACK RIVER)

Private

| | | | |
|---|---|---|---|
| Must See: | 8 | GPS: | N46 38.423 W90 03.017 |
| Height: | 34 feet | | |
| Type: | Series | **Hiking Information** | |
| | | Path: | Improved Footpath |
| **Driving Information** | | Length: | 1/8 mile |
| Signs: | Good Sign | Elev. Change: | Moderate |
| Road: | Secondary | GPS: | N/A |
| Access: | Very Easy | Danger: | Slight |
| 4WD: | N/A | WP Boots: | N/A |

This is a nicely presented waterfall from the viewing deck that is furthest downstream. Don't be confused with the deck upstream that doesn't show the main drop.

The area between Potawatomi and Gorge Falls has been tastefully built up with wooden walkways, stairways, benches, vault toilets and the like. Continuing both up and downstream, however, the North County Trail (here a primitive footpath) quietly beckons adventurers to follow it on its 4,600 mile long journey.

129

# Black River Falls Area

### Rainbow Falls Hike

There are two ways to get to Rainbow Falls. The easiest, most common route is from the Rainbow Falls parking area. A footpath leads from there to a wooden overlook. The second option follows the North Country Trail, crossing the Black River near its mouth, and then following the river back upstream to the falls. This route is much longer, and there are no guard rails to protect from falling into the river gorge. I only recommend this route for highly experienced hikers during ideal conditions.

**Rainbow Falls:** Rainbow Falls plunges into a narrow gorge that quickly widens out as it heads down river. On sunny days, rainbows can sometimes be seen in the mist that rises from the base of the falls.

Directions:
**(Standard)** The most common and easiest hike to Rainbow Falls starts at the parking lot off of CR 513. Follow the well groomed trail. A sign at the trail head says that it is a 1/2 mile walk from the parking area (it's actually only .19 miles). At the end of the trail there are 159 steps down to the wooden viewing deck.

**(Alternate)** Viewing from the other side of the river is best. To get there, park in the Harbor Parking Lot where the Black River empties into Lake Superior. Walk across the suspension bridge that spans the river. Follow the North Country Trail back upstream from there. It about a 3/4 mile hike with some decent elevation changes and lots of steps!

## RAINBOW FALLS (BLACK RIVER)                               Private

| | | | |
|---|---|---|---|
| Must See: | 8 | GPS: | N46 39.540 W90 02.612 |
| Height: | 45 feet | | |
| Time: | 1/2 to 2 hours | Hiking Information | |
| | | Path: | Improved Footpath |
| Driving Information | | Length: | 1/5 or 3/4 mile |
| Signs: | Good Sign | Elev. Change: | Moderate |
| Road: | Secondary | GPS: | N/A |
| Access: | Very Easy | Danger: | Slight to moderate |
| 4WD: | N/A | WP Boots: | N/A |

The view from the wooden platform located on the west side of the river offers a limited view of the waterfall. The river has cut a narrow groove back from the original precipitous edge. Now the river plunges down into the slit, with little of the drop left visible from this side.

A better view is had from the far side of the river, but getting close to the drop from the top side requires walking on a mass of rock that slants down toward the gorge and the swirling waters below. Use extreme caution if venturing over to the east side of the falls. It is possible to get down to the river's edge. I have seen trout fishermen working the river below the falls. I'm not sure if there is enough of a bank to walk along to view the falls from down there. It may be necessary to wade up the river to get to the base of the waterfall. (Consider bringing hip-waders if attempting this.)

The waterfall splits into two separate drops when the river is higher and shrinks back to a single drop during low water conditions.

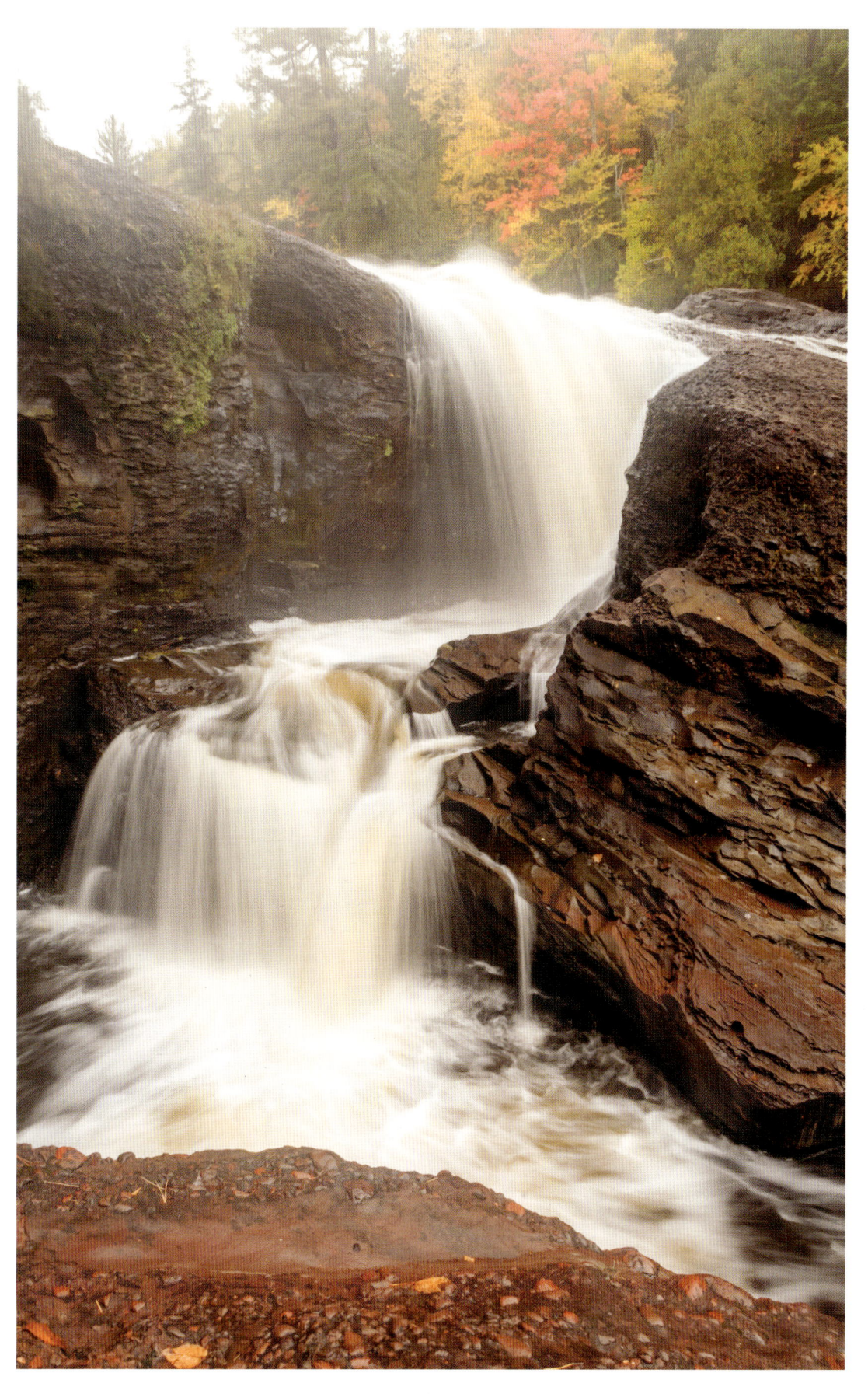

Black River Falls Area

GOGEBIC COUNTY

Rainbow Falls

# Black River Falls Area

### Sandstone Falls Hike

*Sandstone Falls:* The waterfall is full of conglomerate stone. You can walk all around the falls for an up-close and intimate experience with this less frequently visited waterfall. Be careful of stepping in holes created by the swirling water. Some are quite deep, and all could cause a nasty fall or twisted ankle.

*Directions:* Between Potawatomi Falls and Rainbow Falls is a short drive marked "Sandstone Falls". Park at the trail head. There are 138 steps down to the river at the end of the 1/4 mile long, nicely maintained trail.

## SANDSTONE FALLS (BLACK RIVER)    Private

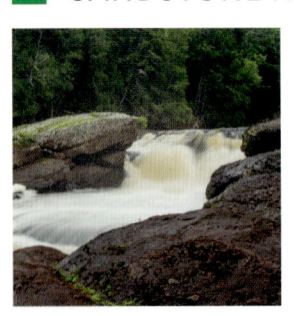

| | |
|---|---|
| Must See: | 7 |
| Height: | 15 feet |
| Time: | 30-60 minutes |

**Driving Information**
| | |
|---|---|
| Signs: | Good Sign |
| Road: | Secondary |
| Access: | Very Easy |
| 4WD: | N/A |

| | |
|---|---|
| GPS: | N46 39.012 W90 02.861 |

**Hiking Information**
| | |
|---|---|
| Path: | Improved Path |
| Length: | 1/4 mile |
| Elev. Change: | Moderate |
| GPS: | N/A |
| Danger: | Slight |
| WP Boots: | N/A |

Of all the popular Black River waterfalls, this is the only one that can be viewed from the riverbed. The trail ends at the river, with no overlook or guard rails. The shortest of the waterfalls, it cascades over a sandstone waterway, with interesting, heaved up bedrock layers bordering either side of the falls. The sandstone is quite pitted, and there are a number of circular impressions below the falls. Pebbles and stones swirling in eddies ground their way down through the somewhat softer material, creating these sometimes dry, sometimes water filled holes.

Gabbro Falls Area

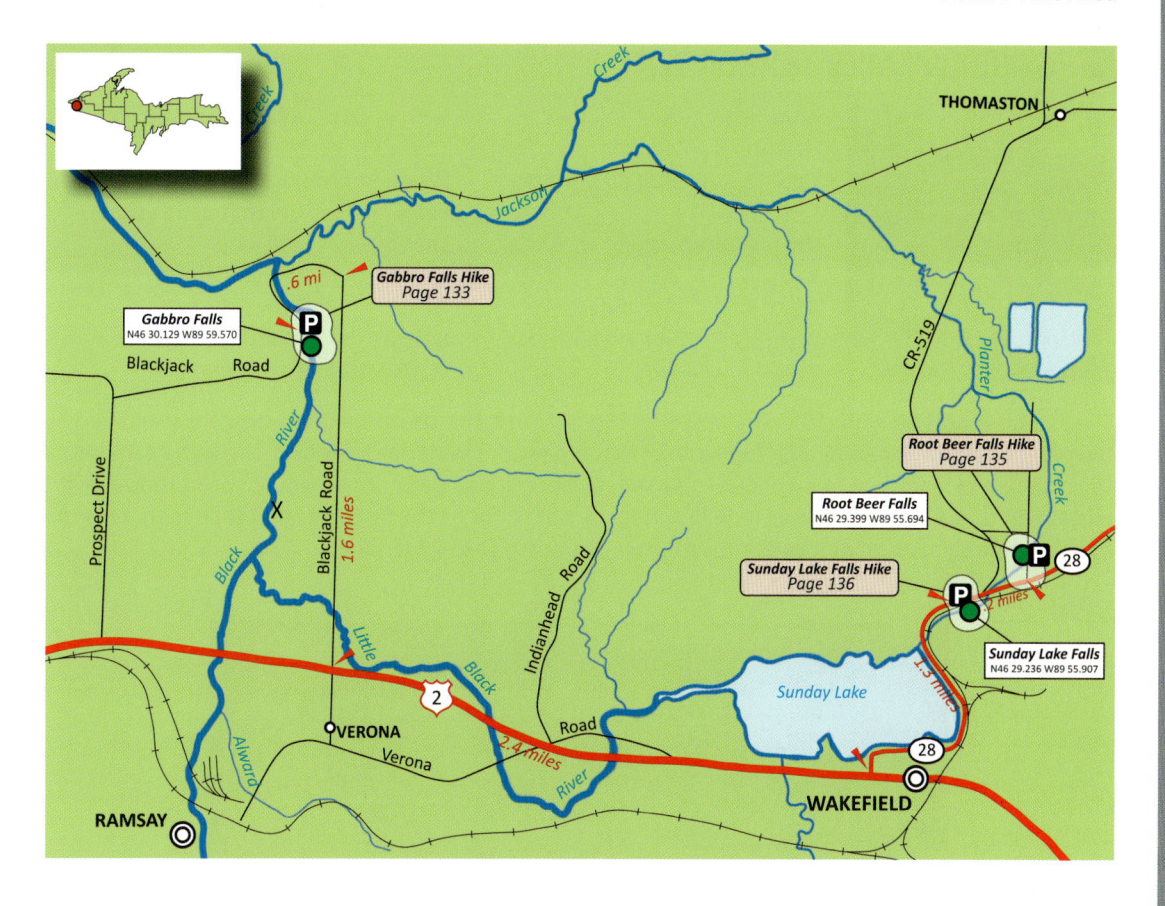

GOGEBIC COUNTY

### Gabbro Falls Hike

*Gabbro Falls:* I had one of those "heart stopping" moments here when I almost slid off of a narrow finger of rock that juts out into the gorge and faces the falls. A light rain and my wife slipping into me at just the wrong moment sent the adrenaline pumping! But hey, I did get a frontal shot after I carefully set up the tripod and camera on the precarious perch!

*Directions:* Turn north onto Blackjack Road from US-2. Drive 1.6 miles. Follow the road to the left, crossing the Black River. Turn left immediately to stay on Blackjack Road. Park on the left .6 miles from where Blackjack Road first turned left. There will be a yellow metal gate on the right. A couple of foot trails lead away into the forest. Both of the trails are quite short; two to three minute walks at the most. The trail to the left heads to the bottom of the gorge. The second path from the parking area leads to the right and stays to the top of the gorge. From up here, the waterfall can be seen dropping down into the deep crevasse. There are no guard rails, and children should not be brought to this waterfall. The drop is about 40 feet straight down into water and solid rock. Use extreme caution, especially when the ground is wet.

## GABBRO FALLS (BLACK RIVER)                              Private

| | | | |
|---|---|---|---|
| Must See: | 8 | GPS: | N46 30.129 W89 59.570 |
| Height: | 40 feet | | |
| Time: | 5 to 20 minutes | Hiking Information | |
| | | Path: | Unimproved Footpath |
| Driving Information | | Length: | 100 yards |
| Signs: | None | Elev. Change: | Moderate |
| Road: | Secondary | GPS: | N/A |
| Access: | Somewhat Easy | Danger: | Moderate |
| 4WD: | N/A | WP Boots: | Recommended |

This is a breathtaking waterfall! The power of the drop and the sheer energy shown are magnified by the rugged terrain and intriguing topography that makes this waterfall possible. The water falls into a split in the rock and then immediately is forced to the right as there is nothing but solid rock straight ahead and to the left. The water then drops again, not so far as the first cascade. Only then does the river become calm again as it continues its journey toward Lake Superior.

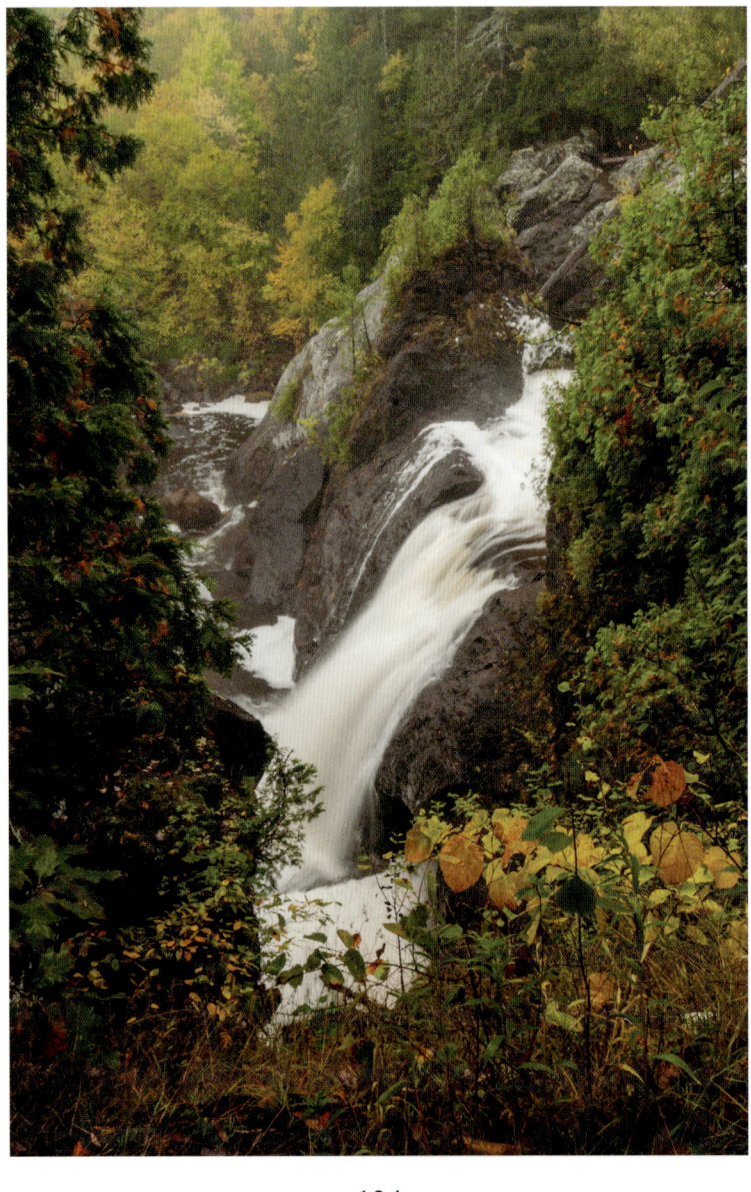

Gabbro Falls Area

### Root Beer Falls Hike

**Root Beer Falls:** A promontory splits the waterfall in two. The river cascades along either side of the bedrock, presenting itself nicely as it rushes down the clean face to a nice sized spill pool. A large smooth boulder sits in the middle of the spill pool where it collects colorful autumn leaves in October.

*Directions:* Take M-28 north out of Wakefield. Follow it along the side of Sunday Lake. It then bends hard to the right (northeast). It will quickly cross Planter Creek. The next road on the left (north) is Wertanen Road. Turn left (north). Park on the side of the road near the bridge that once again crosses Planter Creek. It will be an obvious parking area along the dirt road. The waterfall can be seen through the trees. A well worn trail leads from the road down through an 8 foot high steep ditch to the floodplain.

## ROOT BEER FALLS (PLANTER CREEK)    Private

| | | | |
|---|---|---|---|
| Must See: | 7 | GPS: | N46 29.399 W89 55.694 |
| Height: | 8 feet | | |
| Time: | 10 to 20 minutes | Hiking Information | |
| | | Path: | None |
| Driving Information | | Length: | 100 yards |
| Signs: | None | Elev. Change: | Slight |
| Road: | Secondary | GPS: | N/A |
| Access: | Somewhat Easy | Danger: | Slight |
| 4WD: | N/A | WP Boots: | Helpful |

The falls are segmented by a large boulder planted at the top of the falls. The best viewing angle is on the near side of the creek. This is a nice place for a picnic and playing in the spill pool on a hot summer's day. Make sure the river isn't raging, however. Notice the difference between the two shots shown here. The river was overflowing its banks in the picture below. In the spring, the river overflows its banks and can flood the entire area over to the road.

GOGEBIC COUNTY

Root Beer Falls

Gabbro Falls Area

### Sunday Lake Falls Hike

The Sunday Lake Mine operated from 1885 to 1961. It was located not far from the shores of Sunday Lake in Wakefield and extracted over seventeen million tons of iron ore during its lifetime. For some reason I have not yet discovered, the mine blasted an underground tunnel from Sunday Lake northeasterly for about 1/3 mile to a ravine. Perhaps this was to regulate the height of the Lake, as this ravine seems to be much lower than the natural flow of the lake out of Little Black River on the western end of the lake. Whatever the reason, a gaping hole in solid rock spews out a creek that tumbles and falls through a rock strewn ravine.

*Directions:* Take M-28 north out of Wakefield. Follow it along the side of Sunday Lake. It then bends hard to the right (northeast). It will quickly cross Planter Creek. Find a safe place to park off either side of the road. Hike upstream along the creek (I prefer the southern side).

## ■ SUNDAY LAKE FALLS (PLANTER CREEK)                                   Private

| | | | |
|---|---|---|---|
| Must See: | 7 | GPS: | N46 29.236 W89 55.907 |
| Height: | 10 feet | | |
| Time: | 15 to 30 minutes | **Hiking Information** | |
| | | Path: | None |
| **Driving Information** | | Length: | 100 yards |
| Signs: | None | Elev. Change: | Moderate |
| Road: | Main | GPS: | N/A |
| Access: | Somewhat Easy | Danger: | Moderate |
| 4WD: | N/A | WP Boots: | Helpful |

The creek emerges from a cavernous tunnel in the rock face. It cascades down 4 feet to a roundish spill pool encircled by a 15 foot high rocky embankment. The creek continues to cascade down the black boulder strewn creek bed, sweeping around a teardrop shaped island where several hardwood trees have matured, fed by the ever present water source.

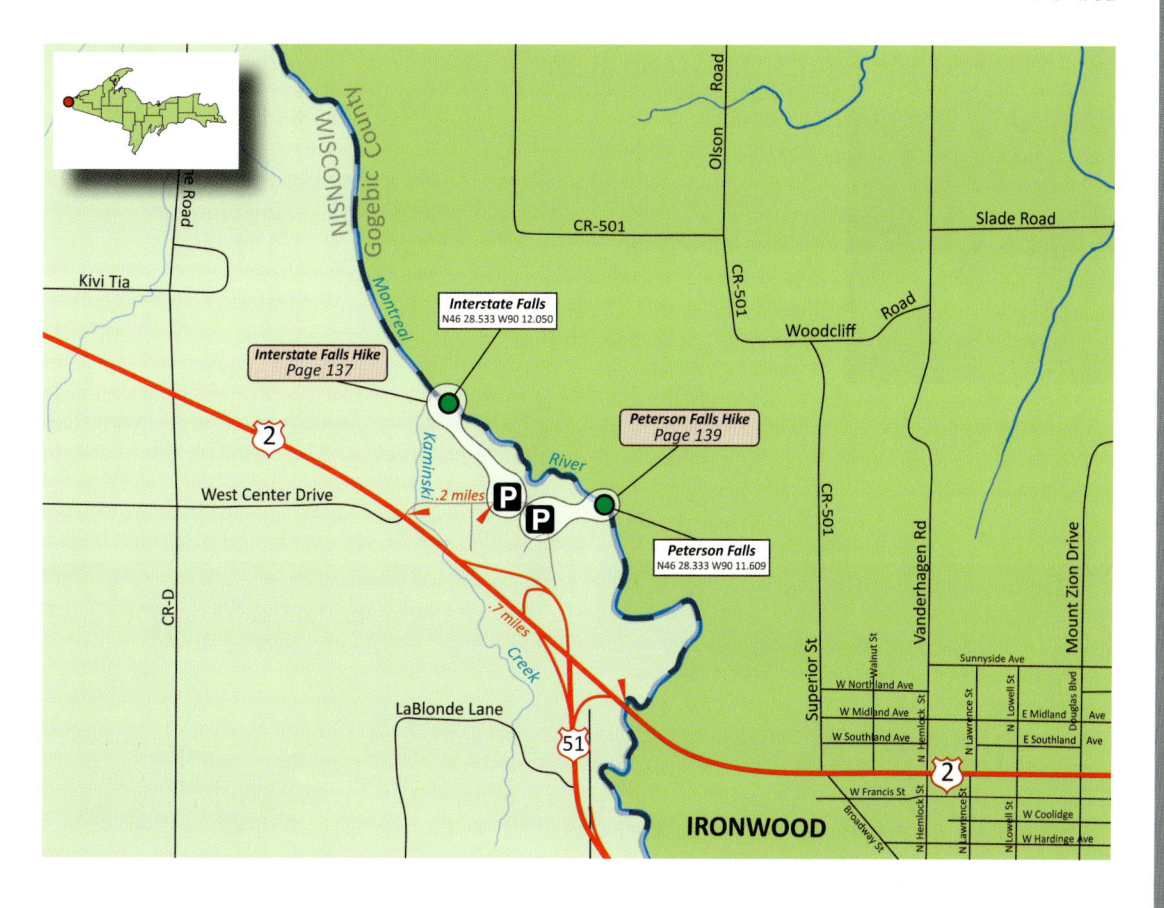

### Interstate Falls Hike

***Interstate Falls:*** This classic cascading waterfall is displayed wonderfully with mist rising up from the force of the pounding water when the river is running well. The trail to the falls is obvious. The hike is easy. The waterfall is gorgeous. But the viewing area is somewhat limited. Be careful near fast moving water.

*Directions:* Drive just into Wisconsin on US-2. Turn right just before "The Country Store". There is a wooden sign - "Peterson Falls" - on the corner. Continue straight ahead on the dirt road that becomes a 2-track until you see a trailhead on the left. Park. Hike northwest to the falls.

Remember that this is private land. Be courteous and respectful of the land.

Interstate Falls Area

## INTERSTATE FALLS (MONTREAL RIVER)   Private

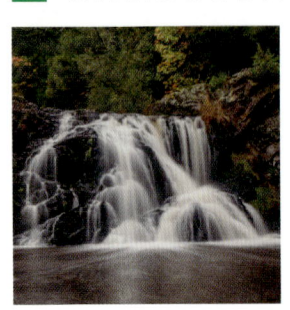

| | | | |
|---|---|---|---|
| Must See: | 9 | GPS: | N46 28.533 W90 12.050 |
| Height: | 20 feet | | |
| Time: | 20 to 40 minutes | **Hiking Information** | |
| | | Path: | Good footpath |
| **Driving Information** | | Length: | 1/4 mile |
| Signs: | Wooden | Elev. Change: | Slight |
| Road: | Dirt | GPS: | N/A |
| Access: | Somewhat Difficult | Danger: | Slight |
| 4WD: | Helpful | WP Boots: | Helpful |

This is best viewed from the Wisconsin side of the river. There signage to help you find the waterfall, a small parking spot, and a trail to the falls. There is a house just above the waterfall on the Michigan side, and no access.

*The look from the top (a house on the Michigan side of the river can be seen peeking through the trees).*

*The river level changes radically. Note the difference from the thumbnail shot to this one!*

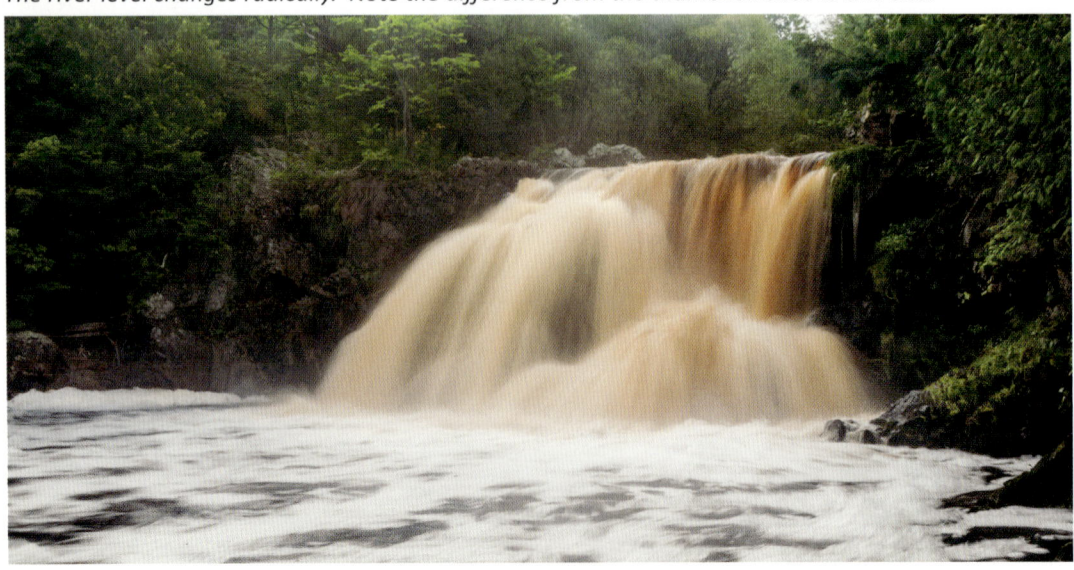

138

### Peterson Falls Hike

***Peterson Falls:*** An island splits the river at the head of the falls. Grasses and trees grasp for footing on the rocky, water-slick outcropping. As the river flows around the island, it pours down over the rock-filled river, merging together again halfway down the falls.

*Directions: These instructions are nearly identical to the directions for Interstate Falls Hike. The Peterson Falls trailhead is not that far past the trailhead to Interstate Falls.* Heading west on US-2, turn to the right just after entering Wisconsin and just before "The Country Store". There is a wooden sign marked "*Peterson Falls*" on the corner. Continue straight and park at GPS location N46 28.309 W90 11.842. An unimproved foot trail starts here. Walk .2 miles to the falls.

Peterson Falls is also on private property, but the owners allow for waterfall visitors. Be respectful of their property.

## PETERSON FALLS (MONTREAL RIVER)  Private

| | | | |
|---|---|---|---|
| Must See: | 8 | GPS: | N46 28.333 W90 11.609 |
| Height: | 15 feet | | |
| Time: | 20 to 40 minutes | Hiking Information | |
| | | Path: | Unimproved footpath |
| Driving Information | | Length: | .2 miles |
| Signs: | Wooden | Elev. Change: | Slight |
| Road: | 2-track | GPS: | Helpful |
| Access: | Somewhat Difficult | Danger: | Slight |
| 4WD: | Helpful | WP Boots: | Helpful |

This is on private property. Be respectful.

Sweeping branches arch over the river as though to protect it from prying eyes, or perhaps to soak up some of the water mist that sometimes plays about the falls. The island divides the river, so the level of water here really makes a large difference in the appearance of the waterfall.

Kakabika Falls Area

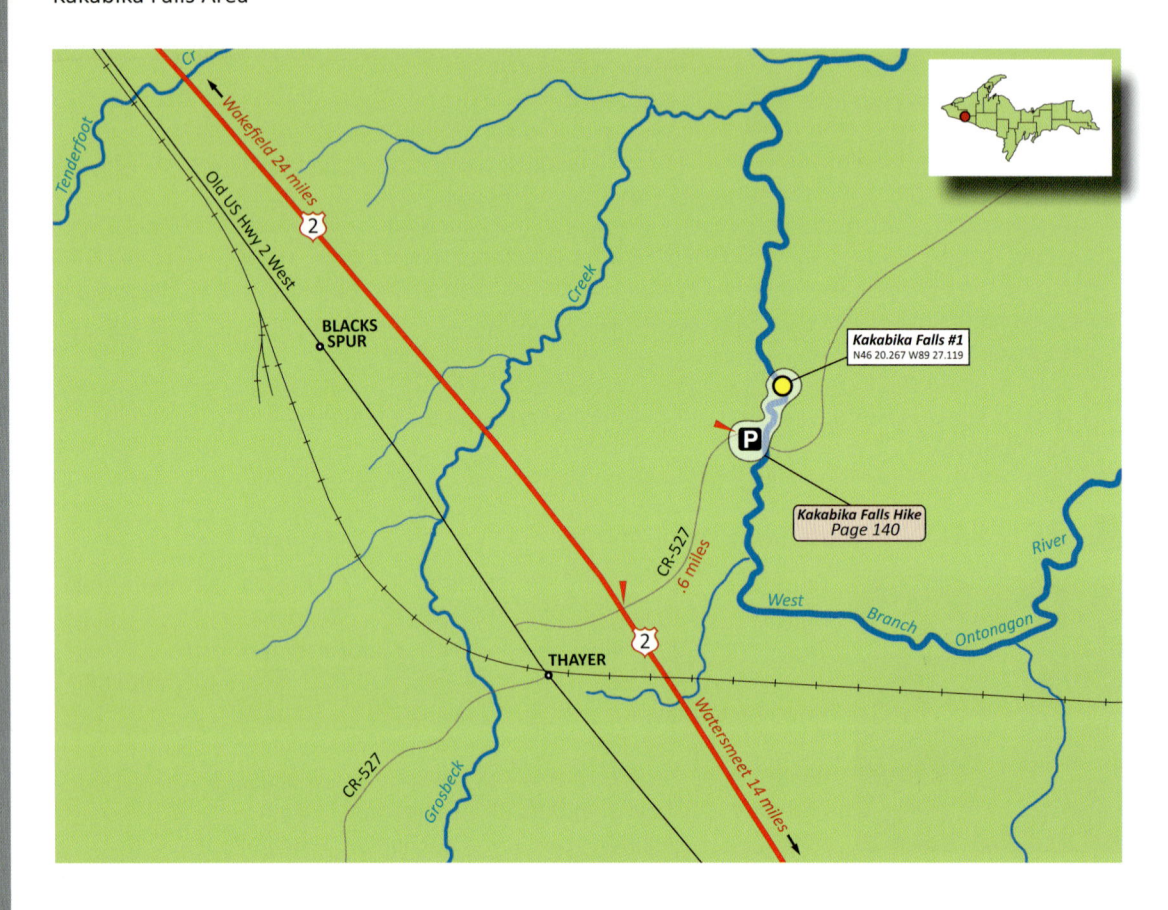

### Kakabika Falls Hike

*Kakabika Falls:* A thunderstorm was brewing as I checked out Kakabika Falls for the first time. Mosquitoes were buzzing around in abundance, as though they knew this was to be their last chance to feed for some time. I was pleasantly surprised when Kakabika Falls turned out to be a series of waterfalls over several hundred yards and not just a single drop! *(In this "Collection" guidebook I only describe one of them. The rest are found in Book 4 of the Waterfalls of Michigan series.)*

Why not follow up a thunderstorm with a snowstorm? My next stop did just that! A freak May snowstorm dumped a foot of snow in Wakefield, and just less than that here. A beautiful combination of snow capped trees and water rushing down the river from the annual spring melt met me for an amazing experience on the swollen West Branch of the Ontonagon River.

*Directions:* Turn east off of US-2 onto County Road 527. Just before the road crosses the West Branch of the Ontonagon River there is a circular turnoff on the left (north) with a sign announcing Kakabika Falls. Park. Hike down the well-worn footpath along the river to the falls.

Kakabika Falls Area

## KAKABIKA FALLS #1 (ONTONAGON RIVER - WEST BRANCH)   Private

| | | | |
|---|---|---|---|
| Must See: | 6 | GPS: | N46 20.267 W89 27.119 |
| Height: | 10 feet | | |
| Time: | 10 to 30 minutes | Hiking Information | |
| | | Path: | Unimproved footpath |
| Driving Information | | Length: | 1/8 mile |
| Signs: | Wooden Sign | Elev. Change: | Slight |
| Road: | Dirt | GPS: | N/A |
| Access: | Somewhat easy | Danger: | Moderate |
| 4WD: | N/A | WP Boots: | Helpful |

A tree shrouded shallow canyon funnels the river between rugged, lichen covered rocky banks. The river quickly descends in the canyon, exiting in a final burst over sharp jagged bedrock. As the river has completed its Kakabika descent it slows down and meanders through a gorgeous mature forest.

GOGEBIC COUNTY

Kakabika Falls #1

141

Mex-i-min-e Falls Area

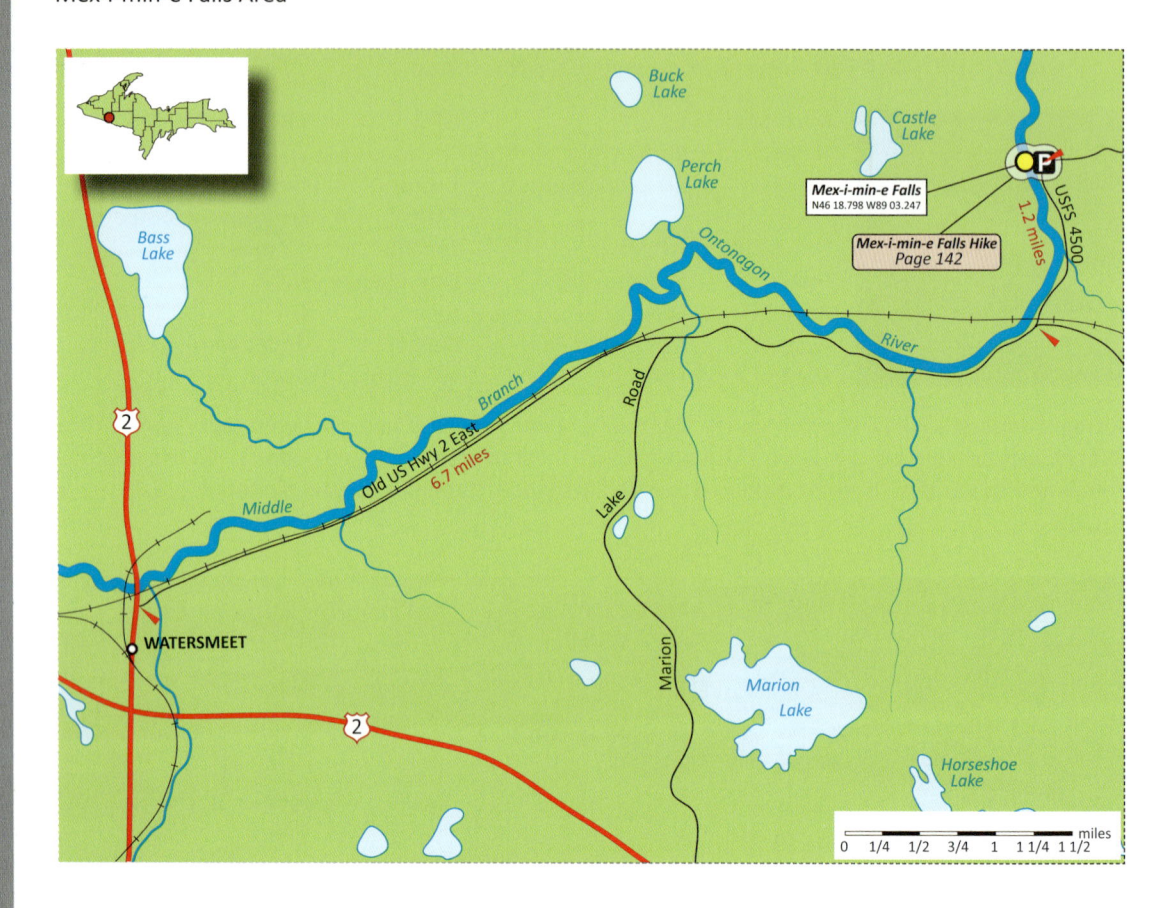

GOGEBIC COUNTY

### Mex-i-min-e Falls Hike

Mex-i-min-e Falls is also known as *"Burned Dam Falls"*. At the end of the 1800's logging was a major industry in this area. A dam was constructed on the river here, and logs floated from upstream were gathered in the backwaters and then transported overland to Interior, a small logging community near Bond Falls. Around 1900 a fire burned through the area, greedily consuming the bone dry slash left from clear cutting and subsequently destroying the dam.

Now, a lightly used rustic Federal Forest campground occupies the grounds. The no fee campground has a pit toilet, but no other facilities.

*Directions:* From Watersmeet, turn north onto US-45 from US-2. In .6 miles, turn right (east) onto Old US-2. Follow it for 6.7 miles to US Forest Road 4500. Turn left (north) and continue for 1.2 miles to the entrance of Burned Dam Camp. Drive around to the back of the campground and look for a sign that describes the history of the area. The river is on the left, and a short 200 foot long hike ends at the falls.

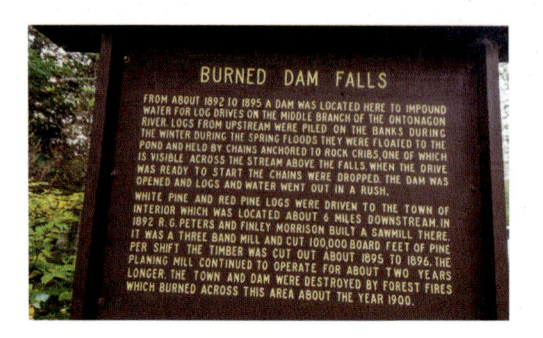

# MEX-I-MIN-E FALLS (ONTONAGON RIVER - MIDDLE BRANCH) Private

| | | | |
|---|---|---|---|
| Must See: | 6 | GPS: | N46 18.798 W89 03.247 |
| Height: | 12 feet | | |
| Time: | 10 to 20 minutes | Hiking Information | |
| | | Path: | Unimproved Footpath |
| Driving Information | | Length: | 200 feet |
| Signs: | None | Elev. Change: | Slight |
| Road: | Dirt | GPS: | N/A |
| Access: | Somewhat difficult | Danger: | Slight |
| 4WD: | N/A | WP Boots: | N/A |

A nice Federal Forest Campground has been built along the Middle Branch of the Ontonagon River with Mex-i-min-e Falls as its main attraction. A short walk through small pines is reminiscent of the hike to Whitefish Falls in Alger County.

The water flows around bedrock and tumbles over and around some misshapen black rocks. A lot of water flows here. In the middle of the falls it is only about 12 feet wide. Below the falls is a rapids area. The total waterfall area is about 150 feet long, with numerous small cascades and four larger drops. The tallest cascade is toward the top of the falls and has one arching trough of water that dumps into the middle of the river. As is quite typical of Michigan waterfalls, rootbeer colored water flows over the falls.

Powderhorn Falls Area

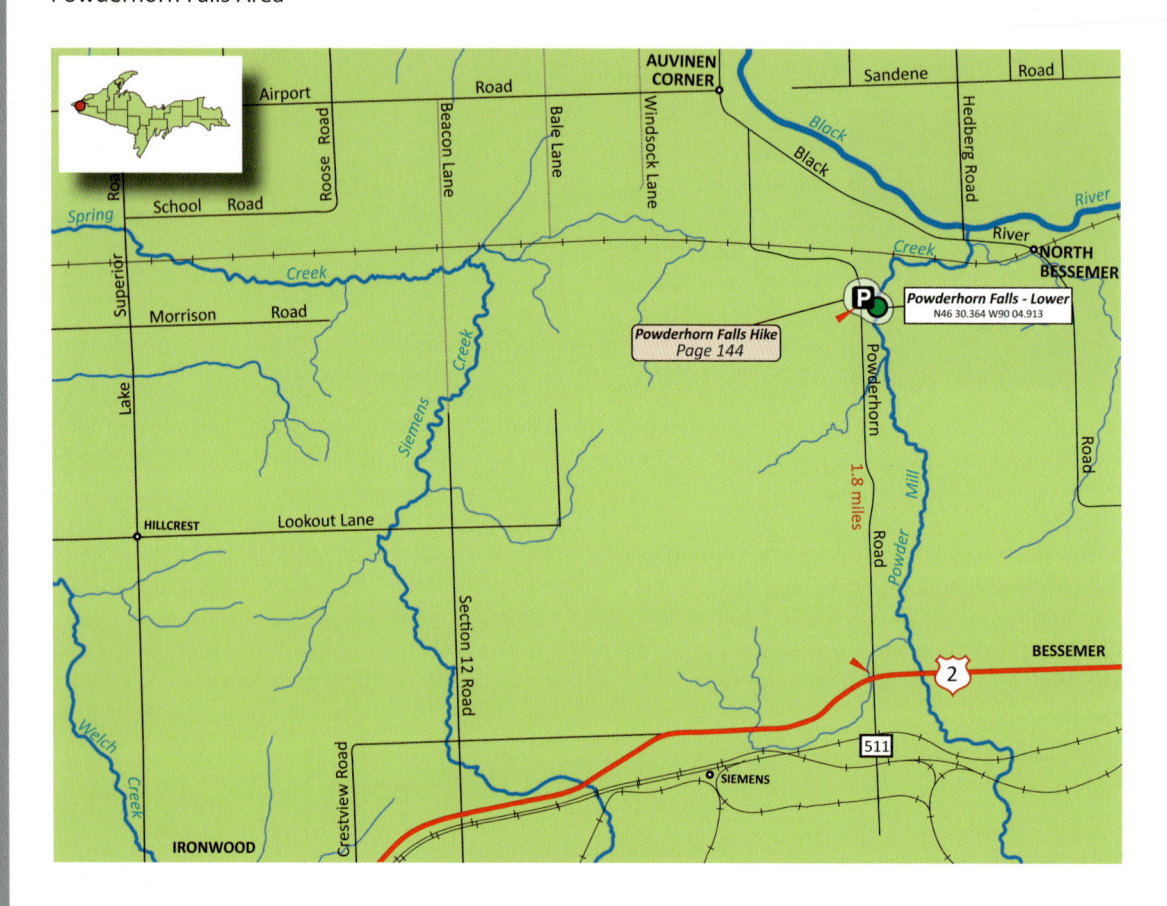

### Powderhorn Falls Hike

Downhill skiing has become an integral part of the tourism industry for the western end of Michigan's Upper Peninsula. Porcupine Mountains Ski Area in the Porcupine Mountains State Park, Indianhead Mountain Resort in Wakefield, along with Blackjack Ski Resort and Big Powderhorn Mountain in Bessemer provide a variety of options for downhill skiers. In the 1960's, Big Powderhorn was considered to be the premier skiing destination in Michigan. Just .7 miles to the east of the Big Powderhorn Mountain peak, Powder Mill Creek plunges down into a ravine over a couple of drops know as the Powderhorn (or Powder Mill) Falls.

Two parallel strings of mountains run in an arc with the northern portion being more dominant and starting basically near Copps Creek by Lake Gogebic and running westerly, swinging gently toward the west/southwest as it crosses the Michigan/Wisconsin line and finally fades out near Mellen, WI. The southern string begins between Wakefield and Bessemer and ends just past Mellen, WI. A smooth valley sits between the slopes for the roughly 40 miles that these parallel ridges interrupt the otherwise flat terrain. Michigan engineers, taking advantage of the relatively level conditions, ran US-2 through the valley. The cities of Wakefield, Bessemer, and Ironwood all lie in this corridor, as well as Hurley, Montreal, Pence, Iron Belt, Upson, and Mellen on the Wisconsin side. Big Powderhorn Mountain is at the northern apex of the arc with the Black River cutting across the countryside just north of the mountain. Nestled between Big Powderhorn Mountain on the west and an unnamed, slightly less steep mountain on the east, Powder Mill Creek runs from the south to the north, joining forces with the much larger Black River less than a mile downstream from the waterfalls.

*Directions:* Turn north onto Powderhorn Road off of US-2 just to the west of Bessemer. In 1.8 miles, just before the road sweeps to the left is a parking spot on the right. Park. Hike the well worn footpath 100 yards to the top of a rocky expanse overlooking Powdermill Creek.

## POWDERHORN FALLS - LOWER (POWDER MILL CREEK) Private

| | | | |
|---|---|---|---|
| Must See: | 8 | GPS: | N46 30.364 W90 04.913 |
| Height: | 20 feet | | |
| Time: | 25-40 minutes | **Hiking Information** | |
| | | Path: | Unimproved Footpath |
| **Driving Information** | | Length: | 100 yards |
| Signs: | None | Elev. Change: | Moderate |
| Road: | Secondary | GPS: | N/A |
| Access: | Fairly Easy | Danger: | Moderate |
| 4WD: | N/A | WP Boots: | Required |

The river drops into a nice, little pool then quickly falls over the lower falls. There is no good way to view them from the top. A rope with knots strategically spaced for hand-holds was stretched between two trees; one at the top of the knob and the other near the base. The creek falls on the far side of the knob, with the spill pool tucked into a partially hidden corner and then cutting sharply back to the "footpath". To fully appreciate the waterfall, wade across the one to two feet deep creek. Bedrock slopes up steeply on the far side, so walking along the "bank" is not an easy feat.

*One of the knotted ropes tied between trees at the falls, helpful for climbing!*

Saxon Falls Area

### Saxon Falls Hike

I must say that access to Saxon Falls is one of the strangest that I have run across. Saxon Falls Road ends at a small parking area with a portable pit toilet. A heavy chain link fence blocks access to a steep metal stairway that descends many feet to a bridge that spans the river. No trespassing signs make it clear that there is no public access here. However, back down Saxon Falls Road a short way is an access road that heads east to the hydroelectric plant's dam, another port-a-jon, and the Saxon Falls Flowage above the dam. Signage here shows exactly how to get to the waterfalls from the Michigan side! Go, MICHIGAN!

*Directions:* From Ironwood, drive west on US-2 for 9.7 miles into Wisconsin. Turn right (north) onto CR B and follow it until it turns to the left. Continue on straight on Saxon Falls Road (dirt road). Follow it for .36 miles. Turn right (east) and follow the dirt access road for .6 miles to the end. Park. The dam is nearby and is easily seen from the parking area. Hike on top of the large steel tube that carries water from the dam to the hydroelectric plant. The tube runs across the river, taking you to the Michigan side of the river and the viewing areas for the waterfall. This guidebook only details the Lower Falls here. They are the easier to view and rate a little better. See Book 4 in the Waterfalls of Michigan series to get information about more waterfalls in the area.

# SAXON FALLS - LOWER (MONTREAL RIVER)           Private

| | | | |
|---|---|---|---|
| Must See: | 7 | GPS: | N46 32.170 W90 22.760 |
| Height: | 40 feet | | |
| Time: | 5 to 15 minutes | Hiking Information | |
| | | Path: | Footpath |
| Driving Information | | Length: | .43 miles |
| Signs: | None | Elev. Change: | Moderate |
| Road: | Dirt | GPS: | N/A |
| Access: | Fairly Easy | Danger: | Moderate |
| 4WD: | N/A | WP Boots: | Helpful |

From the parking area at the dam, hike over to the large steel tube that begins at the dam. A wooden catwalk with cable handrails is fastened to the top of the tube. Use this walkway to cross the river and then...

1) Stay on the catwalk to the surge tank. Climb down the short steel ladder (watch out for hornets - they like to build nests here) and then down a long steel stairway to the power plant. Walk around to the east side of the building. Another short metal ladder mounted to the concrete base leads down to the riverbed.

2) Follow the tube a short distance to an exit. Follow a footpath through the woods to the top of the falls. Be careful as this trail skirts the top of the very deep ravine. There are no guard rails, and the drop could easily be fatal.

In the spring and after very heavy rains the lower waterfall flows over three separate sections of the riverbed. It always flows on the southern side of the river. As the river rises, it also pours over the center section and when the river is at its highest it will also cascade down the northern side as well.

I really recommend viewing this waterfall from the Michigan side. On the Wisconsin side the gorge is VERY deep. Respect it. A wrong step along the edge could be deadly.

*The access to the waterfalls from Michigan*

*Looking downstream from the base of the fall*

*This shot shows the Upper and Lower Falls together*

*The signage on the Wisconsin side*

147

Saxon Falls Area

### Superior Falls Hike

There is a path that heads back up the road to the right (south). Cross the cable and walk about 100 feet. A foot path wanders through the woods on the right. Follow it along a fence for about 100 feet to a viewing area. To get to the top of the falls, go back on the foot path to the trail. Follow the trail to the right (away from the parking area) for another 100-150 feet to another foot path on the right. The path is steep and slippery when wet, but worth the view!

*Directions:* From the Saxon Falls area, continue west on CR B. It will end at CR 122. Turn right (north) and follow CR 122 across the Montreal River and back into the state of Michigan. In about a half mile, a small sign on the left of the road marks Superior Falls. Turn left onto the dirt road and drive to the Power Plant. Park.

## SUPERIOR FALLS (MONTREAL RIVER) — Private

| | | | |
|---|---|---|---|
| Must See: | 8 | GPS: | N46 33.826 W90 24.914 |
| Height: | 70 feet | | |
| Time: | 15 to 30 minutes | **Hiking Information** | |
| | | Path: | Unimproved Footpath |
| **Driving Information** | | Length: | 100 yards |
| Signs: | Small Sign by Road | Elev. Change: | Moderate |
| Road: | Dirt | GPS: | N/A |
| Access: | Fairly Easy | Danger: | Moderate |
| 4WD: | N/A | WP Boots: | N/A |

The waterfall slides into a channel that feeds directly into Lake Superior just a couple hundred yards down river. Hike down the steep access road down to the mouth of the river and then back upstream, past the power generation plant, and nearly to the spill pool at the base of the falls for a river's edge viewing of the waterfall. (This view is not be accessible when the river is running high as the river floods the narrow footpath along the edge of the gorge wall.) The thumbnail picture was taken from the river's edge while the lower shot was from the top of the gorge.

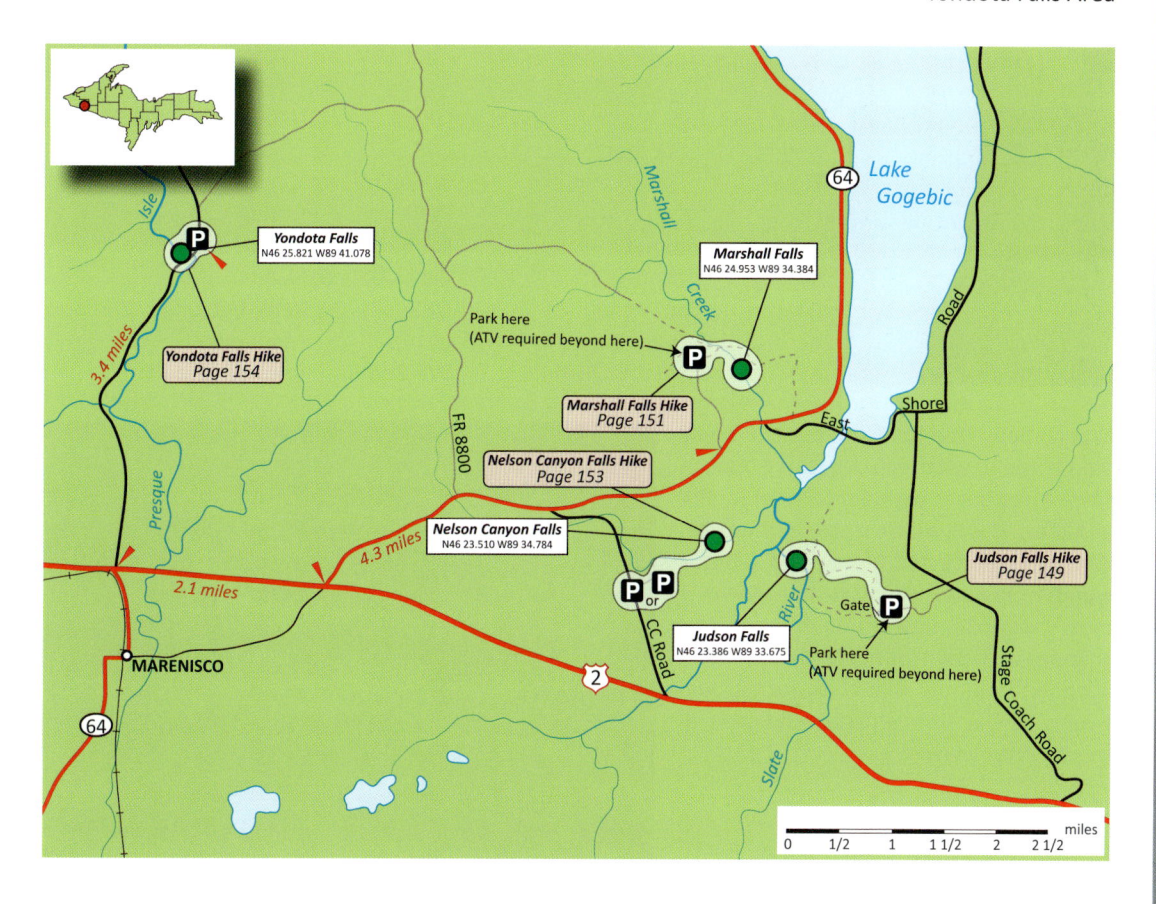

## Judson Falls Hike

Prepare for a rugged hike! This is in keeping with the historical context of the area. The eastern shore of Lake Gogebic, one of Michigan's largest inland lakes, didn't begin to be developed until the 1960's. The last stagecoach robbery recorded in US history took place on Stage Coach Road on August 16, 1889. It fits that there should be a wild, untamed feel here near the headwaters of the Ontonagon and Presque Isle Rivers.

*Judson Falls:* This classic, nearly vertical drop has multiple cascades frothing white into a large spill pool ringed with rocks of basalt. The main falls are 10 feet wide with a smaller, possibly seasonal 1 foot wide fall on the right side. Ancient cedar trees overlook the falls, conforming to the solid rock out of which it appears they are growing.

*Directions:* Turn north on Stagecoach Road off of US-2. In 2.8 miles turn left (southwest) onto dirt road (N46 23.176 W89 31.801). This requires an ATV. Plan on hiking 2 miles in otherwise. In .98 miles there is a fork in the road. The left hand trail is gated. Take the right trail at N46 23.012 W89 32.605. Turn right at N46 23.292 W89 33.365. Turn hard left at N46 23.358 W89 33.488. Turn left at N46 23.383 W89 33.581. This will take you to the river and the falls.

Yondota Falls Area

## JUDSON FALLS (SLATE RIVER)

Private

| | |
|---|---|
| Must See: | 9 |
| Height: | 12 feet |
| Time: | 15-30 minutes |

**Driving Information**
| | |
|---|---|
| Signs: | None |
| Road: | ATV trail |
| Access: | Very difficult |
| 4WD: | ATV required |

| | |
|---|---|
| GPS: | N46 23.386 W89 33.675 |

**Hiking Information**
| | |
|---|---|
| Path: | None |
| Length: | 100 yards |
| Elev. Change: | Slight |
| GPS: | Required |
| Danger: | Moderate |
| WP Boots: | Recommended |

Expectations are funny things. I really didn't know what to expect at Judson Falls. I had never seen a picture of it. For all I knew, it was a little ripple in the river! What an unexpected blessing to see this wonderful waterfall cascading down a mostly vertical face through a narrow channel and then bursting down into a widened spill pool that then turned and wound its way through scattered rocks in the shallow riverbed.

Although the terrain is rugged, and the trails getting out here are muddy, rutted and overgrown, this is a locally popular destination, and with good cause! The beauty of this waterfall is a magnet, drawing adventurous souls back, time and time again.

### Marshall Falls Hike

***Marshall Falls:*** Marshall Falls consists of two drops: first, an 8 foot cascade, followed by a 4 foot drop. This is not a place for children. The terrain is quite rugged. Look for the upthrust of a large plate of rock just downstream from here.

*Directions:* Follow M-64 south along Lake Gogebic. At the southern end of the lake the road sweeps to the west. About 1 mile later there is a dirt road to the right (northwest). Follow it to the north and a bit west for 1 mile. Park here at the "T". Walk about .3 miles down the snowmobile trail (2-track) to the east. When it crosses the bridge, follow it across and along the eastern side of the creek down river to Marshall Falls.

## MARSHALL FALLS (MARSHALL CREEK)   Private

| | | | |
|---|---|---|---|
| Must See: | 7 | GPS: | N46 24.953 W89 34.384 |
| Height: | 12 feet | | |
| Time: | 40 to 60 minutes | Hiking Information | |
| | | Path: | 2-track then none |
| Driving Information | | Length: | .66 miles |
| Signs: | None | Elev. Change: | Moderate |
| Road: | Dirt | GPS: | Required |
| Access: | Difficult | Danger: | Moderate |
| 4WD: | Recommended | WP Boots: | Recommended |

There is always a sense of excitement mixed with apprehension when getting close to where a waterfall is "supposed to be". Too often I have been engaged in wild goose chases, with either no waterfall anywhere in the area, or else up to 1/2 mile away from the target destination. Sometimes the "waterfall" is nothing more than some aggravated ripples in the water. Other times they are on obviously private property with "No Trespassing" signs posted. Let me tell you how the search for Marshall Falls transpired.

It was August 7, 2010. It had been a long day of waterfall hunting. I had started at the western end of Gogebic County, taking pictures of Interstate, the upper falls and Peterson Falls between 8:51 and 9:48 AM. From there I travelled to Maple Creek and hiked from Manakiki Falls to Maple Creek Falls #9, taking about two hours to document those eleven waterfalls (12:50 - 2:56 PM). Next I visited Rootbeer Falls between 4:00 and 4:03 PM. Gabbro Falls and its lower brother were next between 4:34 and 4:54 PM. I had already been to eighteen waterfalls. Traveling east I really wanted to find Marshall Falls. It had been on my to-do list for some time and now I was at Marshall Creek!

Not only was I fatigued, but mosquitoes were out in force. Oh, and it was soon going to be dark. Driving as far as I dared with my truck down deteriorating 2-tracks, I finally parked when the trail ahead looked like a snowmobile trail. Not daring to risk getting stuck I struck out on foot. After hiking nearly

Yondota Falls Area

a 1/2 mile I found a small drop. I took some pictures between 7:00 and 7:02 PM. I wasn't sure if this was Marshall Falls. I was 1/4 mile upstream from where I thought Marshall Falls was supposed to be so I plunged on. No trail, and sometimes rugged terrain slowed the progress. But finally, success! The creek dropped down into a lower grade. I had to get to the base of the falls for some shots, but it was tricky going with very uneven footing and slippery rocks throughout the descent. The creek twisted and fell in an interesting S-curve as it started to run down to the lower grade. I took several pictures between 7:15 and 7:16 PM, then headed further down. There was an obvious lower fall. After taking a shot of that drop at 7:20 PM, I headed back up to Marshall Falls for some wider shots. I took another 5 pictures between 7:30 and 7:32 PM. By now I was happy to head back to the truck and drive over to L'Anse for dinner!

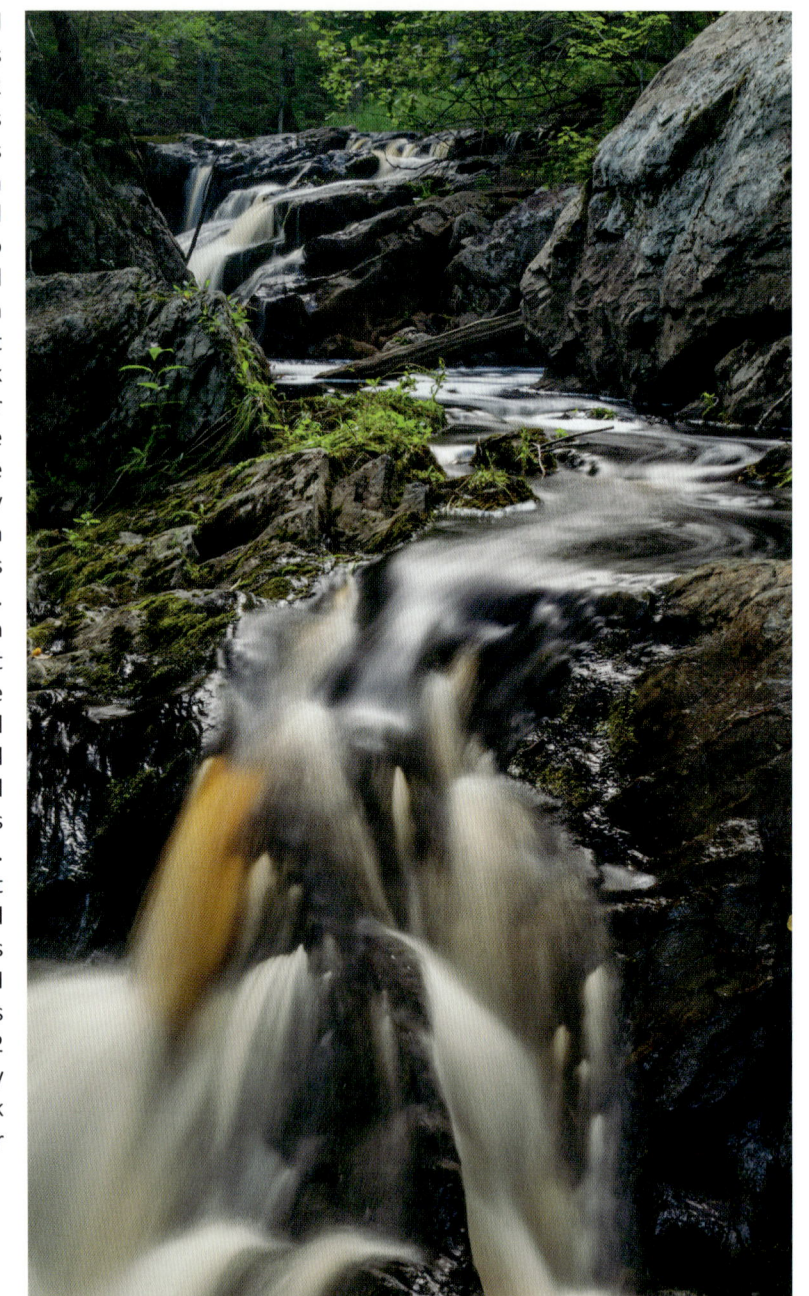

### Nelson Canyon Falls Hike

***Nelson Canyon Falls:*** Canyon Falls has been described as the "Grand Canyon of Michigan". If so, Nelson Canyon Falls must be a close runner-up! Twenty to thirty foot sheer rock walls extend for about 100 yards . There are multiple cascades and drops its entire length. As the river enters the canyon, it divides into thirds and drops 15 feet to the canyon floor. The right-hand third pours onto an outstretched slab of rock, sending out a fan of water to the spill pool below.

*Directions:* West of Lake Gogebic, turn onto CC Road. This is a shortcut between M-64 and US-2. Go either 1.3 miles south of M-64 or 1.2 mile north of US-2. Either park off the road near the 2-track that heads east and hike down the trail, or, if you have a vehicle that has good clearance and the trail doesn't look too muddy, follow the 2-track until it fades (about .2 miles from CC Road). This is where it gets a bit tricky. There is a VERY FAINT path that continues. As of this writing, the path had sporadically placed faded ribbons tied to trees along it. Try to stay on this trail. If not, bushwack over to Nelson Creek (hiking toward the coordinates for Nelson Canyon Falls) - you need a GPS for this. After reaching the creek, follow the continuing faint footpath that parallels the creek downstream to Nelson Canyon Falls. There is a smaller but very beautiful canyon to be enjoyed along the way.

## NELSON CANYON FALLS (NELSON CREEK)                                  Private

| | | | |
|---|---|---|---|
| Must See: | 9 | GPS: | N46 23.510 W89 34.784 |
| Height: | 15 feet | | |
| Time: | 1.5 to 2 hours | Hiking Information | |
| | | Path: | VERY FAINT |
| Driving Information | | Length: | .64 to .92 miles |
| Signs: | None | Elev. Change: | Slight |
| Road: | Secondary | GPS: | Required |
| Access: | Somewhat difficult | Danger: | Moderate |
| 4WD: | N/A | WP Boots: | Recommended |

The canyon is not "a" canyon, but rather several canyons, spaced out over 3/4 mile. There are small drops along the way, but keep going. This beautiful waterfall will be obvious when you see it. The creek enters this canyon in dramatic fashion, dividing and plunging to the creek below. Numerous cascades follow for the length of the canyon (over 100 yards). The best viewing of the main drop is from the far side of the creek. I like to enjoy the lower end of the canyon from the near side, however. There is no bridge over the creek, but a large tree has fallen across the creek up above the waterfall. If the creek is running low, stones below the falls may be used to carefully cross.

A wonderful undergrowth free flat area is perfect for picnics at the top of the falls; the babbling creek off to the side disappears into the canyon, the sound of it a constant companion. The rising hillside on the far side of the canyon is awash in golden splendor during early October as maple and birch trees color the canopy.

*From the far side of the canyon*

*Looking down the canyon*

Yondota Falls Area

### Yondota Falls Hike

***Yondota Falls:*** A footpath leads to an outcropping at the top of the falls. Yondota Falls is a nice, clean plunge bordered by basalt masses.

***Directions:*** At Marenisco, turn north onto County Road 105 from US-2. In 3.3 miles a bridge spans the Presque Isle River. Park on the far side of the bridge. The NCT runs along the river here. A spur off of the trail need to be taken to get to the waterfall. There is a lot of uneven terrain along this hike. Use caution.

## YONDOTA FALLS (PRESQUE ISLE RIVER)    Private

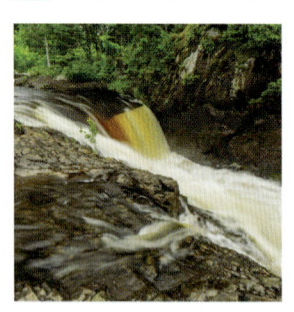

| | | | |
|---|---|---|---|
| Must See: | 8 | GPS: | N46 25.821 W89 41.078 |
| Height: | 6 feet | | |
| Time: | 15-25 minutes | Hiking Information | |
| | | Path: | Footpath |
| Driving Information | | Length: | .14 miles |
| Signs: | By bridge | Elev. Change: | Moderate |
| Road: | Dirt | GPS: | N/A |
| Access: | Easy | Danger: | Moderate |
| 4WD: | N/A | WP Boots: | Recommended |

The path to the falls, though well defined, requires climbing around on rocks and over uneven ground. The river above the falls, cradled in the bare rocked riverbed, can appear as a calm enlarged swimming pool. And then, the seemingly serene scene changes to a frothing, turbulent river, churning through a narrow chasm.

Pink and gray stone line the banks that are covered in several hues of green moss and pastel greenish lichen. The rugged banks make viewing the waterfall tricky. A sheer wall on the far side of the top drop makes a great backdrop for the beginning of this 30 yard long waterfall.

After a sweeping bend, the river narrows to 10 feet. It then plunges over a sheer drop into a straight edged slot. This narrows the river even more - down to 5 feet at its narrowest. Emerging from the short canyon, it widens out again.

# CHAPTER 7
# HOUGHTON COUNTY

# Houghton County Map

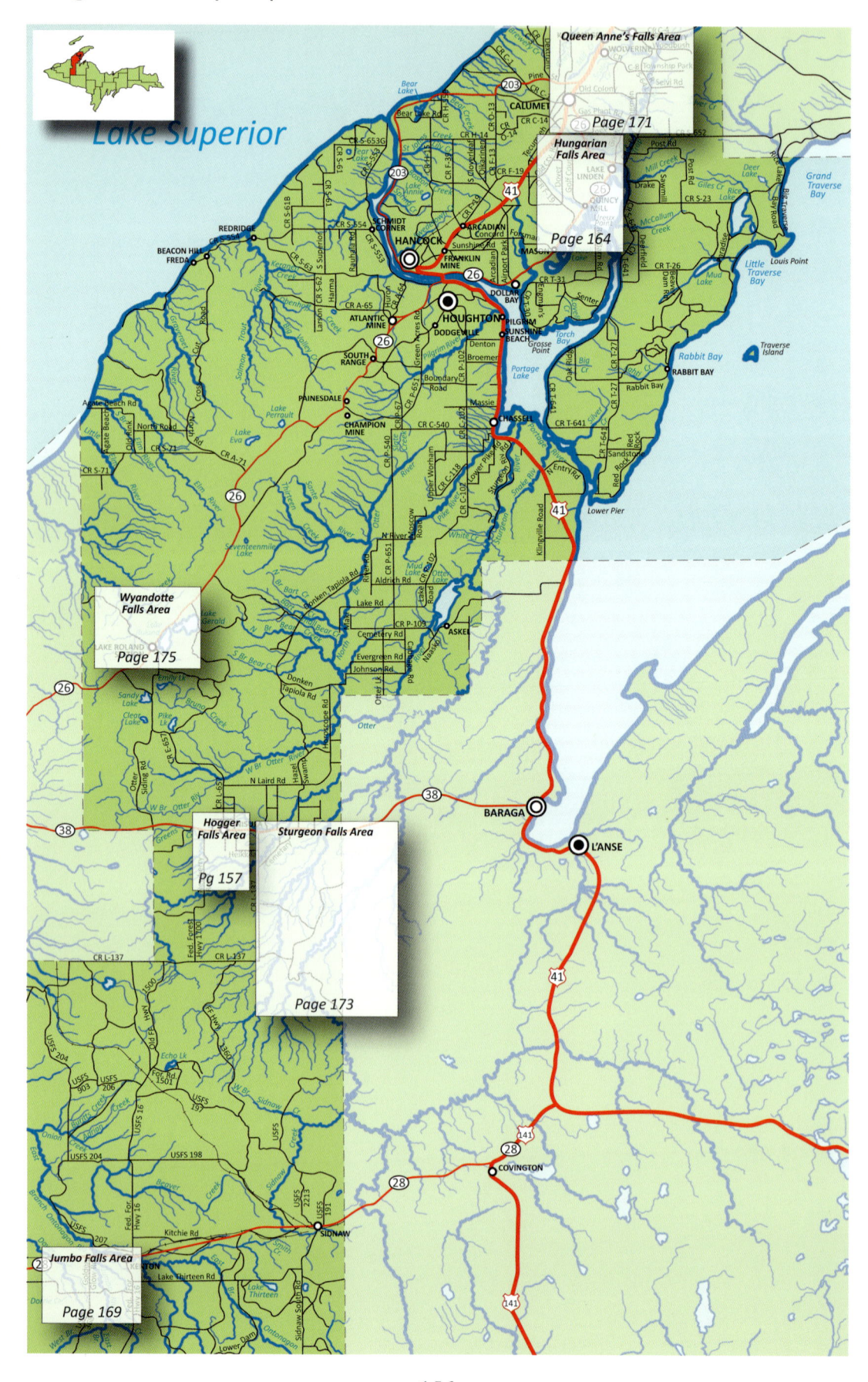

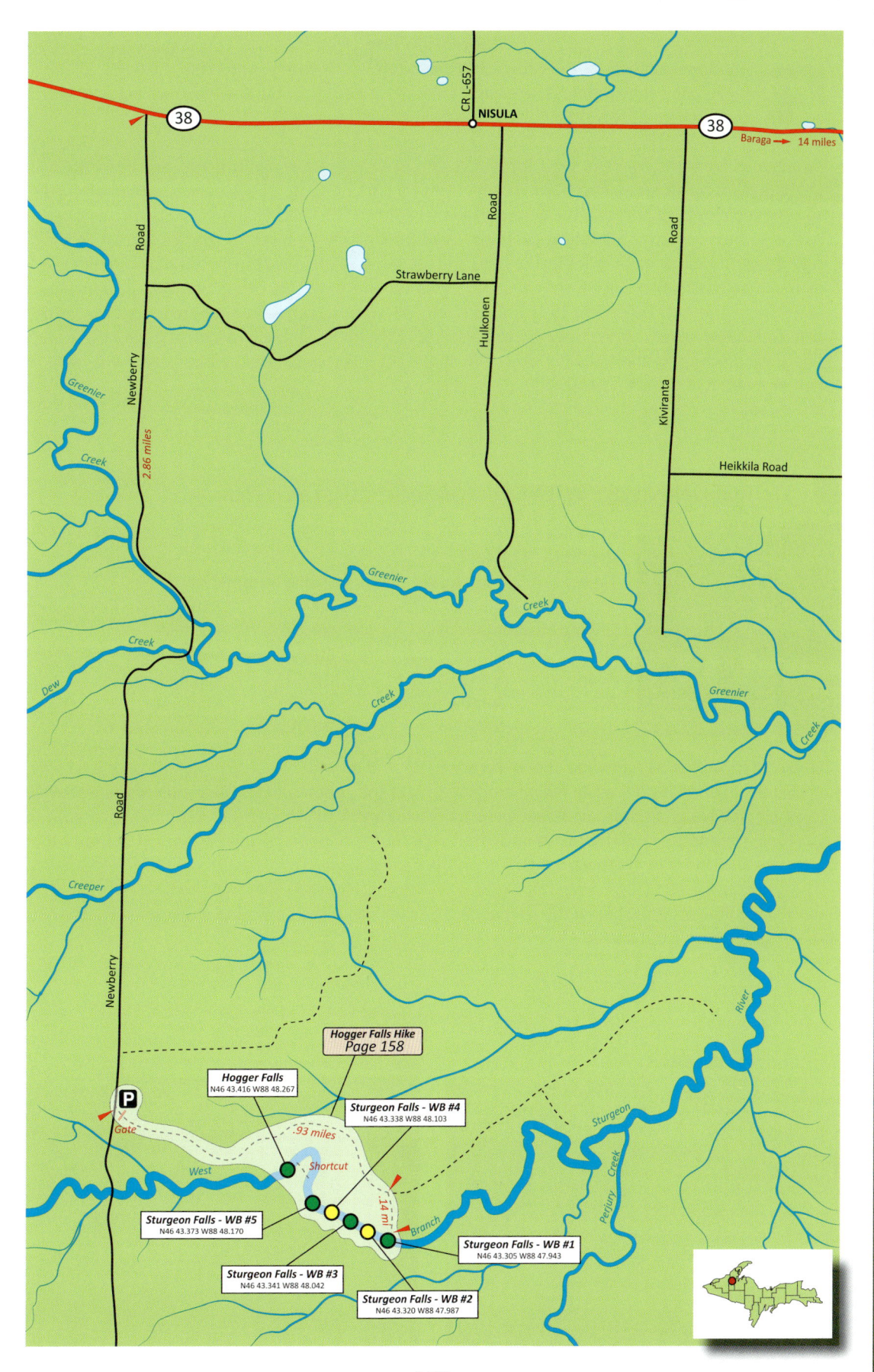

Hogger Falls Area

HOUGHTON COUNTY

Hogger Falls Area

### Hogger Falls Hike

The West Branch of the Sturgeon River hosts some lovely waterfalls. It takes a little hiking, and they are not the easiest to traverse between, but for those willing and able there are great rewards.

*Directions:* From Nisula, head west for .9 miles on M-38. Turn left (south) onto Newberry Road. In 2.9 miles turn left into a short 2-track that is now a parking spot. The 2-track has been blocked to keep vehicles from entering the Ottawa National Forest. The parking area is just before a bridge over the West Branch of the Sturgeon River. Hike the 2-track .93 miles to another 2-track to the right (south). Follow it .14 miles to the river and Sturgeon Falls - WB #1. Hike directly up the river as much as possible to keep from having to climb up and down the steep gorge walls between waterfalls. The only exception to this is between #5 and Hogger Falls. Cut cross country for a considerable shortcut. After Hogger Falls, use your GPS and hike back toward the parking spot. There will be no trail through the forest. In about .13 miles you should be back to the 2-track. Follow it about .4 miles to the vehicle.

## STURGEON FALLS - WB #1 (WEST BRANCH - STURGEON RIVER) *Private*

| | | | |
|---|---|---|---|
| Must See: | 7 | GPS: | N46 43.305 W88 47.943 |
| Height: | 6 feet | | |
| Time: | 1-1.5 hours | Hiking Information | |
| | | Path: | 2-track |
| Driving Information | | Length: | 1.1 miles |
| Signs: | None | Elev. Change: | Moderate |
| Road: | Gravel | GPS: | Recommended |
| Access: | Somewhat Easy | Danger: | Moderate |
| 4WD: | N/A | WP Boots: | Recommended |

The river starts about 25 feet wide above the waterfall. It then widens out, particularly on the far side, tapering down on that side, while falling more sharply in the center and the near side of the waterfall. The base of the waterfall is about 40 feet wide, narrowing again quickly between sandbars covered with sandstone, river debris, and thick undergrowth. Large chunks of bedrock have broken off of the 12 foot high gorge wall and fallen in toward the river on the near side.

Beautiful wildflowers grow below the spill pool. The river can often be waded easily, allowing the falls to be explored from both banks.

*The 2-track to the falls*

*Spotted touch-me-nots cluster below the waterfall*

# STURGEON FALLS - WB #2 (WEST BRANCH - STURGEON RIVER) Private

| | | | |
|---|---|---|---|
| Must See: | 5 | GPS: | N46 43.320 W88 47.987 |
| Height: | 6 feet | | |
| Time: | 1-1.5 hours | Hiking Information | |
| | | Path: | 2-track |
| Driving Information | | Length: | 1.13 miles |
| Signs: | None | Elev. Change: | Moderate |
| Road: | Gravel | GPS: | Recommended |
| Access: | Somewhat Easy | Danger: | Moderate |
| 4WD: | N/A | WP Boots: | Recommended |

A faint but followable footpath between #1 and #2 follows the top of the gorge wall. It is only about 75 yards between the waterfalls. Feel free to hike up the river if it feels safe.

The river slants back hard to the near bank, rushing down in a slide/cascade. The river compresses from a 50 foot wide river to just 20 feet at the waterfall in normal conditions. It's a little tough to view the waterfall easily, as it snuggles up against the 10 to 20 foot bluff that you are standing on. If you can ford the river, there's a good viewing area on the far side, above and below the waterfall. After the slide, the river slows down and flows calmly around a corner downstream.

*Shot of the waterfall - taken from the far side of the river*

Hogger Falls Area

## STURGEON FALLS - WB #3 (WEST BRANCH - STURGEON RIVER) Private

| | | | |
|---|---|---|---|
| Must See: | 7 | GPS: | N46 43.341 W88 48.042 |
| Height: | 3 feet | | |
| Time: | 1.25 to 1.75 hours | **Hiking Information** | |
| | | Path: | 2-track |
| **Driving Information** | | Length: | 1.19 miles |
| Signs: | None | Elev. Change: | Moderate |
| Road: | Gravel | GPS: | Recommended |
| Access: | Somewhat Easy | Danger: | Moderate |
| 4WD: | N/A | WP Boots: | Recommended |

The gorge wall dramatically rises between #2 and #3. It is often easier to walk the 100 yards right up the normally shallow river between these falls.

It's not tall, but this waterfall has a lot of character. The 50 foot wide waterfall is a sandstone ledge that is constantly being undercut. When the ledge becomes too thin, a section breaks off and the undercutting starts over. It looks somewhat like a miniature Tahquamenon Falls. A slow moving spill below the falls narrows and then cascades down another foot or so. Numerous moss covered fragments of broken off sandstone line the sides of the waterway, forcing it ever narrower below the waterfall.

*This is from the far side of the river*

160

# STURGEON FALLS - WB #4 (WEST BRANCH - STURGEON RIVER) Private

| | | | |
|---|---|---|---|
| Must See: | 5 | GPS: | N46 43.338 W88 48.103 |
| Height: | 2 feet | | |
| Time: | 1.5-2 hours | **Hiking Information** | |
| | | Path: | 2-track then none |
| **Driving Information** | | Length: | 1.23 miles |
| Signs: | None | Elev. Change: | Aggressive |
| Road: | Gravel | GPS: | Recommended |
| Access: | Somewhat Easy | Danger: | Moderate |
| 4WD: | N/A | WP Boots: | Recommended |

Cross over the river (if possible) to the far side below #3. Climb up above the waterfall. Hike along the flat bank on the far side most of the way to #4. Otherwise you'll need to climb up to the top of the 40 foot gorge wall between the falls. It's 100 yards to #4.

This is another wide, but short waterfall. A high bluff overlooks the far side of the waterfall. Chunks of sandstone, broken off of the bedrock, litter the riverbed below the spill pool. A nice viewing/picnic area presents itself above and below the waterfall.

This is quite similar to #3, just shorter and narrower, and with a softer top layer. This waterfall is eroding through the top layers, making a cascade, and then a plunge. It runs mostly over two lower sections of the shelf, filling a wide but short spill pool before narrowing and flowing along the base of the far gorge wall. A large sandstone debris field makes a great viewing area just below the waterfall.

*Note the encroaching gorge wall on the far side of the river*

Hogger Falls Area

## STURGEON FALLS - WB #5 (WEST BRANCH - STURGEON RIVER) Private

| | | | |
|---|---|---|---|
| Must See: | 7 | GPS: | N46 43.373 W88 48.170 |
| Height: | 6 feet | | |
| Time: | 1.75-2.25 hours | Hiking Information | |
| | | Path: | 2-Track Then None |
| Driving Information | | Length: | 1.27 miles |
| Signs: | None | Elev. Change: | Aggressive |
| Road: | Gravel | GPS: | Recommended |
| Access: | Somewhat Easy | Danger: | Moderate |
| 4WD: | N/A | WP Boots: | Recommended |

Once again, hike along the river's edge at the base of the gorge on the near side upstream to the waterfall. Ford the river over to the "island" below the waterfall and then to the far side and upstream to the base of the waterfall. The near side rises up tall with a 20 foot wall directly above the waterfall.

The river has carved out a path through a rocky outcropping, with the remaining rock guarding the left side of the river. The waterfall runs down over a multitude of thin rock layers, each one sticking out slightly further than the one above it, something like a deck of cards fanned out.

*Looking downstream from up above the waterfall*

The waterfall is a lovely cascade rushing down layers of sandstone. Although the riverbed is 75 feet across, the waterfall snuggles up against the near side, widening out as the river rises.

*Eroded sandstone has made a small "island" below the waterfall*

162

Hogger Falls Area

# HOGGER FALLS (WEST BRANCH - STURGEON RIVER)  Private

| | | | |
|---|---|---|---|
| Must See: | 8 | GPS: | N46 43.416 W88 48.267 |
| Height: | 8 feet | | |
| Time: | 2-2.5 hours | Hiking Information | |
| | | Path: | 2-Track Then None |
| Driving Information | | Length: | 1.41 miles |
| Signs: | None | Elev. Change: | Aggressive |
| Road: | Gravel | GPS: | Recommended |
| Access: | Somewhat Easy | Danger: | Moderate |
| 4WD: | N/A | WP Boots: | Recommended |

HOUGHTON COUNTY

If possible, hike the river upstream from #5 until the bank on the far side looks inviting. Hike along the bank a little ways. The river is going to make a huge "U", doubling back on itself. If you see the tall sand bank across the river, cut straight away from the river and take the shortcut to the other side of the "U". You don't have to climb up the gorge wall as you cut across. If you're tempted to do so, turn a bit to the right and stay on the low ground until you reach the river again. Continue upstream. You should hear the waterfall almost instantly. Cross the river when possible and follow the "near" bank to the waterfall.

The gorgeous waterfall cascades down with the backdrop a 15 foot rock gorge wall on the far side. A sheet of solid sandstone arches over space vacated below the waterfall where softer, fractured stone has now eroded away. Trees grow thick on this precarious formation. It's a beautiful setting for a beautiful waterfall!

*The softer layers below the harder rock are eroding away below the waterfall*

Hogger Falls

# Hungarian Falls Area

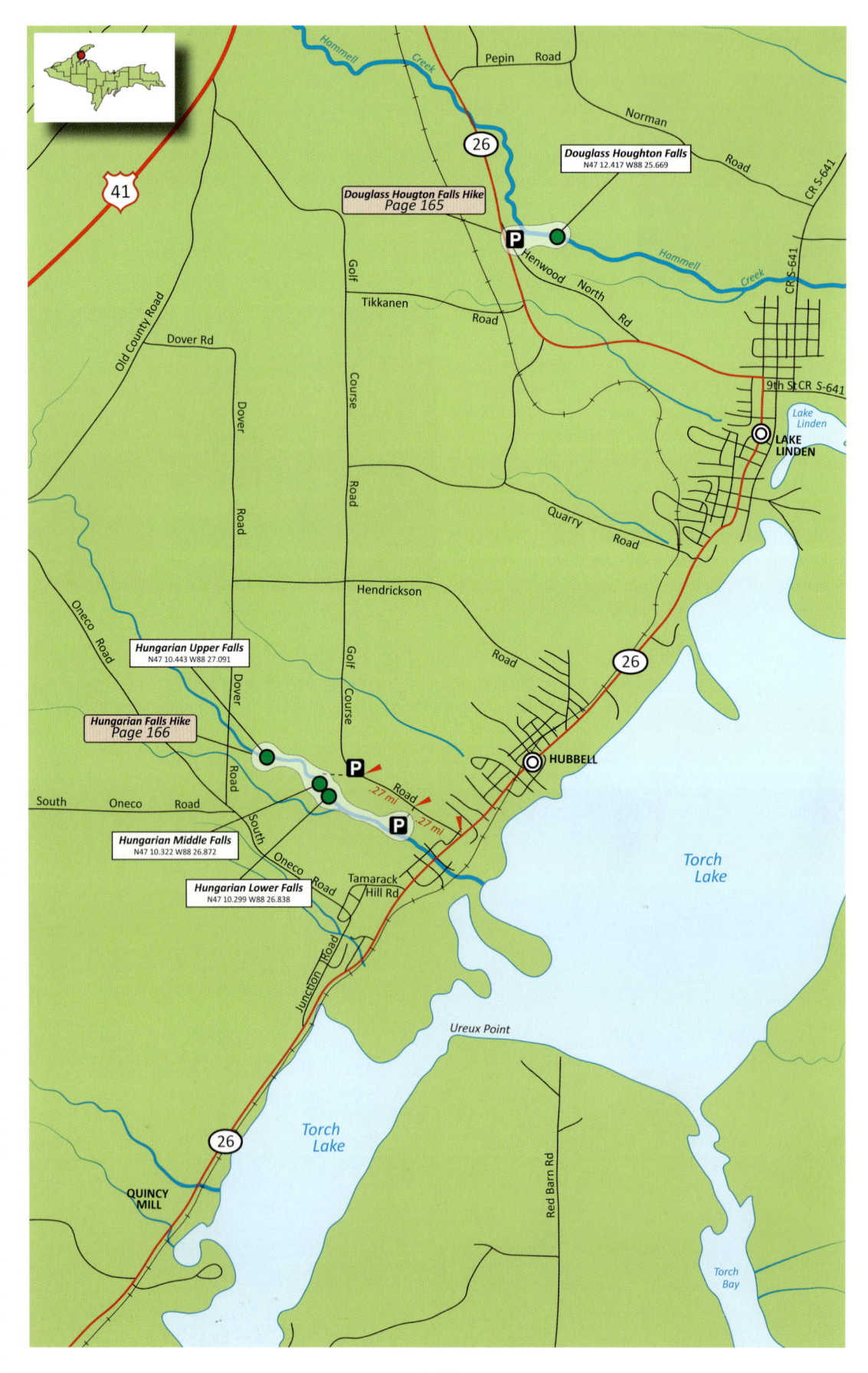

Hungarian Falls Area

## Douglass Houghton Falls Hike

***Douglass Houghton Falls:*** The highest waterfall in Michigan, Douglass Houghton Falls was a favorite haunt of Michigan Tech students for years. I remember my brother taking me to see it back in the 1980's while he was attending college in Houghton. However, since the 1990's it has been closed to the public. Trash was being left behind. Individuals were rappelling down the unstable, crumbling face down into the gorge. Several people had died by falling over the edge to the unforgiving rock floor below. The gorge walls seem to have become steeper and more dangerous over time.

Hammell Creek, the small creek that feeds the falls, runs through a flat field before suddenly plunging over the cliff. Multiple cascades send the creek tumbling over one rock face after another. The creek gathers itself together again at the base of the gorge. It follows the relatively narrow split in the earth, eventually merging with Trap Rock River before dumping into the northern end of Torch Lake.

As of this printing, the State of Michigan has approved funding to purchase the waterfall and surrounding land. It is hoped that the transfer will take place in the spring of 2017. Afterwards, there will need to be construction of appropriate safeguards before public access will be allowed.

*Directions:* From Lake Linden, head west on M-26 about 1.5 miles. After the DNR has opened the waterfall to the public, I'm assuming that there will be appropriate signage to the parking area and waterfall.

As of this printing, this waterfall is still on private land, and the landowner has expressly forbidden trespassing. As always, respect landowners' wishes. Do not enter without permission.

## ■ DOUGLASS HOUGHTON FALLS (HAMMELL CREEK)   Private

| | | | |
|---|---|---|---|
| Must See: | 8 | GPS: | N47 12.417 W88 25.669 |
| Height: | 143 feet | | |
| Time: | 20-60 minutes | **Hiking Information** | |
| | | Path: | Overgrown Footpath |
| **Driving Information** | | Length: | .2 miles from the road |
| Signs: | None | Elev. Change: | Extremely Steep Gorge |
| Road: | Secondary | GPS: | N/A |
| Access: | N/A | Danger: | Extreme |
| 4WD: | N/A | WP Boots: | Recommended |

The State of Michigan is in the process of purchasing Douglass Houghton Falls. After it is opened to the public, it stands to be a great tourist draw, with waterfall lovers and geologists alike flocking to enjoy this wonderful Michigan treasure.

Note the black oval shaped hole near the base of the waterfall. This is all that remains of an old mining attempt.

Do not attempt to visit this waterfall until it is owned by the State of Michigan and made available to the public. Until then, it is private, and access is strictly prohibited.

Hungarian Falls Area

### Hungarian Falls Hike

The Hungarian Falls are a very popular set of waterfalls to visit. Many rock climbers enjoy rappelling down the face of the lower falls, they are fairly easy to access, and they are clustered together over only about .3 miles.

*Directions:* From M-26, near Hubbell, turn northwest onto Golf Course Road (dirt). The road splits almost immediately. Take the left branch. The road rises up quickly into the highlands. About .25 miles up from M-26, turn left (southwest) onto a 2-track. Follow it for about .10 miles. There is a widened out parking area along the 2-track. Park. Follow the 2-track to the edge of the gorge. A footpath follows the gorge. Hike upstream (northwest). Soon, a "mountain goat" spur trail "Y"s off down into the gorge. If desiring to get to the base of the gorge to the Lower Falls from its base, follow this trail. (Note: This is a VERY steep and narrow trail. Beware!) Otherwise, stay on the top path to get to the top of the Lower Falls as well as the rest of the Hungarian waterfalls upstream.

*Alternate route:* About .5 miles up from M-26 there is a gate on the left. Park off of the side of the road (not blocking the gate). Hike past the gate (southwest) for about .2 miles. There is lacework of dirt roads here. The general idea is to find the creek and follow the road that leads along it. Hiking in should bring you about to the middle of the waterfall area. Hike both directions to see all the waterfalls.

## HUNGARIAN LOWER FALLS (DOVER CREEK)  Private

| | | | |
|---|---|---|---|
| Must See: | 9 | GPS: | N47 10.299 W88 26.838 |
| Height: | 50 feet | | |
| Time: | 60-90 minutes | **Hiking Information** | |
| | | Path: | Steep, Narrow Footpath |
| **Driving Information** | | Length: | .36 miles |
| Signs: | None | Elev. Change: | Extremely Steep Gorge |
| Road: | 2-track | GPS: | Helpful |
| Access: | Somewhat Easy | Danger: | Extreme |
| 4WD: | N/A | WP Boots: | Recommended |

The highest waterfall in the Hungarian Falls is also the furthest downstream. It sports a fanned out, bridal veil look over a solid rock face. A jumbled pile of rock slabs and dead tree trunks lie at the foot of the falls. The deep ravine is guarded with steep side walls, making it very difficult to access the base of the falls. Unfortunately, this is the best way to view the waterfall, since there is very little to see from the top. Water seeps down from the surrounding land, saturating the seemingly sheer walls, making for a muddy and slippery climb. It is recommended to take the "mountain goat" footpath from downstream as described in the "Hungarian Falls Hike" above.

*The view from the base of the steep and deep gorge*

Keep in mind that the trail can be washed out by mud slides.

Note: Hiking Information is based on parking down the 2-track, not by the gate.

Hungarian Falls Area

## ■ HUNGARIAN MIDDLE FALLS (DOVER CREEK)  Private

| | | | |
|---|---|---|---|
| Must See: | 9 | GPS: | N47 10.322 W88 26.872 |
| Height: | 20 feet | | |
| Time: | 30-120 minutes | Hiking Information | |
| | | Path: | Narrow Footpath |
| Driving Information | | Length: | .38 miles |
| Signs: | None | Elev. Change: | Moderate |
| Road: | 2-track | GPS: | Helpful |
| Access: | Somewhat Easy | Danger: | Moderate |
| 4WD: | N/A | WP Boots: | Recommended |

The Middle Falls are only about 200 feet upstream from the Lower Falls. It requires a little bit of climbing (nothing like the Lower Falls, however) to get down to the base of the waterfall, but the view is wonderful, and with the spill pool ringed by rock walls, it feels like the ultimate, intimate, private garden. What a great place for a family picnic! The spill pool is shallow enough for children to splash around in. Just be careful in getting them down the rocky edge to this little piece of paradise.

Note: Hiking Information is based on parking down the 2-track, not by the gate.

*Note the many looks during the seasons!*

HOUGHTON COUNTY

Hungarian Middle Falls

Hungarian Falls Area

## HUNGARIAN UPPER FALLS (DOVER CREEK)    Private

| | | | |
|---|---|---|---|
| Must See: | 7 | GPS: | N47 10.443 W88 27.091 |
| Height: | 20 feet | | |
| Time: | 60-145 minutes | Hiking Information | |
| | | Path: | 2-track |
| Driving Information | | Length: | .62 miles |
| Signs: | None | Elev. Change: | Moderate |
| Road: | 2-track | GPS: | Helpful |
| Access: | Somewhat Easy | Danger: | Moderate |
| 4WD: | N/A | WP Boots: | N/A |

From the dam, follow the northern side of the reservoir. About 200 yards upstream from the dam, the Upper Falls cascade down just above the top of the back waters. This is a two-tiered waterfall. The top tier is a 15 foot nearly sheer plunge over a rocky face. The creek flattens out over a debris field for 20 yards, then drops another 5 feet (the second tier) over cascades. It fills the creek bed from side to side during spring melt. The waterfall is much less impressive during dry summer months.

Note: Hiking Information is based on parking down the 2-track, not by the gate.

*This waterfall needs a good deal of water to present itself well. Compare these widely different looks!*

168

Jumbo Falls Area

HOUGHTON COUNTY

### Jumbo Falls Hike

***Jumbo Falls:*** A short, but nicely presented cascading waterfall greets you after a short hike through a mature section of forest. Beautiful wildflowers grow along the edges of the waterfall, adding a splash of color.

Directions: Travel 1.75 miles west on M-28 from Kenton. Turn left (south) on Golden Glow Road (the next road west of Jumbo River). After 1.63 miles follow the road to the left (east). In .31 miles veer to the right (southeast). In about 1 mile, park near the obvious trailhead to the falls. Hike 100 yards on a semi-improved trail to Jumbo Falls.

Jumbo Falls Area

## JUMBO FALLS (JUMBO RIVER)  Private

| | | | |
|---|---|---|---|
| Must See: | 8 | GPS: | N46 26.970 W88 54.779 |
| Height: | 6 feet | | |
| Time: | 10-20 minutes | **Hiking Information** | |
| | | Path: | Semi-improved Footpath |
| **Driving Information** | | Length: | 100 yards |
| Signs: | None | Elev. Change: | Slight |
| Road: | Dirt | GPS: | N/A |
| Access: | Somewhat Easy | Danger: | Slight |
| 4WD: | N/A | WP Boots: | N/A |

This rates as a "kid-friendly" waterfall since it is a short hike down the well-travelled path that is normally not too muddy, and the river isn't especially deep and there are no major stumbling spots along the way.

The Jumbo River, a little over 3 miles downstream from the Duppy Falls in Iron County, runs quietly through a beautiful forest. The minimally banked river turns a bend and cascades down 6 feet to a shallow, widened spill pool. A lovely viewing area is several dozen yards downstream as the river narrows below the pool.

*Beware! The dirt road to the falls is not plowed in the winter.*

HOUGHTON COUNTY

Jumbo Falls

170

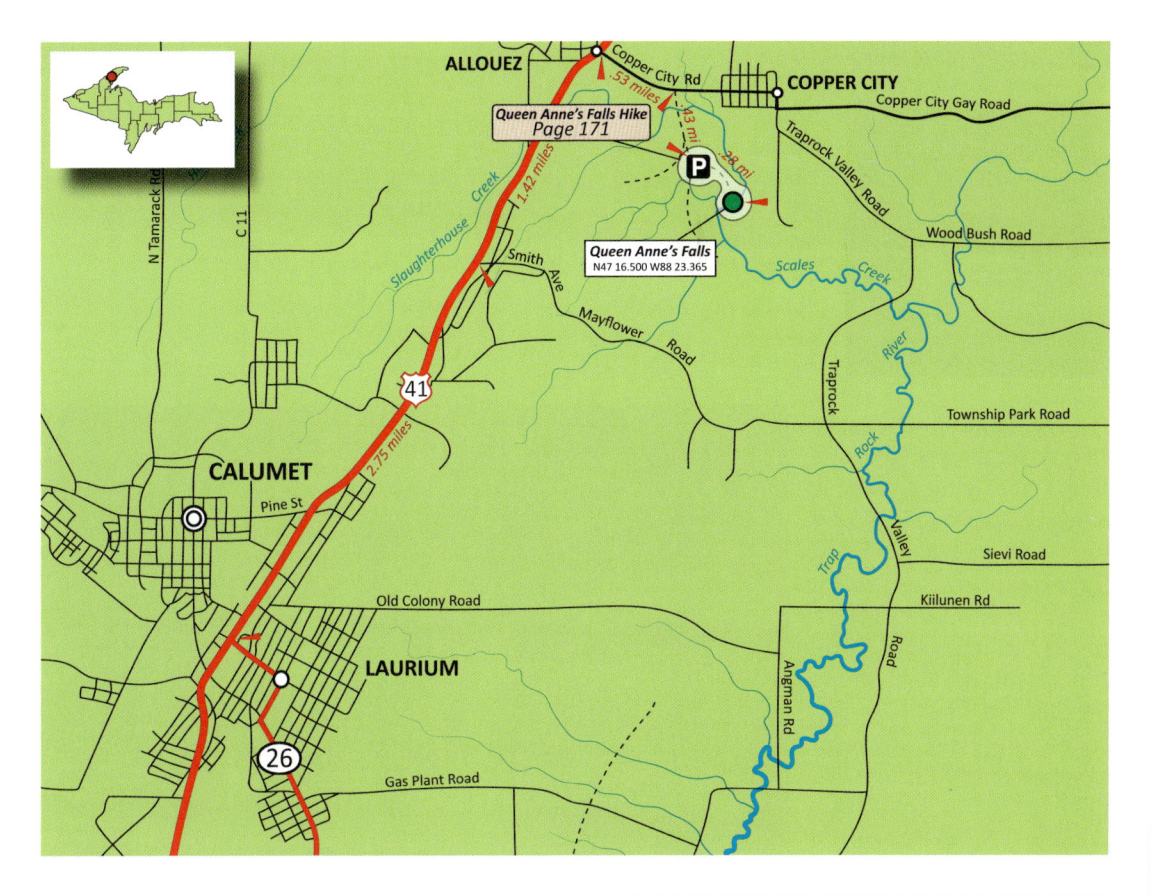

### Queen Anne's Falls Hike

***Queen Anne's Falls:*** The tall, narrow, zig-zag shaped waterfall is channelled down into a gorge through rough, exposed basalt bedrock. A popular spill pool awaits at the bottom of the falls before the creek continues on its way through the boulder strewn creek bed downstream. There is a dangerous climb down to the base of the falls. There is about 50 feet of elevation change. After leaving the ATV turnaround, the trail rapidly descends down a clay footpath. It can be very slippery - especially after a rain. After reaching the river at the top of the waterfall the trail mostly dissapears. Scramble down the rocky side of the waterfall to the base.

Several smaller cascades greet you at the top of the main drop as you first approach the creek. They're not large, but they are nice! Numerous small drops can be found for the next several hundred yards upstream.

*Directions:* On US-41 in Allouez, turn southeast onto Copper City Road. In less than .53 miles, turn right (south) onto a dirt road at N47 17.012 W88 23.688 (if you pass the bar on the right, you've gone too far). Drive .23 miles. Stay left and drive another .19 miles. Park on the left at the base of a steep 2-track. Hike up the 2-track 150 feet. Turn slight right at N47 16.654 W88 23.533. Turn right at N47 16.646 W88 23.494. Turn right at N47 16.621 W88 23.439. The narrow 2-track ends at N47 16.528 W88 23.357. A well-worn footpath begins at the circle turnaround. (There is not much room to turn around. A very small vehicle is required, preferably a 4-wheeler.) Hike down the footpath. Slippery clay eventually gives way to steep rock at the waterfall. (The total hike length from vehicle to waterfall is .28 miles.)

## QUEEN ANNE'S FALLS* (SLAUGHTERHOUSE CREEK)    Private

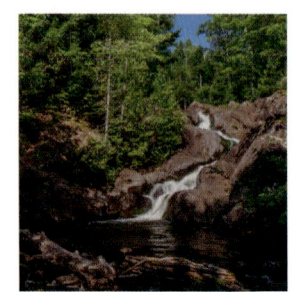

| | | | |
|---|---|---|---|
| Must See: | 7 | GPS: | N47 16.500 W88 23.365 |
| Height: | 30 feet | | |
| Time: | 20-40 minutes | Hiking Information | |
| | | Path: | Footpath |
| Driving Information | | Length: | .28 miles |
| Signs: | None | Elev. Change: | Moderate |
| Road: | Dirt | GPS: | Helpful |
| Access: | Difficult | Danger: | Elevated |
| 4WD: | Recommended | WP Boots: | Recommended |

The dirt road off of Copper City Road is very sandy in places and getting stuck is a real possibility. Be very careful when trying to turn around or park. I very nearly buried my 4WD truck a couple of times out here. The shot to the right shows the top of the waterfall. Follow the creek upstream to view more small drops like this one.

*AKA  Queen Annie's Falls*

*Several drops like this are found up above the waterfall*

*The look from the far side of the creek*

172

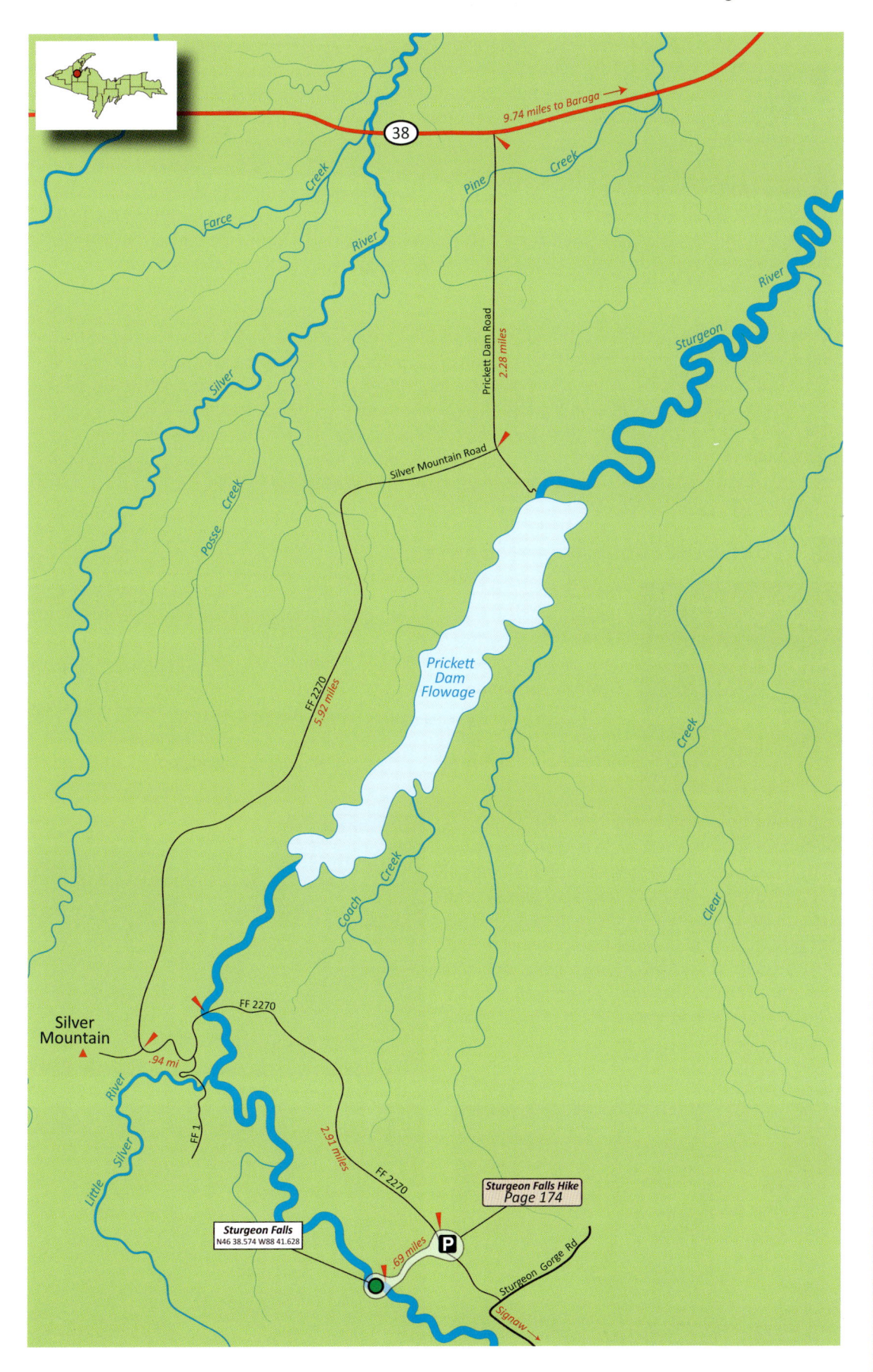

Sturgeon Falls Area

HOUGHTON COUNTY

Sturgeon Falls Area

### Sturgeon Falls Hike

This is a popular back country hike, but since it is quite a distance from major population centers, it is seldom crowded. Make sure that you are in good physical shape before attempting this hike. The narrow footpath is plainly visible, but the hike back out of the Sturgeon River Gorge is strenuous.

*Sturgeon Falls:* The switch-backing hike down into the deepest gorge in Michigan is rewarded with wonderful sights: overlooking an expanse of hardwoods, hiking through a mature forest with its sights and smells, and at last - the majestic Sturgeon Falls. Mist swirls through the air downstream from the pounding of thousands of gallons of water struggling to race over the falls on its way to Portage Lake.

*Directions:* In Baraga, turn west onto M-38 off us US-41. Follow M-38 for 9.7 miles to Prickett Dam Road. Turn left (south) on Prickett Dam Road. In 2.3 miles turn right onto Silver Mountain Road at N46 43.804 W88 40.562. After 5.9 miles stay left at N46 40.075 W88 43.891 for another 3.8 miles to the trailhead parking area on the left. Park. Hike in on the obvious trail back across FF 2270, through a flat stretch of forest, then along the top of the gorge until the trail plunges down into the gorge and switchbacks back and forth to get to the bottom where it then flattens out again until getting close to the river. The trail meets the river at the top of Sturgeon Falls.

## STURGEON FALLS (STURGEON RIVER)  Private

| | | | |
|---|---|---|---|
| Must See: | 10 | GPS: | N46 38.574 W88 41.628 |
| Height: | 30 feet | | |
| Time: | 1-2 hours | **Hiking Information** | |
| | | Path: | Semi-improved Footpath |
| **Driving Information** | | Length: | .69 miles |
| Signs: | None | Elev. Change: | Major |
| Road: | Gravel | GPS: | Recommended |
| Access: | Difficult | Danger: | Moderate |
| 4WD: | N/A | WP Boots: | N/A |

Rugged and bold. This remote waterfall, located at the bottom of the deepest gorge in Michigan, shows off its power with a spray that can drift hundreds of feet downstream. Massive boulders, angular and black, make up the face of the waterfall. Twenty foot cliffs, topped with cedar trees, rise higher still on either side of the falls. Rough hewn boulders litter the river downstream. A sandy, flat beach below the falls shows traces of old campfires and tent sites.

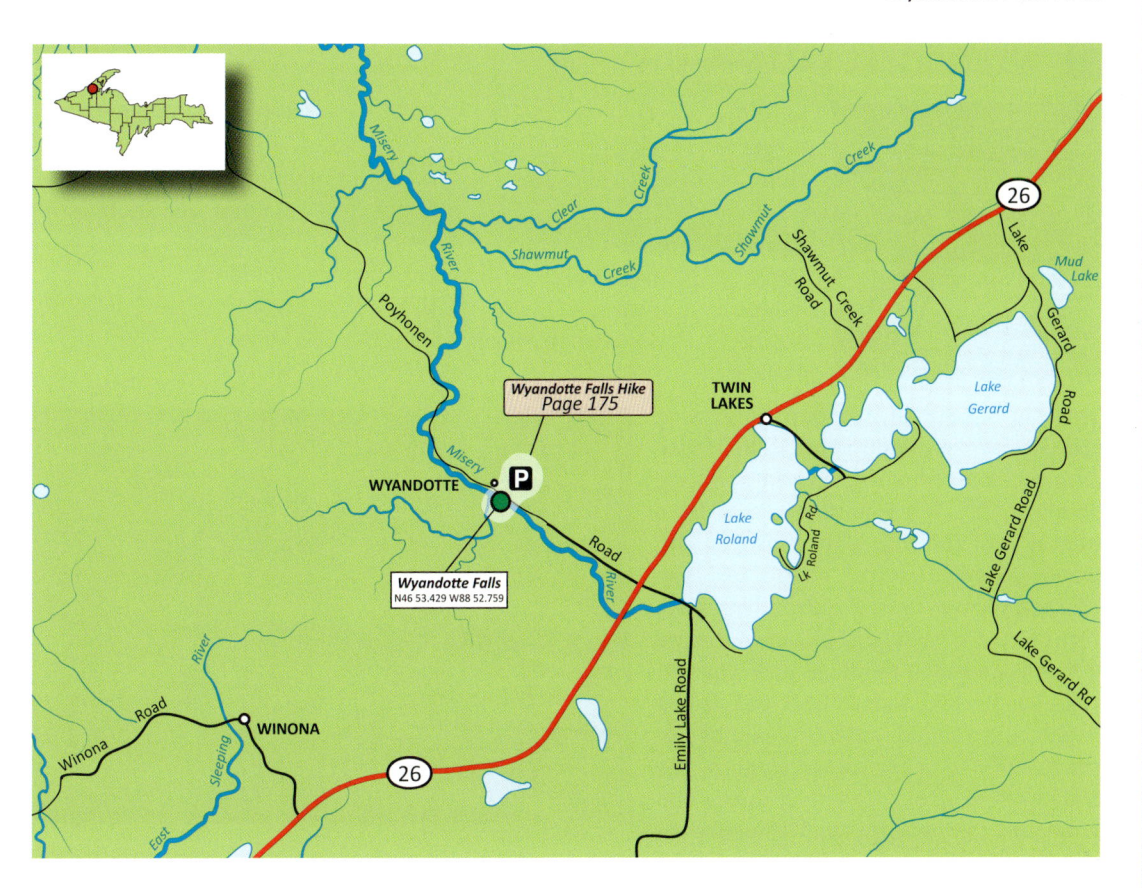

### Wyandotte Falls Hike

The falls are on the Misery River. It is thought that early traders living along the river suffered from starvation, giving it the name "Misery River". Lake Roland empties via Misery River, and during summer months when the lake level is low the river can dry up completely. During spring snow melt, the river can rage. So the waterfall has a wide range of looks over the course of a year.

Wyandotte Falls: Angled mossy bedrock slabs separate the upper river with its little pools from the rock strewn continuation of the river below the falls. Slippery clay is found along the side and base of the falls.

*Directions:* Take M-26 to Lake Roland. Turn west/northwest onto Poynonen Road, traveling past Wyandotte Hills Golf Course. The blacktop deteriorates into a dirt road just past the golf course. Several hundred yards later is a parking area and an old wooden sign "promoting" the falls. Park. Hike 160 yards through the forest on an obviously travelled footpath. The trail drops down several times as it gets close to the falls. Be careful. There is a lot of clay in this area, and the ground is extremely slippery when wet.

## WYANDOTTE FALLS (MISERY RIVER)

Private

| | | | |
|---|---|---|---|
| Must See: | 7 | GPS: | N46 53.429 W88 52.759 |
| Height: | 13 feet | | |
| Time: | 5-15 minutes | Hiking Information | |
| | | Path: | Unimproved Footpath |
| Driving Information | | Length: | 150 yards |
| Signs: | Wooden | Elev. Change: | Moderate |
| Road: | Dirt | GPS: | N/A |
| Access: | Somewhat Difficult | Danger: | Minor |
| 4WD: | Helpful | WP Boots: | Helpful |

This can be a great, wonderfully flowing river. Or it can dry up to a trickle. Make sure you come after a good rain or during spring melt. The waterfall is split by a narrow outcropping with most of the water pouring over the near side. The cascade plunges into a narrow crevasse, turns to the far side, rushes out of a mere 2 foot wide gap in the ridge wall where it cascades while it widens back out, falling 4 feet and running around a number of fractured bedrock chunks lying in the shallow spill pool. The river turns and continues to cascade down a number of small drops over the next 30 feet or so.

Follow the river upstream for 100 yards to see more small drops.

*Wildly different looks between these winter, summer, and autumn pictures!*

176

# CHAPTER 8
# IRON COUNTY

# Iron County Map

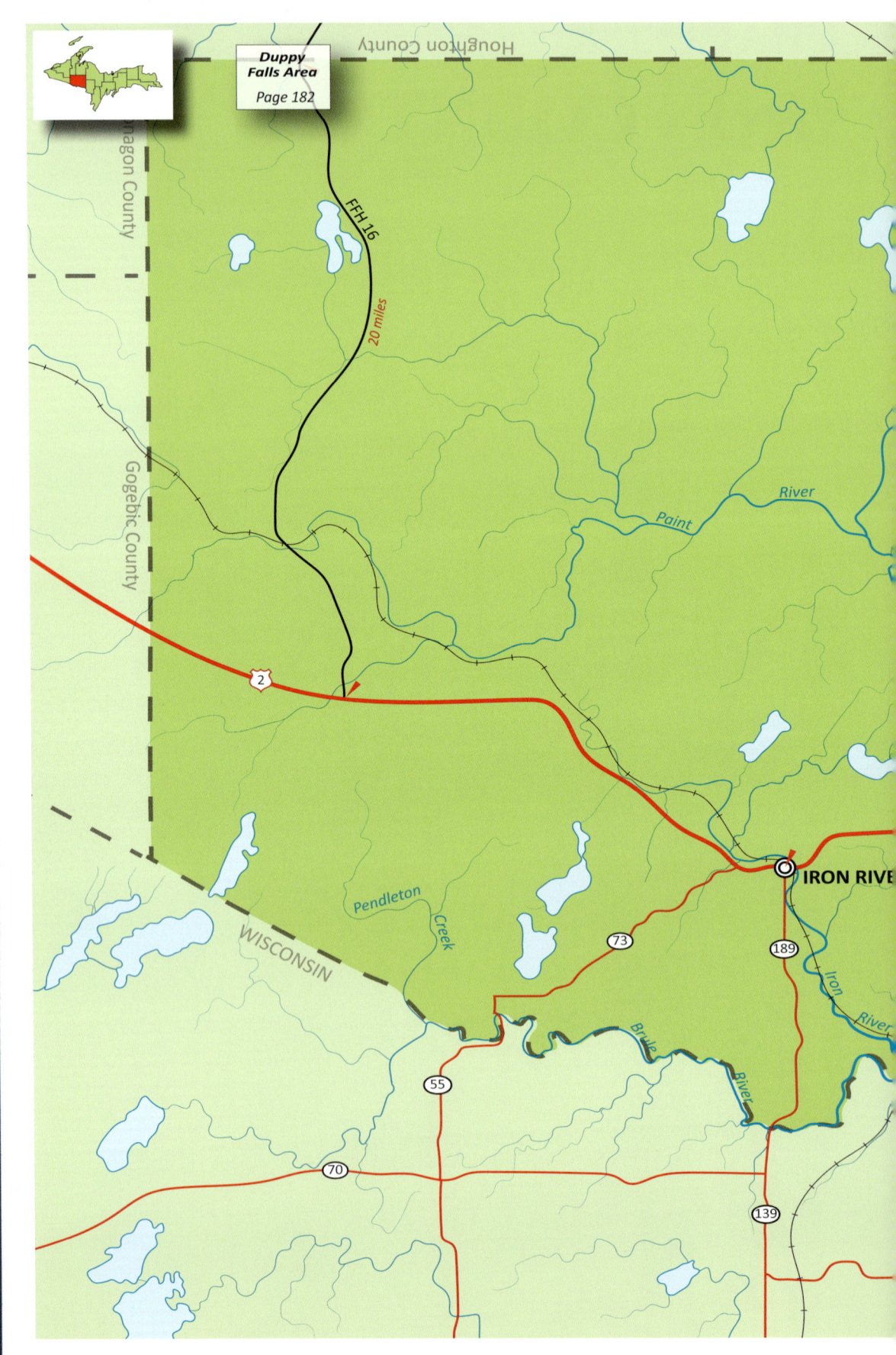

**Crystal Falls Area**

Page 180

**Horserace Rapids Area**

Page 186

IRON COUNTY

Crystal Falls Area

## Chicagon Falls Hike

***Chicagon Falls:*** Throughout a stand of cedar trees next to the waterfall are massive squarish boulders lying strewn about. Even the riverbed is full of boulders. This is one of the settings that seems to take on an unearthly quality. The trail to the falls deteriorates as you go. Park before getting into a portion of the trail that you are concerned about. Hike from there.

*Directions:* From Crystal Falls, take US-2 west about 4.5 miles to Long Lake Road. Turn right (north). Follow the winding road for 3.1 mile around to the north side of Long Lake. Turn right (northwest) on the unmarked 2-track. In .2 miles turn right (northeast). Stay to the right (northeast) in another .2 miles and drive .16 miles. Turn left (north) and drive .11 miles (this stretch is very bumpy, but most cars can probably make it). Turn left (northwest) for .16 miles (this is a VERY steep grade - a 4WD is required). Turn left (northwest) and drive to the end of the 2-track (a VERY high clearance vehicle is needed here - this is worse than the last segment). Park in the small parking area and hike 100 yards down the obvious footpath to the falls.

# CHICAGON FALLS (CHICAGON CREEK)

Private

| | | | |
|---|---|---|---|
| Must See: | 7 | GPS: | N46 08.042 W88 27.180 |
| Height: | 20 feet | | |
| Time: | 15-30 minutes | **Hiking Information** | |
| | | Path: | Footpath |
| **Driving Information** | | Length: | 100 yards |
| Signs: | Small Hand Painted | Elev. Change: | Moderate |
| Road: | 2-track | GPS: | Helpful |
| Access: | Difficult | Danger: | Moderate |
| 4WD: | Recommended | WP Boots: | Recommended |

A dilapidated footbridge may still cross the creek at the top of the falls, but don't count on it. Either cross at the base of the falls from rock to rock or wade across with a good pair of waterproof boots.

Large, chiselled blocks of bedrock run along both sides of the waterfall. The fractured rocks tilt down toward the creek below the falls. They resemble a peeled orange, with sections being pulled outwards, splaying open. Cedars grow in clusters among the fragments. These trees tend to fall into the creek, sometimes blocking the view of the waterfall.

*The steep 2-track - last portion of the drive*

# Duppy Falls Area

*The Parking Spot*

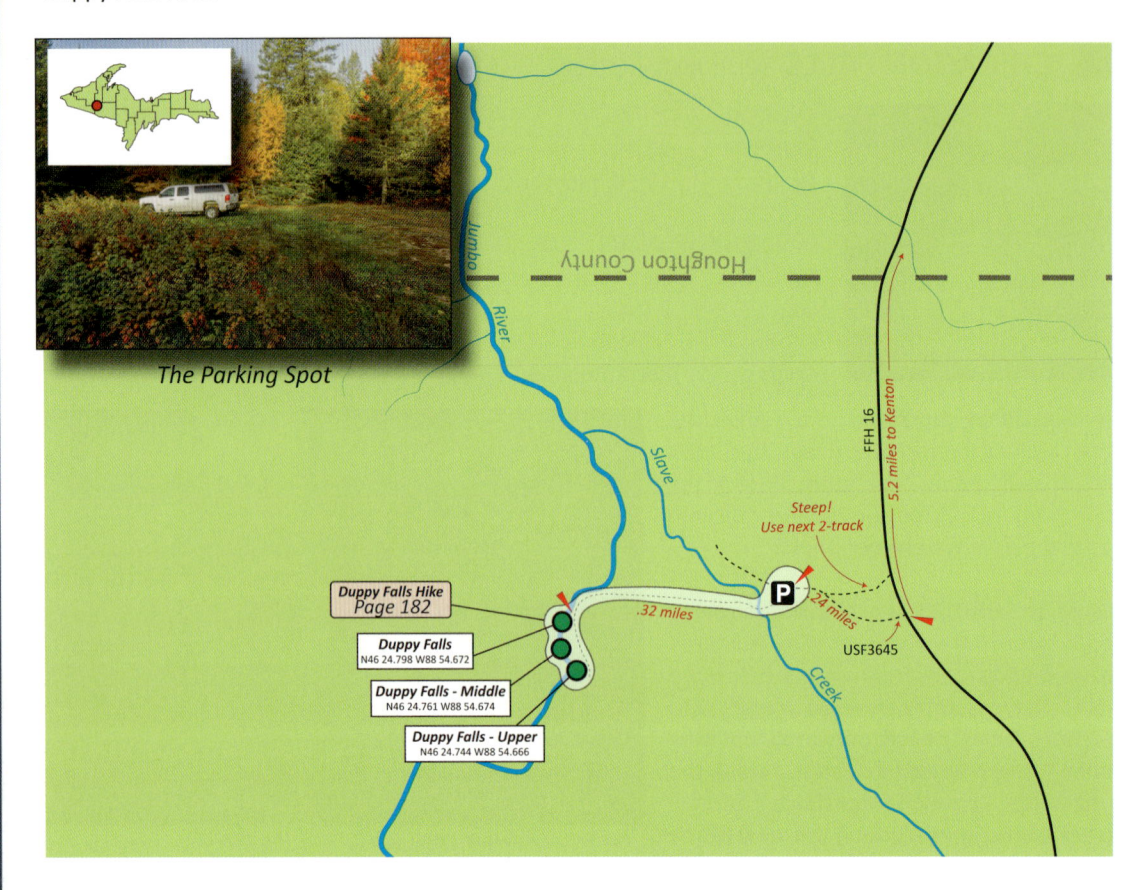

## Duppy Falls Hike

**Duppy Falls:** The main cascade is split in half. Most of the water runs to the left side. A secondary drop is just below the spill pool.

**Duppy Falls - Middle:** The middle waterfall is a triple cascade that pours over black rocks. The first two drops are lined up while the final fall is around a small bend in the river.

**Duppy Falls - Upper:** The last of the Duppy Falls along the hike is the furthest up river. An easily identifiable trail leads all the way from the parking area to here and beyond, although it does diminish somewhat after the first drop.

*Directions:* Turn south onto FFH 16 at the light in Kenton off of M-28. In 5.3 miles, just after entering Iron County, turn right (west) onto USF 3645 at N46 24.813 W88 54.116 (2-track). Drive .22 miles to a clearing at N46 24.863 W88 54.380 (on the left at the base of a steep part of the 2-track just before it turns hard to the right and enters the forest). Park. A well traveled footpath heads into the trees left of the 2-track. Follow it to a small creek (Slave Creek). Cross on the small wooden foot bridge. The trail heads westerly until it joins up with Jumbo River. The trail then turns to the southwest and continues along the east side of Jumbo River to the falls. This stretch of the hike is relatively flat. But after approaching Duppy Falls #1 from below the waterfall, the trail climbs up the rocky hillside (this section can be quite slippery and more difficult to navigate) to the upper two waterfalls.

## DUPPY FALLS (JUMBO RIVER)

Private

| | | | |
|---|---|---|---|
| Must See: | 8 | GPS: | N46 24.798 W88 54.672 |
| Height: | 12 feet | | |
| Time: | 30-45 minutes | **Hiking Information** | |
| | | Path: | Footpath |
| **Driving Information** | | Length: | .32 miles |
| Signs: | None | Elev. Change: | Slight |
| Road: | 2-track | GPS: | Helpful |
| Access: | Somewhat Difficult | Danger: | Moderate |
| 4WD: | Helpful | WP Boots: | Recommended |

I had the hardest time finding these three waterfalls for some reason. I tried in vain four times over three years. Twice I dragged my kids through miles of forest, over rolling and sometimes steep hillsides, breaking through dead pine branches and thick undergrowth. We would either end up in beaver flooded sections of Slave Creek, fighting through chest high wild flowers covered with bumble bees, or come in on a wrong 2-track, only to be heading to the wrong GPS coordinates. I finally got good information from the owner of Hoppy's Bar in Kenton. I'm glad I didn't give up! These are great waterfalls! I'm sure that you'll love them as well.

*The bridge over Slave Creek*

## DUPPY FALLS - MIDDLE (JUMBO RIVER)       Private

| | | | |
|---|---|---|---|
| Must See: | 7 | GPS: | N46 24.761 W88 54.674 |
| Height: | 14 feet | | |
| Time: | 40-60 minutes | **Hiking Information** | |
| | | Path: | Footpath |
| **Driving Information** | | Length: | .36 miles |
| Signs: | None | Elev. Change: | Moderate |
| Road: | 2-track | GPS: | Helpful |
| Access: | Somewhat Difficult | Danger: | Moderate |
| 4WD: | Helpful | WP Boots: | Recommended |

The trail between Duppy Falls and here climbs up some steep rocks. These can be quite slippery when wet or icy. Be careful!

Halfway up the "Duppy Series" is this lovely triple drop. It starts with a 5 foot plunge into a heavily shaded shallow pool. Moss covered gnarled roots cling to the rock face next to this drop. Twenty feet later the river drops again, this time sliding down another 5 feet into a slightly deeper pool, churning before turning and cascading down a final 4 feet.

*It can be very beautiful with snow! But the rocky trail can be treacherous in the winter. Be careful!*

## DUPPY FALLS - UPPER (JUMBO RIVER)

Private

| Must See: | 7 | GPS: | N46 24.744 W88 54.666 |
|---|---|---|---|
| Height: | 8 feet | | |
| Time: | 45-60 minutes | | |

**Hiking Information**
- Path: Footpath
- Length: .40 miles
- Elev. Change: Moderate
- GPS: Helpful
- Danger: Moderate
- WP Boots: Recommended

**Driving Information**
- Signs: None
- Road: 2-track
- Access: Somewhat Difficult
- 4WD: Helpful

Climb up to the top of the Middle Falls. The viewing area below the Upper Falls will quickly come into sight.

Slightly terraced black slate makes up the face of this cascading/sliding waterfall. In high water, the river runs from side to side. At the base of the waterfall, the river checks down to just 4 feet. It then enters a large, circular pool. The exit is like the entrance, only 4 feet wide. Cedars and yellow birch surround the waterfall and pool. Golden leaves are found in abundance in the surrounding forest during October hikes.

There is a small slate quarry just 20 feet from the waterfall. More areas of rock removal from days gone by can be seen further downstream along the trail.

Horserace Rapids Area

*The Rocky Overlook*

### Horserace Rapids Hike

**Horserace Rapids:** Although not an official waterfall, this aggressive set of rapids is locally quite popular, with signage and a designated park assigned to it.

*Directions:* Head south from Crystal Falls on US-2 for about 6 miles. Turn left (east) at the signs for "Horserace Rapids" and the airport. The road is gravel, but should be navigable by most vehicles. Stay to the right at every intersection. After 3.6 miles the road ends at the parking lot. Hike .25 miles to the rocky overlook of the rapids.

### HORSERACE RAPIDS (PAINT RIVER)                Private

| | | | |
|---|---|---|---|
| Must See: | 5 | GPS: | N45 59.414 W88 16.152 |
| Height: | 10 feet | | |
| Time: | 15-30 minutes | Hiking Information | |
| | | Path: | Improved Footpath |
| Driving Information | | Length: | .25 miles |
| Signs: | Metal Road Sign | Elev. Change: | Moderate |
| Road: | Gravel | GPS: | Helpful |
| Access: | Somewhat Easy | Danger: | Moderate |
| 4WD: | N/A | WP Boots: | N/A |

The river runs through a canyon with a 40 foot high rock wall on the far side. A short trail heading downhill from a parking lot with a pit toilet ends at an outcropping of jumbled basalt rocks overlooking the rapids. Smaller ripples occur down river from the viewing area, but the main feature is perfectly situated upstream. On the far side of the river a massive face of vertical, flat basalt shows off its profile. Pine trees grow straight and tall from thin soil coverings. The near side isn't so rugged, but it still has numerous rock outcroppings and boulders strewn about.

186

# CHAPTER 9
# KEWEENAW COUNTY

# Keweenaw County Map

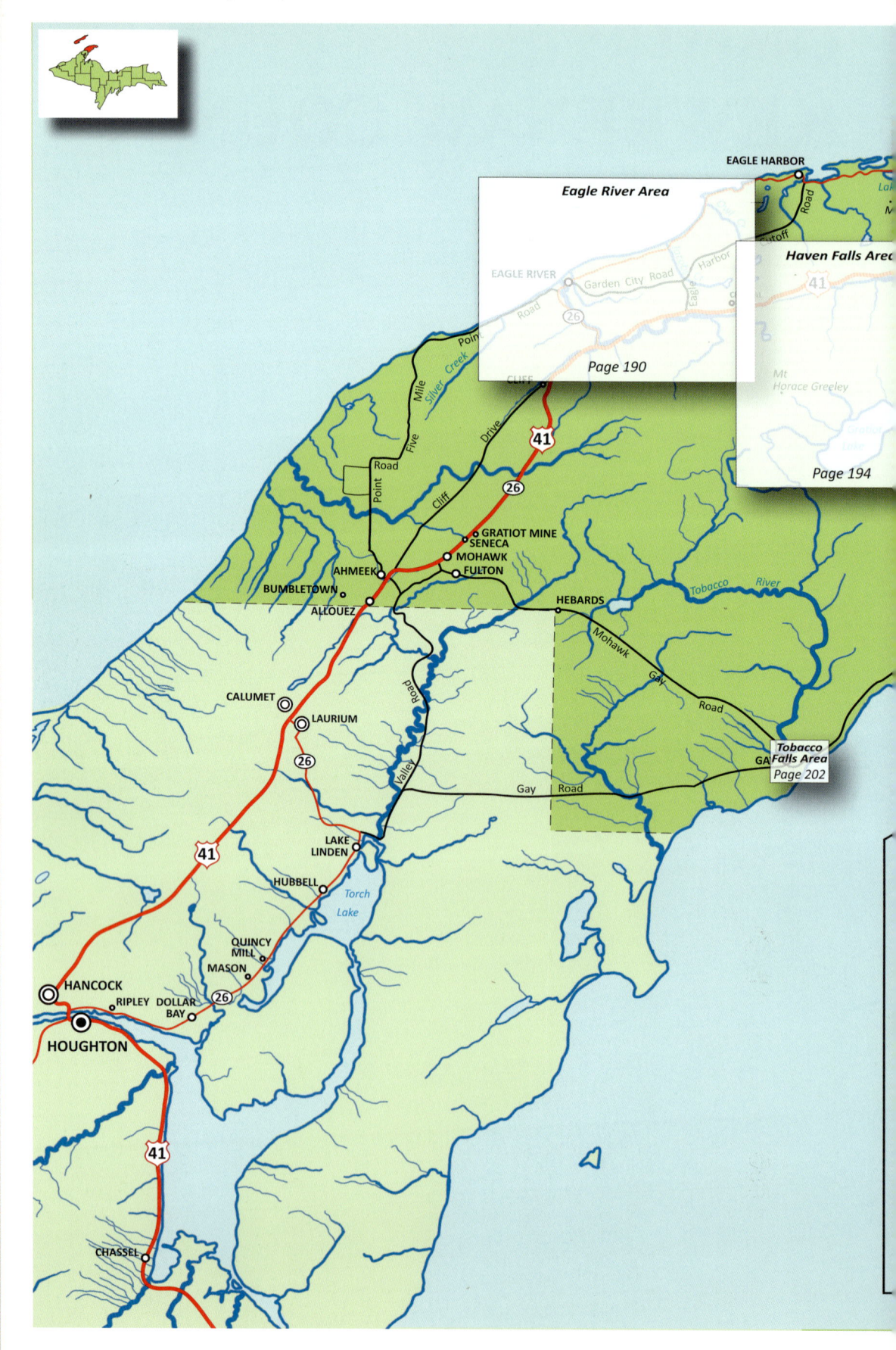

KEWEENAW COUNTY

Eagle River Area

## Eagle River Falls Hike

**Eagle River Falls:** The falls are extremely easy to find as they can be seen upon entering Eagle River on M-26. The original bridge that was built in 1915 is now a pedestrian bridge from which to view the falls. An old dam that spans the top of the falls was built to power the Lake Superior Safety Fuse Factory that was established in 1862. The plant that made safety fuses used in the mining industry burned to the ground in 1957. The bulging dam built 150 years ago diverts the river to the right side of the riverbed until the river rises to levels typically associated with spring melt and runoff.

*Directions:* The falls are in "downtown" Eagle River and can be seen from M-26 while driving over the Eagle River. Park in the good sized parking area just east of the river. Walk along the pedestrian bridge for a perfect viewing opportunity.

## EAGLE RIVER FALLS (EAGLE RIVER)  Private

| | | | |
|---|---|---|---|
| Must See: | 8 | GPS: | N47 24.747 W88 17.783 |
| Height: | 60 feet | | |
| Time: | 5-15 minutes | Hiking Information | |
| | | Path: | N/A |
| Driving Information | | Length: | 100 feet |
| Signs: | None | Elev. Change: | Slight |
| Road: | Main | GPS: | N/A |
| Access: | Very Easy | Danger: | Slight |
| 4WD: | N/A | WP Boots: | N/A |

This waterfalls is the largest in the Keweenaw in terms of width times height. When the river is running high with spring melt or after some intense rains the waterfall is amazing!

# Eagle River Area

## Fenners Falls Hike

The most dangerous of the hikes on the Eagle River ends at an amazing double drop waterfall. If you can manage the steep climb down into the gorge you will enjoy the sight that awaits you!

*Directions:* Drive south on M-26 from Eagle River Falls for .8 miles. Park safely off of the road (there is a narrow shoulder in this area - find an acceptable place to park). The trailhead to the falls is across from a driveway at N47 24.195 W88 17.629. A short, white post marks the beginning of the faint trail. Hike 80 yards to the top of the gorge. Follow the top of the gorge downstream for about 50 yards. The top of the gorge narrows to a point. Follow the end of the point down, paralleling the river. When you feel it's safe, head down the still steep bank to the river. It's not easy. Make sure you are up to the task. Follow the river back upstream to the falls. Waterproof boots are highly recommended, as you may need to walk partly in the river on the way back to the waterfall.

## FENNERS FALLS (EAGLE RIVER)                           Private

| | | | |
|---|---|---|---|
| Must See: | 8 | GPS: | N47 24.244 W88 17.617 |
| Height: | 25 feet | | |
| Time: | 45-90 minutes | Hiking Information | |
| | | Path: | Faint |
| Driving Information | | Length: | 150 yards |
| Signs: | None | Elev. Change: | Major |
| Road: | Main | GPS: | Helpful |
| Access: | Somewhat Difficult | Danger: | Elevated |
| 4WD: | N/A | WP Boots: | Recommended |

The Eagle River narrows to 10 feet wide and passes through a perfectly square, short canyon. A rope dangles from a cedar bough above, proof of playful activity in the pool above the falls. The river bursts over the edges of the pool, cascading down to another pool below. Another rope is suspended above this deep pool. From the upper canyon spill pool the river cascades down a jagged mass of slippery black rock. An elongated pool waits at the bottom. From the center of the pool, the river quietly exits, swirling around the rounded rocks that are so familiar in this river.

*The river is choked with rocks below the falls*

*The look down from the top of the canyon*

Eagle River Area

### Jacobs Falls Hike

***Jacobs Falls:*** This popular roadside waterfall attracts many tourists driving along the twisting road between Eagle River and Copper Harbor. A steep, unimproved footpath climbs quickly up the hillside following the creek upstream. Above Jacobs Falls are several more waterfalls. My favorite is a delightful cascade that spills into a 6 foot deep pool. It is tucked into a steep walled portion of the ravine that Jacobs Creek has cut into the fast descending hillside. In less than a mile, Jacobs Creek descends 400 feet!

*Directions:* Head northeast out of Eagle River (toward Copper Harbor) on M-26. In 3 miles a small parking area is on the right nearly at the base of the falls.

## ■ JACOBS FALLS (JACOBS CREEK)   Private

| | | | |
|---|---|---|---|
| Must See: | 7 | GPS: | N47 25.669 W88 14.256 |
| Height: | 20 feet | | |
| Time: | 5-10 minutes | Hiking Information | |
| | | Path: | N/A |
| Driving Information | | Length: | N/A |
| Signs: | Roadside | Elev. Change: | N/A |
| Road: | Main | GPS: | N/A |
| Access: | Very Easy | Danger: | N/A |
| 4WD: | N/A | WP Boots: | N/A |

The waterfall presents itself nicely as it slides down toward the road along the steep rocky waterway. The creek then passes beneath M-26 on its way to Lake Superior.

**The Jampot**, a gift store just 100 yards up the road from Jacobs Falls, is well known for their sweet treats and preserves. It's run by the monks from the nearby monastery. For more information, check out www.societystjohn.com.

192

Eagle River Area

## Ten Foot Falls Hike

**Ten Foot Falls:** As long as the river is calm this is a great place to take the family for a cool dip in the river and a picnic beneath the trees. However, when the river is raging, it is a force to be reckoned with.

*Directions:* Head north on M-26 off of US-41 in Phoenix. In .8 miles there is a dirt parking area on the right. Park and walk down the short trail to the falls.

## TEN FOOT FALLS (EAGLE RIVER)   Private

| | | | |
|---|---|---|---|
| Must See: | 6 | GPS: | N47 23.855 W88 17.073 |
| Height: | 8 feet | | |
| Time: | 10-30 minutes | Hiking Information | |
| | | Path: | Unimproved Footpath |
| Driving Information | | Length: | 25 yards |
| Signs: | None | Elev. Change: | Minor |
| Road: | Main | GPS: | N/A |
| Access: | Easy | Danger: | Slight |
| 4WD: | N/A | WP Boots: | N/A |

The original basalt bedrock has eroded and fractured over the years into what looks like an artistic assortment of closely placed boulders over which the river cascades to a popular swimming hole just yards off of M-26.

The relatively flat and open space at the top of the falls can be seen in the shot to the right.

*This is the first of the waterfalls on the Eagle River between US-41 and the city of Eagle River. The last waterfall on the river is the much better known Eagle River Falls.*

KEWEENAW COUNTY

Ten Foot Falls

193

Haven Falls Area

## Haven Falls Hike

***Haven Falls:*** Haven Falls is another of the "view from the vehicle" waterfalls. Easy to drive to, easy to find, and easy to view; this is a great place to take the family.

***Directions:*** From US-41, turn south onto Lac La Belle Road. 4.3 miles later, turn right (southwest) at the sharp bend just beyond where Bete Grise Road veers off to the left. In .47 miles turn right (north) into the roadside park. The waterfall will be visible from the road.

## HAVEN FALLS (HAVEN CREEK)                                          Private

| | | | |
|---|---|---|---|
| Must See: | 6 | GPS: | N47 22.911 W88 01.720 |
| Height: | 20 feet | | |
| Time: | 5-15 minutes | Hiking Information | |
| | | Path: | N/A |
| Driving Information | | Length: | N/A |
| Signs: | Clearly Marked | Elev. Change: | N/A |
| Road: | Main | GPS: | N/A |
| Access: | Very Easy | Danger: | N/A |
| 4WD: | N/A | WP Boots: | N/A |

This is a great family park with pit toilets, picnic tables and charcoal grills. The falls can be viewed from the vehicle, making this a great spot to check out for those wanting an easily accessed waterfall. Climb to the top of the falls up the clay bank for a small drop at the top that can't be seen from below. The bedrock tilts at the top of the falls between highly eroded banks, then suddenly tips to nearly vertical, ending in a very small spill pool. The creek then runs down another small stretch of rock before it meanders through Haven Park, passes beneath the road and ends up flowing into Lac La Belle.

## Fanny Hooe Falls Hike

Fanny Hooe Creek runs the short distance from Lake Fanny Hooe into Lake Superior, passing through Fort Wilkins State Park, under US-41, alongside the parking area for viewing Copper Harbor Lighthouse from across the bay, and into Lake Superior. It's in this short stretch that Fanny Hooe Falls occurs.

*Directions:* Follow US-41 through Copper Harbor to the east. Signage for Fort Wilkins State Park will be seen on the right. Immediately after crossing the bridge over Fanny Hooe Creek, turn left (north) into the parking lot for viewing the lighthouse. The waterfall is easily seen just yards into the woods next to the parking area.

## FANNY HOOE FALLS (FANNY HOOE CREEK)    Private

| | | | |
|---|---|---|---|
| Must See: | 5 | GPS: | N47 28.046 W87 51.986 |
| Height: | 4 feet | | |
| Time: | 5-10 minutes | **Hiking Information** | |
| | | Path: | N/A |
| **Driving Information** | | Length: | 50 feet |
| Signs: | None | Elev. Change: | Slight |
| Road: | Main | GPS: | N/A |
| Access: | Very Easy | Danger: | Slight |
| 4WD: | N/A | WP Boots: | N/A |

The creek cascades over cobbled bedrock just 100 yards before entering Lake Superior. There is a short, but steep bank on either side of the creek.

Manganese Falls Area

### Manganese Falls Hike

***Manganese Falls:*** This unique waterfall drops a long ways over several precipices at various angles into a narrow gorge. It is difficult to view due to the extremely narrow and steep gorge.

*Directions:* Turn south off of US-41 onto Manganese Road. In .7 miles, there will be a sign on the left for the falls. Park on the right, cross the road and follow the short path to the falls overlook.

## MANGANESE FALLS (MANGANESE CREEK)                    Private

| | | | |
|---|---|---|---|
| Must See: | 6 | GPS: | N47 27.699 W87 52.722 |
| Height: | 30 feet | | |
| Time: | 5-30 minutes | Hiking Information | |
| | | Path: | Footpath/None |
| Driving Information | | Length: | 50 feet/100 yards |
| Signs: | Wooden | Elev. Change: | Slight/Moderate |
| Road: | Secondary | GPS: | N/A |
| Access: | Somewhat easy | Danger: | Slight/Moderate |
| 4WD: | N/A | WP Boots: | None/Required |

The split hiking information is for "The Viewing Deck" and "Base of the Falls". To get to the base of the falls, drive back toward Copper Harbor from the falls. Immediately on the right (east) will be a dirt road. Follow it down a good sized hill. At the bottom is a bridge. Park here. Wade up the creek, over an old, short dam, and to the base of the falls. Even from here, there is not much to see. The way that the rock is split, much of the falling water is hidden from any one vantage point.

*Looking down at the top of the waterfall as the creek tumbles into the narrow gorge about 75 feet upstream from the viewing deck*

*I took this shot from the "official overlook"*

*This is down at the base of the winding drops*

KEWEENAW COUNTY

Manganese Falls

196

Montreal Falls Area

KEWEENAW COUNTY

### Montreal Falls Hike

Prepare for a wilderness walk. These falls are at the end of the Keweenaw Peninsula. There is nothing past here but water - until ending up in Canada! The trail through rugged forest is not well maintained. Fallen trees often block the trail, forcing short, alternate routes. The trail skirts the edge of Lake Superior, but not at beach level. The lake is sometimes 10-15 feet below the ground level and a couple of times the trail comes to the very edge of the drop-off. All of these facts contribute to the sense of adventure and ruggedness that this hike embodies. Don't come to these waterfalls if you are looking for a short trip. Allow 3 to 4 hours at least. There is a great picnic spot at the lower falls, as the trail widens out at the beach, just as the waterfall also meets Lake Superior.

*Directions:* In Bete Grise, there will be a sign for the Smith Fishery. Please note that this is a private road. Be respectful. Follow that dirt road for the next 5 miles, keeping to the right. Just after the Smith Fisheries, the road ends. There are spaces for a dozen or so vehicles to park here. A 2-track continues to the east paralleling Lake Superior. Hike down the 2-track. After about 1/2 mile, the 2-track ends, and a footpath enters the forest, still running parallel with Lake Superior. There are times that the path becomes narrow. Keep Lake Superior to the right and don't wander too far inland. After a total of 1.16 miles of hiking, the lower falls come into view. Follow the river upstream for another .44 miles to see the middle falls. In another .34 miles are the upper falls. The trail to the upper falls is faint and sometimes nonexistent. Once again, follow the river and don't wander far from it, in order to keep from getting lost.

Montreal Falls Area

## MONTREAL FALLS - LOWER (MONTREAL RIVER)    Private

| | | | |
|---|---|---|---|
| Must See: | 7 | GPS: | N47 23.556 W87 50.497 |
| Height: | 25 feet | | |
| Time: | 1.5-2 hours | Hiking Information | |
| | | Path: | Narrow footpath |
| Driving Information | | Length: | 1.16 miles |
| Signs: | None | Elev. Change: | Slight |
| Road: | Gravel Road | GPS: | Helpful |
| Access: | Difficult | Danger: | Moderate |
| 4WD: | Helpful | WP Boots: | Helpful |

The waterfall drops directly into Lake Superior alongside a small beach. This makes for a nice camping location or picnic area.

Rugged basalt forms the 40 foot wide riverbed. The river cascades down this rough blackened rock, forming various rivulets as the water level changes. A 25 foot long cascade that drops about 5 feet starts the waterfall about 50 yards above an 8 foot descent that is followed by 30 feet of relative calm. The river then narrows to 15 feet and rushes down another 5 feet before a final 2 foot cascade that falls directly into Lake Superior.

*Looking out over Lake Superior from the trail*

*The scene heading back from the waterfall*

*Thimbleberries line a portion of the trail*

*Looking down from the top of the waterfall*

Montreal Falls Area

## MONTREAL FALLS - MIDDLE (MONTREAL RIVER)

Private

| | | | |
|---|---|---|---|
| Must See: | 8 | GPS: | N47 23.739 W87 50.133 |
| Height: | 20 feet | | |
| Time: | 2-3 hours | Hiking Information | |
| | | Path: | Rough Path |
| Driving Information | | Length: | 1.6 miles |
| Signs: | None | Elev. Change: | Moderate |
| Road: | Gravel Road | GPS: | Helpful |
| Access: | Difficult | Danger: | Moderate |
| 4WD: | Helpful | WP Boots: | Helpful |

Follow the faint footpath upstream .44 miles from the Lower Falls. It wanders over, under, and around trees and undergrowth before ending up at this wonderful waterfall!

A 25 foot tall reddish-brown-black mass stands next to the waterfall on the near side. The river is dramatically narrower up here than it is downstream from the waterfall. At the top of the waterfall the river is 8 feet wide, narrowing at the base of the waterfall to just 3 feet, as the jagged basalt on the far side encroaches on the waterfall, pushing it back onto itself. A "V" shaped spill pool widens back out suddenly, filling a small cove lined with rough bedrock that's perfect for viewing the waterfall. The river turns and narrows again over a short rapids and then cascades down a 2 foot drop around a corner.

*My son, Andrew, sets up for a shot on a lovely overcast July evening*

KEWEENAW COUNTY

Montreal Falls - Middle

Montreal Falls Area

## MONTREAL FALLS - UPPER (MONTREAL RIVER)    Private

| | | | |
|---|---|---|---|
| Must See: | 7 | GPS: | N47 23.877 W87 50.183 |
| Height: | 13 feet | | |
| Time: | 2.5-4 hours | **Hiking Information** | |
| | | Path: | Rough Path/None |
| **Driving Information** | | Length: | 1.94 miles |
| Signs: | None | Elev. Change: | Elevated |
| Road: | Gravel Road | GPS: | Recommended |
| Access: | Difficult | Danger: | Elevated |
| 4WD: | Helpful | WP Boots: | Helpful |

The dwindling trail between the Middle and Upper Falls must be taken into account when deciding to hike out to this furthest of the Montreal River Falls. Also, the waterfall is difficult to observe from the base.

A large spill pool widens out immediately below the waterfall with dense undergrowth running down to the water's edge. If you can pick your way along the base of the large bluff that stands up next to the waterfall, you'll see a smaller bluff that forms the actual edge of the waterfall. It's steep, but there are some stair-like hand holds that can be used to get to the top and observe the waterfall from above. The river, placid before the waterfall, suddenly drops 1.5 feet just after it enters a steep, rocky ravine. The bluffs rise on both sides with the river squeezed in between. Fifty yards after the initial drop, a second 1.5 foot drop occurs where the river has been channeled down to just 2 feet across (in most river conditions). In another 25 yards the river exits the gorge with a frothy 10 foot descent, cascading down the crumbly conglomerate face in dramatic fashion.

*It's a tough bust through a ton of thick undergrowth to get to this vantage spot. But I love it!*

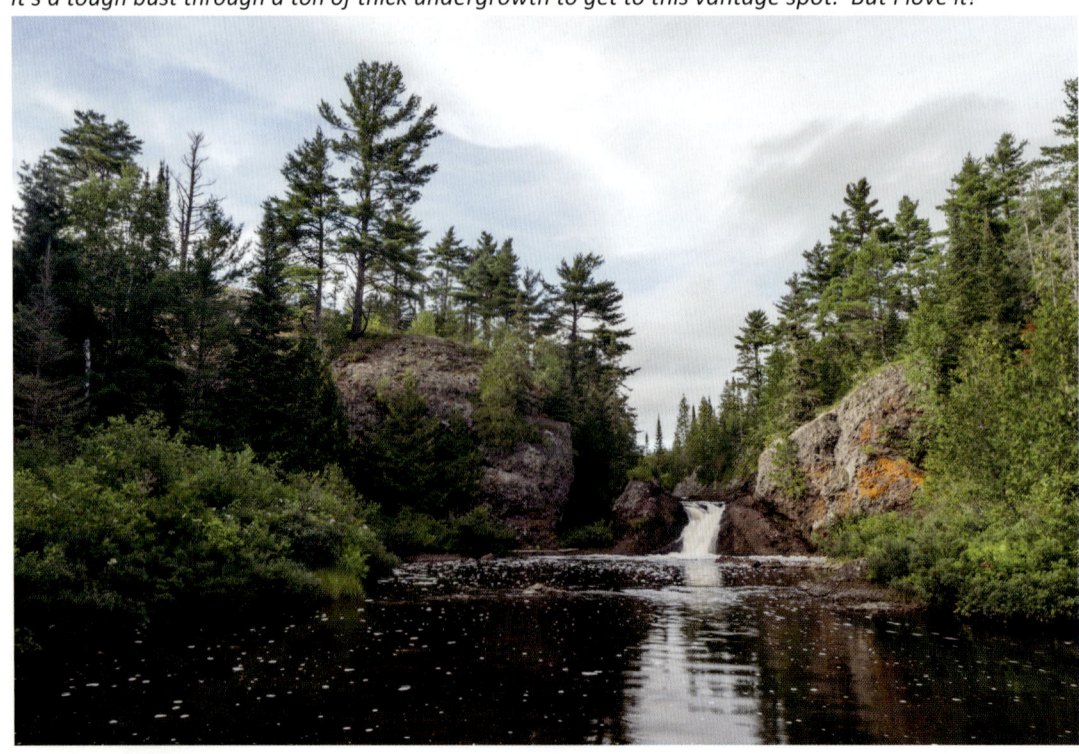

KEWEENAW COUNTY

Montreal Falls - Upper

200

Silver River Falls Area

### Silver River Falls Hike

**Silver River Falls:** A rough cascading drop flows just below the bridge. Continue downstream along an easy to follow footpath on the west side of the river to the lower drop. They both present themselves nicely, if not dramatically.

*Directions:* On M-26, 12.5 miles east of Eagle River and 9.5 miles west of Copper Harbor is an obvious pull-off by the Silver River Bridge. Park and hike downstream 100 feet from the bridge on a well travelled footpath to view Silver River Falls as the river emerges from beneath the road.

## SILVER RIVER FALLS (SILVER RIVER)    Private

| | | | |
|---|---|---|---|
| Must See: | 6 | GPS: | N47 27.798 W88 04.378 |
| Height: | 15 feet | | |
| Time: | 10-20 minutes | **Hiking Information** | |
| | | Path: | Footpath |
| **Driving Information** | | Length: | 100 feet |
| Signs: | Clearly Marked | Elev. Change: | Minor |
| Road: | Main | GPS: | N/A |
| Access: | Very Easy | Danger: | Slight |
| 4WD: | N/A | WP Boots: | N/A |

Climb down the west side of the river to view the falls. The riverbed and tilted bedrock walls bordering the river are composed of conglomerate. The bridge, which sits just above the main sloped drop is made of precisely cut stone. After the first drop of 7 feet, the river continues to descend down at a gentle angle over the next 30 yards. A variety of shrubs and evergreens blanket both sides of the river.

Tobacco Falls Area

### Tobacco Falls Hike

Water fills the riverbed from side to side. Undergrowth lines the sides of the river. Either wade up the normally shallow river or be prepared to contend with uneven terrain and flora between the lower and upper falls.

*Directions:* From Hancock, take M-26 to the east. Follow it to Lake Linden. Turn right (east) on 9th Street one block before M-26 turns to the left. Follow 9th Street for .6 miles. Turn left (northeast) onto Traprock Valley Road (S 641). In 1.4 miles turn right (east) onto Gay Road. It will take you into Gay in about 10.5 miles. Stay on Gay Road which runs along Lake Superior to the northeast. In .8 miles there is a small campground on the right (southeast) side of the road just before Tobacco River. Park in the day use area and hike along the river upstream. The lower waterfall is easily seen from the bridge and the upper drop is only about 75 yards up river from there.

## TOBACCO FALLS - LOWER (TOBACCO RIVER)  Private

| | | | |
|---|---|---|---|
| Must See: | 4 | GPS: | N47 13.886 W88 08.929 |
| Height: | 5 feet | | |
| Time: | 10-20 minutes | Hiking Information | |
| | | Path: | Well Worn Path |
| Driving Information | | Length: | 50 yards |
| Signs: | None | Elev. Change: | Slight |
| Road: | Secondary | GPS: | N/A |
| Access: | Easy | Danger: | Slight |
| 4WD: | N/A | WP Boots: | Helpful |

Several small drops cascade the river over red rock slabs. A wavy ledge of black and red sandstone creates a vertical drop of 1 foot, then a second, larger cascading drop of 4 feet just upstream from the bridge.

# TOBACCO FALLS - UPPER (TOBACCO RIVER)  Private

| | | | |
|---|---|---|---|
| Must See: | 5 | GPS: | N47 13.916 W88 08.961 |
| Height: | 3 feet | | |
| Time: | 15-30 minutes | **Hiking Information** | |
| | | Path: | Well Worn Path |
| **Driving Information** | | Length: | 150 yards |
| Signs: | None | Elev. Change: | Slight |
| Road: | Secondary | GPS: | N/A |
| Access: | Easy | Danger: | Slight |
| 4WD: | N/A | WP Boots: | Helpful |

Hike up alongside the river for about 75 yards.

The river gathers itself to the center of the bed and then falls over a horseshoe shaped stair stepping cascade just 200 feet up river from the lower falls.

203

# KEWEENAW COUNTY

# CHAPTER 10
# MARQUETTE COUNTY

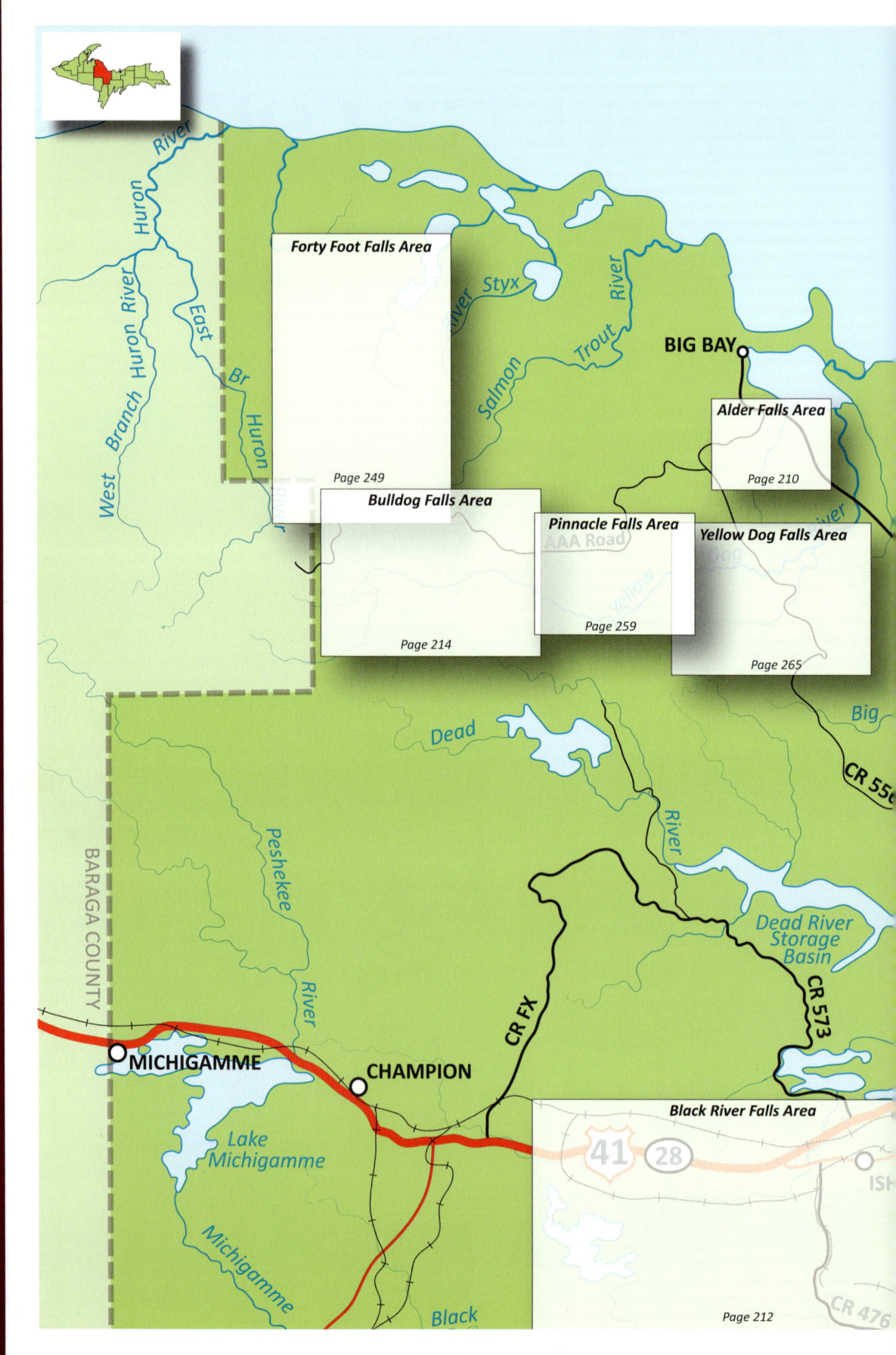

# Marquette County (North)

- Forty Foot Falls Area — Page 249
- Alder Falls Area — Page 210
- Bulldog Falls Area — Page 214
- Pinnacle Falls Area — Page 259
- Yellow Dog Falls Area — Page 265
- Black River Falls Area — Page 212

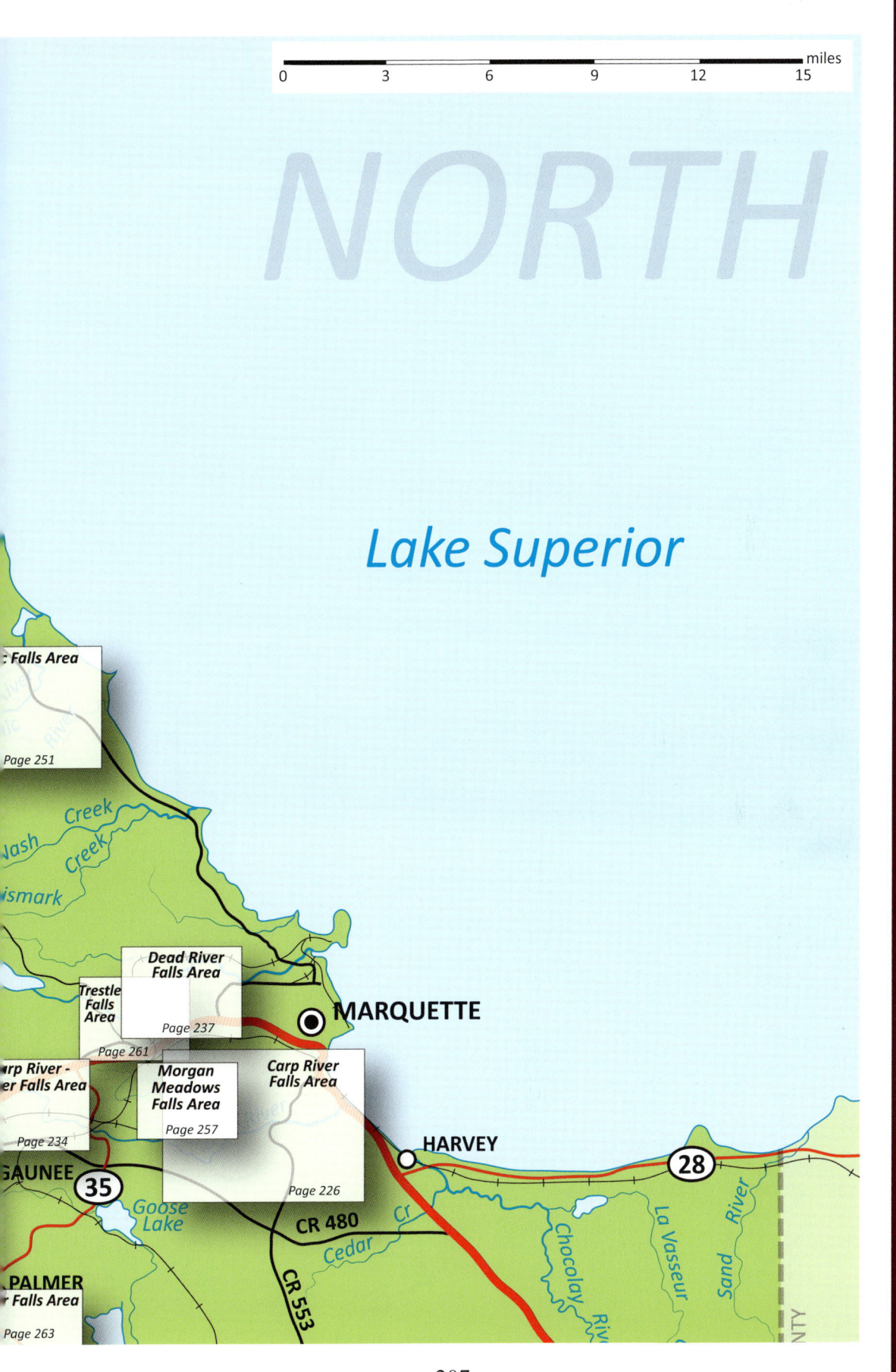

# MARQUETTE COUNTY

## NORTH

**Lake Superior**

- Falls Area — Page 251
- Dead River Falls Area — Page 237
- Trestle Falls Area — Page 261
- Carp River - ... Falls Area — Page 234
- Morgan Meadows Falls Area — Page 257
- Carp River Falls Area — Page 226
- PALMER Falls Area — Page 263

MARQUETTE

HARVEY

ISHPEMING/NEGAUNEE area: M-35, Goose Lake, CR 480, CR 553, Cedar Cr, Chocolay River, La Vasseur, Sand River, US-28

# Marquette County (South)

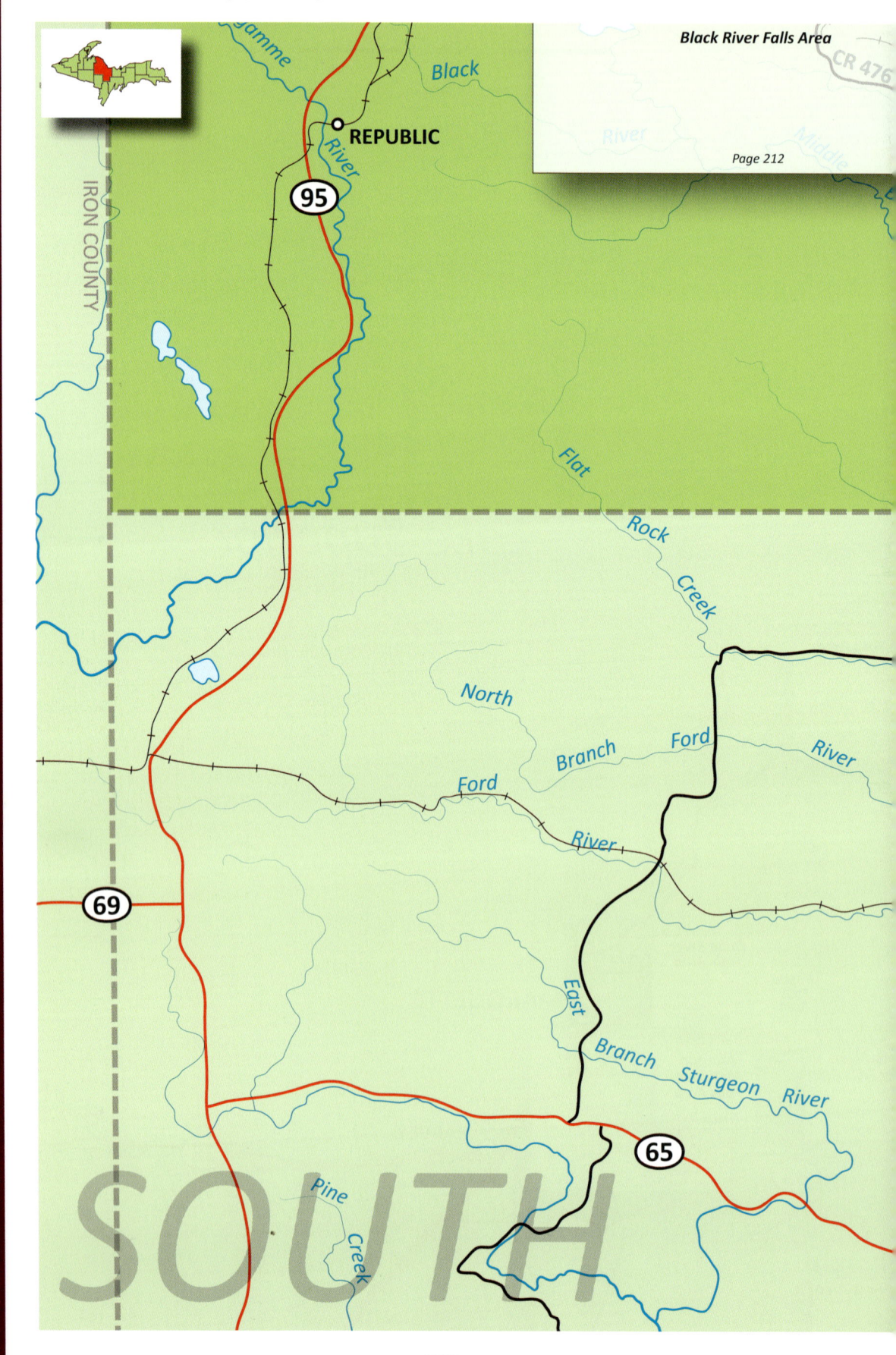

er Falls Area
Page 263
CR 553
CR 565
East Branch
Escanaba
River
Gwinn Area
Page 255
94
94
41
River
Creek
Sand
ALGER COUNTY
35
West Branch
Little West Branch
Escanaba
River
Ford
River
Hunters
Brook
DELTA COUNTY
Tacoosh
River
Days
River
MENOMINEE COUNTY
0
3
6
9
12
15
miles

Alder Falls Area

## Alder Falls Hike

Alder Falls should be on the list of all waterfall enthusiasts. Just southeast of the quaint little town of Big Bay, Alder Falls is somewhat difficult to find. These waterfalls are on private property. However, a sign at the parking area implies that visitors are welcome but must not leave traces of having been there. As always, access to waterfalls can change over time. Obey the wishes of land owners and be considerate.

*Directions:* Drive on CR 550 from Marquette toward Big Bay. Approximately 2.5 miles before entering Big Bay, Alder Creek Truck Trail is on the left (west). This is the last road before crossing Alder Creek. The road is a very sandy 2-track. (A 4WD vehicle is helpful, but not normally required.) Follow the road for .7 miles to the parking area. There is room for a couple of vehicles on either side of the trail. Park. Hike down the nice footpath that ends with a somewhat precarious hillside approaching the river. The falls are just upstream from where the trail deposits you on the riverbank and can be viewed from both sides of the river, if you dare to cross on the rocks and fallen trees that present themselves for the more adventurous among us!

# ALDER FALLS (ALDER CREEK)                                    Private

| | | | |
|---|---|---|---|
| Must See: | 8 | GPS: | N46 46.913 W87 42.443 |
| Height: | 20 feet | | |
| Time: | 15-30 minutes | Hiking Information | |
| | | Path: | Unimproved footpath |
| Driving Information | | Length: | .13 miles |
| Signs: | None | Elev. Change: | Moderate |
| Road: | Sandy 2-track | GPS: | Helpful |
| Access: | Somewhat difficult | Danger: | Moderate |
| 4WD: | Helpful | WP Boots: | Helpful |

A 3 foot wide channel at the top of the falls widens out to a veil about 15 feet wide as it slides over the bedrock. Black rocks backdrop the 20 foot falls that end in the shallow 30 foot wide river that is strewn with boulders and tree trunks. In the U.P. it is rare to meet fellow waterfall adventurers at all but the most popular waterfalls. So it was surprising to run across Douglas Feltman here as he was also photographing the falls. Check out his videos on the internet at https://vimeo.com/feltphoto1.

*The steep side of the waterfall can be a little treacherous to climb*

*Beautiful wildflowers can be seen along the rocky base of the waterfall in late spring*

**MARQUETTE COUNTY**

*Alder Falls*

Black River Falls Area

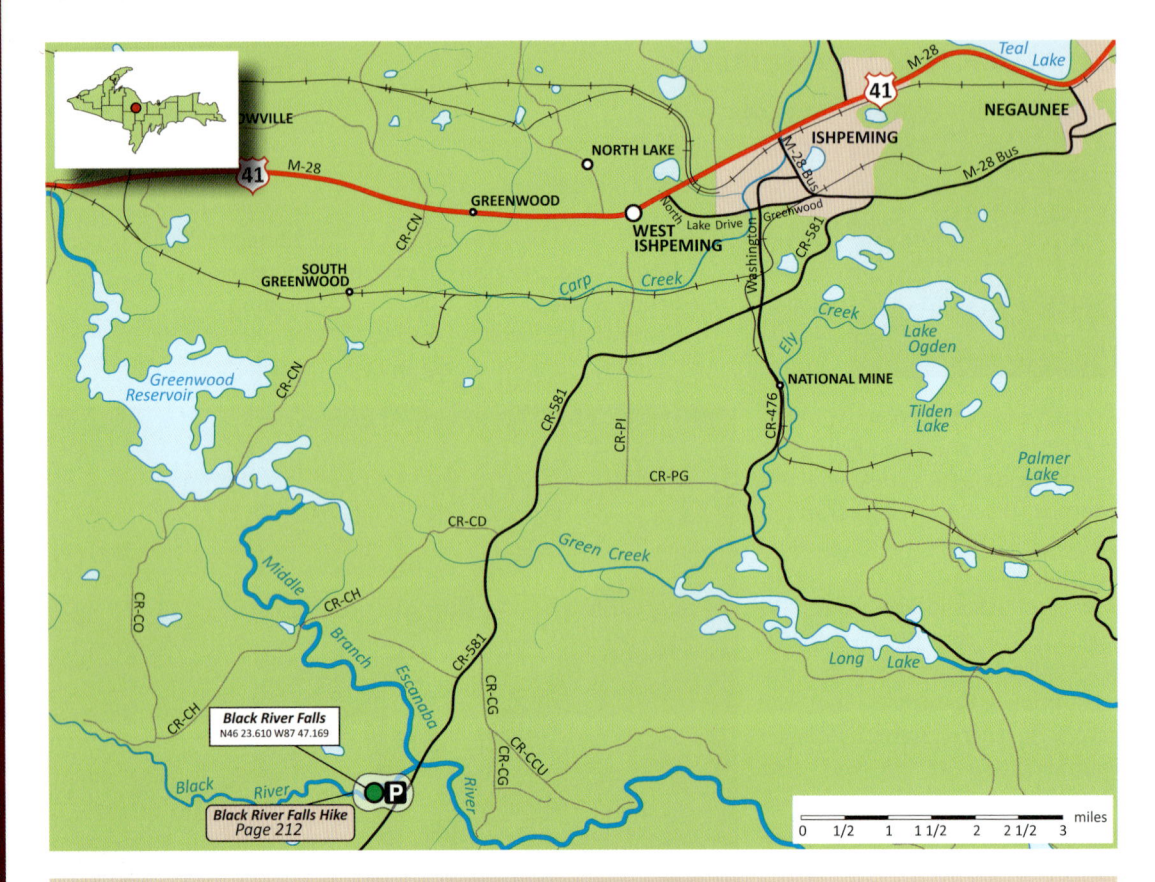

## Black River Falls Hike

***Black River Falls:*** The Black River runs through a narrow, shallow canyon; vertical walls rising on either side of the raging river. The trail from the parking area leads to the top of the cliff on the south side of the river. There is an old wooden footbridge that crosses the river to get down to the river level below the falls.

*Directions:* Off of US-41 in Ishpeming, turn southeast onto the western end of the Business M-28 Loop which heads easterly through downtown Ishpeming. In 1 mile after turning onto the Business Loop, turn right (south) onto CR 581 (South Pine Street). In about 9.9 miles turn right (west) onto an unimproved dirt road (N46 23.264 W87 46.784). Drive .6 miles to N46 23.134 W87 47.508. Turn right (north) and drive .2 miles. Turn right (northeast) @ N46 23.321 W87 47.653 and drive for .4 miles to a circular parking area on the left (north). Park @ N46 23.536 W87 47.218. Hike 200 yards down a well-worn footpath to the falls.

# BLACK RIVER FALLS (BLACK RIVER)

Private

|  |  |  |  |
|---|---|---|---|
| Must See: | 7 | GPS: | N46 23.610 W87 47.169 |
| Height: | 20 feet | | |
| Time: | 15-30 minutes | Hiking Information | |
| | | Path: | Unimproved footpath |
| Driving Information | | Length: | 200 yards |
| Signs: | Small - well marked | Elev. Change: | Moderate |
| Road: | Unimproved dirt | GPS: | N/A |
| Access: | Somewhat difficult | Danger: | Slight |
| 4WD: | Helpful | WP Boots: | Helpful |

This is a popular picnic and camping area. There is evidence of campfires between the trailhead and the rocky knoll overlooking the falls. White bubbles churned up from the falls sit in vivid contrast to the black waters of the river. Wearing waterproof boots allows for some wading in the river to find new vantage points for viewing the waterfall.

*Looking through the trees at the drop from the cliff edge.*

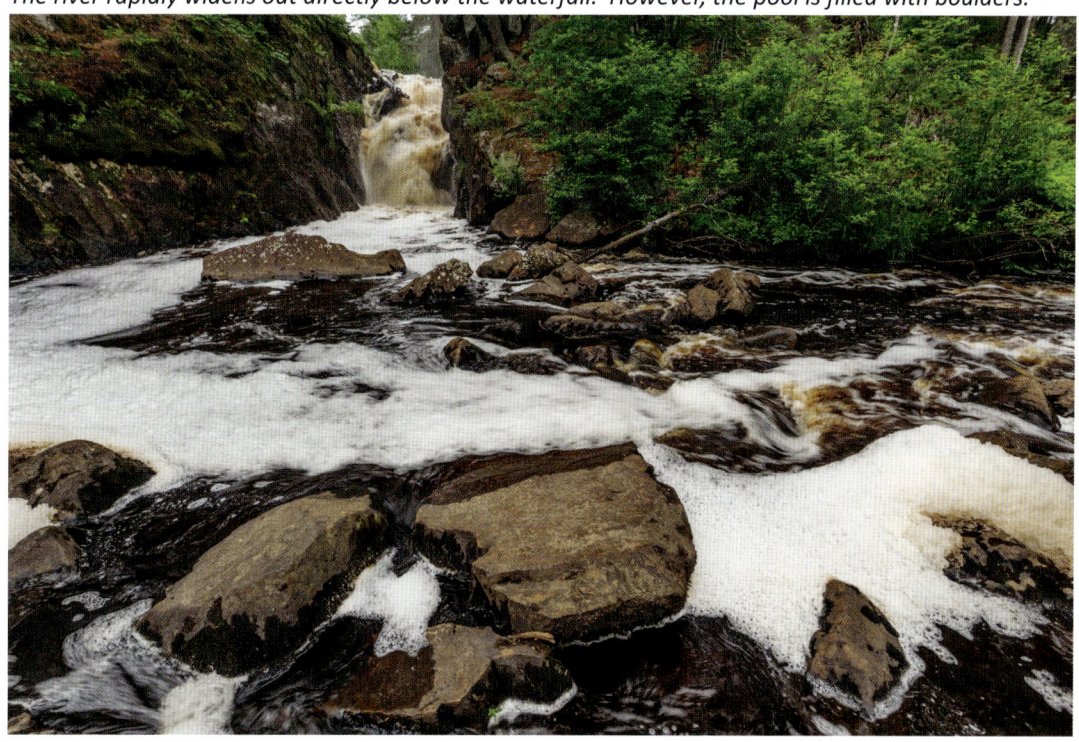

*The river rapidly widens out directly below the waterfall. However, the pool is filled with boulders.*

MARQUETTE COUNTY

Black River Falls Area

Black River Falls

213

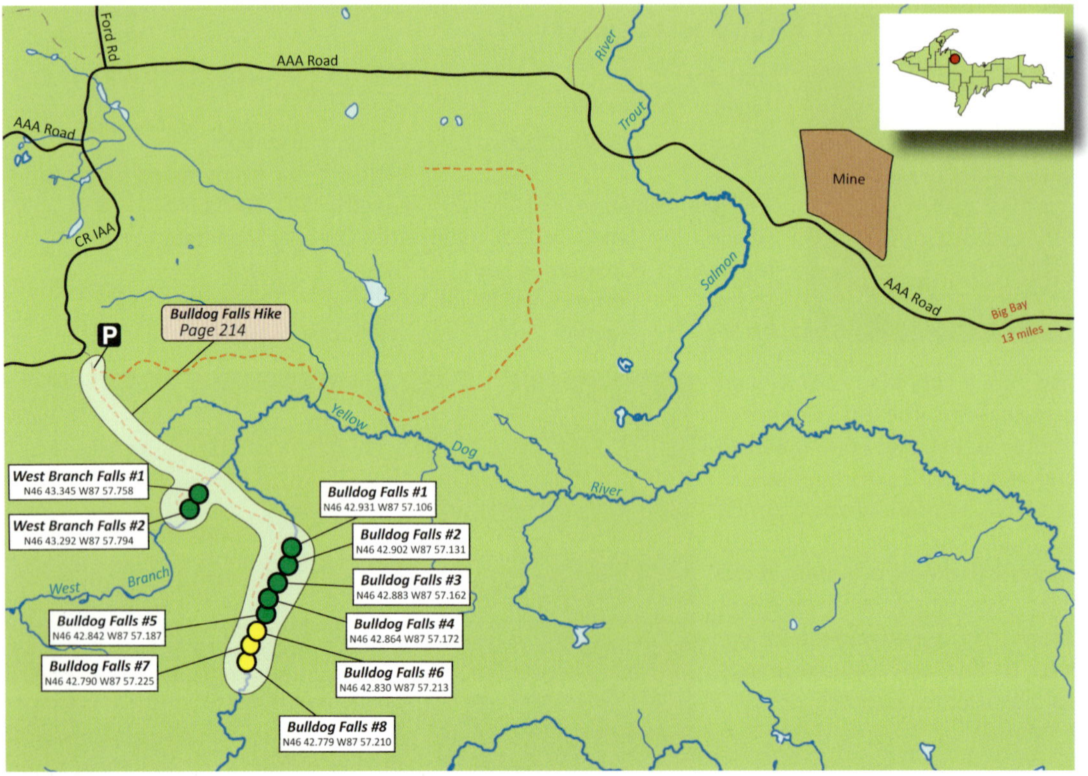
Ford Rd
AAA Road
AAA Road
CR IAA
River
Trout
Mine
Salmon
AAA Road
Big Bay
13 miles
P
Bulldog Falls Hike
Page 214
Yellow
Dog
River
West
Branch
West Branch Falls #1
N46 43.345 W87 57.758
West Branch Falls #2
N46 43.292 W87 57.794
Bulldog Falls #1
N46 42.931 W87 57.106
Bulldog Falls #2
N46 42.902 W87 57.131
Bulldog Falls #3
N46 42.883 W87 57.162
Bulldog Falls #4
N46 42.864 W87 57.172
Bulldog Falls #5
N46 42.842 W87 57.187
Bulldog Falls #6
N46 42.830 W87 57.213
Bulldog Falls #7
N46 42.790 W87 57.225
Bulldog Falls #8
N46 42.779 W87 57.210

## Bulldog Falls Hike

I will never forget my experience finding the Bulldog falls. It was the afternoon of October 12, 2009, and after cataloging twelve waterfalls that day, I was trying to get in one last batch of falls before heading home. Unfortunately, every attempt at locating the falls was coming up fruitless. I was driving down CR AAA and ckecking out every 2-track that looked promising, only to find each of them ending 2 to 3 miles from the waterfalls (assuming that the GPS coordinates that I was using were correct). I continued heading west on CR AAA with my GPS telling me that the waterfalls were getting further away and my hopes of finding them were diminishing as well. Suddenly, the road turned south and the waterfalls once again were getting closer. I found what must have been the only house within a 10 mile radius with a gentleman working outside and asked him if he knew where the Bulldog Falls were. To my surprise, he told me that I was close to the trail head!

Following the rough 2-track that he had told me about, I found the trail head and quickly started down the nearly 2 mile hike to the falls. This late in the fall the sun was setting at 7:08 PM and I was just getting underway at 3:40 PM. Since I had never been to these waterfalls and didn't know what kind of terrain to expect, I hoped that I had enough time to explore the waterfalls, photograph and write down my observations, and make it back to the truck before the sun went down.

The hike was golden! The entire landscape took on a yellowish hue with beautiful autumn leaves dropping all around. In contrast with the gorgeous walk, what a disappointment it was to finally make it to the river, only to discover that the first two "drops" that I encountered were both small rapids and certainly not worth the long walk.

After the initial disappointment, I continued upstream with some trepidation. Fortunately, I was greeted with a magnificent sight! Bulldog Falls #1 appeared as a tumbling cascade of white water flowing over and around black rocks that were topped with green moss and newly fallen golden leaves. The sight was awe-inspiring! I clambered up to the top of the steep hill and found Bulldog Falls #2 hiding over the crest. It was one glorious sight after another.

If only I would have had more time to explore I would have discovered that there were many more falls up river. But the relentless hands of time were swiftly bringing an end to the day, and I had 2 miles to hike back to my truck. To complicate matters, the slight mist that had accompanied me on my walk to the falls turned into an October snowstorm. What a relief to see the truck through the trees at 6:35 PM, having beaten the elements and the clock once again!

*Directions:* From Big Bay, drive south on CR 550 for about 2 miles to CR 510. Turn right (CR 510 only goes to the right). After about 2.6 miles, stay to the right to merge onto CR AAA. Drive 12.9 miles (this will take you past the mine after which CR AAA turns into a dirt road). At this point, turn left and head south. CR AAA has merged with Ford Road (CR IAA). In another 1/2 mile, CR AAA turns to the right. DON'T TURN! Continue on straight for another .4 miles. The road will fork here. Stay to the right. Keep going for another 1.2 miles. There will be a 2-track to the left. Follow this until it ends. There is a display board with a small roof over it that gives information regarding the wilderness area that you are about to enter. There is also a locked box that is for contact information and anticipated dates for entering and exiting the forest in case of emergency situations. Hike 1.1 miles to the West Branch. The two West Branch falls are only a short distance up river from the trail. After viewing these two falls, come back to the original trail. Ford the West Branch River. Continue another .7 miles to the Yellow Dog River. The trail becomes very faint. Follow the river upstream. An ancient bridge spans the river near the base of the first falls. An island stands in the middle of the river. A second bridge runs from the island to the far side of the river. The terrain gets very steep at this point. Both sides of the river rise rapidly. The second falls occur in a bend in the river just above #1 falls. Continue climbing up to the top of the gorge. Follow a raised aquaduct-like bedrock channel to view the next four waterfalls. The final two waterfalls are in a flatter space with larger spill pools around which wild grasses grow profusely.

Bulldog Falls Area

## BULLDOG FALLS #1 (YELLOW DOG RIVER)    Private

| | | | |
|---|---|---|---|
| Must See: | 8 | GPS: | N46 42.931 W87 57.106 |
| Height: | 35 feet | | |
| Time: | 2.5-3.5 hours | Hiking Information | |
| | | Path: | Footpath then none |
| Driving Information | | Length: | 1.8 miles |
| Signs: | None | Elev. Change: | Elevated |
| Road: | 2-track | GPS: | Required |
| Access: | Very difficult | Danger: | Elevated |
| 4WD: | Helpful | WP Boots: | Required |

A multitude of moss covered rocks fill the riverbed. Be careful as you climb around on the hill that is the foundation for this waterfall. The steep and sometimes slippery sides can be dangerous.

There is about a 35 foot total drop as the river cascades over green, mossy rocks. When those mossy rocks are covered in red and yellow leaves, so much the better! The river comes tumbling down amongst 2 to 4 foot diameter rounded boulders. The base of the waterfall ends by splitting around an elongated island. There are very old bridges dating back to the original McCormick owners. These bridges span both sides of the river onto the island. Passing over these bridges is the easiest way to cross the river at this point. The far side of the bridge is at N46 42.969 W87 57.088.

*Looking up from near the base of the tumbling waterfall*

# BULLDOG FALLS #2 (YELLOW DOG RIVER)

Private

| | | | |
|---|---|---|---|
| Must See: | 8 | GPS: | N46 42.902 W87 57.131 |
| Height: | 20 feet | | |
| Time: | 2.5-3.5 hours | Hiking Information | |
| | | Path: | Footpath then none |
| Driving Information | | Length: | 1.8 miles |
| Signs: | None | Elev. Change: | Elevated |
| Road: | 2-track | GPS: | Required |
| Access: | Very difficult | Danger: | Elevated |
| 4WD: | Helpful | WP Boots: | Required |

Climb to the top of the hill that Bulldog Falls #1 tumbles down and you will be greeted by this wonderful waterfall. Unfortunately, Bulldog Falls #2 is not easily viewed. You will find yourself perched on the edge of a cliff as you gaze over and down into this beauty. Cross the river down below Falls #1 and climb up the far side of the ravine. Follow the steep incline up around the bend in the river to where the #2 falls start. It's possible to view the waterfall more closely from here.

*Peering down into gorge from the east side*

*Up near the top of the waterfall on the western side with lovely wildflowers in bloom*

## BULLDOG FALLS #3 (YELLOW DOG RIVER)

Private

| | | | |
|---|---|---|---|
| Must See: | 7 | GPS: | N46 42.883 W87 57.162 |
| Height: | 12 feet | | |
| Time: | 2.75-4.0 hours | Hiking Information | |
| | | Path: | Footpath then none |
| Driving Information | | Length: | 1.9 miles |
| Signs: | None | Elev. Change: | Elevated |
| Road: | 2-track | GPS: | Required |
| Access: | Very difficult | Danger: | Elevated |
| 4WD: | Helpful | WP Boots: | Required |

The wide angular drop is best viewed from the west side of the river. A large fern covered boulder sits above the left side of the falls.

Bulldog Falls #3 is a fast cascade with a mostly vertical drop of 5 feet before the river turns to the left and cascades eight more times over flat rock shelves. The river then flattens out.

*What a strange rock perched up above the waterfall!*

218

Bulldog Falls Area

## BULLDOG FALLS #4 (YELLOW DOG RIVER)

Private

| | | | |
|---|---|---|---|
| Must See: | 7 | GPS: | N46 42.864 W87 57.172 |
| Height: | 18 feet | | |
| Time: | 3-4 hours | **Hiking Information** | |
| | | Path: | Footpath then none |
| **Driving Information** | | Length: | 1.9 miles |
| Signs: | None | Elev. Change: | Elevated |
| Road: | 2-track | GPS: | Required |
| Access: | Very difficult | Danger: | Elevated |
| 4WD: | Helpful | WP Boots: | Required |

Just up above #3 the Yellow Dog River slides down rapidly along an angled rock that tips the river back toward tilted bedrock that creates a trough.

This is a LONG slide with exposed rock all around. Angled bedrock forces the river through an elevated channel of rock. It seemingly defies gravity as the river is actually above the surrounding valleys.

*Where did these amazing chunks of bedrock come from?*

MARQUETTE COUNTY

Bulldog Falls #4

219

## BULLDOG FALLS #5 (YELLOW DOG RIVER)

Private

| | | | |
|---|---|---|---|
| Must See: | 7 | GPS: | N46 42.842 W87 57.187 |
| Height: | 10 feet | | |
| Time: | 3-4 hours | **Hiking Information** | |
| | | Path: | Footpath then none |
| **Driving Information** | | Length: | 2.0 miles |
| Signs: | None | Elev. Change: | Elevated |
| Road: | 2-track | GPS: | Required |
| Access: | Very difficult | Danger: | Elevated |
| 4WD: | Helpful | WP Boots: | Required |

Rusty brown, gray and black boulders sit next to a severely angled smooth layer of bedrock. The river flows through a backward "C" shaped trough that results from their intersection. More of the boulders are set along the side of the river as it continues through a deep spill pool.

*The hike along this series of waterfalls on the Yellow Dog River is a thoroughly unique experience!*

Bulldog Falls Area

## BULLDOG FALLS #6 (YELLOW DOG RIVER)

Private

| | |
|---|---|
| Must See: | 6 |
| Height: | 8 feet |
| Time: | 3.25-4.25 hours |

**Driving Information**
| | |
|---|---|
| Signs: | None |
| Road: | 2-track |
| Access: | Very difficult |
| 4WD: | Helpful |

| | |
|---|---|
| GPS: | N46 42.830 W87 57.213 |

**Hiking Information**
| | |
|---|---|
| Path: | Footpath then none |
| Length: | 2.0 miles |
| Elev. Change: | Elevated |
| GPS: | Required |
| Danger: | Elevated |
| WP Boots: | Required |

This is another of the classic Bulldog slide falls. A large gray lichen covered rocky mass stands next to bedrock slanted up with the river wedged between them. The river runs through the by-now-familiar crevasse. Angled bedrock with boulders lined up against the downhill side creates a narrow path for the river to travel through. It narrows down to about 1 foot at its narrowest point. At the base of the fast slide is a 30 foot long spill pool.

*I love the peanut shaped boulder that lies planted in the center of the narrow river.*

221

MARQUETTE COUNTY

Bulldog Falls #6

## BULLDOG FALLS #7 (YELLOW DOG RIVER)

Private

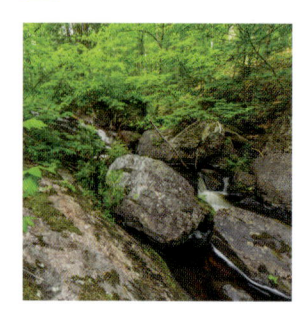

| | | | |
|---|---|---|---|
| Must See: | 4 | GPS: | N46 42.790 W87 57.225 |
| Height: | 9 feet | | |
| Time: | 3.25-4.25 hours | Hiking Information | |
| | | Path: | Footpath then none |
| Driving Information | | Length: | 2.1 miles |
| Signs: | None | Elev. Change: | Elevated |
| Road: | 2-track | GPS: | Required |
| Access: | Very difficult | Danger: | Elevated |
| 4WD: | Helpful | WP Boots: | Required |

Water flows over uneven surface, narrowing from 15 feet wide at the top to just 4 feet across as it approaches the base of the slide. Boulders below the slide narrow the river further, until it's down to 1 foot wide and looks like a long funnel. More nice rocks below the falls support large ferns, other grasses and even a small cedar tree.

During the summer, undergrowth starts to dominate the area, making it difficult to appreciate the waterfall.

*This is getting close to the plateau, where the terrain flattens out a bit.*

222

# BULLDOG FALLS #8 (YELLOW DOG RIVER)

Private

| | | | |
|---|---|---|---|
| Must See: | 6 | GPS: | N46 42.779 W87 57.210 |
| Height: | 8 feet | | |
| Time: | 3.25-4.25 hours | Hiking Information | |
| | | Path: | Footpath then none |
| Driving Information | | Length: | 2.1 miles |
| Signs: | None | Elev. Change: | Elevated |
| Road: | 2-track | GPS: | Required |
| Access: | Very difficult | Danger: | Elevated |
| 4WD: | Helpful | WP Boots: | Required |

The Yellow Dog River divides around a pine covered island, sliding over black basalt to a deep dark pool to form the furthest of the falls on this river. In drier times the right fork of the river may dry up.

This is the top of the Bulldog waterfall series. The terrain is now quite leveled out and the river runs slowly up above this drop.

*The large calm spill pool below the waterfall slide is good sized and ringed by large delicate fern.*

MARQUETTE COUNTY

Bulldog Falls #8

Bulldog Falls Area

## WEST BRANCH FALLS #1 (YELLOW DOG RIVER - WEST BRANCH) Private

| | | | |
|---|---|---|---|
| Must See: | 8 | GPS: | N46 43.345 W87 57.758 |
| Height: | 30 feet | | |
| Time: | 1.5-2.25 hours | Hiking Information | |
| | | Path: | Footpath |
| Driving Information | | Length: | 1.0 miles |
| Signs: | None | Elev. Change: | Moderate |
| Road: | 2-track | GPS: | Required |
| Access: | Very difficult | Danger: | Elevated |
| 4WD: | Helpful | WP Boots: | Required |

The main falls tucked along a high rock wall are shaped in a half moon configuration. The waterfall starts at the top, cascading down and running over bedrock. Halfway down the arc it drops in terraces about 6 feet into a channel that funnels down along a face of bedrock that is about 10 feet high. The wall is pinkish-brown with lichen and moss growing on the side of it. It narrows down into a slot that at one point is about only 1 foot wide.

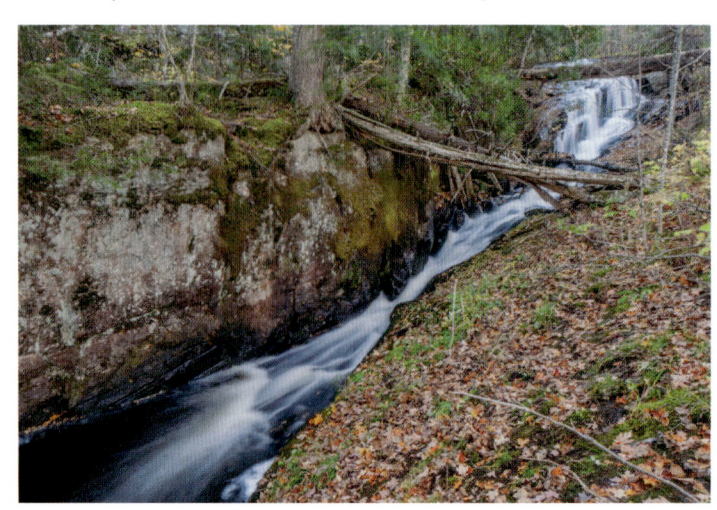

*Be careful walking along the side of the waterfall. It's quite a steep hillside and can be VERY slippery.*

Bulldog Falls Area

## WEST BRANCH FALLS #2 (YELLOW DOG RIVER - WEST BRANCH) Private

| | | | |
|---|---|---|---|
| Must See: | 7 | GPS: | N46 43.292 W87 57.794 |
| Height: | 20 feet | | |
| Time: | 1.5-2.25 hours | Hiking Information | |
| | | Path: | Footpath then none |
| Driving Information | | Length: | 1.0 miles |
| Signs: | None | Elev. Change: | Moderate |
| Road: | 2-track | GPS: | Required |
| Access: | Very difficult | Danger: | Moderate |
| 4WD: | Helpful | WP Boots: | Required |

MARQUETTE COUNTY

This is a winding "S" curving waterfall. Large squared off blocks of basalt rise 30 feet from the opposite side of the river. The riverbed angles toward the rock wall, keeping the river wedged in a narrow channel 2 to 4 feet wide. It tumbles and slides over a 70 yard stretch of river. Pines overlook both side of the river. There is no free drop on these falls - rather they slide and cascade in a fast elevation change. The waterfall area is surrounded with cedar trees that stand like sentinels amongst the rocks on the far side of the river.

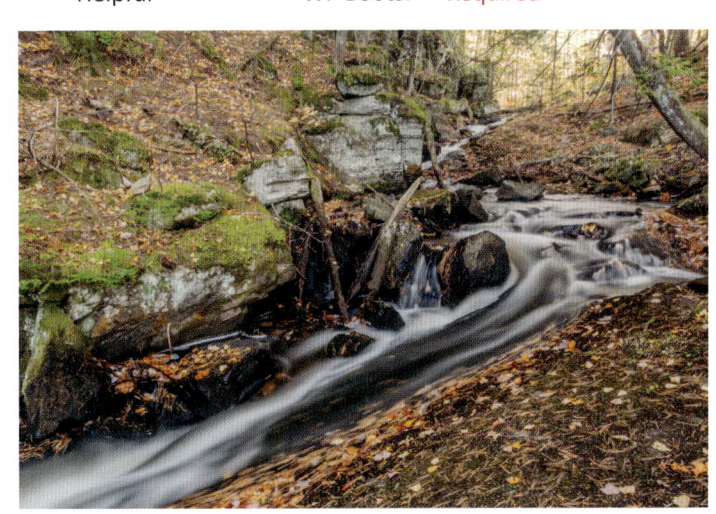

*Look for beautiful greenery in spring and early summer*

West Branch Falls #2

225

Carp River Falls Area

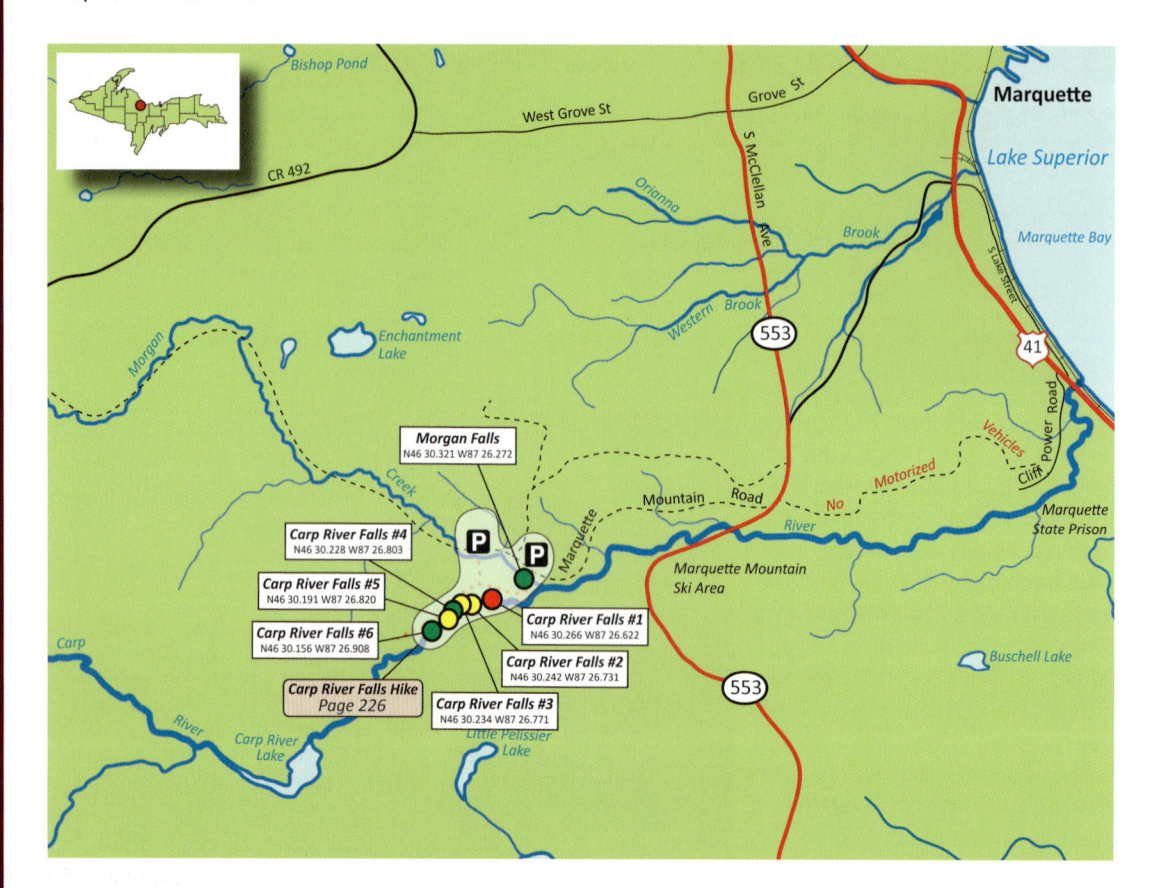

### Carp River Falls Hike

The Carp River Falls Area is an interesting study in contrasts. Marquette is a thriving college city with bustling streets and large box stores. And yet just a couple of miles south from the heart of the city is the Carp River, sporting beautiful waterfalls and rugged terrain. Morgan Falls, one of my favorites, is easily accessed and very photogenic (in fact, I met a photographer and model setting up for a shoot on one of my many trips to Morgan Falls). For those desiring longer and more daring hikes, following the Carp River upstream provides added adventure.

*Directions:* The key feature to look for is Marquette Mountain, a ski area that has been in operation since 1957. It is located on M-553 about 3 miles south of Marquette and 10 miles north of Sawyer International Airport. Running to the north of Marquette Mountain is the Carp River. Follow M-553 north, crossing the bridge over the river. Look to the left. Almost immediately past the bridge is a dirt road that cuts back hard to the west. Turn left and follow the dirt road for 1.3 miles. There is space for a couple of vehicles to pull off to the left (south) between sandy banks. The trail to Morgan Falls drops off quickly down to the creek. In the past couple of years a set of stairs have been constructed to make the climb safer and easier. At the creek, either walk across logs that span the creek, or wade through the knee deep waters. Climb down the 15 foot high hill to the base of the falls, which is on a plateau between Morgan Creek and Carp River. This flat area is perfect for viewing the falls and having a picnic!

There are two ways to get to the Carp River Falls. The most obvious is also the longest and more difficult. From Morgan Falls follow the creek to the Carp River, a short 100 yards or so. Then hike along the Carp River back up river along steep hillsides, climbing down whenever possible to view the falls. There is a labyrinth of narrow footpaths along the river, most likely made by college students. This route is 1.4 miles round trip. The other hike is shorter (1 mile), but has more involved directions.

This shorter, 1 mile round trip hike starts by driving from the Morgan Falls parking area further west (away from M-553) for about .2 miles. Park off of the road at a sandy area on the right. Hike to the left (southwest) atop a half-buried large water pipe that is used to transport water from the dam up river to the power generation plant miles from here. Follow the "pipe" for .4 miles. Along the way it will cross Morgan Creek with a minimal handrail added for protection along this span. At N46 30.268 W87 26.898 there is a 2-track that turns to the left. A concrete and steel ramp may be seen at this juncture. This 2-track ends in about 700 feet at Carp River Falls #6. From here, follow the river down river for .28 miles along the narrow footpaths that follow the top and side of the ravine. This stretch of river houses the six waterfalls described here. After getting to the #1 falls, cut back north for about 700 feet to get back to the buried water pipe. Follow the pipe to the northeast back to the vehicle.

## MORGAN FALLS (MORGAN CREEK)

Private

| | | | |
|---|---|---|---|
| Must See: | 9 | GPS: | N46 30.367 W87 26.356 |
| Height: | 20 feet | | |
| Time: | 10-30 minutes | Hiking Information | |
| | | Path: | Footpath |
| Driving Information | | Length: | 100 yards |
| Signs: | None | Elev. Change: | Moderate |
| Road: | Dirt road | GPS: | Helpful |
| Access: | Somewhat difficult | Danger: | Moderate |
| 4WD: | Helpful | WP Boots: | Helpful |

I rate this as "kid-friendly". It can be tricky getting young children across the creek, but once to the base of the falls, they will have a great time wading in the sandy shallow spill pool and creek or playing in the flat, somewhat open area between the creek and the river.

Carp River Falls Area

## CARP RIVER FALLS #1 (CARP RIVER)    Private

| | | | |
|---|---|---|---|
| Must See: | 3 | GPS: | N46 30.266 W87 26.622 |
| Height: | 4 feet | | |
| Time: | 30-60 minutes | Hiking Information | |
| | | Path: | Unimproved footpath |
| Driving Information | | Length: | .34 miles |
| Signs: | None | Elev. Change: | Moderate |
| Road: | Dirt road | GPS: | Recommended |
| Access: | Somewhat difficult | Danger: | Elevated |
| 4WD: | Helpful | WP Boots: | Helpful |

After hiking past nearly continuous rapids from downstream where Morgan Falls joins the Carp River, the first of the Carp River Falls offers a little taste of what's to come.

The river runs through a shallow gorge, flaking pink-gray bedrock lying exposed on either side. Pinching down a bit, the river turns in a subtle "S" curve, the main portion of the waterfall found at the second curve. Here, the turbulent river surges down 3 feet over moss covered rounded boulders. Then the river turns to the left, flowing around several rocks, narrows down and then drops another foot. Cedar, birch, poplar, and maple comprise the bulk of the trees that hug up close to the river.

228

# CARP RIVER FALLS #2 (CARP RIVER)

Private

| | | | |
|---|---|---|---|
| Must See: | 5 | GPS: | N46 30.242 W87 26.731 |
| Height: | 5 feet | | |
| Time: | 40-60 minutes | Hiking Information | |
| | | Path: | Unimproved footpath |
| Driving Information | | Length: | .44 miles |
| Signs: | None | Elev. Change: | Moderate |
| Road: | Dirt road | GPS: | Recommended |
| Access: | Somewhat difficult | Danger: | Elevated |
| 4WD: | Helpful | WP Boots: | Helpful |

The trail between #1 and #2 rises rapidly. It drops back down at the waterfall to only about 15 feet above the river. The far side, however, is 50 to 60 feet high. This horseshoe shaped waterfall is nearly a vertical plunge, with overflow water running through a maze of black basalt on the near side of the river. A large smoothish boulder, nearly 5 feet high, sits in the viewing area below the waterfall. Several more, smaller but of similar build, are found around the waterfall. Where did they come from? They look nothing like the bedrock.

This classic cascading waterfall can be viewed from river level. A small strip of land juts out into the river, giving just enough room for several people to stand along its edge, looking out past a small rise to view the left side of the falls. This waterfall would be best viewed from the other side of the river but there is no good way to get there.

*The tight, horseshoe shape is evident in the bedrock. Above shot: the far side of the river rises sharply!*

Carp River Falls Area

## CARP RIVER FALLS #3 (CARP RIVER)     Private

| | | | |
|---|---|---|---|
| Must See: | 4 | GPS: | N46 30.234 W87 26.771 |
| Height: | 4 feet | | |
| Time: | 50-75 minutes | Hiking Information | |
| | | Path: | Unimproved footpath |
| Driving Information | | Length: | .47 miles |
| Signs: | None | Elev. Change: | Moderate |
| Road: | Dirt road | GPS: | Recommended |
| Access: | Somewhat difficult | Danger: | Elevated |
| 4WD: | Helpful | WP Boots: | Helpful |

It's any easy hike along the river's edge between #2 and #3. The gorge walls on either side rise 40 feet, towering over the river. Fierce rapids mark its course to the next waterfall. A narrow footpath leads along the river's edge, providing close access to the waterfall.

Walking along the river and seeing the water channelled down to only 2 to 3 feet across, rushing down the short causeway and tumbling over lovely rapids is a beautiful sight! This drop is just below #4. That waterfall is so magnificent, it would be easy for this unique little waterfall to get lost in what's just around the corner.

*The spill pool for #4 is just above the channel*

# CARP RIVER FALLS #4 (CARP RIVER)

Private

| | | | |
|---|---|---|---|
| Must See: | 9 | GPS: | N46 30.228 W87 26.803 |
| Height: | 40 feet | | |
| Time: | 60-90 minutes | **Hiking Information** | |
| | | Path: | Unimproved footpath |
| **Driving Information** | | Length: | .50 miles |
| Signs: | None | Elev. Change: | Moderate |
| Road: | Dirt road | GPS: | Recommended |
| Access: | Somewhat difficult | Danger: | Elevated |
| 4WD: | Helpful | WP Boots: | Helpful |

This spectacular waterfall widens out to 40 feet, falling in a triple drop cascade. Frothing white water dominates the river, from side to side. Two final drops arc toward each other at the base of the falls, combining their collective water in a final burst of large white bubbles that are carried downstream. The same footpath at the river's edge from #3 can be hiked the additional 100 feet to view #4 from below the spill pool. The top drop is magnificent in its own right! It's a 15 foot drop that's 10 feet wide. Torrents of water cascade in a very pleasing way to a large spill pool which fans out to slide over the second set of drops, sliding and cascading down another 18 feet. One third of the circumference of the spill pool is involved in this drop as the water follows a cone shaped extension of the pool to its base. The river quickly narrows back down to 10 feet for its final plunge of 7 feet. Clamber up the muddy side next to the falls to view each drop closer.

*The three drops can be seen in this shot. The above picture is looking down from above the waterfall.*

MARQUETTE COUNTY

Carp River Falls #4

Carp River Falls Area

## CARP RIVER FALLS #5 (CARP RIVER)  Private

| | | | |
|---|---|---|---|
| Must See: | 5 | GPS: | N46 30.191 W87 26.820 |
| Height: | 10 feet | | |
| Time: | 60-90 minutes | Hiking Information | |
| | | Path: | Unimproved footpath |
| Driving Information | | Length: | .54 miles |
| Signs: | None | Elev. Change: | Moderate |
| Road: | Dirt road | GPS: | Recommended |
| Access: | Somewhat difficult | Danger: | Elevated |
| 4WD: | Helpful | WP Boots: | Helpful |

Continue on the footpath next to the river for another 150 feet past the top of #4. The trail narrows to a precarious rocky ledge just inches wide for about 6 feet. A small landing beyond ends at the base of the waterfall. Two irregularly shaped mounds in the center of the river are covered with grasses and flowers. The second drop can just be seen past an imposing crumbling rock edifice. Thimble berries grow along the water and delicate Spotted Touch-me-nots seemingly grow from the rock itself. Back track along the trail and climb to the top of the cliffs to see the rest of the waterfall through pine boughs. The cliff is sheer to the river 40 feet below. The top cascade can be seen 50 feet further upstream from here, but once again, obscured by tree branches. Continue on the trail to the top drop. Climb down the ravine and follow a narrow ledge back to the second drop. There are three drops total in this waterfall, the first two are each 4 feet high and the third is 2 feet for a total of 10 feet.

*It's nice to enjoy the waterfall from the river's edge. The view from atop the cliff is seen above.*

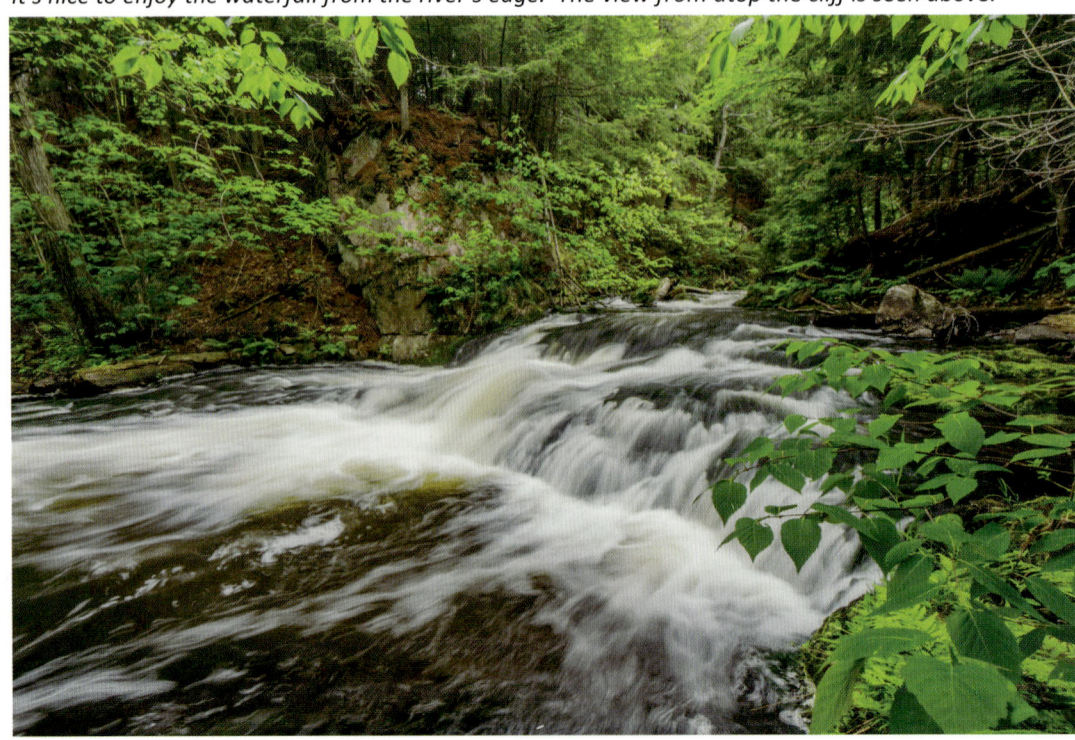

Carp River Falls Area

## CARP RIVER FALLS #6 (CARP RIVER)  Private

| | | | |
|---|---|---|---|
| Must See: | 7 | GPS: | N46 30.156 W87 26.908 |
| Height: | 10 feet | | |
| Time: | 60-90 minutes | Hiking Information | |
| | | Path: | Unimproved footpath |
| Driving Information | | Length: | .65 miles |
| Signs: | None | Elev. Change: | Moderate |
| Road: | Dirt road | GPS: | Recommended |
| Access: | Somewhat difficult | Danger: | Elevated |
| 4WD: | Helpful | WP Boots: | Helpful |

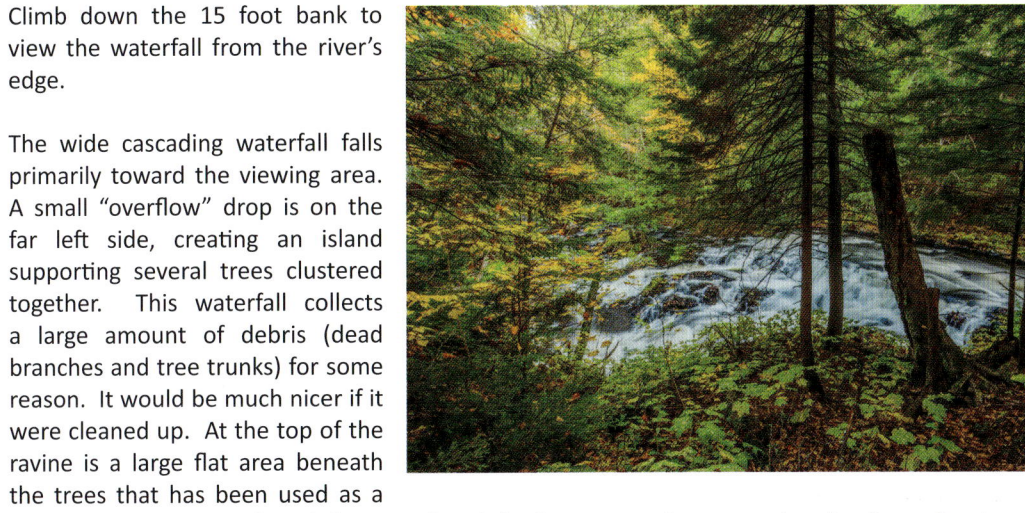

Climb down the 15 foot bank to view the waterfall from the river's edge.

The wide cascading waterfall falls primarily toward the viewing area. A small "overflow" drop is on the far left side, creating an island supporting several trees clustered together. This waterfall collects a large amount of debris (dead branches and tree trunks) for some reason. It would be much nicer if it were cleaned up. At the top of the ravine is a large flat area beneath the trees that has been used as a camping area. A 2-track ends here. Follow it back to get to the water pipe that is used to transport water for the hydroelectric plant.

*A typical collection of debris around the waterfall*

MARQUETTE COUNTY

Carp River Falls #6

233

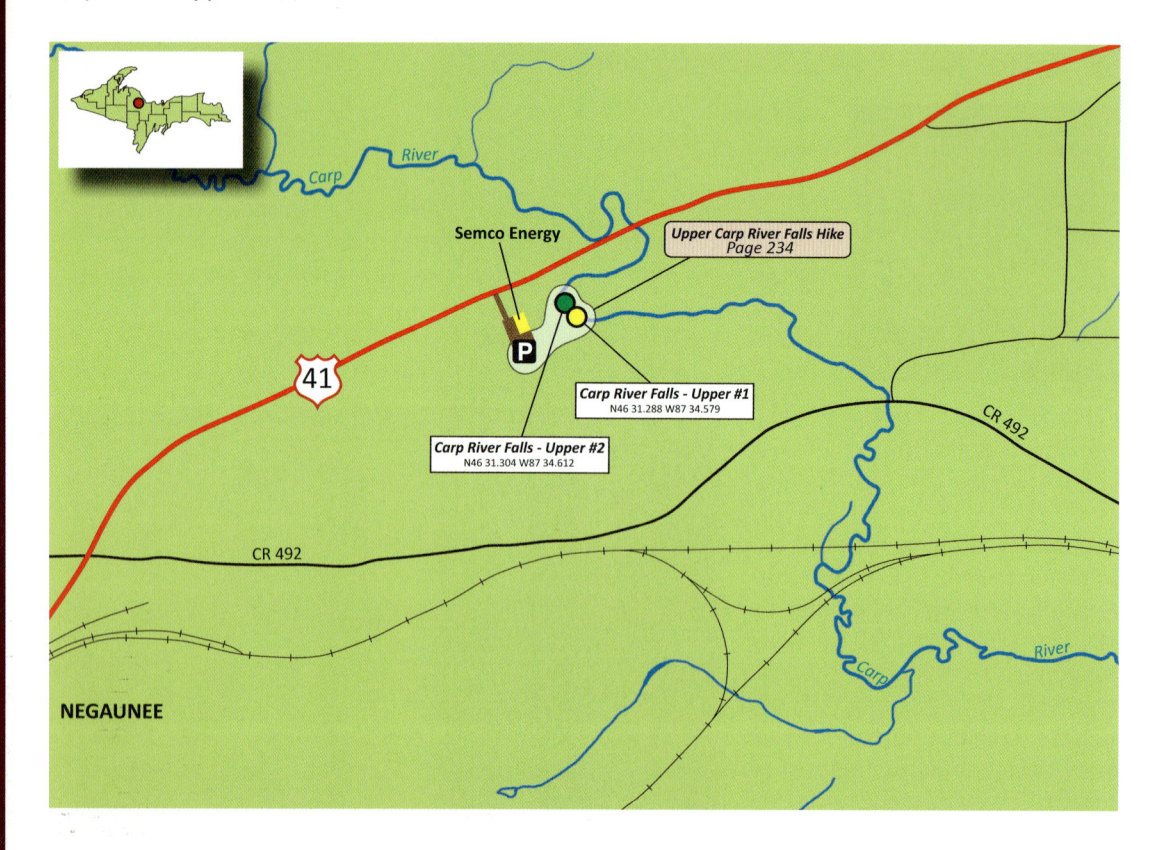

Carp River - Upper Falls Area

Map labels:
- Carp River
- Semco Energy
- Upper Carp River Falls Hike Page 234
- 41
- Carp River Falls - Upper #1 N46 31.288 W87 34.579
- Carp River Falls - Upper #2 N46 31.304 W87 34.612
- CR 492
- CR 492
- NEGAUNEE
- Carp River

MARQUETTE COUNTY

### Upper Carp River Falls Hike

The Carp River has its beginning as the drain for Deer Lake, a mere 2 miles north of Ishpeming. Running easterly with a slight southern movement, the Carp River passes beneath US-41, 6 miles further on. The river is now about 1 mile east of Negaunee. In the middle of turning a hard S-curve there are a couple waterfalls fairly close together. They are very nice waterfalls, and equally as nice, they are the closest to the parking area!

*Directions:* If coming in on US-41 headed west, look for the bridge over the Carp River. Turn left (south) soon afterwards into the parking lot for the Semco Power Company. If driving east on US-41, the road bends left (northwest) right after running next to Teal Lake between Ishpeming and Negaunee. Two miles after that bend, the Semco Power Company will be seen on the right (south). Park in the back of the parking lot. Make sure that you are not interfering with the operations of the power company. Be considerate. Hike to the east behind the fenced-in area of the company. A footpath will be obvious. It runs across a slight ditch and then through a narrow strip of field before entering the woods. Follow the trail to the river. It will lead you directly to the #1 Falls. Follow the trail up river to the #2 Falls. They are not as easily viewed at the #1 Falls.

# CARP RIVER FALLS - UPPER #1 (CARP RIVER)

Private

| | | | |
|---|---|---|---|
| Must See: | 6 | GPS: | N46 31.288 W87 34.579 |
| Height: | 5 feet | | |
| Time: | 20-40 minutes | Hiking Information | |
| | | Path: | Narrow footpath |
| Driving Information | | Length: | .15 miles |
| Signs: | None | Elev. Change: | Minor |
| Road: | Main | GPS: | Helpful |
| Access: | Easy | Danger: | Slight |
| 4WD: | N/A | WP Boots: | Recommended |

The river splits around black, moss covered rocks and beside a 25 foot tall massive rock outcropping. The vertical, striated cliff serves as a nice backdrop for the falls. This really has a nice, small, private viewing area. It has a better viewing area than #2.

*The wooden looking cliff behind the waterfall has vertical lines*

Carp River - Upper Falls Area

## CARP RIVER FALLS - UPPER #2 (CARP RIVER)             Private

| | | | |
|---|---|---|---|
| Must See: | 7 | GPS: | N46 31.304 W87 34.612 |
| Height: | 5 feet | | |
| Time: | 20-40 minutes | Hiking Information | |
| | | Path: | Narrow footpath |
| Driving Information | | Length: | .20 miles |
| Signs: | None | Elev. Change: | Moderate |
| Road: | Main | GPS: | Helpful |
| Access: | Easy | Danger: | Moderate |
| 4WD: | N/A | WP Boots: | Recommended |

This is a classic lovely symmetrical cascading waterfall made up of hundreds of little rocky plateaus to catch the water falling. Along the river banks are elegant ferns and thimble berries. Spotted touch-me-nots are interspersed with maple saplings. Cedars overlook the falls, casting green boughs like protective wings over the river.

It requires a bit of a scramble over a rocky ledge to get down to the river's edge. And then there's not much of a ledge on which to stand.

*The waterfall lays out nicely as seen from down river*

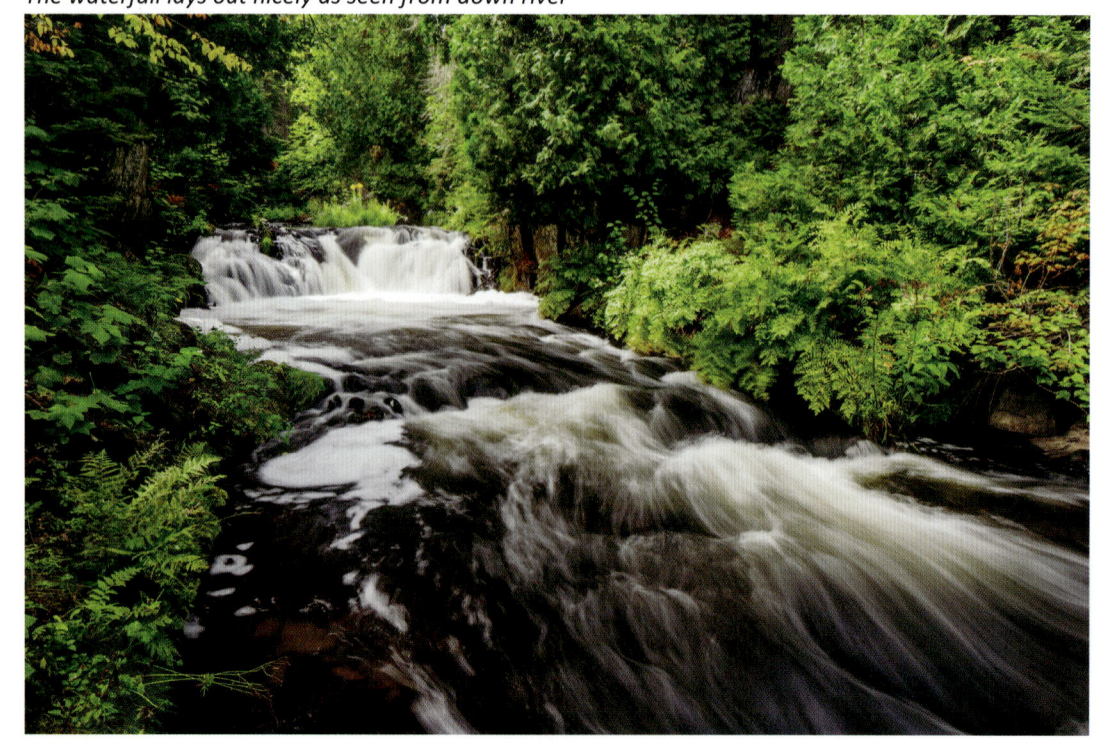

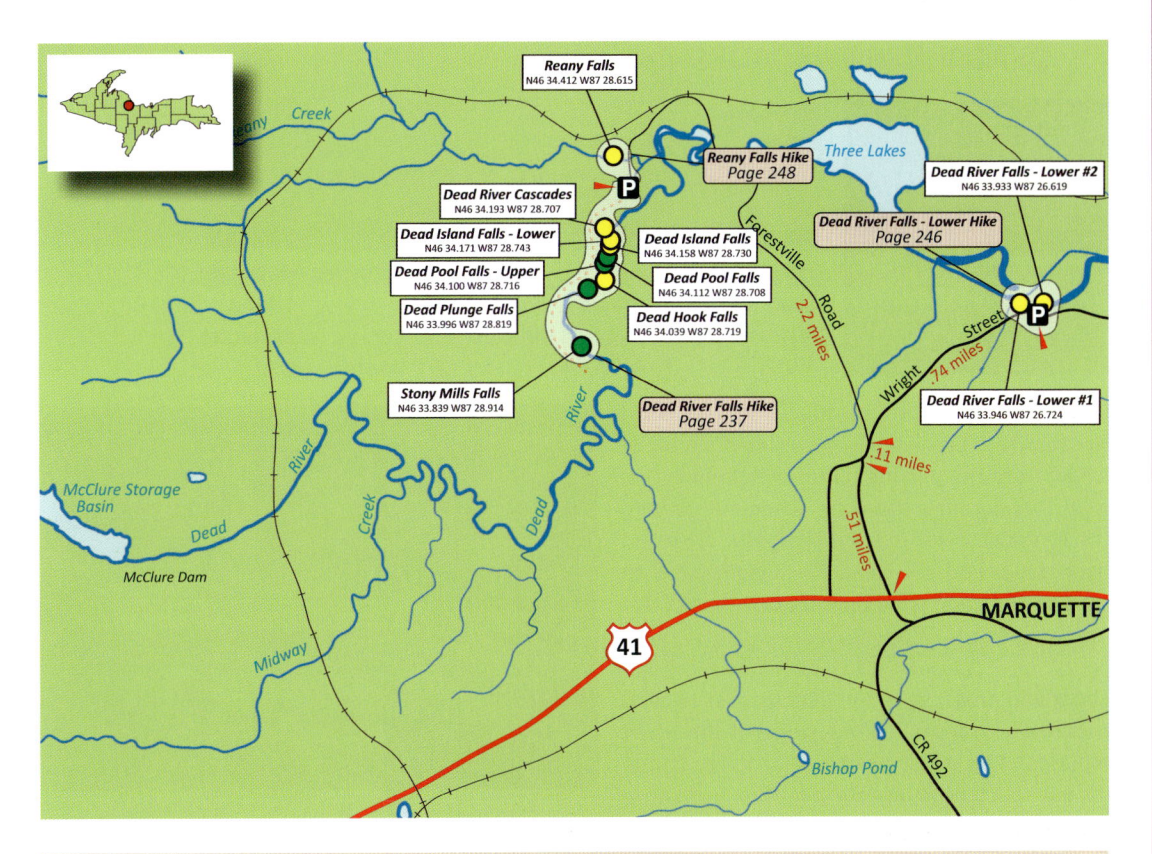

## Dead River Falls Hike

The Dead River Falls are best accessed by hiking from the parking lot at the Dead River Power Plant. This is the same place to park for the Reany Falls Hike. The Dead River Falls are often visited and are quite popular. Several of them have wonderful drops in the 15 to 20 foot height range. Be prepared. There is some decent elevation change along the unimproved trail.

College students from Marquette frequent this stretch of river. It is close to town and a couple of the falls have splash pools deep enough to allow diving from rocky perches above the falls.

*Directions:* Turn north onto Wright Street (CR 492) from US-41. The Westwood Mall Shopping Center is on the northeast corner, Starbucks is on the southwest, with a Culvers to the southeast and a Quiznos on the northwest. In .51 miles turn right to stay on Wright Street. In .11 miles turn left (northwest) onto Forestville Road. After about 1 mile the road makes several sharp bends, crossing the Dead River on an old bridge. From Wright Street to the end of the road is 2.2 miles. The road ends at a parking lot not far from a hydroelectric power plant. Park. (The Reany Falls Hike also begins at this parking lot.) Hike along an obvious dirt road that is to the right of the power plant (DON'T approach the building - it is strictly OFF LIMITS). A footpath cuts off to the left after passing by the power house and soon intersects the Dead River. Follow the trail up river, following close to the shoreline. After viewing the seven "Dead River Falls", continue past a large pond that bulges the river to over 300 feet wide. The western shore of the pond is about 350 yards long. The "Stony Mills Falls" are found within the next 800 feet. All told, the hike from the vehicle to the 8th waterfall on the hike, "Stony Mills Falls" is .84 miles (one way).

Dead River Falls Area

## DEAD RIVER CASCADES (DEAD RIVER)     Private

| | | | |
|---|---|---|---|
| Must See: | 5 | GPS: | N46 34.193 W87 28.707 |
| Height: | 4 feet | | |
| Time: | 20-30 minutes | Hiking Information | |
| | | Path: | Footpath |
| Driving Information | | Length: | .23 miles |
| Signs: | None | Elev. Change: | Moderate |
| Road: | Secondary road | GPS: | Helpful |
| Access: | Somewhat difficult | Danger: | Moderate |
| 4WD: | N/A | WP Boots: | N/A |

It's good to get to this introductory waterfall. I like to take a break here. After all, it's a bit of a hike from the parking lot up the steep gravel road that parallels the river. Then cut over to the forest at a well marked footpath. Descend back down into the Dead River Gorge and to the top of a good sized bluff that overlooks this first waterfall.

The river drops in a semi-circle over jagged bedrock with ferns topping some of the rocky mounds. This is just a taste of what's to come. It's not spectacular, but the overlook from atop the knobby basalt mass provides a great viewing location. The river splits into several streams as it flows around the matching bedrock some 20 feet below the viewing area. Spindly wildflowers grasp at the sparse soil on the rocky crag, their delicate beauty offering a splash of color to the otherwise gray floor.

*The view from the top of the bluff*

## DEAD ISLAND FALLS - LOWER (DEAD RIVER)   Private

| | | | |
|---|---|---|---|
| Must See: | 5 | GPS: | N46 34.171 W87 28.743 |
| Height: | 4 feet | | |
| Time: | 25-40 minutes | **Hiking Information** | |
| | | Path: | Footpath |
| **Driving Information** | | Length: | .28 miles |
| Signs: | None | Elev. Change: | Moderate |
| Road: | Secondary road | GPS: | Helpful |
| Access: | Somewhat difficult | Danger: | Moderate |
| 4WD: | N/A | WP Boots: | N/A |

Follow the footpath down from the Dead River Cascades to the river's edge along calm waters. A small tributary enters the river and must be crossed. A cluster of logs is typically strategically placed to accommodate this. Follow the base of the ravine (beyond the tributary, another trail climbs the swiftly rising bank) to the bottom of the waterfall. The river here has cut a channel through a 30 foot high mass of bedrock. Several huge chunks have since fallen into the narrow cut. The water pours around the sides of these displaced masses.

*Notice the calm waters below the waterfall in this shot and the one above*

Dead River Falls Area

## DEAD ISLAND FALLS (DEAD RIVER)    Private

| | | | |
|---|---|---|---|
| Must See: | 6 | GPS: | N46 34.158 W87 28.730 |
| Height: | 15 feet | | |
| Time: | 30-45 minutes | Hiking Information | |
| | | Path: | Footpath |
| Driving Information | | Length: | .28 miles |
| Signs: | None | Elev. Change: | Moderate |
| Road: | Secondary road | GPS: | Helpful |
| Access: | Somewhat difficult | Danger: | Moderate |
| 4WD: | N/A | WP Boots: | N/A |

The Dead River splits into two streams as it flows around a large island that rises as much as 20 feet above the river and is nearly 100 yards wide. The far stream flows through a channel and ends in a subdued cascade. The near stream has two main drops. The first bursts over a 5 foot ledge to a short pool beneath a smooth rounded mass. The final drop falls about 7 feet through a 3 foot wide opening with sharp black rock dramatically contrasting the nearby smooth basalt.

*To the right is the 2nd drop on the near side stream. On the left side, the far side cascades can be seen.*

MARQUETTE COUNTY

Dead Island Falls

Dead River Falls Area

## DEAD POOL FALLS (DEAD RIVER)    Private

| | | | |
|---|---|---|---|
| Must See: | 7 | GPS: | N46 34.112 W87 28.708 |
| Height: | 15 feet | | |
| Time: | 35-50 minutes | Hiking Information | |
| | | Path: | Footpath |
| Driving Information | | Length: | .33 miles |
| Signs: | None | Elev. Change: | Moderate |
| Road: | Secondary road | GPS: | Helpful |
| Access: | Somewhat difficult | Danger: | Moderate |
| 4WD: | N/A | WP Boots: | N/A |

A favorite of college kids, the pool below the main waterfall is often dived into. I'm not recommending this as a safe practice, but I have witnessed it several times on my trips here. When the river is high, it divides and flows heavily over two distinct waterfalls some yards apart. The "black when wet" rock nicely offsets the white frothing river as it cascades down the nearly vertical face. The waterfall tumbles over a long cliff face. At the base of the cliff is a trough. It starts at just a couple feet wide and expands to about 30 feet across at the "main" waterfall. The river then continues around the side of the perfect viewing area to the Dead Island Falls further downstream.

*The two waterfalls are running well in this shot, but only the "main" one in the picture above.*

MARQUETTE COUNTY

Dead Pool Falls

241

Dead River Falls Area

## ■ DEAD POOL FALLS - UPPER (DEAD RIVER)    Private

| | | | |
|---|---|---|---|
| Must See: | 7 | GPS: | N46 34.100 W87 28.716 |
| Height: | 15 feet | | |
| Time: | 40-60 minutes | Hiking Information | |
| | | Path: | Footpath |
| Driving Information | | Length: | .35 miles |
| Signs: | None | Elev. Change: | Moderate |
| Road: | Secondary road | GPS: | Helpful |
| Access: | Somewhat difficult | Danger: | Moderate |
| 4WD: | N/A | WP Boots: | N/A |

Lovely smooth mounds of bedrock lay out before you. Three larger waterfalls and a very tiny one on the left have eroded their way through the basalt and present themselves beautifully. This waterfall is just above Dead Pool Falls. Picnic perfect rock is at the ideal viewing area below the waterfall and at the top of Dead Pool Falls.

This picture was taken up at the top of Dead Pool Falls. It's an amazing place to enjoy both waterfalls.

Dead River Falls Area

## DEAD HOOK FALLS (DEAD RIVER)  Private

| | | | |
|---|---|---|---|
| Must See: | 6 | GPS: | N46 34.039 W87 28.719 |
| Height: | 10 feet | | |
| Time: | 50-75 minutes | Hiking Information | |
| | | Path: | Footpath |
| Driving Information | | Length: | .44 miles |
| Signs: | None | Elev. Change: | Moderate |
| Road: | Secondary road | GPS: | Helpful |
| Access: | Somewhat difficult | Danger: | Moderate |
| 4WD: | N/A | WP Boots: | N/A |

Hike up along the river from Dead Pool Falls - Upper about .1 miles. Up above the waterfall the river runs along to the edge of a plateau. It angles to the right and then back hard to the left, avoiding a surprisingly hard section of black shiny bedrock. As it "hooks" around the bedrock it cascades, building to a final frothy climax as it enters a large squarish pool.

*An enlarged pool below the waterfall gives the river a chance to slow down before heading downstream.*

MARQUETTE COUNTY

Dead Hook Falls

243

## DEAD PLUNGE FALLS (DEAD RIVER)    Private

| | | | |
|---|---|---|---|
| Must See: | 8 | GPS: | N46 33.995 W87 28.819 |
| Height: | 20 feet | | |
| Time: | 60-90 minutes | Hiking Information | |
| | | Path: | Footpath |
| Driving Information | | Length: | .55 miles |
| Signs: | None | Elev. Change: | Moderate |
| Road: | Secondary road | GPS: | Helpful |
| Access: | Somewhat difficult | Danger: | Moderate |
| 4WD: | N/A | WP Boots: | N/A |

Continue hiking .11 miles upstream from Dead Hook Falls. Approaching Dead Plunge Falls, it looks like a beautiful waterfall that is plunging down in a very open space. What a difference there is when actually getting up close! The river courses through a narrow 3 foot wide channel, launching the water in a descending arc into a fairly narrow chasm. The perpetual spray mists the black wall and waters delicate fern and small trees that are growing along the river. It is an intimate setting with a multitude of fractured rocks scattered along the bank, perfect for sitting and contemplating.

*The difference between the front and side view of this waterfall is amazing!*

MARQUETTE COUNTY

Dead River Falls Area

Dead Plunge Falls

244

# STONY MILLS FALLS (DEAD RIVER)

Private

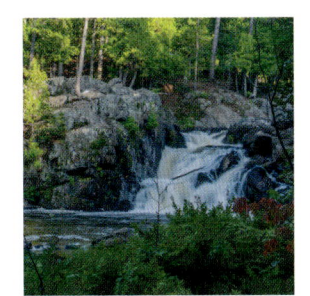

| | | | |
|---|---|---|---|
| Must See: | 8 | GPS: | N46 33.839 W87 28.914 |
| Height: | 15 feet | | |
| Time: | 80-120 minutes | Hiking Information | |
| | | Path: | Footpath |
| Driving Information | | Length: | .84 miles |
| Signs: | None | Elev. Change: | Moderate |
| Road: | Secondary road | GPS: | Helpful |
| Access: | Somewhat difficult | Danger: | Moderate |
| 4WD: | N/A | WP Boots: | N/A |

Hike another .35 miles upstream from Dead Plunge Falls, passing around a good sized pond until once again finding waterfall conducive terrain. Here you'll find another locally favorite waterfall! It is a great cascading waterfall with a wall of rock on the left and piles of boulders on the right. Local youth dive into the spill pool from the bluff on the left of the falls. There is a way to get to this end of the Dead River without walking so far, but it involves riding an ORV or ATV along power lines and 2-tracks. There is also a way to drive to the far side of the river, coming out at Stony Mills Falls, but I have not been there yet.

*A lovely large spill pool extends downstream below the waterfall*

MARQUETTE COUNTY

Dead River Falls Area

Stony Mills Falls

# MARQUETTE COUNTY

Dead River Falls Area

**Lower Dead River Falls Hike**

The Lower Dead River Falls are on the outskirts of Marquette. Wright Street runs around the west and north border of the city. The Dead River runs further south at one point on its journey from west to east. It is at this southern bend that it comes quite close to Wright Street. The two lower falls are located within easy walking distance of the street.

*Directions:* Turn north onto Wright Street (CR 492) from US-41. The Westwood Mall Shopping Center is on the northeast corner, Starbucks is on the southwest, with a Culvers to the southeast and a Quiznos on the northwest. In .51 miles turn right to stay on Wright Street. In .85 miles there is a dirt road to the left (north). Turn and park before the gate that blocks the road. This is an access road for the Upper Peninsula Power Company to work on their water lines. If the gate happens to be open, DO NOT DRIVE BEYOND as it may be closed and locked at any time. Hike past the gate and across the bridge to the falls. The #2 falls are to the right (east) of the bridge and the #1 falls are to the left (west) by a bridge that spans the river right at the base of the falls.

## ■ DEAD RIVER FALLS - LOWER #1 (DEAD RIVER)   Private

| Must See: | 6 | GPS: | N46 33.946 W87 26.724 |
| --- | --- | --- | --- |
| Height: | 18 feet | | |
| Time: | 10-15 minutes | Hiking Information | |
| | | Path: | N/A |
| Driving Information | | Length: | 150 yards |
| Signs: | None | Elev. Change: | Moderate |
| Road: | Secondary road | GPS: | N/A |
| Access: | Easy | Danger: | Slight |
| 4WD: | N/A | WP Boots: | Helpful |

The #1 falls are comprised of three main drops spread over 75 yards. At the top of the waterfall, the river widens out and cascades down 5 feet. It then gathers itself together, passes below the concrete bridge, cascades down another 4 feet, flows alongside the base of a rocky cliff and then drops another 4 feet before turning and heading downstream to the #2 falls.

## DEAD RIVER FALLS - LOWER #2 (DEAD RIVER)   Private

| | | | |
|---|---|---|---|
| Must See: | 5 | GPS: | N46 33.933 W87 26.619 |
| Height: | 6 feet | | |
| Time: | 10-15 minutes | Hiking Information | |
| | | Path: | N/A |
| Driving Information | | Length: | 100 yards |
| Signs: | None | Elev. Change: | Moderate |
| Road: | Secondary road | GPS: | N/A |
| Access: | Easy | Danger: | Slight |
| 4WD: | N/A | WP Boots: | Helpful |

Follow the far side of the river downstream. Climb down the rocky, craggy bank to the river's edge. The 6 foot drop splits around a 30 foot wide island in the middle of the river with several trees growing on it. The bridge over the river can be seen in the distance behind the falls. Be sure to walk down the 2-track (it parallels the river) far enough to get past the most inhospitable area of undergrowth and downed trees before cutting cross country down to the river.

*Park by the bridge seen in these shots*

Dead River Falls Area

### Reany Falls Hike

Reany Falls is located on Reany Creek just north of the parking lot for the Dead River Falls. It is very easily accessed small, but nicely presented waterfall.

*Directions:* Turn north onto Wright Street (CR 492) from US-41. The Westwood Mall Shopping Center is on the northeast corner, Starbucks is on the southwest, with a Culvers to the southeast and a Quiznos on the northwest. In .51 miles turn right to stay on Wright Street. In .11 miles turn left (northwest) onto Forestville Road. After about 1 mile the road makes several sharp bends, crossing the Dead River on an old bridge. From Wright Street to the end of the road is 2.2 miles. The road ends at a parking lot not far from a hydroelectric power plant. Park. Hike 100 yards back up the road until reaching the creek that flows beneath the road. Reany Falls is 50 feet to the left (west) of the road.

## REANY FALLS (REANY CREEK)   Private

| | | | |
|---|---|---|---|
| Must See: | 6 | GPS: | N46 34.412 W87 28.615 |
| Height: | 9 feet | | |
| Time: | 10-15 minutes | Hiking Information | |
| | | Path: | N/A |
| Driving Information | | Length: | 50 yards |
| Signs: | None | Elev. Change: | Moderate |
| Road: | Secondary road | GPS: | N/A |
| Access: | Somewhat difficult | Danger: | Slight |
| 4WD: | N/A | WP Boots: | Helpful |

Moss and lichen covered bedrock is thrust up in a vertical wall 10 feet high on the far side of the creek. A nice three split drop over a nearly hidden mass in the center of the creek is the culmination of three drops in a 100 foot stretch in the creek. Each drop is about 3 feet high for a total of 9 feet.

248

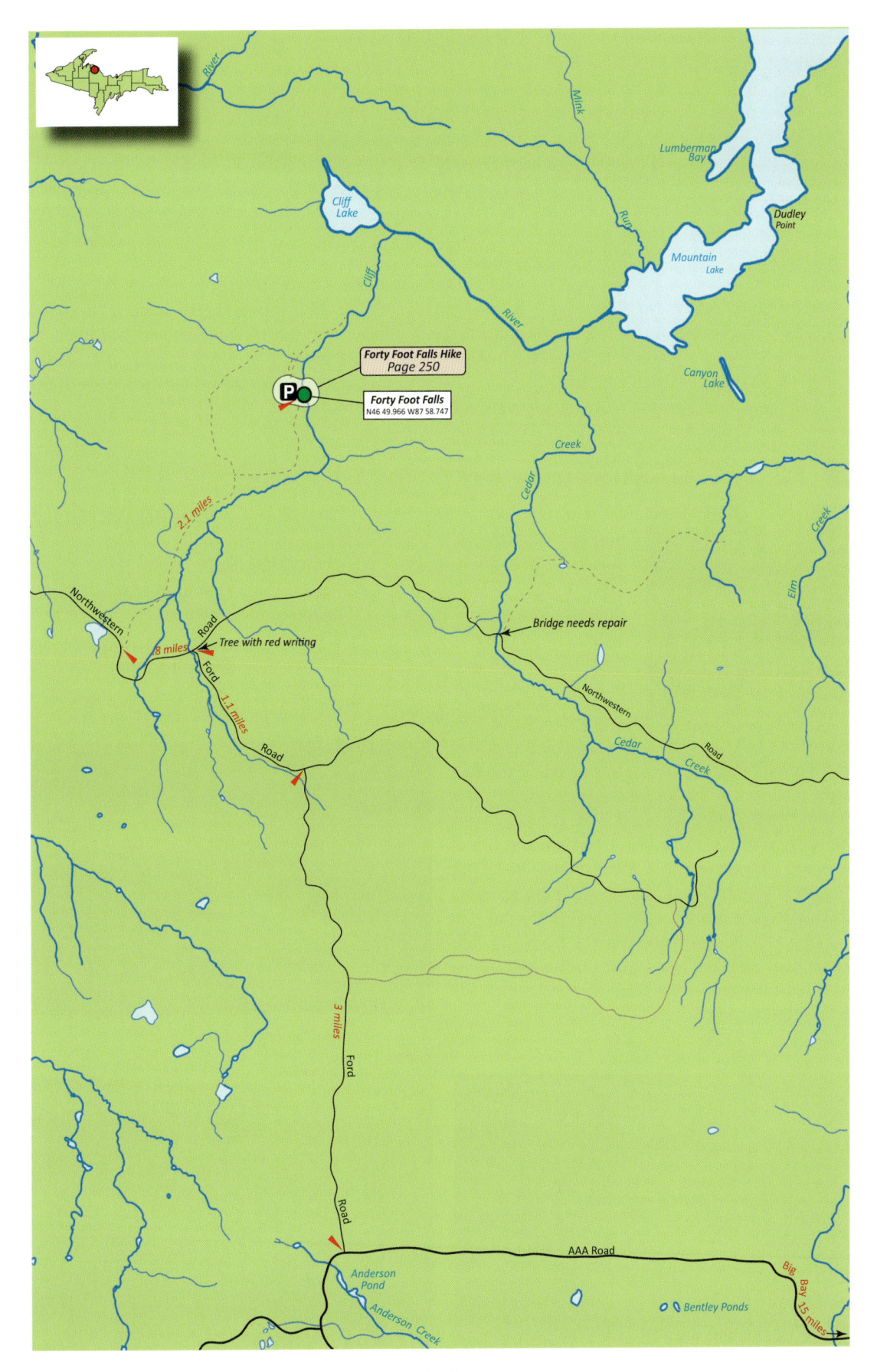

Forty Foot Falls Area

MARQUETTE COUNTY

Forty Foot Falls Area

### Forty Foot Falls Hike

Forty Foot Falls is in the Huron Mountains. When you haven't seen a road sign for 20 miles, and the best indication of where to turn is by memorizing the number of beer cans piled at a corner or by looking for painted trees, you know that you have left civilization in the dust some time ago. The winding roads keep degenerating until you arrive near the top of the waterfall some 2 miles down a pot-holed 2-track. Don't be discouraged, however. On most days any vehicle with decent clearance should be able to get to the falls. I would recommend having a GPS unit with you in case you lose track of exactly where you are on the route. There really are NO road signs out here!

*Directions:* After driving west on CR AAA Road for just under 3 miles (this is the only real straight stretch on CR AAA) turn north (right) at N46 45.510 W87 58.418 just before CR AAA turns to the south. Follow Ford Road (not marked) north for 3 miles. Turn left to continue on Ford Road. After 1.1 miles turn left (west) onto Northwestern Road. In .8 miles there is a 2-track on the right (northeast). Follow the 2-track for 2.1 miles. Park at the small parking area near the top of the falls. The waterfall is less than 100 yards from the parking area.

## FORTY FOOT FALLS (CLIFF RIVER)    Private

| | | | |
|---|---|---|---|
| Must See: | 8 | GPS: | N46 49.966 W87 58.747 |
| Height: | 40 feet | | |
| Time: | 5-20 minutes | Hiking Information | |
| | | Path: | Unimproved footpath |
| Driving Information | | Length: | 50 yards |
| Signs: | None | Elev. Change: | Slight |
| Road: | 2-track | GPS: | Recommended |
| Access: | Difficult | Danger: | Slight |
| 4WD: | Recommended | WP Boots: | N/A |

Forty Foot Falls, or Cliff Falls, has to rank as one of my more interesting discoveries. Finding the falls right next to the 2-track was a special treat. But unexpectedly, there were assorted pots and pans hanging from the trunk of a tree near the top of the falls. A grill was also there. These were not "accidently" left there, but looked quite at home in this remote setting. My guess is that an old hunting club located not too far from the falls keeps cooking utensils for some on-the-spot eating of fish caught below the falls. Be considerate and do not touch them.

*At the base of the main cascade*

*Looking down the fast running waterfall*

Garlic Falls Area

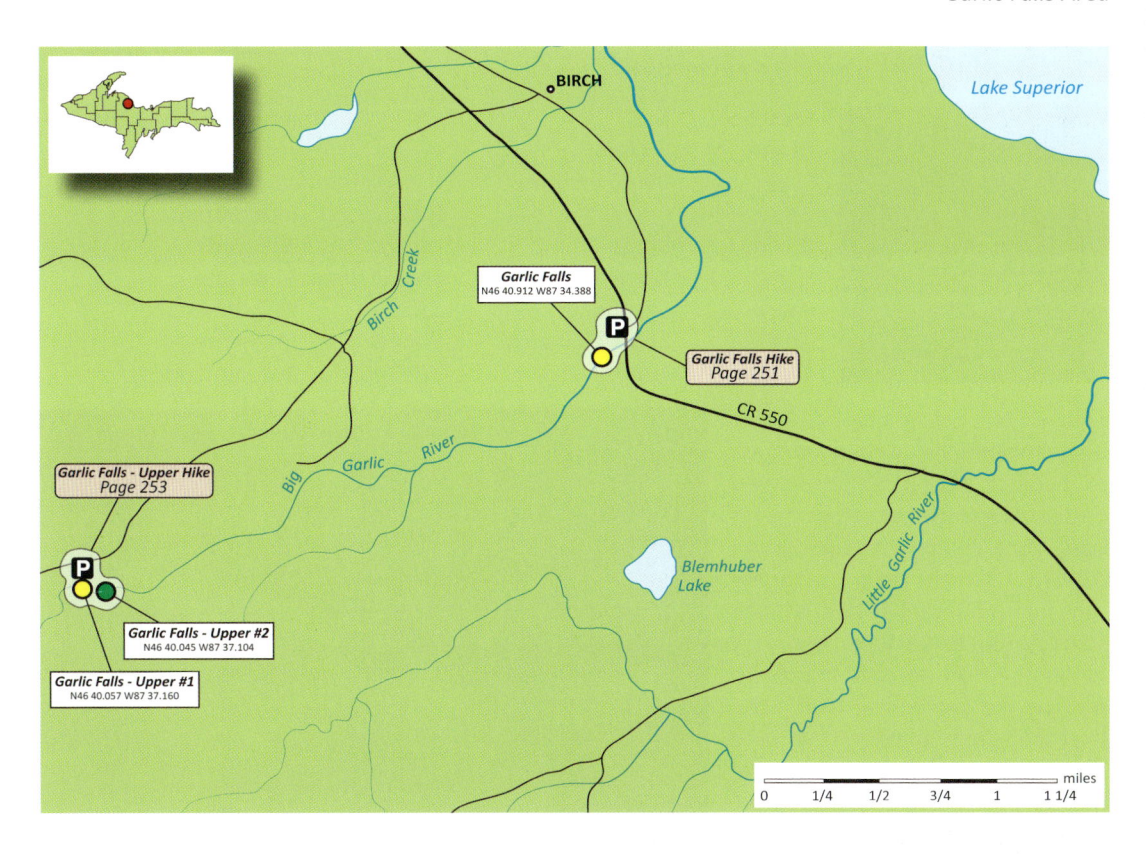

## Garlic Falls Hike

Big Garlic River runs through a swampy area between CR 550 and Lake Superior. But higher, dry ground lies just up river from the bridge. It is through this land that the Big Garlic River flows down a sheet of bedrock in a sweeping, sliding waterfall.

*Directions:* Drive 11.5 miles on CR 550 north from Marquette to the Big Garlic River. Park safely along the roadside. Hike through waist to shoulder high grasses, goldenrod, ferns, and thimbleberries as you parallel the river on the north side, heading upstream. In about 100 yards you'll be in the forest proper, and the thick undergrowth will dwindle. The river splits into several branches and you many need to ford one or more to find the easiest route to the waterfall.

*Standing at the top of the waterfall, looking down*

Garlic Falls Area

## GARLIC FALLS (BIG GARLIC RIVER)   Private

| | | | |
|---|---|---|---|
| Must See: | 6 | GPS: | N46 40.921 W87 34.388 |
| Height: | 15 feet | | |
| Time: | 30-45 minutes | **Hiking Information** | |
| | | Path: | Intermittent |
| **Driving Information** | | Length: | 300 yards |
| Signs: | None | Elev. Change: | Moderate |
| Road: | Secondary | GPS: | Recommended |
| Access: | Somewhat easy | Danger: | Moderate |
| 4WD: | N/A | WP Boots: | Recommended |

This is one of Michigan's more unique waterfalls. A rounded mass of bedrock set at a fairly steep decline ushers the river down the far side of the hump (both sides when the river is high) until it abruptly runs into a bulwark of layered rock standing up to 15 feet high. This forces the river to turn sharply to pass by the descending bluff. The river then drops another 3 feet over a small tiered ledge. After this, the river runs quietly on its short journey to Lake Superior.

*Looking straight up the main slide*

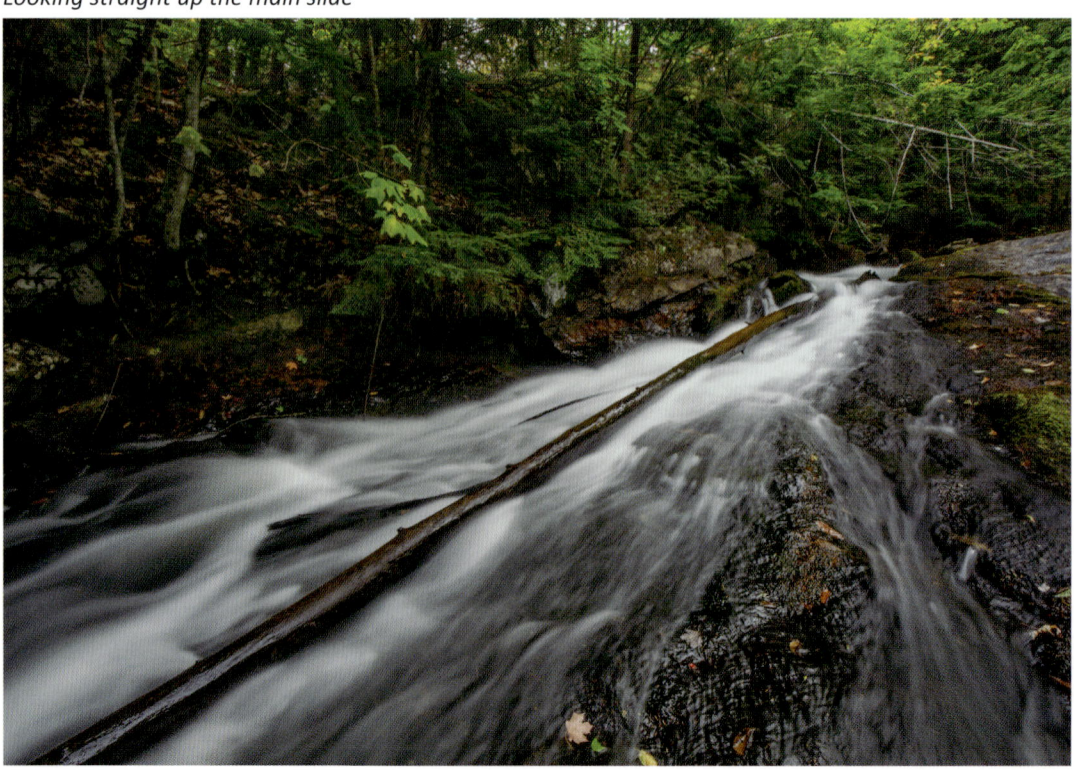

252

**Garlic Falls - Upper Hike**

A walk through thick pines abruptly ends at the river with the Upper #1 Falls. The forest in this area is quite thick, with the lower dead branches of evergreens seemingly everywhere!

*Directions:* Follow CR 550 north from Marquette about 13 miles. Turn left (west) off of CR 550 onto the dirt road that is just past Birch Creek (N46 41.854 W87 35.077). Follow the dirt road for 2.8 miles. Turn left (south) at N46 40.150 W87 37.104. Drive 100 yards to the end of the 2-track. Hike the well-worn trail to the river. Upper #1 is there. Upper #2 is downstream 85 yards in a small ravine.

## GARLIC FALLS - UPPER #1 (BIG GARLIC RIVER)   Private

| | | | |
|---|---|---|---|
| Must See: | 6 | GPS: | N46 40.057 W87 37.160 |
| Height: | 15 feet | | |
| Time: | 15-30 minutes | **Hiking Information** | |
| | | Path: | Well-worn footpath |
| **Driving Information** | | Length: | 150 yards |
| Signs: | None | Elev. Change: | Moderate |
| Road: | 2-track | GPS: | Recommended |
| Access: | Somewhat difficult | Danger: | Minor |
| 4WD: | Helpful | WP Boots: | Recommended |

Although this set of waterfalls is in a somewhat remote area, there is a relatively nice path to the falls. These falls are much easier to get to than the "regular" Garlic Falls!

This waterfall is a multi-tiered cascade pouring around a rounded mass of rock in the center of the river. Water-warn boulders look like they were strategically placed in the river just below the falls. The rock walls and boulders are covered with moss. Sit on the bare rocks and absorb the feeling of antiquity and timelessness as the waterfall babbles and the unchanging river rushes on.

## GARLIC FALLS - UPPER #2 (BIG GARLIC RIVER)   Private

| | | | |
|---|---|---|---|
| Must See: | 7 | GPS: | N46 40.045 W87 37.104 |
| Height: | 18 feet | | |
| Time: | 30-45 minutes | **Hiking Information** | |
| | | Path: | Well-worn footpath |
| **Driving Information** | | Length: | 250 yards |
| Signs: | None | Elev. Change: | Moderate |
| Road: | 2-track | GPS: | Recommended |
| Access: | Somewhat difficult | Danger: | Moderate |
| 4WD: | Helpful | WP Boots: | Recommended |

The Garlic River runs down a narrow chute to a 20 foot long pool and then plunges another 2 feet over moss covered rocks for a nice end to this waterfall. It is much more challenging to get to this waterfall than the Upper #1 Falls. But the view makes it worth the extra work!

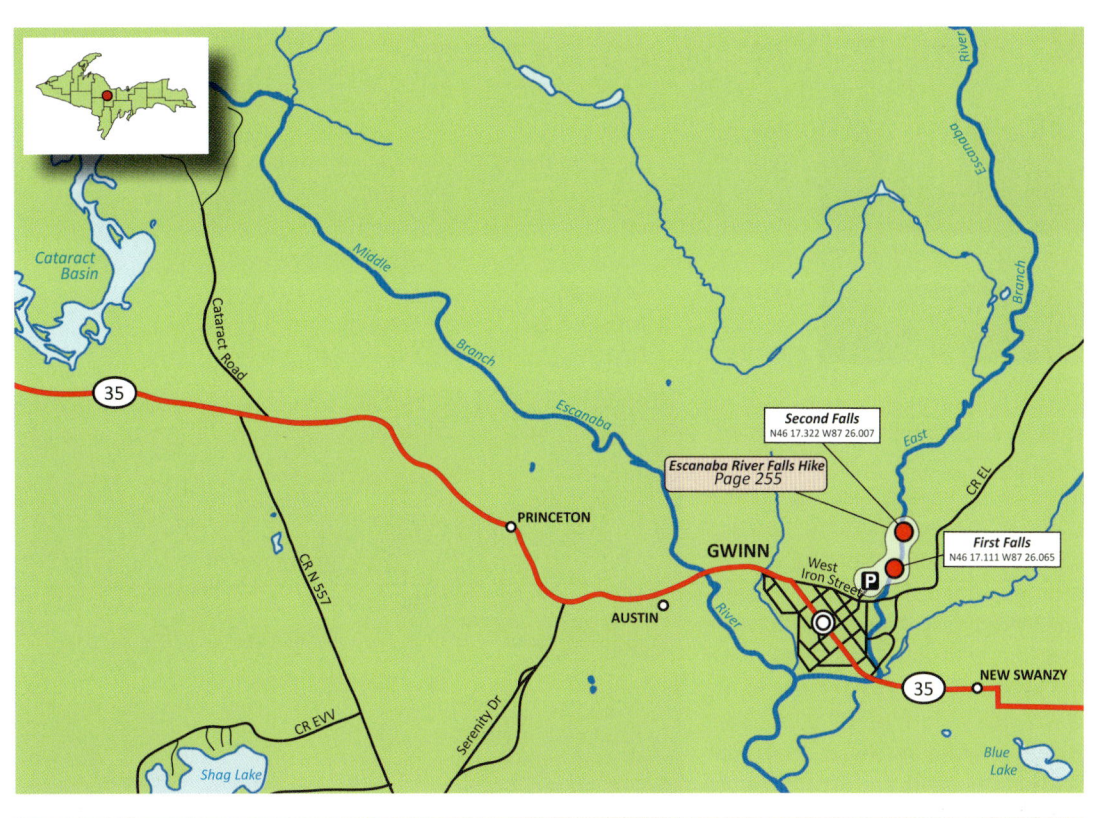

## Escanaba River Falls Hike

Farquar-Metsa Tourist Park is several blocks north of Gwinn on the west side of the East Branch of the Escanaba River. It underwent a large renovation in 2012. A large unsupervised swimming area on the river is just down river from First Falls. Both of the falls in the park are really just a couple of rapids, but since they are located in a nice park in Gwinn, they're included in this collection.

*Directions:* From the northwestern end of Gwinn, take West Iron Street sharply to the east for .35 miles. The park is on the left (north). Drive past the camping area to behind the building on the left (I think it's a bathhouse). Park in the parking lot back there. Head down to the river (east) which is only about 100 yards. First Falls are at the mouth of the swimming area. It should be easy to find. Follow the narrow footpath north 1/4 mile along the river to Second Falls. The trail heads through a forest of mostly evergreens.

## FIRST FALLS (EAST BRANCH ESCANABA RIVER)

| | | | |
|---|---|---|---|
| Must See: | 1 | GPS: | N46 17.111 W87 26.065 |
| Height: | 2 feet | | |
| Time: | 10-20 minutes | **Hiking Information** | |
| | | Path: | Mowed fields |
| **Driving Information** | | Length: | 100 yards |
| Signs: | None | Elev. Change: | Slight |
| Road: | Secondary | GPS: | N/A |
| Access: | Mostly Easy | Danger: | Slight |
| 4WD: | N/A | WP Boots: | N/A |

With mowed grass along the river and several structures visible from the falls, this feels like a tamed waterfall compared to the vast majority in Michigan! It does make it more kid friendly, however. Enjoy frisbee in the open field next to the river or maybe a picnic on the bedrock next to the falls.

255

Gwinn Area

## SECOND FALLS (EAST BRANCH ESCANABA RIVER)  Private

| | | | |
|---|---|---|---|
| Must See: | 1 | GPS: | N46 17.322 W87 26.007 |
| Height: | 2 feet | | |
| Time: | 30-45 minutes | Hiking Information | |
| | | Path: | Mowed fields |
| Driving Information | | Length: | .3 miles |
| Signs: | None | Elev. Change: | Slight |
| Road: | Secondary | GPS: | N/A |
| Access: | Mostly Easy | Danger: | Slight |
| 4WD: | N/A | WP Boots: | N/A |

These falls are almost a third of a mile back from "civilization", so imagine my amazement when, after taking several pictures here in October, I turned around, startled to hear someone speaking to me. A hunter wanted to know if I'd seen any black bears. I hadn't, which was just fine with me. But it did make me keep a closer eye and ear to my surroundings for the rest of the day! It was a good reminder that bear season was open, and I really should keep that in mind.

*The minor rapids are found in the necked down section of the river, the same as First Falls*

256

Morgan Meadows Falls Area

MARQUETTE COUNTY

### Morgan Meadows Falls Hike

Bad data is a bummer! I had information to look for these falls about a mile downstream from here. So... after hiking to the creek from Lake Enchantment Road, I followed it down river all the way to Morgan Falls. Of course, there were no waterfalls. It was on my third attempt that I finally had it right... somewhat. When I arrived at the correct parking spot, the information I had sent me the wrong way. I hiked over 1/4 mile up the creek before coming back to the vehicle only to discover a waterfall just on the other side of the road! What an easy set of waterfalls to find, if you only know where to look!

The drive down the 2-track can be a little bumpy, but most vehicles should be able to make it. The creek makes a hard turn to the right, drops over a set of cascades, meanders through a small flat area and then, as it starts to parallel the road, tumbles down through a wild and steep tangle of undergrowth.

*The dirt road that runs past the waterfall*

*Directions:* Off of US-41 in Marquette, turn south onto CR 492 (next to Starbucks) and drive for 3.5 miles. Turn left (south) onto Morgan Meadow Drive. The road crosses a creek almost immediately. Turn left (southeast) at the first dirt road following the creek. Follow it for .7 miles. Park on the right. The falls are on the left.

Morgan Meadows Falls Area

## MORGAN MEADOWS FALLS (MORGAN CREEK) Private

| | | | |
|---|---|---|---|
| Must See: | 5 | GPS: | N46 31.062 W87 28.796 |
| Height: | 5 feet | | |
| Time: | 5-10 minutes | Hiking Information | |
| | | Path: | None needed |
| Driving Information | | Length: | 100 feet |
| Signs: | None | Elev. Change: | Slight |
| Road: | Dirt road | GPS: | N/A |
| Access: | Somewhat easy | Danger: | Slight |
| 4WD: | N/A | WP Boots: | N/A |

Block shaped rocks push the creek to the right over falls through a three-step cascade to a sandy and pebble filled spill pool. This is only 50 feet from the parking spot! There is a good sized flat area that works for picnicking near the falls and playing with kids!

*The foreground is clear and flat. It's a perfect place to view the waterfall and for kids to play!*

258

Pinnacle Falls Area

MARQUETTE COUNTY

Map labels:
- AAA Road (Paved)
- N46 44.227 W87 49.098
- Turn E @ N46 43.367 W87 49.379
- Turn E @ N46 43.301 W87 49.068
- Turn S onto a small dirt road at a 3-way corner at N46 43.294 W87 48.650
- 1.2 miles
- .28 mi
- .35 miles
- .63 miles
- Turn south on a 2-track at N46 42.760 W87 48.571
- Pinnacle Falls Hike Page 259
- Yellow Dog River
- Pinnacle Falls N46 42.377 W87 48.397
- miles 0 1/4 1/2 3/4 1 1 1/4

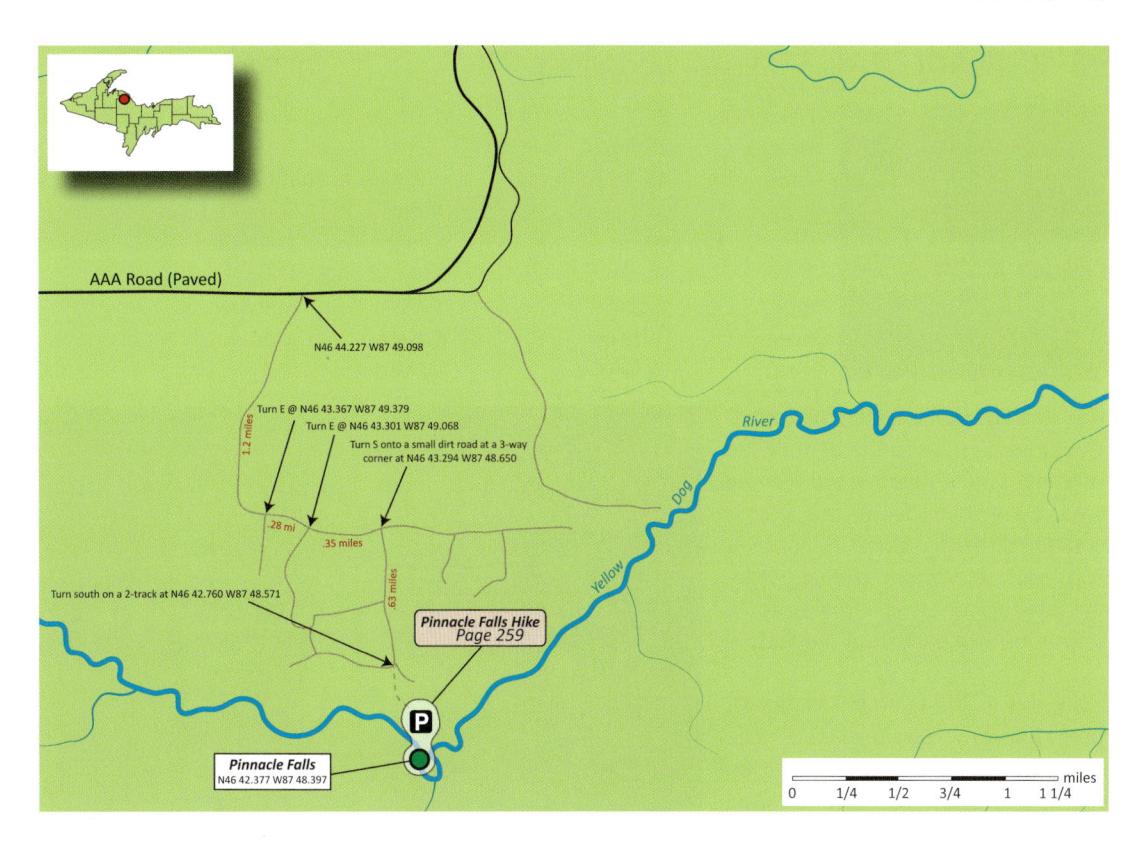

## Pinnacle Falls Hike

Pinnacle Falls has a rich history that still impacts us today. In fact, I heard that the Yellow Dog River was named by an event that took place at Pinnacle Falls hundreds of years ago. Several bands of Chippewa Indians were trapped at the bend in the river by a superior force of Iroquois warriors. It was only by an ingenious plan crafted by the chief which relied on the brave actions of five young members of the "Yellow Dog" family that the Chippewas were able to escape under cover of darkness.

Pinnacle Falls is also unique in that it retains relics from the logging days. At the top of the falls are rings of iron that are fastened to the solid granite. They were used to create a sluice gate that kept logs lined up correctly as they tumbled over the falls in the late 1800's. Countless pine trees made their way from the Yellow Dog Plains down the Yellow Dog River and across Lake Independence to the sawmill at Big Bay.

We are fortunate to have Pinnacle Falls now under the ownership of the Yellow Dog Watershed Preserve, a land trust that is designed to keep the falls open to the general public for generations to come. To learn more about the Yellow Dog Watershed Preserve please visit their website at http://www.yellowdogwatershed.org

*Directions:* Turn off of CR AAA Road to the southwest @ N46 44.227 W87 49.098. There are a couple of excavation areas after turning off of CR AAA. Continue past this area. Turn east 1.2 miles after leaving CR AAA Road. In .28 miles turn east again. After .35 miles turn south at a 3-way corner. The road here is a smaller dirt road. In another .63 miles turn south onto a 2-track that will dead end at a small parking area for the falls. Hike down the obvious footpath. It descends about 100 feet into the Yellow Dog Gorge on the hike. The path loops along the side of the river back to the north until opening up beneath hardwoods and a beautiful place for a picnic below the falls.

## PINNACLE FALLS (YELLOW DOG RIVER)

Private

| | | | |
|---|---|---|---|
| Must See: | 9 | GPS: | N46 42.377 W87 48.397 |
| Height: | 25 feet | | |
| Time: | 45-75 minutes | Hiking Information | |
| | | Path: | Semi-improved footpath |
| Driving Information | | Length: | 1/4 mile |
| Signs: | None | Elev. Change: | Major |
| Road: | 2-track | GPS: | Helpful |
| Access: | Difficult | Danger: | Moderate |
| 4WD: | Helpful | WP Boots: | N/A |

This is a classic cascading waterfall! The Pinnacle rises to the right of the falls about 50 feet above the viewing area. The river below the falls is boulder strewn. There is about a 100 foot elevation change from the parking area. This makes for a strenuous hike back from the falls.

I rate this a "Kid Friendly" waterfall. Take this with a grain of salt! The hike down and especially back up the trail may be too much for little ones. But for those that can handle a steep hike, the river below the falls is shallow and the terrain flat and pleasing.

*Remnants from the logging days are still up above the waterfall*

*The base of the large "pinnacle" of rock can just be seen to the right of the waterfall*

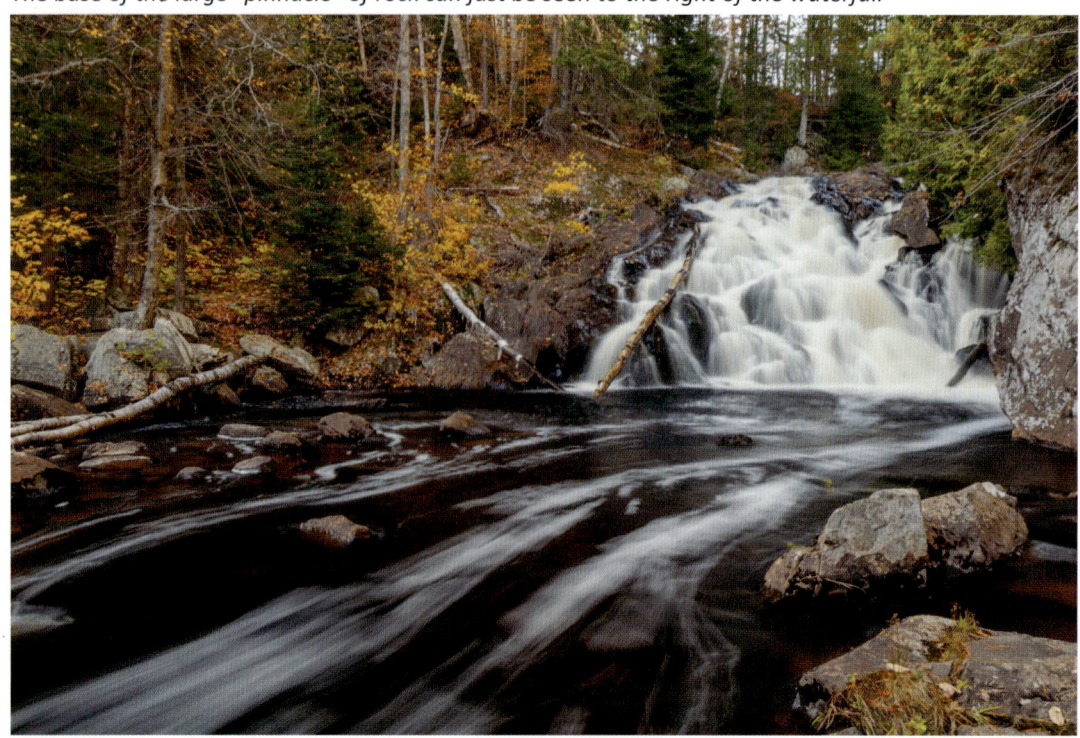

260

Trestle Falls Area

MARQUETTE COUNTY

## Trestle Falls Hike

This lovely waterfall is found below a trestle that spans the Dead River. The steel structure, high overhead, is impressive in its own right.

*Directions:* Off of US-41, turn north into Midway Rentals driveway just west of the overhead railroad tracks. Before the rental company is a large propane tank. About 100 yards later is a building with a sign for "H&L Mesabi" on the left (west). Turn left (west) just before the building. Drive past the building. There is a dirt road that starts on the far side of the parking lot. Drive down it and into the woods (.9 miles). The road diminishes in size to a narrow 2-track by the end of the drive. Park on the side of the 2-track by another small ATV trail that heads to the right (east).

*The 2-track narrows as it goes*

Park at N46 33.019 W87 30.362. Hike 50 feet down the ATV trail. The trail will suddenly come upon a set of railroad tracks. Turn left and parallel the tracks for .3 miles. DO NOT hike down the tracks. It is dangerous and illegal. The tracks will continue over the trestle. DO NOT go out onto the trestle. It is extremely dangerous. Head east (downstream) along the top of the gorge. Follow a faint trail. The gorge wall will descend down to the riverbed in a couple hundred yards. Follow the rocks in the river back upstream to get close to the waterfall.

261

Trestle Falls Area

## TRESTLE FALLS (DEAD RIVER)　　　　　　　　　　　Private

| | | | |
|---|---|---|---|
| Must See: | 7 | GPS: | N46 33.271 W87 30.432 |
| Height: | 20 feet | | |
| Time: | 1-1.5 hours | Hiking Information | |
| | | Path: | Slight Footpath |
| Driving Information | | Length: | .5 miles |
| Signs: | None | Elev. Change: | Major |
| Road: | 2-track | GPS: | Recommended |
| Access: | Quite difficult | Danger: | Increased |
| 4WD: | Helpful | WP Boots: | N/A |

Trestle Falls reminds me of a miniature Agate Falls. There is much less water and the trestle is lower, but the feel is similar. The waterfall is nested below the trestle, crossing the top of the gorge some 60 feet above. The Dead River runs through the gorge with descending walls overlooking the rock strewn river way below. Unlike Agate Falls, this railroad is still active. In fact, as I sat there writing my field notes, I heard a train whistle. I quickly got back to my camera and tripod which was on a large flat rock in the riverbed. I was able to take some pictures of the train over the waterfall! The numerous cars were filled with iron balls headed to the smelters.

262

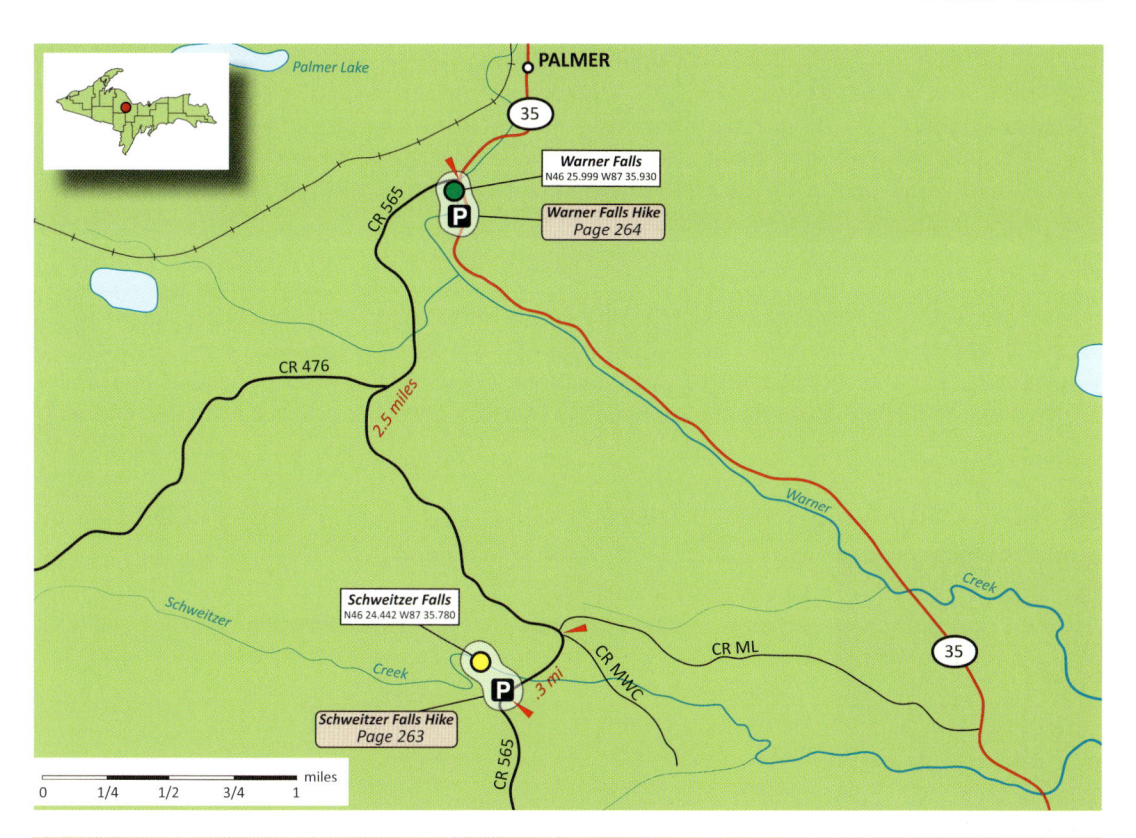

## Schweitzer Falls Hike

It is not a long hike from the small parking area next to the bridge through the pine trees, down the hill and around (or through) the marshy area and undergrowth to the overgrown viewing area situated on high banks above Schweitzer Creek. For as short as the hike is, it is equally difficult! Between the thick undergrowth and profuse cedars boughs, it becomes easy to get turned around on this hike. For that reason, I highly recommend using a GPS or at least marking your path for a safe return trip.

*Directions:* Take CR 565 west and south from Palmer off of M-35. In 2.8 miles park on the right (northwest) side of the road just past the bridge over Schweitzer Creek. Hike to the GPS coordinates for the falls. Warning! This is through thick brush, boughs and undergrowth.

## SCHWEITZER FALLS (SCHWEITZER CREEK)   Private

| | | | |
|---|---|---|---|
| Must See: | 6 | GPS: | N46 24.442 W87 35.780 |
| Height: | 18 feet | | |
| Time: | 30-45 minutes | Hiking Information | |
| | | Path: | None |
| Driving Information | | Length: | 200 yards |
| Signs: | None | Elev. Change: | Moderate |
| Road: | Secondary | GPS: | Required |
| Access: | Somewhat easy | Danger: | Moderate |
| 4WD: | N/A | WP Boots: | Required (to cross creek) |

There is thick undergrowth and downed trees making this short walk difficult to navigate. Use a GPS, a compass, or mark your trail. You don't want to get turned around in these woods! Schweitzer Creek and Warner Creek join 3 miles downstream to create the East Branch of the Escanaba River. Some 60 miles later the Escanaba River empties into Lake Michigan.

Warner Falls Area

### Warner Falls Hike

There are not a large number of waterfalls in Michigan that can be seen from a vehicle. Warner Falls is one of those elite few! The waterfall presents itself beautifully as seen from the road. It cascades down in a widening fan shape as it tumbles over a steep face to the marshy spill pool at the base. The creek then slowly moves through swampy land until it runs right next to M-35 for several miles.

*Directions:* Drive just south of Palmer on M-35. The waterfall will be seen on the right (west), down in a valley. Park just past the bridge off the side of the road. Walk back along the road to view the falls closer. I like to walk on the "dirt" side of the guard rail as the shoulder of the road is not very wide and there can be some traffic in this area. At the north end of the guard rail there is a trail of sorts that heads down the steep hillside over a bed of loose shale to the falls at the bottom.

## WARNER FALLS (WARNER CREEK)  Private

| | | | |
|---|---|---|---|
| Must See: | 7 | GPS: | N46 25.999 W87 35.930 |
| Height: | 20 feet | | |
| Time: | 5-20 minutes | Hiking Information | |
| | | Path: | N/A |
| Driving Information | | Length: | N/A |
| Signs: | None | Elev. Change: | N/A |
| Road: | Main | GPS: | N/A |
| Access: | Easy | Danger: | N/A |
| 4WD: | N/A | WP Boots: | N/A |

This very nice waterfall can be viewed from the bridge area or up close if you carefully pick your way down the loose shale and follow the dirt path to the bottom of the falls.

*It's a steep climb down to the waterfall itself. Staying up at the road, however, still offers a great view!*

Yellow Dog Falls Area

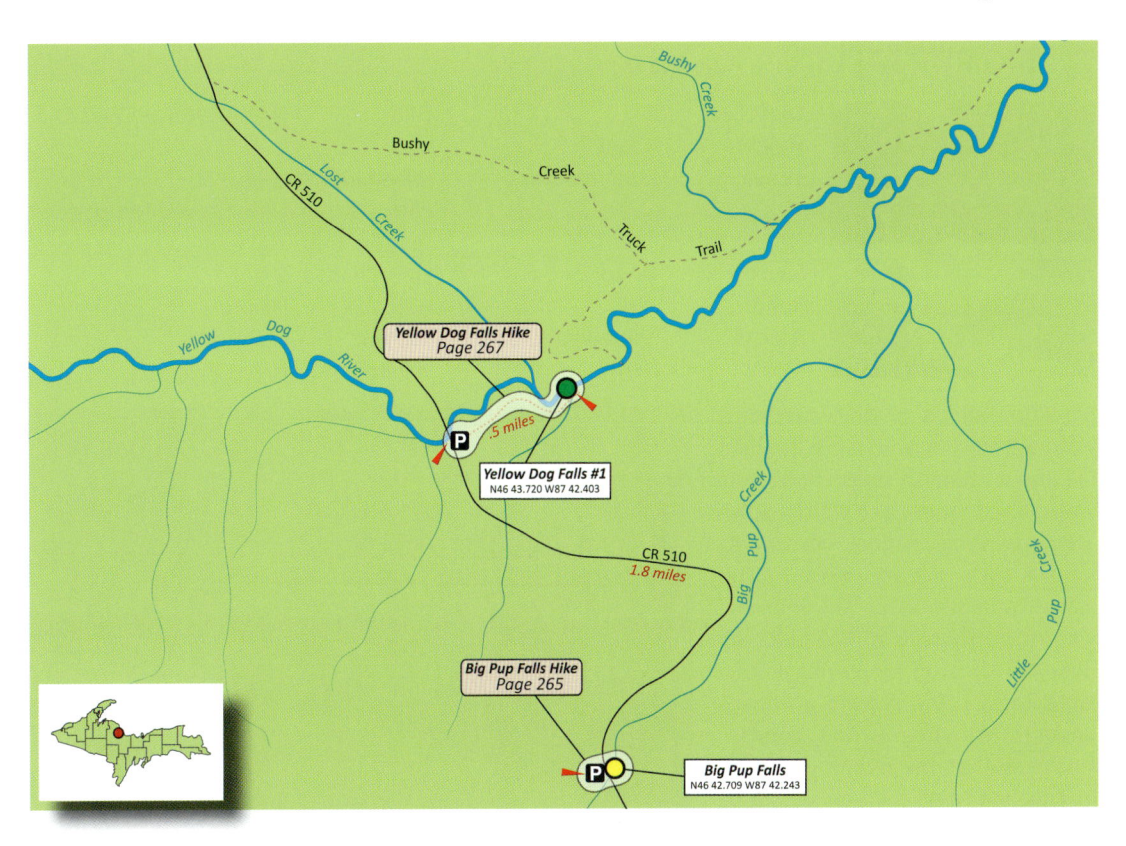

### Big Pup Falls Hike

Although I've been told that a family of otters lives near the falls, I have never had the pleasure of watching them at play. Big Pup Creek starts dropping just after it passes beneath CR 510.

*Directions:* On CR 510, 1.8 miles south of the Yellow Dog River Bridge is a bridge over the Big Pup Creek. Park on the northwest side of the bridge. Big Pup Falls is a short 100 feet from the road.

Yellow Dog Falls Area

## BIG PUP FALLS (BIG PUP CREEK)  Private

| | | | |
|---|---|---|---|
| Must See: | 6 | GPS: | N46 42.709 W87 42.243 |
| Height: | 4 feet | | |
| Time: | 5-15 minutes | Hiking Information | |
| | | Path: | Unimproved footpath |
| Driving Information | | Length: | 100 feet |
| Signs: | None | Elev. Change: | Slight |
| Road: | Dirt | GPS: | Helpful |
| Access: | Somewhat easy | Danger: | Moderate |
| 4WD: | N/A | WP Boots: | N/A |

Big Pup Falls is a long, cascading waterfall starting with a nearly shear fall into a roundish splash pool. The waterfall continues as it churns down a long twisting channel, descending into a rock strewn ravine. This almost qualifies as a "Kid Friendly" waterfall. There is a nice place up near the top drop for playing among large trees. The ground is mostly undergrowth free. The concern I have is that the ravine drops off quickly and small children should be closely supervised in this area.

Fractured bedrock creates a nicely cascading waterfall with 6 foot moss covered walls immediately below the falls. Towering evergreens overshadow the creek and eliminate most ground cover. Therefore, there are lovely, clear viewing areas along both banks.

*The waterfall is close to CR 510, the road seen above*

### Yellow Dog Falls Hike

The Yellow Dog River is over 31 miles in length and by the time it flows below CR 510 it is about 7 miles from Lake Independence. The first 4 miles of the river are designated as a "wild river" by the US Fish and Wildlife Service. The rugged river has its start in Bulldog Lake, within the confines of the McCormick Tract. It then flows over the Bulldog Falls, through the Yellow Dog Plains, over Pinnacle Falls, then over the Yellow Dog Falls and on to Lake Independence.

*(There are many more waterfalls in the area. For information on these, check out Book 2 of the Waterfalls of Michigan guidebook series.)*

Drive down CR 510 to the bridge over the Yellow Dog River. On the far side of the bridge (south) is a parking area on the east side of the road. An obvious trail heads down river, crosses a couple of wet areas (waterproof boots are recommended) and ends at Yellow Dog Falls #1. This is about a 1/2 mile hike.

*Looking down from up above the popular waterfall*

Yellow Dog Falls Area

## 🟩 YELLOW DOG FALLS #1 (YELLOW DOG RIVER)   Private

| | | | |
|---|---|---|---|
| Must See: | 8 | GPS: | N46 43.720 W87 42.403 |
| Height: | 11 feet | | |
| Time: | 30-40 minutes | Hiking Information | |
| | | Path: | Footpath |
| Driving Information | | Length: | .45 miles |
| Signs: | None | Elev. Change: | Moderate |
| Road: | Dirt | GPS: | Recommended |
| Access: | Easy | Danger: | Moderate |
| 4WD: | N/A | WP Boots: | Recommended |

Smooth, wildly curved bedrock below the falls makes for a great viewing or picnicking platform when the river is low. A large rock outcropping juts forward in the middle of the falls, forcing the river to split around it, cascading down either side. A secondary drop of 3 feet is below the irregularly shaped spill pool.

There are a number of waterfalls on the Yellow Dog River, but this one displays itself in such a way as to feel more powerful than many of the other ones. Ferns and even a hardwood tree grow on the bulwark of rock in the center of the waterfall. It splits wide (about 75 feet), a white frothy cascade on both sides rushing down to a second level of pitted yellowish-brown bedrock. The waterfall then rushes back together in front of the exposed face, finishing the drop with a final 2 foot plunge into the river below.

# CHAPTER 11
# MENOMINEE COUNTY

# Menominee County Map

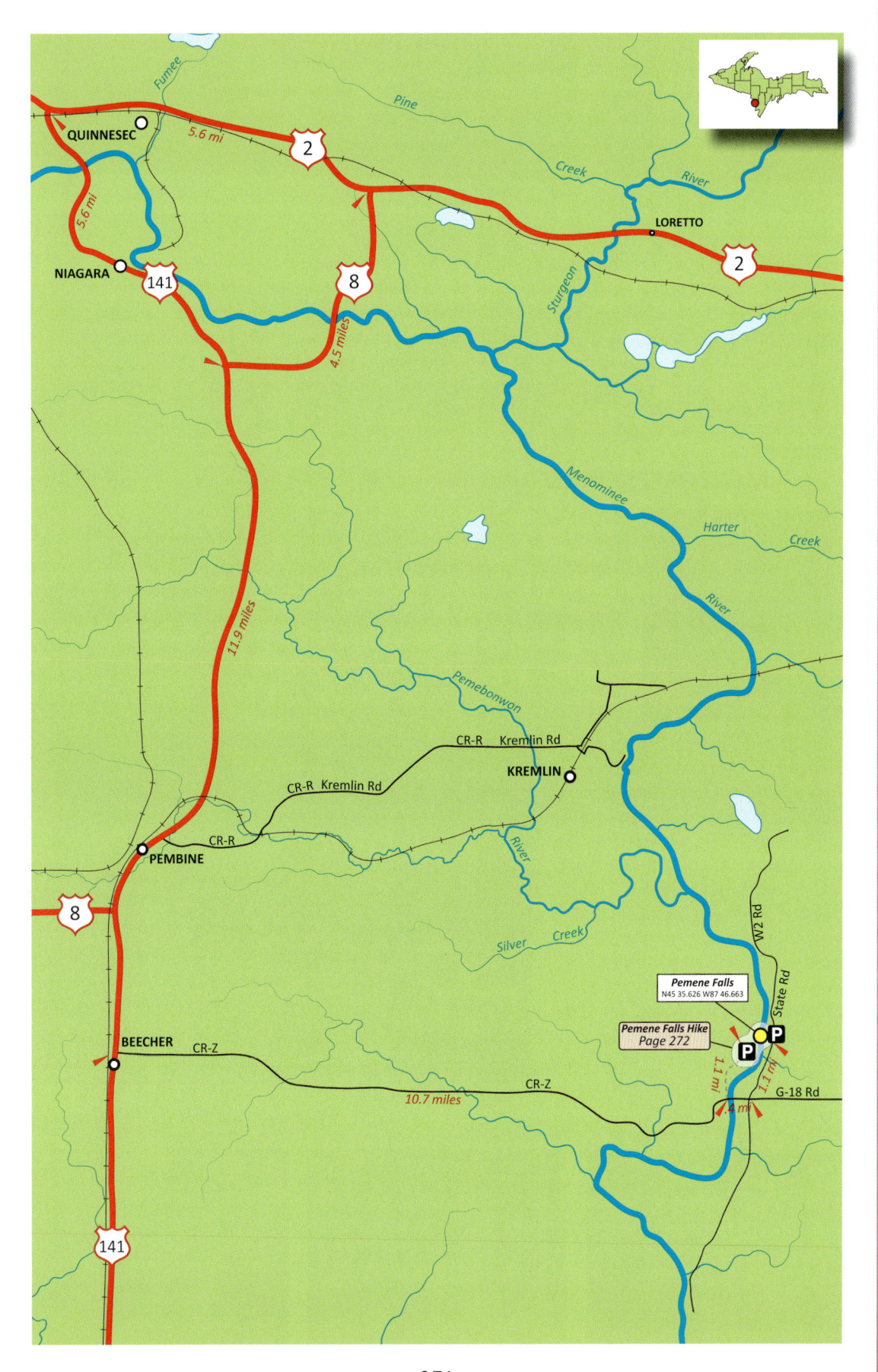

Pemene Falls Area

MENOMINEE COUNTY

Pemene Falls Area

### Pemene Falls Hike

After having been to the Wisconsin side of the river, I have discovered that there is an easy looking access point on the Michigan side. I haven't verified it, so I will give you directions to the Wisconsin side. Use the area map on the previous page to see my directions on viewing from Michigan via State Road.

*Directions:* From US-2, head south into Wisconsin on US-141 to Beecher. Turn left (east) onto County Road Z. In 10.7 miles, just before getting to the Menominee River, turn left (north) on Verheyen Road. Travel about 1.1 miles on a deteriorating dirt road to the trailhead in the Wisconsin State Park. Some signage is there describing the area. The footpath begins at the shaded parking area with a narrow, but easily hiked trail. It heads straight to the river, turning quickly to the left once the river comes in view. Presently, it descends to the shore level and as the trail drops, the undergrowth increases. At several places, the trail is barely discernible, but since it follows the river, there is no fear of becoming lost. Two hundred yards before the rapids, an outcropping rises to offer a great initial view. Continue on the footpath around a small cove and up again to a higher bluff up above the rapids.

## PEMENE FALLS (MENOMINEE RIVER)                                Private

| | | | |
|---|---|---|---|
| Must See: | 5 | GPS: | N45 35.626 W87 46.663 |
| Height: | 8 feet | | |
| Time: | 45-70 minutes | Hiking Information | |
| | | Path: | Footpath - faint at times |
| Driving Information | | Length: | .35 miles |
| Signs: | None | Elev. Change: | Minor |
| Road: | 2-track | GPS: | Helpful |
| Access: | Somewhat difficult | Danger: | Minor |
| 4WD: | N/A | WP Boots: | N/A |

The river runs in a narrows, constricted between masses of rock. A rib of rock further splits the river. Concrete remains of an old bridge or dam are still in place, now billboards for graffiti. The river widens dramatically after the rapids, opening up in an expanse that is viewed generously from a 30 foot outcropping along the riverbed.

I'd like to check this out from the Michigan side. It looks like a short dirt road heads almost to the old concrete abutments at the river.

*Part of the trail by the river*

*The better part of the footpath*

*The 2-track to the trailhead*

272

# CHAPTER 12
# ONTONAGON COUNTY

# Ontonagon County Map

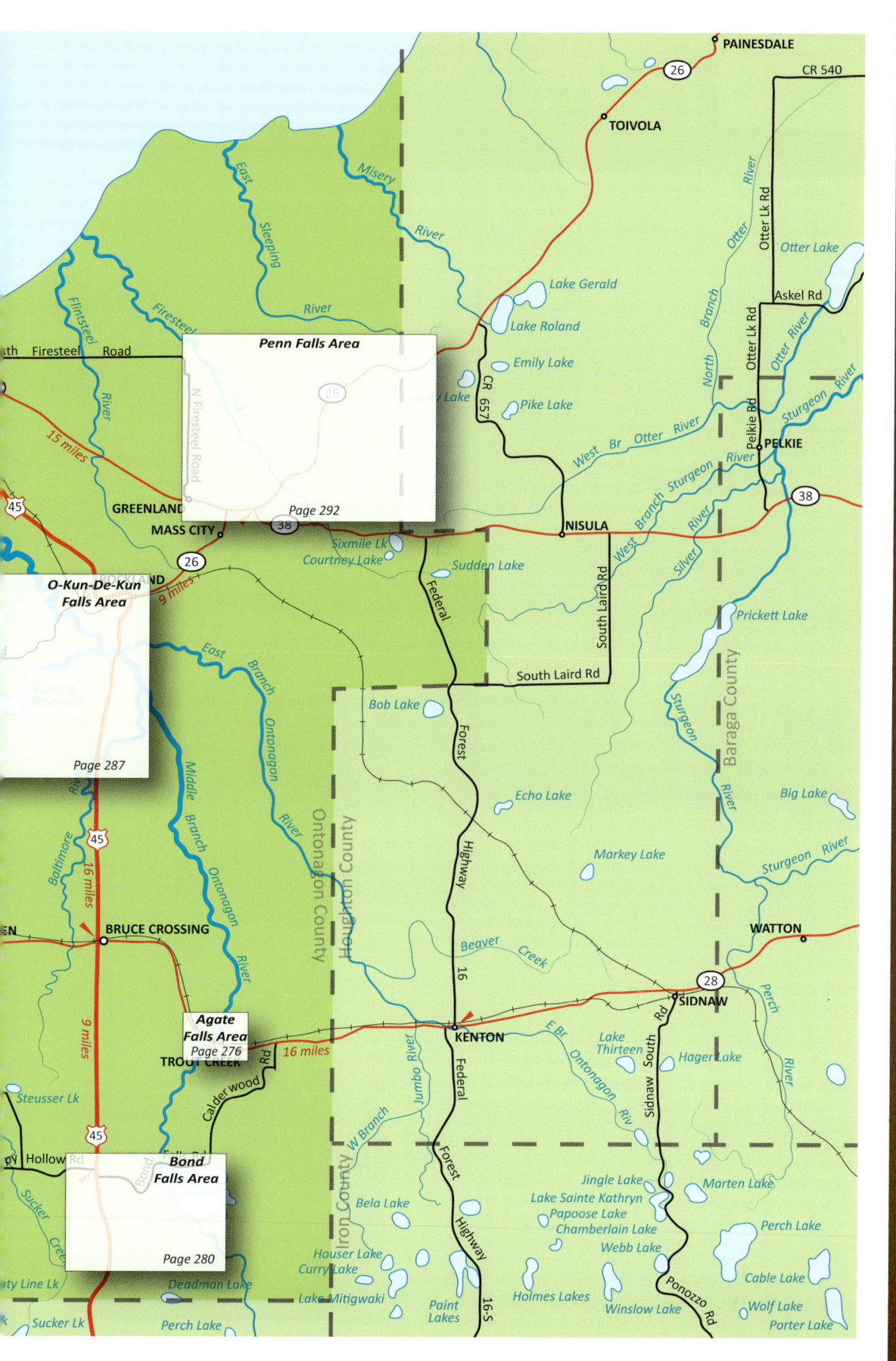

ONTONAGON COUNTY

Agate Falls Area

### Agate Falls Hike

Agate Falls is one of the most beautiful waterfalls in Michigan! And fortunately, it is an easy, short hike to view it from the top. The Middle Branch of the Ontonagon River flows over a multi-stepped sandstone ledge resulting in numerous cascades. The quiet waters below the falls are favored by local fishermen.

The Michigan DNR maintains the Agate Falls Scenic Site which is located on the south side of M-28 while Agate Falls is on the north. A vehicle pass is required at the Scenic Site. It is a tastefully maintained park, with toilets, water and picnic tables available. There are plenty of paved parking spots and a wide sidewalk follows the river to the north, passing beneath the highway and continuing to a waterfall overlook above the falls.

In 1900 a railroad trestle was constructed high above the falls. It has since been converted for snowmobile use. It is a common site in the winter to see snowmobilers stop and peer over the side rail to catch an overhead view of the waterfall.

*The steep trail down into the ravine*

*Directions:* About 4 miles west of Trout Creek on M-28 is the Agate Falls Scenic Site on the left (south) side of the road just before the bridge that crosses the Middle Branch of the Ontonagon River. Park (a Recreation Passport is required). Follow the walkway a short distance to the river then turn and continue on the wide path under M-28 and over to the waterfall viewing area. A steep unimproved fisherman's trail continues down into the ravine below the falls. This trail is not easy to navigate, so it is not recommended for children.

# AGATE FALLS (WEST BRANCH - ONTONAGON RIVER) Private

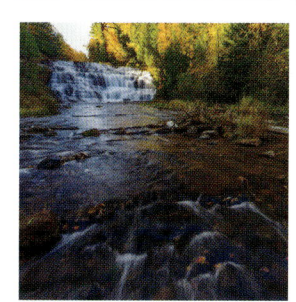

| | | | |
|---|---|---|---|
| Must See: | 10 | GPS: | N46 28.858 W89 05.418 |
| Height: | 30 feet | | |
| Time: | 10-40 minutes | Hiking Information | |
| | | Path: | *Paved then Dirt |
| Driving Information | | Length: | *.15 miles or .25 |
| Signs: | Roadside | Elev. Change: | *Moderate or Elevated |
| Road: | Main | GPS: | N/A |
| Access: | Very Easy | Danger: | *Slight or Elevated |
| 4WD: | N/A | WP Boots: | *N/A or Recommended |

*The first set of data is to the overlook - the second is to climb down to the base of the falls.

It is my understanding that a large hotel was situated on the site over 100 years ago. Tourists would catch a train from downstate, arriving in the logging community of Trout Creek. Photography was a recent phenomena and men and women would climb down a wooden set of stairs dressed in their finest to have their photographs taken at the base of the falls. The lure and charm of this waterfall remains and many take advantage of the relatively easy access to enjoy Agate Falls to this day!

*The 1929 bridge carries M-28 over the river*

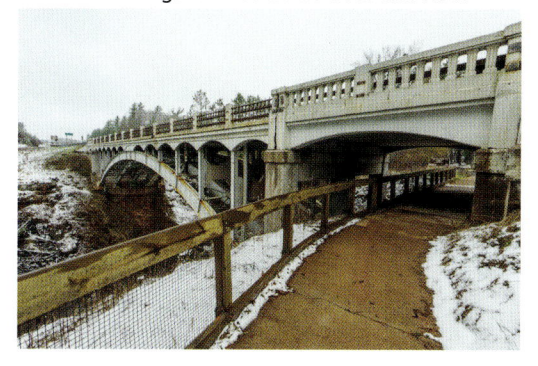

*The viewing deck at Agate Falls*

ONTONAGON COUNTY

Agate Falls

Bonanza Falls Area

ONTONAGON COUNTY

## Bonanza Falls Hike

Bonanza Falls, also known as "Greenwood Falls", is not a typical Michigan waterfall. The Big Iron River runs against the grain of the angled rock layers. This forces the river to pool and then drop over the ledges. During periods of lower water it is possible to walk nearly across the river on the exposed rock ridges. There are drops for several hundred yards downstream.

A silver mine was established here in 1872 but was closed by 1876. The initial anticipation for a "Bonanza" of silver gave the nearby waterfall its name. Later on, in the early 1900's, the Greenwood Lumber Company built their headquarters on the premises. The waterfall then started to take on the name "Greenwood Falls". It currently goes by both names, but it is most often referred to as "Bonanza Falls".

*The history of Bonanza Falls - a sign on the drive to the falls*

*Directions:* Drive south on M-64 from the intersection of M-107 for .9 miles. Turn right (west) on a 2-track and follow it to the end. Park. The main drop is nearly straight ahead. Climb down about 6 feet to the river's edge.

278

## BONANZA FALLS (BIG IRON RIVER)

Private

| | | | |
|---|---|---|---|
| Must See: | 7 | GPS: | N46 49.057 W89 34.204 |
| Height: | 14 feet | | |
| Time: | 5-30 minutes | Hiking Information | |
| | | Path: | Unimproved path |
| Driving Information | | Length: | 100 feet |
| Signs: | Roadside | Elev. Change: | Slight |
| Road: | Main | GPS: | N/A |
| Access: | Very Easy | Danger: | Slight |
| 4WD: | N/A | WP Boots: | N/A to helpful |

Bonanza Falls is a family paradise! The numerous small pools and countless miniature drops can keep an inquisitive individual occupied for hours. What better way to spend a hot summer day than wading in the cool water and listening to the rush of falling water along the Big Iron River. My youngest son loves to slide down the "main" plunge. He typically comes up covered in small leeches, but he thinks half of the fun is pulling them off!

*Looking back toward the parking area*

*High water in spring*

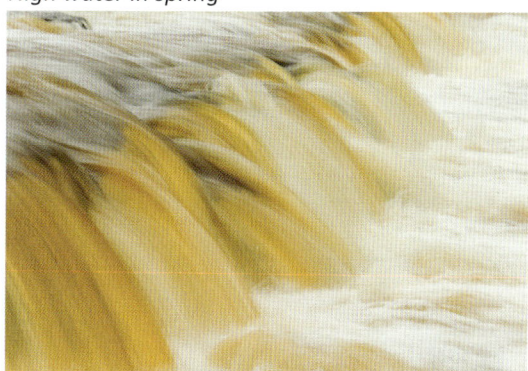

*Low water on a gorgeous autumn day*

279

Bond Falls Area

ONTONAGON COUNTY

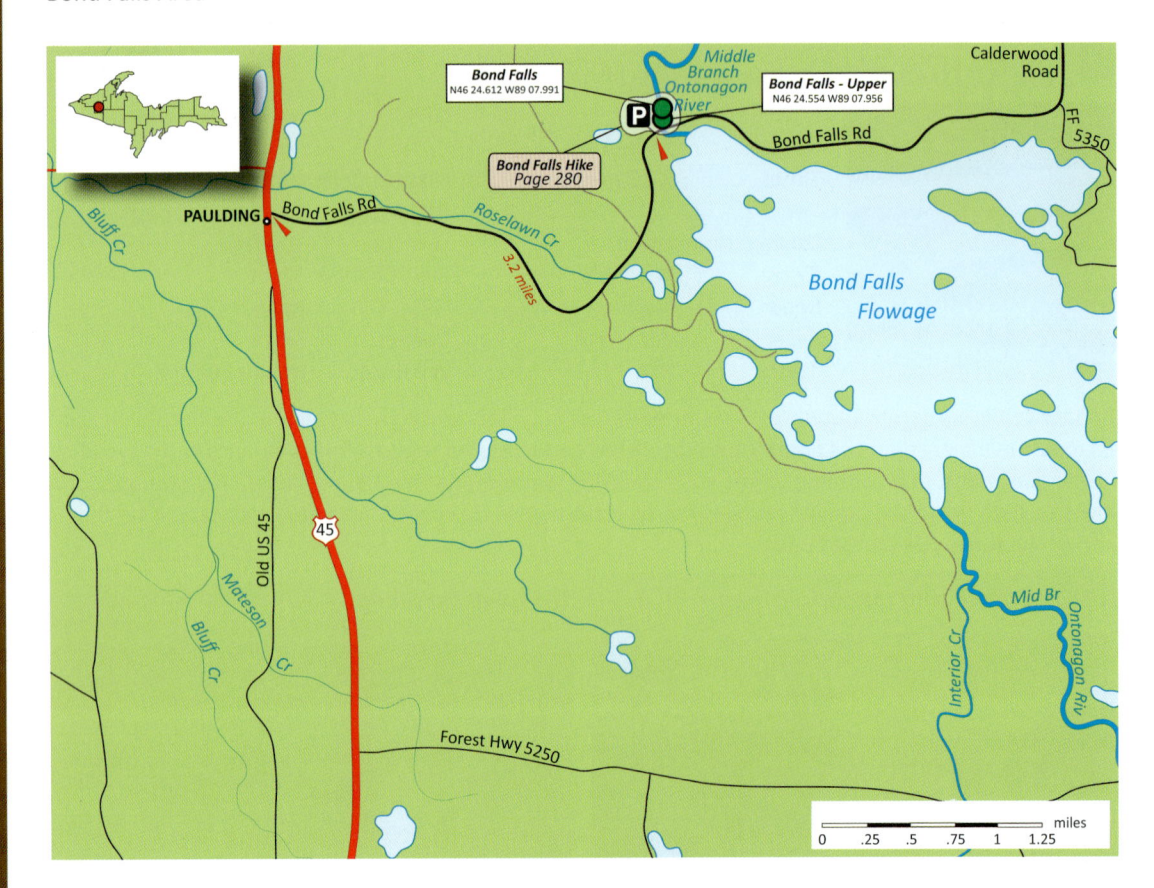

## Bond Falls Hike

What a waterfall! A number of smaller drops conclude with the main drop that is so well known. About 500 gallons of water flow over the falls every second. This supports a thriving brook trout population.

Six viewing locations along an expansive boardwalk allow for a number of visitors to enjoy a multitude of perspectives of this top-rated waterfall. This is the easiest of the waterfalls with my "10" ratings to hike to. It is only about 200 yards to the falls on a fairly level wheelchair accessible path.

There are more rustic paths leading away from the observation deck along both sides of the waterfall. These lead to the Upper Falls. The trail on the west side is the better of the two and passes by the famous "Z" that is a favorite stopping spot for photographers.

A Recreational Passport is required for access to the site. For current information check the DNR website at http://www.michigandnr.com/parksandtrails/Details.aspx?id=412&type=SPRK or call (906) 353-6558.

*Directions:* About 10 miles north of US-2 and 9 miles south of M-28 on US-45 is the ghost town of Paulding. A gas station on the corner serves as a landmark for Bond Falls Road. Turn east and follow Bond Falls Road for 3.2 miles to the well marked entrance to Bond Falls on the left (north). A short steep paved drive descends to the base level below the falls. Park in the ample lot. Hike 200 yards to the observation deck. Climb up the trails on either side of the waterfall to access the Upper Falls.

Bond Falls Area

# BOND FALLS (MIDDLE BRANCH - ONTONAGON RIVER)   Private

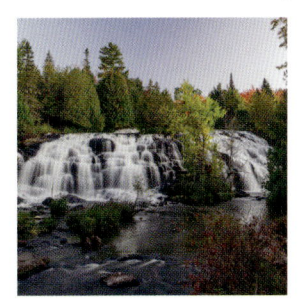

| | | | |
|---|---|---|---|
| Must See: | 10 | GPS: | N46 24.612 W89 07.991 |
| Height: | 50 feet | | |
| Time: | 5-60 minutes | **Hiking Information** | |
| | | Path: | Boardwalk |
| **Driving Information** | | Length: | 200 yards |
| Signs: | Large Entrance | Elev. Change: | Slight |
| Road: | Secondary | GPS: | N/A |
| Access: | Easy | Danger: | Slight |
| 4WD: | N/A | WP Boots: | N/A to helpful |

Bond Falls has been attracting sightseers since the 1800's. In the 1930's the Bond Falls Dam project was begun. The idea was to divert water from the Ontonagon River's Middle Branch to the South Branch by means of Roselawn, Sucker and Bluff Creeks. This would increase the water flow to the Victoria Power Plant by as much as 35 percent, allowing for a decent increase in the amount of electricity produced there. Nearby mines were demanding more and more cheap power and this seemed like the perfect fix. Unfortunately, when the diversion took place in 1937, the ENTIRE Middle Branch was stopped for years as the flowage filled up. This killed all the fish down river and created a huge outcry from fishermen and environmentalists as well as the local population. Plans for several more dams scheduled for construction along the river were scrapped. Finally, in 1940, water was again flowing over Bond and Agate Falls. Much has been done in the years since to restore the public trust. Just recently, a $5 million upgrade to the dam and spillway has improved the safety of the dam and allows for a greater flow of water over the falls.

ONTONAGON COUNTY

Bond Falls

281

Bond Falls Area

ONTONAGON COUNTY

Bond Falls

282

## BOND FALLS - UPPER (MIDDLE BRANCH - ONTONAGON RIVER)   Private

| | | | |
|---|---|---|---|
| Must See: | 7 | GPS: | N46 24.554 W89 07.956 |
| Height: | 20 feet | | |
| Time: | 20-75 minutes | Hiking Information | |
| | | Path: | Boardwalk, Stairs, Path |
| Driving Information | | Length: | 300 yards |
| Signs: | Large Entrance | Elev. Change: | Moderate |
| Road: | Secondary | GPS: | N/A |
| Access: | Easy | Danger: | Slight |
| 4WD: | N/A | WP Boots: | N/A to helpful |

Climb up the improved side of Bond Falls (west side). Concrete stairways with rails assist in the ascent. Keep in mind that in the winter, spray from the falls ices the stairway, making it extremely dangerous.

Once at the top of Bond Falls, the Upper falls come into view. There are a series of drops that can be seen as you walk along the river's edge. Autumn viewing is iconic and you will likely join other tourists enjoying the breath taking beauty of one of Michigan's most visited waterfalls.

Remember: A Michigan Recreational Passport is required for admittance to Bond Falls. They can be purchased on site.

# Cascade Falls Area

### Cascade Falls Hike

A spur off of the North Country Trail extends southward to Cascade Falls. Take either the "High" or "Low" trail for various looks at the terrain along the hike.

*Directions:* From Bergland, drive 1.3 miles east on M-28. Turn left (north) onto Forest Road 400 (a dirt road). Follow it for about 7.1 miles. A well marked road to the right ends at the trailhead. There is plenty of room for parking. Hike down the groomed trail to the falls.

## CASCADE FALLS (CASCADE CREEK)   Private

| | | | |
|---|---|---|---|
| Must See: | 7 | GPS: | N46 39.087 W89 26.762 |
| Height: | 20 feet | | |
| Time: | 45-60 minutes | **Hiking Information** | |
| | | Path: | Well traveled |
| **Driving Information** | | Length: | 1/2 mile |
| Signs: | Roadside | Elev. Change: | Minor |
| Road: | Dirt | GPS: | Required |
| Access: | Somewhat Easy | Danger: | Slight |
| 4WD: | N/A | WP Boots: | Helpful |

As the name implies, Cascade Falls is made up of multiple cascades. Wildflowers grow profusely on a multitude of rocks scattered down river from the falls.

One of my most embarrassing waterfall experiences occurred here! I didn't know there was a trail to the falls, so I trekked cross-country with one of my sons along the southern side of the river. The nearly mile long hike led through dense undergrowth, wet areas, briars, and thick pines. We finally made it to this seemingly remote waterfall only to find a family at the top of the falls wearing flip-flops! We were glad to hike the extra mile back to the vehicle via the newly discovered trail!

### Little Trap Falls Hike

Two thirds of the way north between Lake Gogebic and the shore of Lake Superior lies the settlement of White Pine, created by the owners of the nearby White Pine Mine. The mine began operations in 1955 and was closed in 1995. In its glory days the mine employed over 3,000 workers. Now White Pine is down to less than 500 residents, consisting more and more of retirees looking for affordable solitude in beautiful northern Michigan.

It is just south of White Pine that Old M-64 veers off to the south. Not far off of this dirt road flows the upper reaches of an unnamed tributary of the Big Iron River. Little Trap Falls occurs as the stream pours down a fractured face into a short walled canyon.

*Directions:* From White Pine, drive south on M-64 for 2.5 miles to Old M-64. Follow Old M-64 (dirt road) for 2.2 miles. Park. Hike 250 yards to the falls using a GPS. Along the short hike you will cross a couple short but steep drainage channels. There is no trail and care needs to be taken in choosing good footing along in the uneven terrain.

Little Trap Falls Area

## LITTLE TRAP FALLS (ANDERSON CREEK)                                    Private

| | | | |
|---|---|---|---|
| Must See: | 7 | GPS: | N46 41.395 W89 33.380 |
| Height: | 25 feet | | |
| Time: | 20-40 minutes | Hiking Information | |
| | | Path: | None |
| Driving Information | | Length: | 250 yards |
| Signs: | None | Elev. Change: | Moderate |
| Road: | Gravel Road | GPS: | Required |
| Access: | Somewhat Difficult | Danger: | Minor |
| 4WD: | N/A | WP Boots: | Required |

Walk up the creek bed through the canyon with its 30 foot high walls to view the falls from its base. The creek slides down a steep face of moss-covered angular rocks. Various small plants line the sides of the falls.

The volume of water flowing over this waterfall varies greatly during the year. I recommend visiting after a good rain, or early in the spring. One note of caution, however: Old M-64 is not plowed in the winter. In fact, it is used as a snowmobile trail. This packs the snow down and takes a long time to melt. This will delay accessibility via automobile. Don't get stuck trying to push through the slowly melting snow!

*The waterfall can slow to a trickle as seen in this August picture*

ONTONAGON COUNTY

Little Trap Falls

286

O-kun-de-kun Falls Area

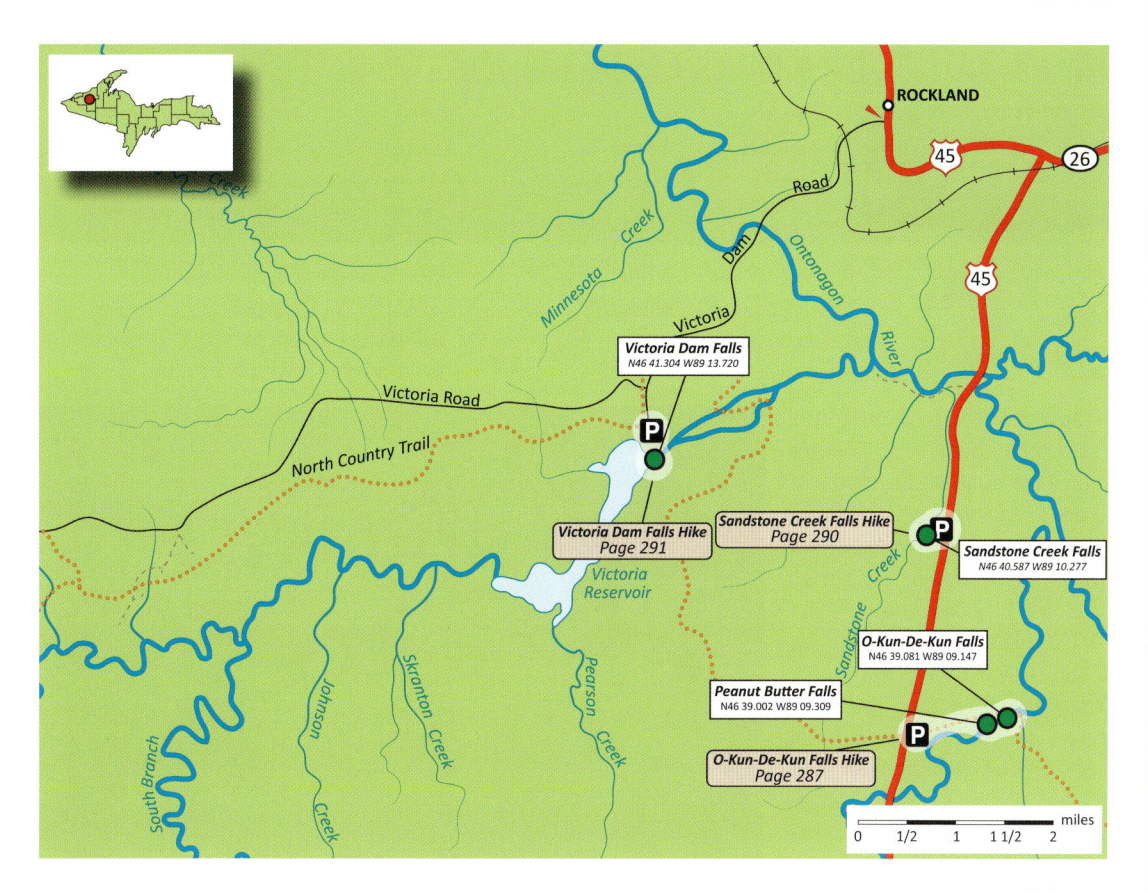

ONTONAGON COUNTY

### O-kun-de-kun Falls Hike

It is always a joy to be able to hike along a section of the North Country Trail! This hike is no exception. Follow the trail, just wide enough for one person, through briar thickets, over sometimes muddy areas, beneath mature hardwoods, and finally along the Baltimore River to the waterfalls. A well constructed footbridge crosses the river just below O-kun-de-kun Falls. Near the bridge are several primitive campsites within earshot of the falls.

*Directions:* Drive 6.1 miles south from the junction of M-26 and US-45 or north 8 miles from Bruce Crossing on US-45. Turn east into a short parking area at the trailhead to the falls. Park. Hike to the falls. Peanut Butter Falls is 1.1 miles from the parking area. The main falls is another 300 yards down river.

O-kun-de-kun Falls Area

## PEANUT BUTTER FALLS (BALTIMORE RIVER)    Private

| | | | |
|---|---|---|---|
| Must See: | 7 | GPS: | N46 39.002 W89 09.309 |
| Height: | 8 feet | | |
| Time: | 60-90 minutes | Hiking Information | |
| | | Path: | Narrow but well kept |
| Driving Information | | Length: | 1.1 miles |
| Signs: | None | Elev. Change: | Slight |
| Road: | Main | GPS: | Helpful |
| Access: | Easy | Danger: | Slight |
| 4WD: | N/A | WP Boots: | Recommended |

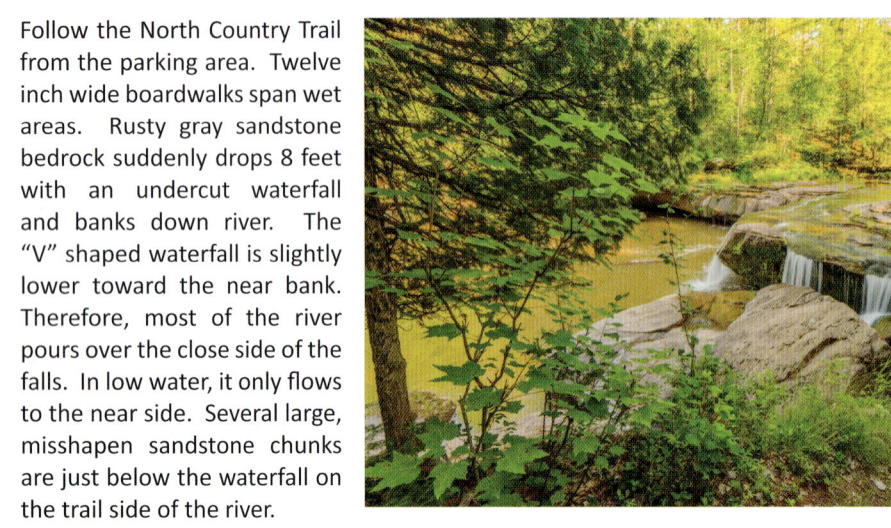

Follow the North Country Trail from the parking area. Twelve inch wide boardwalks span wet areas. Rusty gray sandstone bedrock suddenly drops 8 feet with an undercut waterfall and banks down river. The "V" shaped waterfall is slightly lower toward the near bank. Therefore, most of the river pours over the close side of the falls. In low water, it only flows to the near side. Several large, misshapen sandstone chunks are just below the waterfall on the trail side of the river.

ONTONAGON COUNTY

Peanut Butter Falls

288

# O-KUN-DE-KUN FALLS (BALTIMORE RIVER)

Private

| | | | |
|---|---|---|---|
| Must See: | 9 | GPS: | N46 39.081 W89 09.147 |
| Height: | 18 feet | | |
| Time: | 75-120 minutes | **Hiking Information** | |
| | | Path: | Narrow but well kept |
| **Driving Information** | | Length: | 1.3 miles |
| Signs: | None | Elev. Change: | Moderate |
| Road: | Main | GPS: | Helpful |
| Access: | Easy | Danger: | Slight |
| 4WD: | N/A | WP Boots: | Recommended |

Continue to follow the trail downstream from the Peanut Butter Falls about .16 miles. As is often the case, the sound of the waterfall will be the first evidence that the waterfall is getting close! And then the wonderful waterfall will come into view. It is easily seen from the North Country Trail bridge that spans the Baltimore River below the falls. The waterfall itself is centered in a 70 foot wide sandstone cliff wall. An undercut, 20 feet deep, angles back behind the falls allowing for an exhilarating, if somewhat dangerous view from behind the falls. A large shelf of rock halfway down the falls provides a close-up and personal experience with the waterfall!

*Ice formations in the cave behind the falls*

*Winter highlights the tannins and sediment in the Ontonagon River watershed*

**ONTONAGON COUNTY**

O-Kun-De-Kun Falls Area

**Sandstone Creek Falls Hike**

Put on a thick pair of jeans and some good hiking boots. This short hike down to the falls is through some of the thickest saplings and undergrowth I've encountered! Poplars grow tightly together down the steep hillside. Trees that have succumbed to age or wind lay haphazardly along the route as well. The reward for pressing through is a view that few have witnessed in person!

Driving southerly, US-45 climbs up out of the Ontonagon River Basin after it crosses the Ontonagon River. As the road nears the top of the plateau, it is no longer right next to the creek. The road has taken a fairly straight path while the creek's upstream route comes in further west.

*Directions:* (On US-45) About 1 3/4 miles south of the bridge over the Ontonagon River, a thick, tree covered ravine can be seen on the west side of the road. Just past the ravine is a clear, steep embankment rising to a small field. Park here. Climb up the embankment, heading towards the trees in the middle of the west side of the field. The terrain starts to drop, heading for the river. I have found that it's easier to get down to the creek up above the waterfall. The trees aren't as thick, and the ravine not as steep.

## SANDSTONE CREEK FALLS (SANDSTONE CREEK)    Private

| | | | |
|---|---|---|---|
| Must See: | 7 | GPS: | N46 40.587 W89 10.277 |
| Height: | 12 feet | | |
| Time: | 60-75 minutes | Hiking Information | |
| | | Path: | None |
| Driving Information | | Length: | .23 miles |
| Signs: | None | Elev. Change: | Elevated |
| Road: | Main | GPS: | Required |
| Access: | Easy | Danger: | Elevated |
| 4WD: | N/A | WP Boots: | Recommended |

Set amongst some of the thickest undergrowth I have seen, this seldom seen waterfall cascades down over stair-stepped sandstone, widening out below the falls to run wall to wall between rusty brown canyon walls. A small tributary cuts through the rocks on the near side of the creek, forming a small, trickling waterfall.

*The shallow "canyon" can be seen in the lower left photo, although the walls are much higher and intimidating in person! This is another reason to come down above, rather than below, the waterfall. The creek flows from wall to wall downstream, so there is no easy way to get down to the creek below there.*

### Victoria Dam Falls Hike

Victoria Dam was originally built in the early 1900's at the sight of an impressive waterfall. The river has since provided power to the area. Subsequent upgrades to the dam and hydroelectric plant as well as a partial diversion of the Middle Branch of the Ontonagon River brings the capacity to 850 cubic feet per second with a 215 foot head. It is able to operate at about 80% efficiency per year. When the flow of water coming into Victoria Reservoir exceeds this volume, the excess is diverted over what remains of the falls. There are times when there is NO water running over the falls. This occurs primarily in July and August. For the best chance at seeing a substantial torrent of water, check out the waterfall during the spring melt.

*Directions:* From Rockland, turn off of US-45 to the west on Victoria Dam Road (AKA: Elm Street). The road winds and twists through the rugged countryside. In 4 miles Victoria Road turns to the left (west). CONTINUE TO THE SOUTH to stay on Victoria Dam Road for another .8 miles to the parking area slightly below the dam and in plain sight of the discharge tube as it runs down the hillside. Park. View the waterfall from up near the dam or hike past the gate (no driving allowed) along the service drive to see the waterfall closer. Respect the dam property and personnel.

## VICTORIA DAM FALLS (ONTONAGON RIVER - WEST BRANCH)   Private

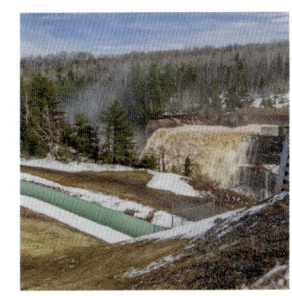

| | |
|---|---|
| Must See: | 9 |
| Height: | 50 feet |
| Time: | 5-20 minutes |

**Driving Information**
| | |
|---|---|
| Signs: | (For the dam) |
| Road: | Dirt |
| Access: | Somewhat Easy |
| 4WD: | N/A |

| | |
|---|---|
| GPS: | N46 41.304 W89 13.720 |

**Hiking Information**
| | |
|---|---|
| Path: | N/A |
| Length: | 100 yards |
| Elev. Change: | Moderate |
| GPS: | None |
| Danger: | Slight |
| WP Boots: | None |

Remember that dams hold large amounts of water behind them. In the event you hear a siren, seek high ground immediately! The "Must See" rating can vary from 2 to 9 depending on water flow. Keep this in mind when deciding to visit the waterfall.

*Spring Melt: so much force there is a rainbow*

*Dry Autumn: barely a trickle runs down the face*

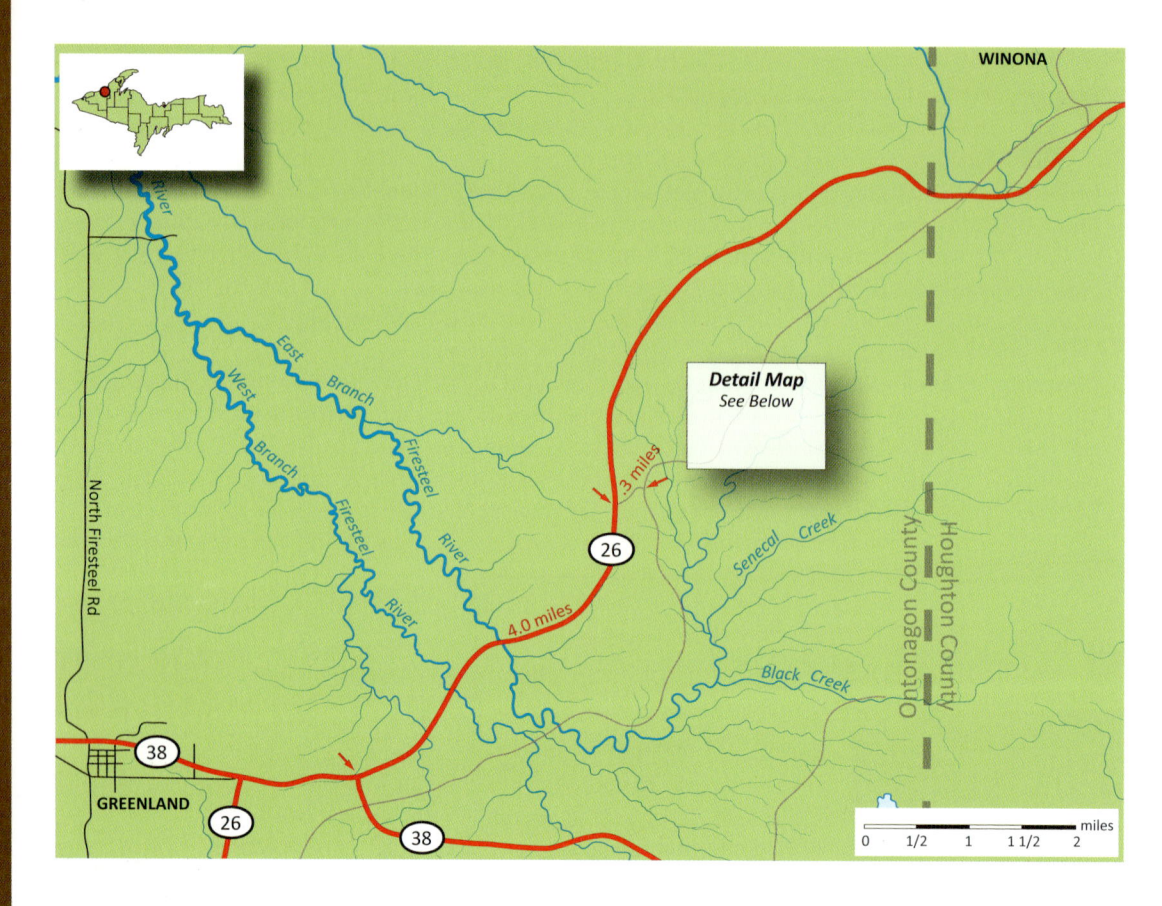

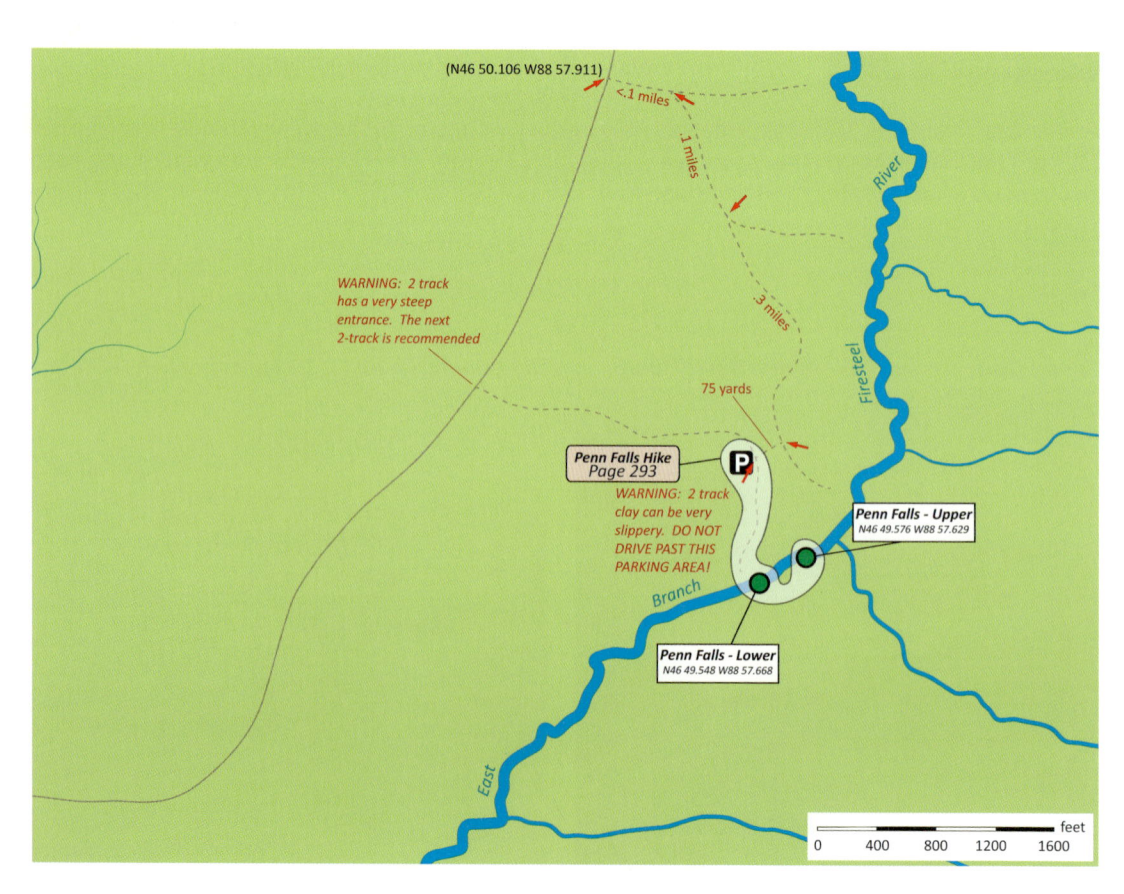

Penn Falls Area

## Penn Falls Hike

One of my most memorable adventures happened here at the Firesteel River. My oldest son was with me on one of the rare occasions we have had to go hiking together. It was a beautiful October day and we had been to a number of waterfalls. I had never been to Penn Falls. In fact, I didn't even know about them until late into my project. Anticipating a long hike, we were pleasantly surprised to find a 2-track that took us upstream from the falls. The waterfalls were still a distance downstream. After finding the waterfalls, we noticed that there was a 2-track that ran right down to the river near the lower drop. So we looked for that 2-track after getting back to the vehicle. It was easy to find, but the trail headed rapidly downhill toward the river. Before it dropped even more sharply I decided to turn around in a small clearing. That's where a problem really presented itself! This whole area is Ontonagon clay based. A thin layer of October leaves covered the wet, slippery mess below. After several hours of trying to get my 4WD Chevy out of the slimy muck it was obvious that it wasn't going to happen without some help. I called AAA to see what type of assistance they could offer. The cell phone signal was poor, and the agent was not helpful at all. This chewed up the last 1/2 hour of precious daylight. By this time, we were ready for a warm shower, a clean bed and some much needed sleep. So we each quickly made an overnight bag out of our camera backpacks and started hiking out of the woods. The sun had completely set during this time so we had a night hike ahead of us. The village of Ontonagon was about 20 miles away. We really hoped that we could find a kind soul or two to drive us partway there. We hiked about 3 miles back to M-26 and there met a vehicle. We had found our kind soul! Here was a hunter heading out from his hunting camp for some supper. After explaining our plight to him, he gave us a ride to Rockland where we had a wonderful Saturday Pizza Buffet with him at *Henry's Never Inn*. From there we went back to see about getting the truck out. After an hour of futile effort, he took us to his nearby hunting lodge where we spent the night. In the morning, he went out hunting with his aging dog and let us drive his truck to a rendezvous he had set up the night before with an off-road towing company from Houghton. We led the tow truck driver to our vehicle. He winched it 100 yards up the 2-track, and then promptly got stuck himself! Now there were two 4WD's in trouble. About this time, our hunter friend and his dog came wandering in. They had hiked the several miles along the river to see how we were doing. Putting all the tow ropes together that we could scrounge up, there were just enough to hook the hunter's truck to the tow truck and pull him out. He then winched me up the rest of the way and we were once again on our way! It's nice to know that there are still helpful people in this world. May we all be like our "guardian angel" yooper!

*Directions:* Drive 4 miles northeast on M-26 from the eastern intersection of M-38. Turn right (east) on a short connector dirt road. It ends at a "T" junction in .3 miles. Turn left (north) onto the old railroad bed made into a dirt road. Follow it for 1.9 miles. Turn right (east) onto a 2-track at N46 50.106 W88 57.911. (Higher clearance is needed - A 4WD is recommended) Veer right in less than .1 miles. Stay right in .1 miles. Stay right in .3 miles. Stay right and park in 75 yards where the 2-track "V's". Walk down the 2-track to the left to the lower waterfall. (DO NOT drive down this 2-track! This is where I became quite stuck!) Wade across the river, climb the far bank and follow it upstream to the upper falls.

Penn Falls Area

## PENN FALLS - LOWER (FIRESTEEL RIVER - EAST BRANCH) Private

| | | | |
|---|---|---|---|
| Must See: | 7 | GPS: | N46 49.548 W88 57.668 |
| Height: | 10 feet | | |
| Time: | 30-60 minutes | Hiking Information | |
| | | Path: | 2-track |
| Driving Information | | Length: | .17 miles |
| Signs: | None | Elev. Change: | Moderate |
| Road: | 2-track | GPS: | Recommended |
| Access: | Difficult | Danger: | Slight |
| 4WD: | Recommended | WP Boots: | Recommended |

The lower fall is a classic cascading face waterfall occurring as the river exits the short canyon. The setting is so idyllic! Looking at the waterfall from the shoreline the canyon wall rises up far above the waterfall, the river hugging the wall's edge. The far side of the river rises much more gently. On the near river's edge a stone fire ring is centered in a naturally flat space. It is an inviting campsite that I'm sure has seen its share of fishermen!

ONTONAGON COUNTY

Penn Falls - Lower

294

# PENN FALLS - UPPER (FIRESTEEL RIVER - EAST BRANCH) Private

| | | | |
|---|---|---|---|
| Must See: | 7 | GPS: | N46 49.576 W88 57.629 |
| Height: | 15 feet | | |
| Time: | 45-75 minutes | Hiking Information | |
| | | Path: | 2-track |
| Driving Information | | Length: | .22 miles |
| Signs: | None | Elev. Change: | Moderate |
| Road: | 2-track | GPS: | Recommended |
| Access: | Difficult | Danger: | Moderate |
| 4WD: | Recommended | WP Boots: | Required |

The steep canyon wall on the northwest side of the river requires crossing the river at the lower falls to be able to get to the upper falls. Once across the river, climb up the embankment to the top of the lower waterfall. The riverbank is easily navigated. There is not much undergrowth and the going is easy.

As the river enters the canyon, a 10 foot drop slides down a steep conglomerate face. An angular spill pool at the base turns hard around a small outcropping, then cascades down another 3 feet to the edge of the canyon wall. Then it bursts down 2 feet to a final black pool beneath the overhanging rock.

*The view from the top*

*Looking upstream*

ONTONAGON COUNTY

# CHAPTER 13
# PORCUPINE MOUNTAINS

# Porcupine Mountains Map

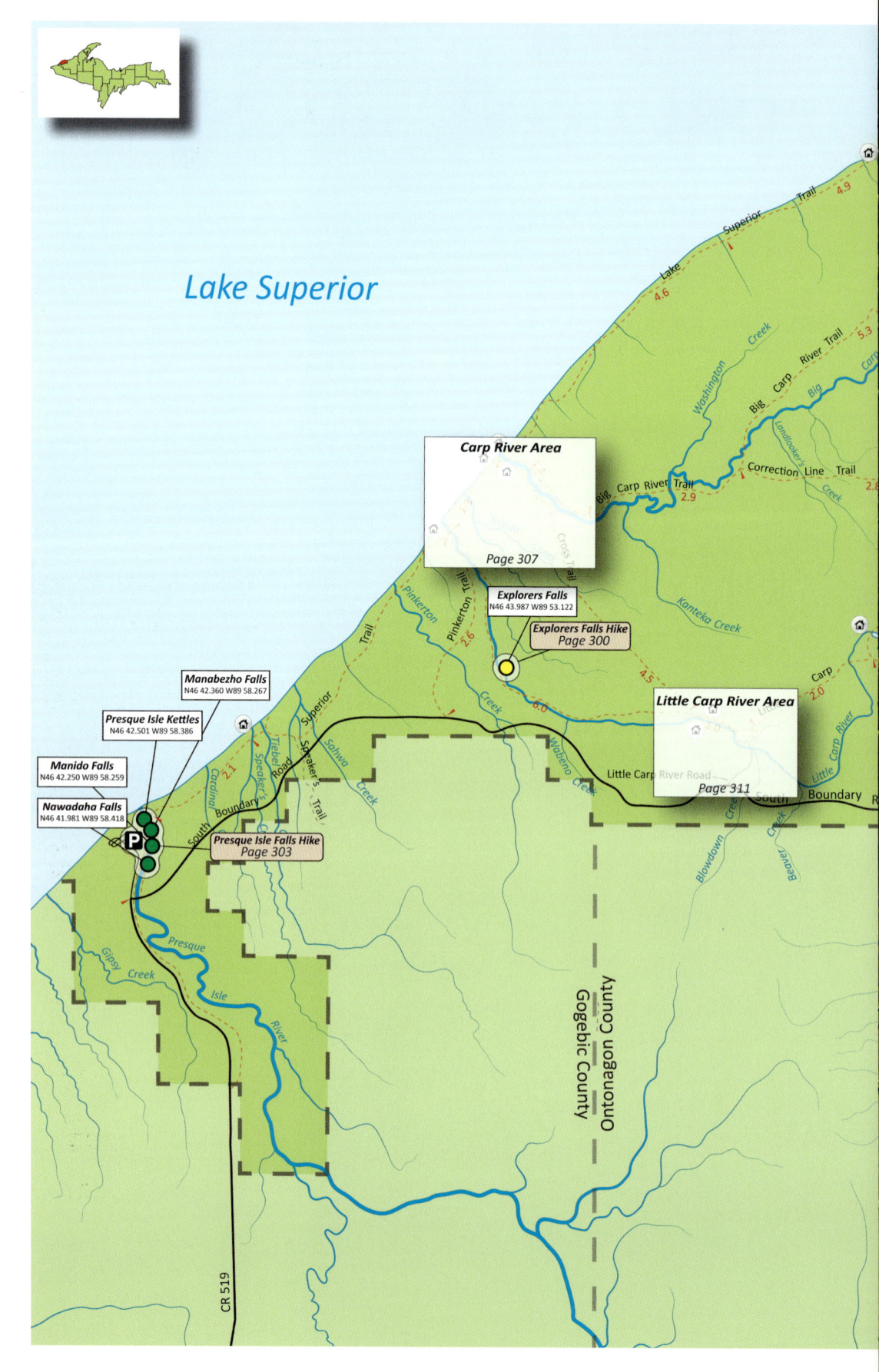

*Lake Superior*

**Carp River Area**
Page 307

**Explorers Falls**
N46 43.987 W89 53.122

**Explorers Falls Hike**
Page 300

**Little Carp River Area**
Page 311

**Manabezho Falls**
N46 42.360 W89 58.267

**Presque Isle Kettles**
N46 42.501 W89 58.386

**Manido Falls**
N46 42.250 W89 58.259

**Nawadaha Falls**
N46 41.981 W89 58.418

**Presque Isle Falls Hike**
Page 303

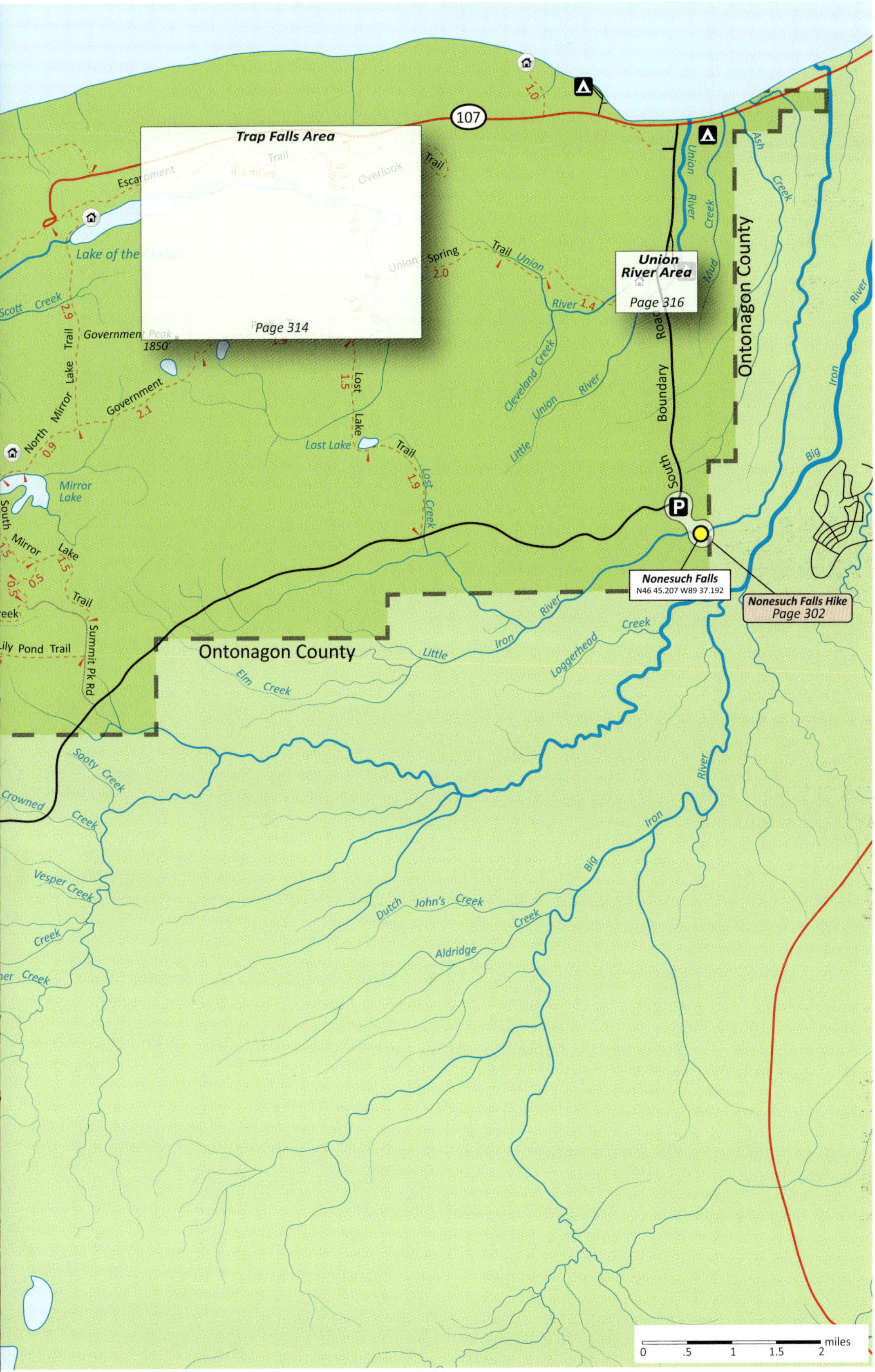
107
Trap Falls Area
Page 314
Union River Area
Page 316
Escarpment
Lake of the
Scott Creek
Government Peak
1850'
North Mirror Lake Trail
Government
2.1
2.9
0.9
Mirror Lake
South Mirror Lake Trail
Lily Pond Trail
Summit Pk Rd
Lost Lake Trail
Lost Lake
Lost Creek
1.5
1.9
Trail
Spring
2.0
Union
Union River 1.4
Trail
Cleveland Creek
Little Union River
South Boundary Road
Union River
Mud Creek
Ash Creek
Ontonagon County
Big Iron River
Nonesuch Falls
N46 45.207 W89 37.192
Nonesuch Falls Hike
Page 302
Little Iron River
Loggerhead Creek
Elm Creek
Sooty Creek
Crowned Creek
Vesper Creek
Dutch John's Creek
Aldridge Creek
Big Iron River
0 .5 1 1.5 2 miles

## Explorers Falls Hike

There is some confusion surrounding this set of waterfalls on the Little Carp River. The long slide has often been referred to as Trappers Falls, but I believe that it is actually Explorers Falls. There is no waterfall properly down river from this waterfall and the little waterfall upstream about 1/3 mile more accurately reflects the proper position for Trappers Falls. I hate to fly in the face of tradition, but I want to be as accurate as possible. In this *"Collection"* book we will only examine "Explorers Falls". *Book 4 of the Waterfalls of Michigan guidebook series covers many more waterfalls on the western end of the Upper Peninsula.*

Quiet. Peaceful. Hiking through miles of Porcupine Mountains' wilderness typically reveals nothing of man's presence other than a narrow footpath and an occasional wooden bridge over a ravine or creek. In this solitude, the only sounds to be heard are those of nature at work. Small feet scurry, carrying a chipmunk with twitching nose and beady eyes to view the surrounding from atop a fallen tree. A scolding black squirrel, hiding from view as it climbs up the backside of a sugar maple, drowns out the tap-tap-tap of a pileated woodpecker looking for a meal in an old hemlock. The Little Carp River gurgles and splashes, supplying flora and fauna alike with a seemingly endless source of life. Leaves and twigs crunch underfoot, especially during the golden autumn season.

*Directions:* There is no "obvious" way to these falls. It really depends on what else you are trying to see along the way. Let me describe the 3 "shortest" ways to the falls:

### The Simplest Way
Park at the end of Little Carp River Road. Remember that there is no place to turn trailers or RV's around here! Follow the Little Carp River Trail. It basically follows the northern side of the river until it gets close to Explorers Falls. You need to ford the river (there is no bridge) as the trail continues along the southern side to the falls. This hike is about 7 miles (round trip) long.

### The Shortest Way
Park on the side of the South Boundary Road between Wabeno Creek and Pinkerton Creek. Hike cross country to the falls. **THERE IS NO TRAIL! A GPS is required.** I have not hiked this route, so I don't know what conditions to expect. Plan on about a 1.5 mile (round trip) hike.

### The Western Route
Park at the trailhead for the Pinkerton Trail on South Boundary Road. Hike the Pinkerton Trail to the Little Carp River. Cross the river on the footbridge that is part of the Superior Trail. This will intersect with the western end of the Little Carp River Trail. Follow it to the east along the northern side of the river to the falls. This route requires about a 9 mile hike to complete.

The advantage to the **Shortest Way** is obviously the much shorter distance. The **Simplest Way** gives you just one trail to follow and is shorter than the **Western Route**. It also passes by a number of waterfalls that are found in the Little Carp River Area. The **Western Route** provides access to Lake Superior as well as the waterfalls found near the mouth of the Little Carp River, but this hike is the longest of the three.

There are many other hiking route options. Take into account your level of experience and ability when planning a hike, especially the longer ones that present themselves in Porcupine Mountains State Park. Enjoy! And be safe!

# EXPLORERS FALLS (LITTLE CARP RIVER) — Private

| | | | |
|---|---|---|---|
| Must See: | 6 | GPS: | N46 43.987 W89 53.122 |
| Height: | 20 feet | | |
| Time: | Varies | **Hiking Information** | |
| | | Path: | Varies |
| **Driving Information** | | Length: | Varies |
| Signs: | None | Elev. Change: | Moderate |
| Road: | Secondary | GPS: | Varies |
| Access: | Somewhat easy | Danger: | Moderate |
| 4WD: | N/A | WP Boots: | Recommended |

This waterfall has traditionally been referred to as Trappers Falls, but as there is no waterfall down river for a ways and there is a drop upstream, I believe that this is the true Explorers Falls; Trappers Falls being further upstream. This follows the USGS pattern.

The conglomerate slide follows the pattern so typical at Porcupine Mountains' waterfalls. The tilted bedrock creates these "slides", many of which are found on the Big Carp River to the north.

*Looking down from the top of the sliding waterfall you get a good view of the conglomerate bedrock*

## Nonesuch Falls Hike

The old birch tree overlooks Nonesuch Falls, its gnarled roots grasping air as the soil, once packed securely around its base, has washed down river over the years during the rush of numerous spring melts. Oh, the countless stories it could tell of when it was but a sapling: The laughter of children splashing below the falls; the sound of steel on rock; the murmur and curses of men's voices as they tried with limited success to wrench stubborn copper from the hard earth; the slowly growing pile of poor rock tailings on the far side of the river; and then... nothing.

The once proud community, lacking the prosperity needed to keep its economic engine running, moved on, its dreams and hopes falling into ruin, much like its buildings would over the years. Slowly the forest reclaimed the land, swallowing up all but the hardiest remnants of the mine.

Now, day after day, the aging birch sits silently, listening to the endless chatter of the falls, interrupted occasionally by the call of a bird, the furtive approach of a white tail deer looking for a drink of water, or the snuffling of a black bear searching out black berries.

My musings are interrupted by the darkening sky leaking a fine mist. I pack away my field notes and take a long last look at the birch. I see that its heart is exposed, foretelling its doom. Any day it will topple over, falling into the river from which it drank these many years.

*Directions:* South Boundary Road runs along two general corridors. The longer of the two is the east/west route that winds along the park's southern border. The north/south portion begins near the park's visitor's center and heads down along the eastern edge of the park. At the point that these two legs of the road meet in a large sweeping bend (4.25 miles south of M-107), a 2-track runs off to the southwest for a short distance. It ends at a small clearing where a number of vehicles may park near a metal gate. Informational signage provides a historical context for the ruins and clearings that are observed on the way to the falls. Follow the nicely mowed path through the woods and finally into a clearing that was once the site of the mining community. The trail angles to the right at the rear of the clearing and reenters the woods. Immediately the trail splits. Head left. The trail divides again. The left path ends at a point down river from the falls. To the right, the trail ends at the base of the falls. Both paths pass by the mining ruins.

## NONESUCH FALLS (IRON RIVER)   Private

| | | | |
|---|---|---|---|
| Must See: | 5 | GPS: | N46 45.207 W89 37.192 |
| Height: | 15 feet | | |
| Time: | 40-70 minutes | Hiking Information | |
| | | Path: | Footpath |
| Driving Information | | Length: | .47 miles |
| Signs: | None | Elev. Change: | Slight |
| Road: | Secondary | GPS: | N/A |
| Access: | Somewhat easy | Danger: | Slight |
| 4WD: | N/A | WP Boots: | N/A |

A rocky riverbed adds an interesting look down river from the angling waterfall. Make sure to spend time at the ruins while here. Imagine what it must have been like living through snowy northern winters, viewing the amazing beauty that was literally just outside the door, working underground for long hours, dragging around heavy steel tools and moving heavier yet stone.

## Presque Isle Falls Hike

Magnificent waterfalls; Coveted camping sites; Towering hemlocks; Ample paved parking lots; Seemingly tame whitetail deer; Numerous boardwalks; Well placed viewing decks: These thoughts flit through my mind as I contemplate the popular Presque Isle waterfall area. "Presque Isle", a French term meaning "almost island", refers to the land mass near the mouth of the river which can become a short lived island during a heavy spring melt. At that time, the river divides around the large, wedge shaped area. A waterfall even forms on the seldom used riverbed on the far side of the "island".

I never tire of hiking along this section of the Presque Isle River. The natural features seen in this 3/4 mile hike are spectacular! The four waterfalls are connected by a series of boardwalks and dirt paths. At the northern end, a suspended bridge spans the river close to Lake Superior. This provides access to the east side of the river as well. There is a trail along that side also, but it is primitive and lacks the viewing platforms, stairs and guardrails that are found in abundance on the commonly traveled side.

Fifty primitive camp sites are within walking distance of the river. There are several vault toilets and a couple hand pumps that provide water. The campground is situated along the 100 foot high cliffs that overlook Lake Superior. Sunsets from this vantage point can be stunning! http://www.michigandnr.com/parksandtrails/Details.aspx?id=75&type=SPCG

Although the Presque Isle Campground is easily accessed, RV'ers often prefer the one hundred sites at the Union Bay Campground where there is electricity at every site, four water spigots are strategically located throughout the campground, and a modern bathhouse is centered among the campsites. *http://www.michigandnr.com/parksandtrails/Details.aspx?id=74&type=SPCG*

*Directions:* At the western end of Porcupine Mountains State Park drive north on CR 519 past South Boundary Road. After passing the small ranger's station (you must confirm that you have a recreational passport here) there are several parking areas to choose from. I prefer the furthest, which is at the end of the road. Park. Signage marks the way to the swinging bridge, which is about 200 yards from the parking lot. The Presque Isle Kettles are located just up river from the bridge. After viewing the "Holes" come back and follow the wooden stairs and walkway up river .7 miles to the 3 other waterfalls.

## PRESQUE ISLE KETTLES (PRESQUE ISLE RIVER)   Private

| | | | |
|---|---|---|---|
| Must See: | 8 | GPS: | N46 42.501 W89 58.386 |
| Height: | 3 feet | | |
| Time: | 20-40 minutes | Hiking Information | |
| | | Path: | Footpath |
| Driving Information | | Length: | 200 yards |
| Signs: | None | Elev. Change: | Moderate |
| Road: | Secondary | GPS: | N/A |
| Access: | Easy | Danger: | Slight |
| 4WD: | N/A | WP Boots: | N/A |

Circular bowls, hollowed out by boulders caught in swirling eddies over the years, display a uniquely beautiful pattern, fashioned as it were by a master artist. When the water level is just right, the river pours from one bowl to the next. During the spring melt and after heavy rainfalls the river may be too high to even see the bowls. When the river is quite low, the riverbed will be dry between some of the bowls.

Porcupine Mountains Area

## ■ MANABEZHO FALLS (PRESQUE ISLE RIVER)  Private

| | | | |
|---|---|---|---|
| Must See: | 10 | GPS: | N46 42.360 W89 58.267 |
| Height: | 22 feet | | |
| Time: | 30-45 minutes | Hiking Information | |
| | | Path: | Footpath |
| Driving Information | | Length: | .25 miles |
| Signs: | None | Elev. Change: | Moderate |
| Road: | Secondary | GPS: | N/A |
| Access: | Easy | Danger: | Slight |
| 4WD: | N/A | WP Boots: | N/A |

There are two viewing decks for Manabezho Falls. The main deck is down river from the falls and provides a sweeping view of the falls and river from atop the gorge walls. The other deck is at the brink of the waterfall. There is not much to see from this vantage point. It is possible to climb down the steep embankment to the riverbed although this is discouraged due to the inherent danger and erosion concerns.

Manabezho, the Ojibwa name for a popular spirit-god, thought by some to enjoy playing tricks, lends its name to this, the most majestic of the Presque Isle waterfalls. In fact, I consider this to be one of the finest waterfalls in Michigan! What is the perfect volume of water for ideal viewing conditions? Perhaps this is the "trickiest" aspect of this waterfall! In the driest times, there are large patches of dry rock at the top of the falls, with no water falling on the eastern side of the river. When the river is raging with spring melt or after heavy downpours, the water levels are so high, that no underlying rocks can be seen at all. I prefer something in between. I love it when water is running across the entirety of the river, and yet the rock outcroppings stand out- water pouring around them like sand sifting through outstretched fingers.

## MANIDO FALLS (PRESQUE ISLE RIVER)

Private

| | | | |
|---|---|---|---|
| Must See: | 7 | GPS: | N46 42.250 W89 58.259 |
| Height: | 8 feet | | |
| Time: | 40-60 minutes | Hiking Information | |
| | | Path: | Footpath |
| Driving Information | | Length: | .30 miles |
| Signs: | None | Elev. Change: | Moderate |
| Road: | Secondary | GPS: | N/A |
| Access: | Easy | Danger: | Slight |
| 4WD: | N/A | WP Boots: | N/A |

Smoothly sculpted into intricately shaped holes and pinnacles, the undulating patterns can only be seen when the river runs low enough to leave the western side of the riverbed above water. Looking like an otherworldly landscape, the milk chocolate colored bedrock gives way below the falls to a small debris field filled with splintered off pieces of rock, eroded from the banks of the river and waterfall cascades up river. In the spring, the river runs from bank to bank, completely covering this entire area!

The Ojibwa people were very impressed by this river. The strong currents, swirling eddies and impressive waterfalls made this a dangerous river to cross. This waterfall was named "ghost" or Manido Falls. Try to view the waterfall as an Ojibwa would have several hundred years ago. What an impressive sight! No boardwalks, no handrails, no roads. Just the thundering river, beautiful waterfalls, and no bridges!

*A circular polarizer knocks down the glare and reveals the rich colors during this misty morning.*

Porcupine Mountains Area

## NAWADAHA FALLS (PRESQUE ISLE RIVER)                                Private

| | | | |
|---|---|---|---|
| Must See: | 8 | GPS: | N46 41.981 W89 58.418 |
| Height: | 10 feet | | |
| Time: | *60-80 minutes | Hiking Information | |
| | | Path: | Footpath |
| Driving Information | | Length: | .60 miles |
| Signs: | None | Elev. Change: | Moderate |
| Road: | Secondary | GPS: | N/A |
| Access: | Easy | Danger: | Slight |
| 4WD: | N/A | WP Boots: | N/A |

The Presque Isle River rushes through a shallow canyon cut through layers of shale and sandstone in the Nonesuch Shale bed. It tumbles over a series of waterfalls in the last mile of its journey to Lake Superior. Nawadaha Falls is the first of these drops, falling about 10 feet, cascading over sheets of bedrock, a haphazardly arranged stair-stepped affair.

Nawadaha, the Ojibwa name meaning "in the midst of the rapids", perhaps marks the beginning of the nearly continuous waterfalls and rapids that stretch down river from here to Lake Superior. This waterfall, like the next one, Manido, are the little kids on the block compared to Manabezho Falls, the spectacular waterfall that many have mistaken for Tahquamenon Falls! Even so, it is a nice waterfall, especially when viewed with a low to medium volume of water flowing.

*Plan on 60-80 minutes if hiking from the far parking lot. This is the furthest of the falls from that spot. There is a parking lot across from the ranger station that provides an easy access to this waterfall. Plan on 10-20 minutes if using this access point.

## Carp River Hike

This is the longest of all the hikes that I have in this Michigan waterfall series! The Porcupine Mountains State Park has a very limited number of roadways within its premises. This is seen by some as limiting access, while others relish the primitive trails and rugged nature of the park. I concur with the latter. As much as my feet may ache after a long day of hiking, it is so rewarding to have intimately viewed the scenery, soaking in the sights and sounds of nature that are little changed after thousands of years.

*Directions:* There are various ways to get to this remote portion of the park. (1)Hike in along the shore from the north or south on the Lake Superior Trail, (2)follow the Carp River from the Lake of the Clouds overlook, (3)hike across the interior of the park on Correction Line Trail from Summit Park Road, (4)follow Little Carp River from the end of Little Carp River Road. (5)The shortest is the one I will describe. Drive along South Boundary Road (northeast) from CR 519 (at the west entrance to the park) about 4.5 miles to the Pinkerton Trailhead. Park off the side of the road in the small gravel parking lot. Hike the well traveled footpath northerly through a mostly flat mature hardwoods forest. Wooden planks attempt to cover wet areas along the way. Eventually the trail bridges Pinkerton Creek and continues cross country to meet up with the Lakeshore Trail and the Little Carp River Trail near the mouth of the Little Carp River. The 1.3 mile hike between Little Carp River and Carp River parallels the Lake Superior shoreline. Hike to the rhythm of the crashing waves that pound the rock strewn beach 100 yards from the trail. Thimbleberries offer August hikers a treat, their large green velvety leaves shading the sour-sweet delicate berries. After crossing the Big Carp River, the trail follows the northern side of the river past several waterfalls, with Shining Cloud Falls making for a wonderful destination point!

Carp River Area

## BATHTUB FALLS (CARP RIVER)                                                        Private

| | | | |
|---|---|---|---|
| Must See: | 7 | GPS: | N46 45.750 W89 52.660 |
| Height: | 15 feet | | |
| Time: | *Variable | Hiking Information | |
| | | Path: | Footpath |
| Driving Information | | Length: | *Variable |
| Signs: | None | Elev. Change: | Moderate |
| Road: | Secondary | GPS: | Recommended |
| Access: | Fairly Easy | Danger: | Moderate |
| 4WD: | N/A | WP Boots: | Recommended |

Bathtub Falls skips and slides down about 15 feet in a series of small cascades. The namesake feature, a hollowed out section of bedrock, looks like it was drilled out with an oversized bit. Actually, it is similar to the Presque Isle Kettles, formed over time by boulders spinning in eddies. I can only imagine that Indians, trappers and miners in days gone by may well have used this as a bathtub!

Looking from downstream, the river falls on the right side of the riverbed, turns 90 degrees to the left and then finishes its drop on the left side. It's a double slanted drop following the angle of the basalt bedrock.

*Time and distance are determined by hiking options. These can vary greatly in this back country hike.

Carp River Area

## BIG CARP FALLS (CARP RIVER)

Private

| | |
|---|---|
| Must See: | 7 |
| Height: | 12 feet |
| Time: | *Variable |

**Driving Information**
| | |
|---|---|
| Signs: | None |
| Road: | Secondary |
| Access: | Fairly Easy |
| 4WD: | N/A |

| | |
|---|---|
| GPS: | N46 45.531 W89 52.309 |

**Hiking Information**
| | |
|---|---|
| Path: | Footpath |
| Length: | *Variable |
| Elev. Change: | Moderate |
| GPS: | Recommended |
| Danger: | Moderate |
| WP Boots: | Recommended |

All the small slides in the "Big Carp" series set the stage for this 12 foot high slide! The river runs down the 30 foot long moss covered decline, divided into two streams unless the water volume is high enough to bring the two together.

At the base of the angled sandstone, the river widens out before surrounding a shallow rock island.

*Time and distance are determined by hiking options. These can vary greatly in this back country hike.*

PORCUPINE MOUNTAINS

Big Carp Falls

309

Carp River Area

## SHINING CLOUD FALLS (CARP RIVER)    Private

| | | | |
|---|---|---|---|
| Must See: | 9 | GPS: | N46 45.471 W89 52.014 |
| Height: | 30 feet | | |
| Time: | *Variable | Hiking Information | |
| | | Path: | Footpath |
| Driving Information | | Length: | *Variable |
| Signs: | None | Elev. Change: | Elevated |
| Road: | Secondary | GPS: | Recommended |
| Access: | Fairly Easy | Danger: | Extreme |
| 4WD: | N/A | WP Boots: | Recommended |

Porcupine Mountains' premier back country waterfall, Shining Cloud Falls, is tucked away into a gorge with 30 foot walls on either side. Climbing down to the base of the falls is difficult and dangerous. The steep hillside drops about 60 feet down from the trail to the cliff's edge. Then comes the dangerous part. A very narrow ledge angles down the face of the cliff with a short 3 foot drop interrupting its continuous descent. *After climbing back out of the ravine I think it may be easier to access the river by climbing down above the waterfall and carefully sliding down the near edge of the waterfall.*

I love mysteries! Several large conglomerate boulders sit in a riverbed that is made of sandstone. Where did THEY come from?

The waterfall is split in half except during periods of high water. The right side slides down the first third of the falls, continues in a sheer drop for the second third, and concludes the drop with another slide. The left side of the falls slides all the way to the river. The main drop is 20 feet high with a smaller, 10 foot double slide just downstream. A large piece of conglomerate sits at the base of the last drop.

*Time and distance are determined by hiking options. These can vary greatly in this back country

*Notice the conglomerate boulder on the right side of the riverbed below the smaller drops.*

310

Little Carp River Area

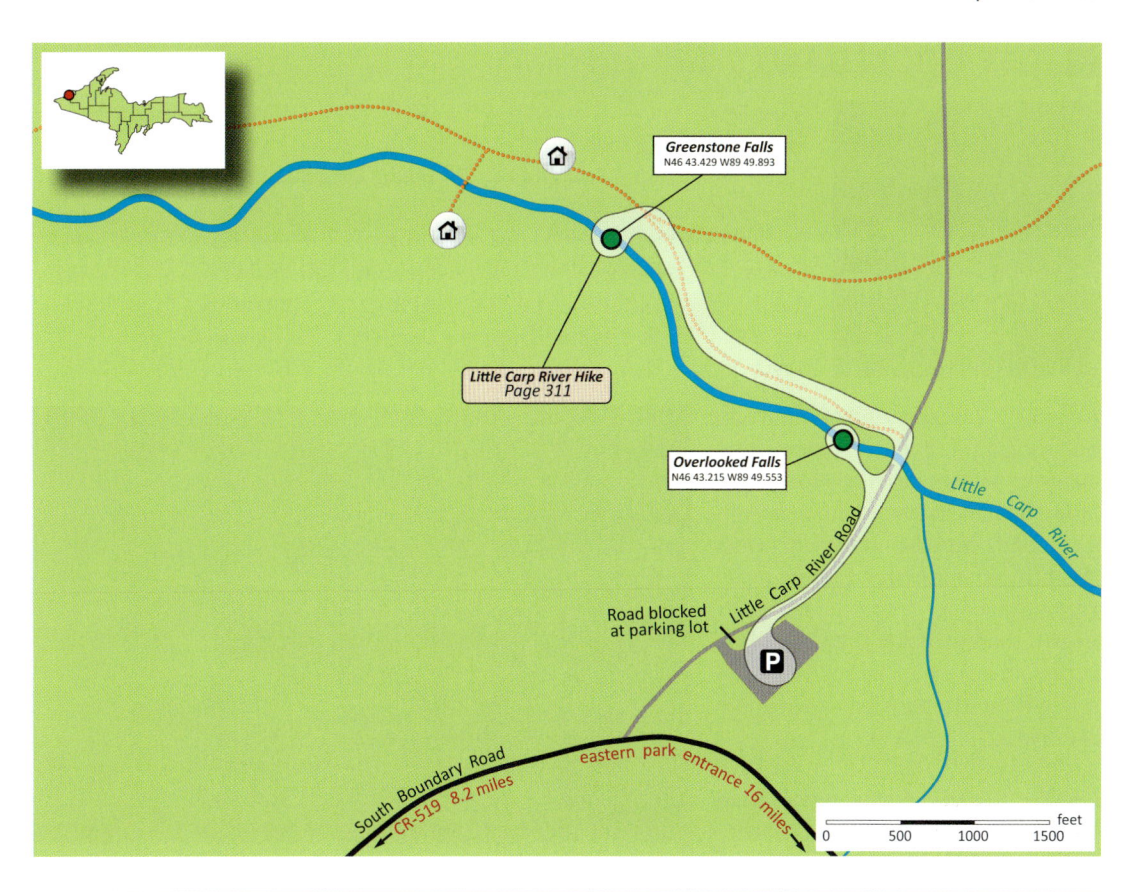

## Little Carp River Hike

Drink in the earthen smell on this hike through interspersed white pine, hemlock, maple and aspen. The muted footfalls of spongy earth underfoot are easily covered by the sound of the rushing, falling river that is ever near! Soak it up. Enjoy. Glory.

Overlooked Falls is probably the most viewed waterfall in the park besides the famous ones on the Presque Isle River. In fact, during one of my many stays at the AmericInn in Silver City a gentleman from the Chicago area showed me pictures of a replica of Overlooked Falls he had built in his garden!

The road continues over the Little Carp River but is gated and is only for use by park Rangers. Parking is set back from the river in an ample lot. The hike along the Little Carp River includes some improvements such as footbridges over small ravines and wet areas. But do be prepared to navigate over tree roots and uneven ground at times. The hike is predominantly level, running about 5 to 15 feet above the rivers edge. Climb down earthen banks at some of the waterfalls along the way to get to the base of the falls for ideal viewing.

*Directions:* Near the western entrance to Porcupine Mountains State Park, at the intersection of CR 519 and South Boundary Road, drive east on South Boundary Road for 8 miles. Turn left (northeast) onto Little Carp River Road. Drive .2 miles to the parking area. Park. Hike .4 miles down the access road to the river. Overlooked Falls is immediately down river. Stay on the near side (south) of the river to view the falls. Hike the short distance back to the road and cross the river on the bridge to pick up the Carp River Trail on the far side of the river. Hike down river (west) to get to Greenstone Falls.

Little Carp River Area

## OVERLOOKED FALLS (LITTLE CARP RIVER)   Private

| | | | |
|---|---|---|---|
| Must See: | 7 | GPS: | N46 43.215 W89 49.553 |
| Height: | 12 feet | | |
| Time: | 30-50 minutes | Hiking Information | |
| | | Path: | N/A |
| Driving Information | | Length: | .4 miles |
| Signs: | None | Elev. Change: | Slight |
| Road: | Dirt | GPS: | None |
| Access: | Somewhat Easy | Danger: | Slight |
| 4WD: | N/A | WP Boots: | None |

A split cascade surrounds an outcropping before connecting again in a roundish spill pool. A little further downstream however, a second cascade, narrower than the first, courses over various rocky knobs, spilling into a narrower angled causeway that then turns just in time to leave a rocky bank situated in a prime location for viewing the waterfall!

I prefer to view this waterfall from the southern side of the river. After viewing, head back to the parking lot, cross the bridge, and double back down river on the Carp River Trail to see Greenstone Falls.

# GREENSTONE FALLS (LITTLE CARP RIVER)   Private

| | | | |
|---|---|---|---|
| Must See: | 7 | GPS: | N46 43.429 W89 49.893 |
| Height: | 6 feet | | |
| Time: | 70-100 minutes | **Hiking Information** | |
| | | Path: | Footpath |
| **Driving Information** | | Length: | .85 miles |
| Signs: | None | Elev. Change: | Moderate |
| Road: | Dirt | GPS: | None |
| Access: | Somewhat Easy | Danger: | Moderate |
| 4WD: | N/A | WP Boots: | None |

The river flows over a nicely presented conglomerate mass with a nice viewing area along the river's edge. A dark spill pool dominates the area below the falls, the cool waters looking inviting on a hot summer's day!

There is little chance of missing Greenstone Falls. The Carp River Trail runs right by the falls with a sign marking the spot. The river has cut through the sediment down to the bedrock, so be prepared to climb down a steep hillside to get down to the river's edge.

313

Trap Falls Area

### Trap Falls Area Hike

One of my boys went with me on this hike. On our way back from Trap Falls something spooked him and he was sure he kept hearing a wolf as we were photographing the lower falls. He spent so much time looking for the wolf that I'm not sure he ever even took a picture! It is a good reminder that we are not alone in the woods and we need to respect our furred and feathered friends as we enter their environment.

Give yourself some time for this hike. It is a 4 mile round trip hike, but more importantly, the trail winds through an old growth forest with majestic trees on display along the Big Carp River.

*Directions:* Drive west on M-107, 3.5 miles past South Boundary Road. Park at the trailhead for Government Trail. There is a steep climb with rocks underfoot at the beginning of the hike. There are several more climbs toward the end of the 2 mile hike. The trail is well marked and maintained by the Park Service. The hike ends at the falls with a bench for resting and viewing the falls.

## TRAP FALLS (CARP RIVER)                                Private

| | | | |
|---|---|---|---|
| Must See: | 8 | GPS: | N46 47.534 W89 41.427 |
| Height: | 12 feet | | |
| Time: | 2-2.5 hours | Hiking Information | |
| | | Path: | Semi-improved footpath |
| Driving Information | | Length: | 2.01 miles |
| Signs: | None | Elev. Change: | Moderate |
| Road: | Secondary | GPS: | Required |
| Access: | Somewhat Easy | Danger: | Moderate |
| 4WD: | N/A | WP Boots: | Recommended |

Government Peak rises to 1,850 feet above sea level. Runoff from its slopes gathers in basins on its eastern and western flanks. These open water areas drain to the southeast and combine to form the beginning of the Carp River. After travelling through relatively flat and marshy terrain, the river begins a steeper descent northward through a low point in the middle ridge of the Porkies. About halfway through this descent is Trap Falls. The lower drops occur at the end of this rapid descent. The river then slows down and enters another marshy area extending to Lake of the Clouds and beyond.

Trap Falls is formed when the river narrows down to 1 foot wide as it slides down bedrock, fanning out like a bridal's veil as it makes its way to the bottom of the rock. A wonderful spill pool dominates the area below the falls before returning to the rock strewn river. This is a great picnic area. From this natural viewing area the waterfall presents itself beautifully with a head-on view.

*Trap Falls is also known as Epidote Falls*

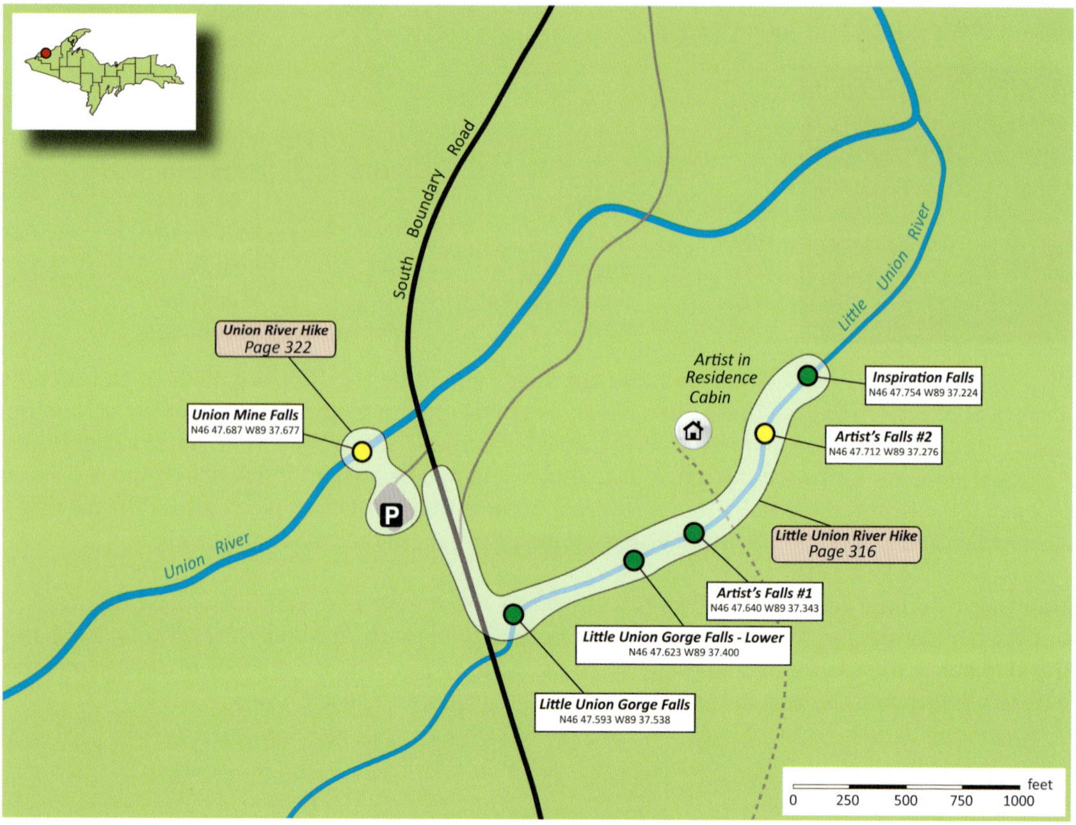
South Boundary Road
Union River Hike
Page 322
Union Mine Falls
N46 47.687 W89 37.677
Union River
Little Union River
Artist in Residence Cabin
Inspiration Falls
N46 47.754 W89 37.224
Artist's Falls #2
N46 47.712 W89 37.276
Little Union River Hike
Page 316
Artist's Falls #1
N46 47.640 W89 37.343
Little Union Gorge Falls - Lower
N46 47.623 W89 37.400
Little Union Gorge Falls
N46 47.593 W89 37.538
feet
0 250 500 750 1000

**Little Union River Hike**

The Little Union River originates between the slopes of the first two mountains on the eastern end of the southern ridge. There is no marshy land along the length of the Little Union River, so as soon as rain falls or snow melts, it rapidly evacuates the slopes, funnels down the river and is gone. Wetlands act as sponges that soak up excess moisture, slowly releasing it back to the waterways and thus moderating the volume of water that flows. Since The Little Union River is lacking this feature, it tends to be a "feast or famine" river. In dry conditions there may be no water at all in the river, the waterfalls looking like stubby, rocky cliffs and the riverbed a worn, wide walkway filled with smooth rock. But, in the spring as the snow is melting, or during a rainy season, the waterfalls come to life and transform this river into a waterfall bonanza!

*Directions:* Turn South on South Boundary Road off of M-107. Drive south for 1.7 miles to the Union Mine Trailhead on the right (west). Pull into the short drive and park in one of the many parking spots. There are often vehicles here, as this is the sole hiking trail access point on the eastern side of the park that leads to the network of trails that crisscross the Porcupine Mountains. Hike back to the road and follow the far side to the south for about 250 yards. A narrow footpath parts the roadside grass and enters the forest. (If the river is running well the Little Union Gorge Falls can be heard distinctly from the road.) The trail leads past the first two waterfalls before cutting across to the Union River. When it veers away from the river, leave the path and stay by the Little Union River to see the rest of the falls.

Union River Area

# LITTLE UNION GORGE FALLS (LITTLE UNION RIVER) Private

| Must See: | 7 | GPS: | N46 47.593 W89 37.538 |
|---|---|---|---|
| Height: | 50 feet | | |
| Time: | 10-20 minutes | Hiking Information | |
| | | Path: | Semi-improved footpath |
| Driving Information | | Length: | .18 miles |
| Signs: | None | Elev. Change: | Slight |
| Road: | Secondary | GPS: | N/A |
| Access: | Somewhat Easy | Danger: | Slight |
| 4WD: | N/A | WP Boots: | N/A |

The 30 foot wide riverbed slides down into the 40 foot deep Little Union Gorge perpendicular to the steep gorge wall. The viewing area with a bench and wooden guard rails is located at the top of the gorge. This works out wonderfully, as the waterfall is viewed head-on as it tumbles down the steeply slanted far wall of the gorge and then turns hard to the left and races along the narrow base of the gorge.

A mature forest maintains a thick canopy overhead. Large hemlock trunks stand tall while soft needles cushion the mostly level ground below.

*Note: This is a seasonal waterfall. During dry periods the Little Union River can completely stop running.*

*When the river flows with a good amount of water, the waterfall is beautiful, fanning out like a peacock displaying its colors!*

*Too often, the Little Union River dries up and becomes a mere ghost of its former self. I have seen this riverbed with no water at all flowing, even less than is shown in this picture which is nearly the same view as the shot shown just above!*

PORCUPINE MOUNTAINS

Union River Area

## LITTLE UNION GORGE FALLS - LOWER (LITTLE UNION RIVER) Private

| | | | |
|---|---|---|---|
| Must See: | 7 | GPS: | N46 47.623 W89 37.400 |
| Height: | 18 feet | | |
| Time: | 15-25 minutes | Hiking Information | |
| | | Path: | Semi-improved footpath |
| Driving Information | | Length: | .28 miles |
| Signs: | None | Elev. Change: | Slight |
| Road: | Secondary | GPS: | Helpful |
| Access: | Somewhat Easy | Danger: | Slight |
| 4WD: | N/A | WP Boots: | N/A |

The footpath that begins at the road runs along the top of the ravine with the Little Union River down at the bottom. It passes by Little Union Gorge Falls and this, the Lower Falls before cutting to the north to meet up with the Union River and then looping back to the parking lot near the Union Mine ruins. To continue on this hike, follow the riverbed down river. There is undergrowth and uneven footing for the rest of the hike.

The 15 foot riverbed couched between 10 foot rock walls drops down suddenly another 18 feet before turning hard to the left as it continues downstream. A viewing area with wooden guard rails is situated on top of the vertical cliff that faces the waterfall. A mining shaft from 1846, sunk by the Boston and North American Mining Company, is enclosed by that same guard rail. It is about 6 by 8 feet across and fifteen feet deep. They were attempting to establish a profitable copper mine here. They failed. This is all that remains of that venture. And yet, the same waterfall that greeted those miners of yesteryear with its calming presence continues to bring joy and tranquility to those that seek it out today!

*Note: This is a seasonal waterfall. During dry periods the Little Union River can completely stop running.*

# ARTISTS FALLS #1 (LITTLE UNION RIVER)

Private

| | | | |
|---|---|---|---|
| Must See: | 7 | GPS: | N46 47.640 W89 37.343 |
| Height: | 10 feet | | |
| Time: | 25-40 minutes | Hiking Information | |
| | | Path: | None |
| Driving Information | | Length: | .34 miles |
| Signs: | None | Elev. Change: | Moderate |
| Road: | Secondary | GPS: | Helpful |
| Access: | Somewhat Easy | Danger: | Slight |
| 4WD: | N/A | WP Boots: | Helpful |

After leaving the nice footpath that leads from South Boundary Road to the first two waterfalls on the hike, leave the path and follow the river downstream to the rest of the falls. To view this waterfall more intimately, continue downstream past the waterfall and canyon until it is safe to climb down to the river's edge. Head back up river to the waterfall, this time down inside the shallow canyon!

A narrow crevasse at the top of the falls pours the river down the face of basalt in a slight zig-zag pattern. A spill pool 30 feet wide sits at the bottom of the nearly encircled, oval shaped canyon with 15 foot walls. The back half of the floor is covered with small stones, making for great picnic and viewing areas.

Thimbleberries in July are working on becoming delicious berries ready to be picked in August! This patch (seen below) drinks up water from the Little Union River below the falls. This fickle river in Porcupine Mountains State Park changes from a wonderful waterfall paradise to a dry riverbed over the course of most summers. Check with the Park Rangers for current conditions.

Note: This is a seasonal waterfall. During dry periods the Little Union River can completely stop running.

Union River Area

## ARTISTS FALLS #2 (LITTLE UNION RIVER)  Private

| | | | |
|---|---|---|---|
| Must See: | 6 | GPS: | N46 47.712 W89 37.276 |
| Height: | 10 feet | | |
| Time: | 30-50 minutes | Hiking Information | |
| | | Path: | None |
| Driving Information | | Length: | .44 miles |
| Signs: | None | Elev. Change: | Moderate |
| Road: | Secondary | GPS: | Helpful |
| Access: | Somewhat Easy | Danger: | Moderate |
| 4WD: | N/A | WP Boots: | Helpful |

The quaint *Artist in Residence* cabin, the temporary home for artists that have been chosen to participate in the Park's *Artist in Residence* program, is nearby. A charming swing overlooks the falls while the faint smell of wood smoke wafts gently in the breeze.

The narrow, channeled river at the top of the falls broadens out and divides halfway down around a misshapen mass of bedrock. The river then continues in a 20 foot wide riverbed full of smallish, red tinged gray rocks.

*Note: This is a seasonal waterfall. During dry periods the Little Union River can completely stop running.*

*Note the thimbleberries again. I love these tart, delicate red berries! Late August hikes can be delicious. Most thimbleberries are found from Marquette to Ironwood and north up the Keweenaw Peninsula.*

320

## INSPIRATION FALLS (LITTLE UNION RIVER)  Private

| | | | |
|---|---|---|---|
| Must See: | 9 | GPS: | N46 47.754 W89 37.224 |
| Height: | 21 feet | | |
| Time: | 45-70 minutes | Hiking Information | |
| | | Path: | None |
| Driving Information | | Length: | .51 miles |
| Signs: | None | Elev. Change: | Moderate |
| Road: | Secondary | GPS: | Helpful |
| Access: | Somewhat Easy | Danger: | Moderate |
| 4WD: | N/A | WP Boots: | Helpful |

The first time I happened upon this set of waterfalls was August 29, 2011. I had hiked over from Union River and found a dry riverbed. I walked right up the middle of the rock strewn "waterway". When I saw this set of three drops I could only imagine what it would look like with water pouring over the ledges! Every time I was in the Porcupine Mountains afterwards I would check the river to see if there was water flowing. Finally, during a surprisingly early spring melt in 2012, I was overjoyed to finally be able to photograph the waterfalls along the Little Union River on March 16, 2012! The photos with lush greenery were taken on July 9, 2013.

The small river slides down a sheet of basalt in a 3-tiered slide. The first steep slide is 10 feet high, the second is 7 feet and the third one drops 4 feet. The three are so close together that I have included them together as a single waterfall.

Note: This is a seasonal waterfall. During dry periods the Little Union River can completely stop running.

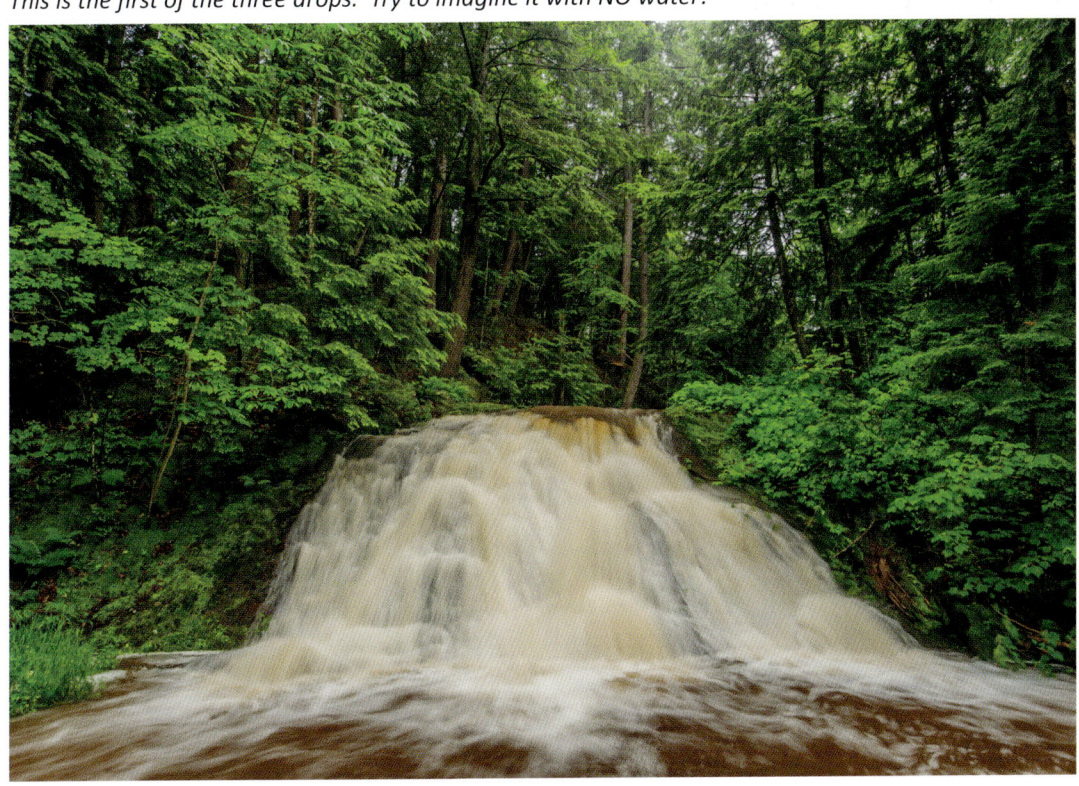

This is the first of the three drops. Try to imagine it with NO water!

Union River Area

### Union River Hike

In 1846 the Union Copper Company began a mining operation along the Union River. Although copper and some silver was mined here, it was not profitable and after a second brief resumption of activities during the Civil war, the mine was closed. In 1908 the Calumet and Hecla Mining Company confirmed the infeasibility of the mine. No further activity has taken place since then.

A 1 mile self guided interpretive trail beginning near the parking area provides glimpses into the mining activity along the Union River.

*Directions:* Use the same driving directions as the Little Union River Hike. Hike northwest to the Union Mine ruins via the interpretive trail.

## UNION MINE FALLS (UNION RIVER)                    Private

| | | | |
|---|---|---|---|
| Must See: | 4 | GPS: | N46 47.687 W89 37.677 |
| Height: | 3 feet | | |
| Time: | 10-15 minutes | Hiking Information | |
| | | Path: | Footpath |
| Driving Information | | Length: | 75 yards |
| Signs: | None | Elev. Change: | Moderate |
| Road: | Secondary | GPS: | Helpful |
| Access: | Somewhat Easy | Danger: | Moderate |
| 4WD: | N/A | WP Boots: | N/A |

The Union Mine was started here in 1846. They dammed the river upstream and carved out the left side of the waterfall to fit a paddle wheel into the river. The dam and paddle wheel have long since gone, but the waterfall lives on!

322

# CHAPTER 14
# PRESQUE ISLE COUNTY

# Presque Isle County Map

# PRESQUE ISLE COUNTY

Lake Huron

gers City

Big Trout Lake
Little Trout Lake
Lake Augusta
Presque Isle
Grand Lake
Possen
N Grand Lake Hwy
Monaghan Creek
Bolton Rd
Long Lake
Leroy

CR 441
Trout River
Little Trout River
US 23
CR 634
M 65
Bay River

Ocqueoc Falls Area

### Ocqueoc Falls Hike

The best know and wonderfully displayed waterfall in the lower peninsula is Ocqueoc Falls. The two drops that make up this lovely set of waterfalls are close to a State Highway. This is a DNR operated park and therefore a Michigan Recreation Passport is required for admission.

*Directions:* Coming in on M-68 from Rogers City, turn right onto Ocqueoc Falls Hwy as M-68 bends to the left (south). The parking lot will be on the right (north) in .4 miles. If coming from Onaway or Millersburg, follow M-68 east. Before the road makes a wide sweeping turn to the east, turn left (stay heading north) on River Rd. It will end at Ocqueoc Falls Hwy in .6 miles. Turn right. The park will be on the left (north) in .2 miles. Park in the nicely paved parking lot. Follow the concrete walkway to the falls.

*The stonework at the overlook*

*At the parking lot*

## OCQUEOC FALLS (Ocqueoc River)

Private

| | | | |
|---|---|---|---|
| Must See: | 6 | GPS: | N45 23.787 W84 03.476 |
| Height: | 5 feet | | |
| Time: | 20-30 minutes | Hiking Information | |
| | | Path: | Wide Concrete Path |
| Driving Information | | Length: | .11 miles |
| Signs: | Small sign | Elev. Change: | Minor |
| Road: | County Road | GPS: | N/A |
| Access: | Easy | Danger: | Slight |
| 4WD: | N/A | WP Boots: | N/A |

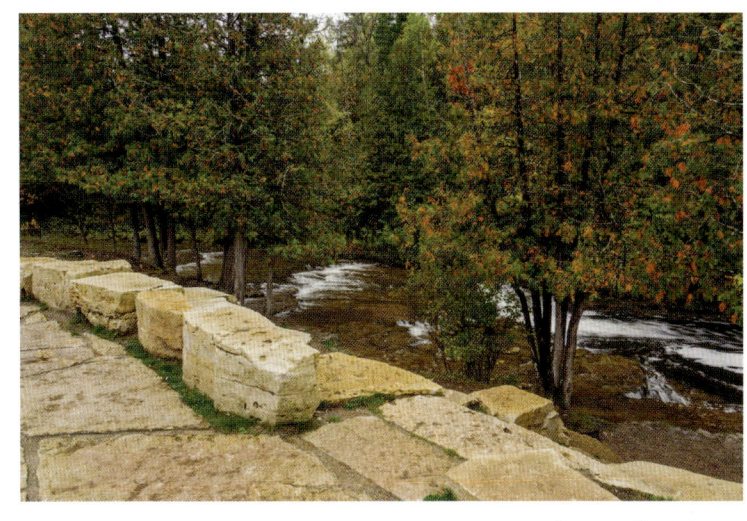

The first and tallest of the three cascades upstream is the only natural drop. The 2 1/2 foot vaguely horseshoe shaped fall has a nice cascading look. Two smaller loose stoned cascades have been added to create a better defined waterfall. This set of cascades is wheelchair accessible. The local park at the waterfall was greatly upgraded in 2011. It was wonderfully landscaped with flagstone steps as well as a gently sloping walkway. These changes provide a beautiful viewing area at the waterfall. Picnic tables, grills and rest room facilities are just a short walk away. A generous paved parking lot greets visitors. It's no wonder that this park is a popular destination.

Did you love "*The Collection*" of Michigan's waterfalls? If so, check out the "*Definitive Guide*" series to discover many more waterfalls. These books are divided by region and contain hundreds more of the waterfalls found in Michigan! Get them all for the ultimate Waterfalls of Michigan collection. www.mifalls.com

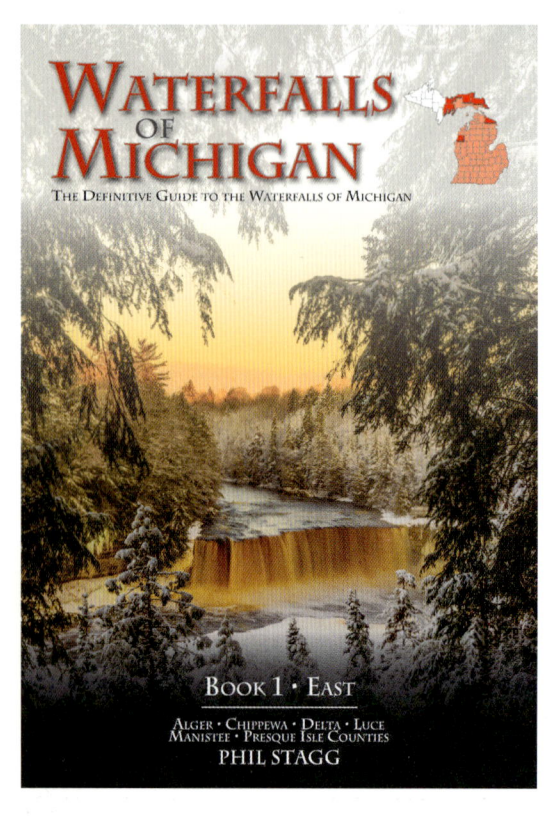

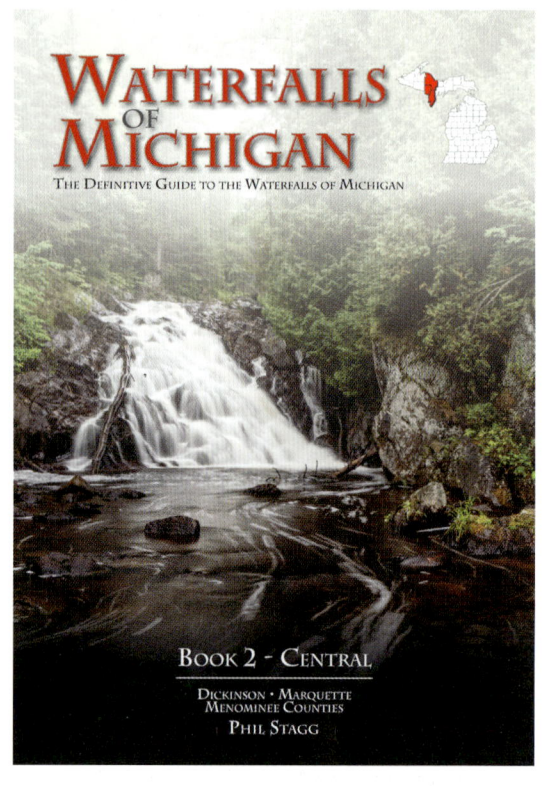

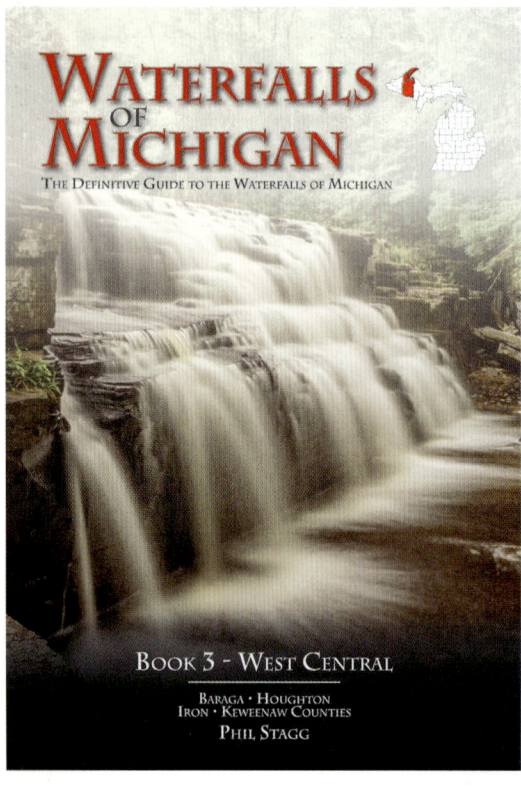

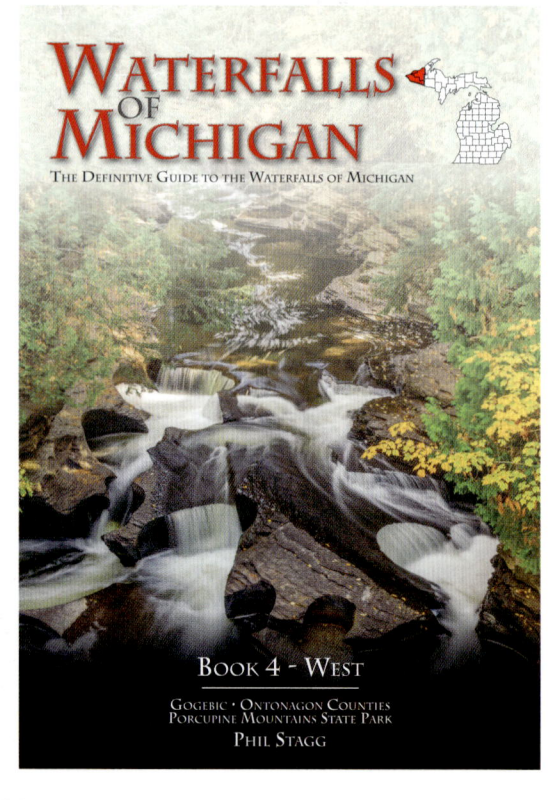

# Index

- ABUTMENT FALLS  (SILVER RIVER) ............................................................................................... 69
- AGATE FALLS  (WEST BRANCH - ONTONAGON RIVER) ......................................................... 277
- ALDER FALLS  (ALDER CREEK) ................................................................................................ 211
- ALGER FALLS  (ALGER CREEK) .................................................................................................. 40
- ARTISTS FALLS #1  (LITTLE UNION RIVER) ............................................................................. 319
- ARTISTS FALLS #2  (LITTLE UNION RIVER) ............................................................................. 320
- AUTRAIN FALLS  (AUTRAIN RIVER) ............................................................................................. 5
- BARAGA FALLS  (SILVER RIVER) ............................................................................................... 78
- BARE HOLE FALLS  (FALLS RIVER) ........................................................................................... 53
- BATHTUB FALLS  (CARP RIVER) .............................................................................................. 308
- BIG CARP FALLS  (CARP RIVER) .............................................................................................. 309
- BIG ERICK'S FALLS  (HURON RIVER) ........................................................................................ 61
- BIG FALLS  (HURON RIVER - EAST BRANCH) ........................................................................... 62
- BIG HOLE FALLS  (FALLS RIVER) ............................................................................................... 56
- BIG PUP FALLS  (BIG PUP CREEK) .......................................................................................... 266
- BLACK RIVER FALLS  (BLACK RIVER) ..................................................................................... 213
- BLACK SLATE FALLS  (SLATE RIVER) ....................................................................................... 82
- BONANZA FALLS  (BIG IRON RIVER) ....................................................................................... 279
- BOND FALLS  (MIDDLE BRANCH - ONTONAGON RIVER) ....................................................... 281
- BOND FALLS - UPPER  (MIDDLE BRANCH - ONTONAGON RIVER) ....................................... 283
- BRIDAL VEIL FALLS  (BRIDAL VEIL CREEK) .............................................................................. 19
- BULLDOG FALLS #1  (YELLOW DOG RIVER) ........................................................................... 216
- BULLDOG FALLS #2  (YELLOW DOG RIVER) ........................................................................... 217
- BULLDOG FALLS #3  (YELLOW DOG RIVER) ........................................................................... 218
- BULLDOG FALLS #4  (YELLOW DOG RIVER) ........................................................................... 219
- BULLDOG FALLS #5  (YELLOW DOG RIVER) ........................................................................... 220
- BULLDOG FALLS #6  (YELLOW DOG RIVER) ........................................................................... 221
- BULLDOG FALLS #7  (YELLOW DOG RIVER) ........................................................................... 222
- BULLDOG FALLS #8  (YELLOW DOG RIVER) ........................................................................... 223
- CANYON FALLS  (STURGEON RIVER) ....................................................................................... 48
- CARP RIVER FALLS #1  (CARP RIVER) .................................................................................... 228
- CARP RIVER FALLS #2  (CARP RIVER) .................................................................................... 229
- CARP RIVER FALLS #3  (CARP RIVER) .................................................................................... 230
- CARP RIVER FALLS #4  (CARP RIVER) .................................................................................... 231
- CARP RIVER FALLS #5  (CARP RIVER) .................................................................................... 232
- CARP RIVER FALLS #6  (CARP RIVER) .................................................................................... 233
- CARP RIVER FALLS - UPPER #1  (CARP RIVER) .................................................................... 235
- CARP RIVER FALLS - UPPER #2  (CARP RIVER) .................................................................... 236
- CASCADE FALLS  (CASCADE CREEK) ..................................................................................... 284
- CASCADING FALLS  (FALLS RIVER) .......................................................................................... 52
- CHAPEL CREEK FALLS  (CHAPEL CREEK) ................................................................................. 7
- CHAPEL FALLS  (SECTION CREEK) ............................................................................................. 9
- CHICAGON FALLS  (CHICAGON CREEK) ................................................................................. 181
- CHUTE FALLS  (FALLS RIVER) ................................................................................................... 58
- DEAD HOOK FALLS  (DEAD RIVER) ......................................................................................... 243
- DEAD ISLAND FALLS  (DEAD RIVER) ....................................................................................... 240
- DEAD ISLAND FALLS - LOWER  (DEAD RIVER) ...................................................................... 239
- DEAD PLUNGE FALLS  (DEAD RIVER) ..................................................................................... 244
- DEAD POOL FALLS  (DEAD RIVER) .......................................................................................... 241
- DEAD POOL FALLS - UPPER  (DEAD RIVER) .......................................................................... 242
- DEAD RIVER CASCADES  (DEAD RIVER) ................................................................................ 238
- DEAD RIVER FALLS - LOWER #1  (DEAD RIVER) ................................................................... 246
- DEAD RIVER FALLS - LOWER #2  (DEAD RIVER) ................................................................... 247
- DOUGLASS HOUGHTON FALLS  (HAMMELL CREEK) ............................................................ 165
- DUPPY FALLS  (JUMBO RIVER) ................................................................................................ 183
- DUPPY FALLS - MIDDLE  (JUMBO RIVER) ............................................................................... 184
- DUPPY FALLS - UPPER  (JUMBO RIVER) ................................................................................ 185
- EAGLE RIVER FALLS  (EAGLE RIVER) ..................................................................................... 190
- EAST BRANCH FALLS  (HURON RIVER - EAST BRANCH) ....................................................... 63
- ECSTASY FALLS - LOWER  (SLATE RIVER) ............................................................................... 84
- ECSTASY FALLS  (SLATE RIVER) ............................................................................................... 85
- ELLIOT FALLS: AKA MINERS BEACH FALLS  (UNNAMED CREEK) .......................................... 20
- ERICK'S FALLS  (HURON RIVER - WEST BRANCH) .................................................................. 64

# Index

- ■ EXPLORERS FALLS (LITTLE CARP RIVER) .................................................................. 301
- ■ FANNY HOOE FALLS (FANNY HOOE CREEK) .......................................................... 195
- ■ FENNERS FALLS (EAGLE RIVER) .............................................................................. 191
- ■ FIRST FALLS (EAST BRANCH ESCANABA RIVER) ................................................... 255
- ■ FORTY FOOT FALLS (CLIFF RIVER) .......................................................................... 250
- FUMEE FALLS (FUMEE CREEK) ................................................................................. 115
- ■ GABBRO FALLS (BLACK RIVER) ............................................................................... 134
- GARLIC FALLS (BIG GARLIC RIVER) ......................................................................... 252
- GARLIC FALLS - UPPER #1 (BIG GARLIC RIVER) .................................................... 253
- ■ GARLIC FALLS - UPPER #2 (BIG GARLIC RIVER) .................................................... 254
- ■ GOMANCHE FALLS (GOMANCHE CREEK) ............................................................... 73
- ■ GORGE FALLS (BLACK RIVER) .................................................................................. 129
- ■ GREAT CONGLOMERATE FALLS (BLACK RIVER) ................................................... 124
- ■ GREENSTONE FALLS (LITTLE CARP RIVER) ........................................................... 313
- HAVEN FALLS (HAVEN CREEK) ................................................................................. 194
- HAYMEADOW FALLS (HAYMEADOW CREEK) ......................................................... 111
- ■ HERMAN FALLS (SILVER RIVER) ............................................................................... 77
- ■ HOGGER FALLS (WEST BRANCH - STURGEON RIVER) ........................................ 163
- HORSERACE RAPIDS (PAINT RIVER) ....................................................................... 186
- ■ HORSESHOE FALLS (STUTTS CREEK) ..................................................................... 41
- ■ HUNGARIAN LOWER FALLS (DOVER CREEK) ........................................................ 166
- ■ HUNGARIAN MIDDLE FALLS (DOVER CREEK) ........................................................ 167
- ■ HUNGARIAN UPPER FALLS (DOVER CREEK) ......................................................... 168
- HURRICANE CASCADES (HURRICANE RIVER) ...................................................... 16
- HURRICANE FALLS (HURRICANE RIVER) ............................................................... 15
- ■ INSPIRATION FALLS (LITTLE UNION RIVER) .......................................................... 321
- ■ INTERSTATE FALLS (MONTREAL RIVER) ................................................................. 138
- ■ JACOBS FALLS (JACOBS CREEK) ............................................................................ 192
- ■ JUDSON FALLS (SLATE RIVER) ................................................................................. 150
- ■ JUMBO FALLS (JUMBO RIVER) ................................................................................. 170
- KAKABIKA FALLS #1 (ONTONAGON RIVER - WEST BRANCH) ............................ 141
- ■ KUCKUK'S FALLS (SLATE RIVER) ............................................................................. 86
- ■ LAKESHORE FALLS #1 (UNNAMED CREEK) ........................................................... 27
- ■ LAKESHORE FALLS #2 (UNNAMED CREEK) ........................................................... 28
- ■ LAUGHING WHITEFISH FALLS (LAUGHING WHITEFISH RIVER) ......................... 18
- ■ LETHERBY FALLS (HURON RIVER - WEST BRANCH) ............................................ 65
- ■ LETHERBY FALLS - UPPER (HURON RIVER - WEST BRANCH) ............................ 66
- ■ LITTLE MINERS FALLS (LITTLE MINERS RIVER) .................................................... 24
- ■ LITTLE TRAP FALLS (ANDERSON CREEK) .............................................................. 286
- ■ LITTLE UNION GORGE FALLS (LITTLE UNION RIVER) .......................................... 317
- ■ LITTLE UNION GORGE FALLS - LOWER (LITTLE UNION RIVER) ......................... 318
- LOWER TAHQUAMENON FALLS #1 (TAHQUAMENON RIVER) .............................. 100
- LOWER TAHQUAMENON FALLS #2 (TAHQUAMENON RIVER) .............................. 102
- LOWER TAHQUAMENON ISLAND FALLS #1 (TAHQUAMENON RIVER) ................ 101
- LOWER TAHQUAMENON ISLAND FALLS #2 (TAHQUAMENON RIVER) ................ 103
- ■ MANABEZHO FALLS (PRESQUE ISLE RIVER) ......................................................... 304
- ■ MANAKIKI FALLS (MAPLE CREEK) ............................................................................ 125
- MANGANESE FALLS (MANGANESE CREEK) ........................................................... 196
- ■ MANIDO FALLS (PRESQUE ISLE RIVER) .................................................................. 305
- ■ MAPLE CREEK FALLS #1 (MAPLE CREEK) .............................................................. 126
- ■ MARSHALL FALLS (MARSHALL CREEK) .................................................................. 151
- ■ MEMORIAL FALLS (UNNAMED CREEK) .................................................................... 29
- MEX-I-MIN-E FALLS (ONTONAGON RIVER - MIDDLE BRANCH) ........................... 143
- ■ MINERS FALLS (MINERS RIVER) ............................................................................... 22
- MISICOT FALLS AKA: THIRD PIER (MENOMINEE RIVER) ...................................... 117
- MITTEN HOLE FALLS (FALLS RIVER) ....................................................................... 55
- ■ MONTREAL FALLS - LOWER (MONTREAL RIVER) .................................................. 198
- ■ MONTREAL FALLS - MIDDLE (MONTREAL RIVER) .................................................. 199
- ■ MONTREAL FALLS - UPPER (MONTREAL RIVER) ................................................... 200
- ■ MORGAN FALLS (MORGAN CREEK) ......................................................................... 227
- MORGAN MEADOWS FALLS (MORGAN CREEK) ..................................................... 258
- ■ MOSQUITO FALLS (MOSQUITO RIVER) ................................................................... 10
- ■ MOSQUITO FALLS - UPPER (MOSQUITO RIVER) ................................................... 12

# Index

- MUNISING FALLS (MUNISING FALLS CREEK) ........................................................................... 31
- NAWADAHA FALLS (PRESQUE ISLE RIVER) ........................................................................ 306
- NELSON CANYON FALLS (NELSON CREEK) ........................................................................ 153
  - NONESUCH FALLS (IRON RIVER) .................................................................................... 302
  - OCQUEOC FALLS (OCQUEOC RIVER) ............................................................................. 327
- OGEMAW FALLS (OGEMAW CREEK) ..................................................................................... 49
- O-KUN-DE-KUN FALLS (BALTIMORE RIVER) ....................................................................... 289
- OLSON FALLS AKA: TANNERY FALLS (TANNERY CREEK) ................................................... 30
- OVERLOOKED FALLS (LITTLE CARP RIVER) ....................................................................... 312
- PEANUT BUTTER FALLS (BALTIMORE RIVER) .................................................................... 288
  - PEMENE FALLS (MENOMINEE RIVER) ............................................................................. 272
- PENN FALLS - LOWER (FIRESTEEL RIVER - EAST BRANCH) ............................................. 294
- PENN FALLS - UPPER (FIRESTEEL RIVER - EAST BRANCH) ............................................. 295
- PETERSON FALLS (MONTREAL RIVER) ............................................................................... 139
- PINNACLE FALLS (YELLOW DOG RIVER) ............................................................................ 260
- POTATO PATCH FALLS (UNNAMED CREEK) ........................................................................ 21
- POTAWATOMI FALLS (BLACK RIVER) ................................................................................... 127
- POWDERHORN FALLS - LOWER (POWDER MILL CREEK) .................................................. 145
- POWER HOUSE FALLS (FALLS RIVER) .................................................................................. 59
- PRESQUE ISLE KETTLES (PRESQUE ISLE RIVER) ............................................................. 303
- QUARTZITE FALLS (SLATE RIVER) ......................................................................................... 81
- QUEEN ANNE'S FALLS (SLAUGHTERHOUSE CREEK) ........................................................ 172
- RAINBOW FALLS (BLACK RIVER) .......................................................................................... 130
  - RAPID RIVER FALLS (RAPID RIVER) ................................................................................ 112
  - RAVINE RIVER ROAD FALLS (UNNAMED TRIBUTARY) ..................................................... 67
  - REANY FALLS (REANY CREEK) ........................................................................................ 248
  - ROCK DAM FALLS (PINE CREEK) ..................................................................................... 119
- ROCK RIVER FALLS (ROCK RIVER) ........................................................................................ 33
- ROOT BEER FALLS (PLANTER CREEK) ............................................................................... 135
- SABLE FALLS (SABLE CREEK) ................................................................................................ 36
- SANDSTONE CREEK FALLS (SANDSTONE CREEK) ........................................................... 290
- SANDSTONE FALLS (BLACK RIVER) ..................................................................................... 132
- SAXON FALLS - LOWER (MONTREAL RIVER) ..................................................................... 147
  - SCHWEITZER FALLS (SCHWEITZER CREEK) .................................................................. 263
  - SCOTT FALLS (SCOTT CREEK) ........................................................................................... 38
- ■ SECOND FALLS (EAST BRANCH ESCANABA RIVER) ........................................................ 256
  - SECOND PIER (MENOMINEE RIVER) ............................................................................... 116
- SECRET HOLE FALLS (FALLS RIVER) .................................................................................... 57
  - SECTION CREEK FALLS (SECTION CREEK) ....................................................................... 8
- SHINING CLOUD FALLS (CARP RIVER) ................................................................................ 310
  - SILVER FALLS AKA: SILVER BELL FALLS (NELSON CREEK) ............................................ 34
- SILVER FALLS - LOWER (SILVER RIVER) .............................................................................. 70
- SILVER FALLS - MIDDLE #8 (SILVER RIVER) ........................................................................ 72
- SILVER FALLS - UPPER (SILVER RIVER) ............................................................................... 79
  - SILVER RIVER FALLS (SILVER RIVER) ............................................................................. 201
- SLATE RIVER FALLS (SLATE RIVER) ...................................................................................... 83
- SPRAY FALLS (SPRAY CREEK) ............................................................................................... 13
- STONY MILLS FALLS (DEAD RIVER) ..................................................................................... 245
- STURGEON FALLS (STURGEON RIVER) .............................................................................. 174
- STURGEON FALLS - WB #1 (WEST BRANCH - STURGEON RIVER) .................................. 158
  - STURGEON FALLS - WB #2 (WEST BRANCH - STURGEON RIVER) ............................... 159
- STURGEON FALLS - WB #3 (WEST BRANCH - STURGEON RIVER) .................................. 160
  - STURGEON FALLS - WB #4 (WEST BRANCH - STURGEON RIVER) ............................... 161
- STURGEON FALLS - WB #5 (WEST BRANCH - STURGEON RIVER) .................................. 162
- SUNDAY LAKE FALLS (PLANTER CREEK) ............................................................................ 136
- SUPERIOR FALLS (MONTREAL RIVER) ................................................................................ 148
- TAHQUAMENON FALLS - UPPER (TAHQUAMENON RIVER) ............................................... 104
  - TEN FOOT FALLS (EAGLE RIVER) .................................................................................... 193
- THE GRADE FALLS (UNNAMED TRIBUTARY) ........................................................................ 88
  - TIBBETS FALLS (STURGEON RIVER) ................................................................................ 91
  - TIOGA PARK FALLS (TIOGA RIVER) ................................................................................... 93
  - TOBACCO FALLS - LOWER (TOBACCO RIVER) ............................................................... 202
  - TOBACCO FALLS - UPPER (TOBACCO RIVER) ................................................................ 203

## Index

- ■ TRAP FALLS  (CARP RIVER) ................................................................................. 315
- ■ TRESTLE FALLS  (DEAD RIVER) .......................................................................... 262
- ■ UNION MINE FALLS  (UNION RIVER) .................................................................. 322
- ■ VICTORIA DAM FALLS  (ONTONAGON RIVER - WEST BRANCH) .................. 291
- ■ VICTORY FALLS  (SLATE RIVER) ........................................................................... 89
- ■ WAGNER FALLS  (WAGNER CREEK) ..................................................................... 42
- ■ WARNER FALLS  (WARNER CREEK) ................................................................... 264
- ■ WEST BRANCH FALLS #1  (YELLOW DOG RIVER - WEST BRANCH) ............ 224
- ■ WEST BRANCH FALLS #2  (YELLOW DOG RIVER - WEST BRANCH) ............ 225
- ■ WHITEFISH FALLS  (WEST BRANCH - WHITEFISH RIVER) .............................. 43
- ■ WYANDOTTE FALLS  (MISERY RIVER) ............................................................... 176
- ■ YELLOW DOG FALLS #1  (YELLOW DOG RIVER) ............................................. 268
- ■ YONDOTA FALLS  (PRESQUE ISLE RIVER) ....................................................... 154

# NOTES

# NOTES